The Best American
Travel Writing 2015

GUEST EDITORS OF
THE BEST AMERICAN TRAVEL WRITING

2000 BILL BRYSON
2001 PAUL THEROUX
2002 FRANCES MAYES
2003 IAN FRAZIER
2004 PICO IYER
2005 JAMAICA KINCAID
2006 TIM CAHILL
2007 SUSAN ORLEAN
2008 ANTHONY BOURDAIN
2009 SIMON WINCHESTER
2010 BILL BUFORD
2011 SLOANE CROSLEY
2012 WILLIAM T. VOLLMANN
2013 ELIZABETH GILBERT
2014 PAUL THEROUX
2015 ANDREW MCCARTHY

The Best American Travel Writing™ 2015

Edited and with an Introduction
by **Andrew McCarthy**

Jason Wilson, Series Editor

A Mariner Original

HOUGHTON MIFFLIN HARCOURT

BOSTON • NEW YORK   2015

www.hmhco.com

ISSN 1530-1516
ISBN 978-0-544-56964-5

Printed in the United States of America
DOC 10 9 8 7 6 5 4 3 2 1

Contents

Foreword

TRAVEL HAS the singular ability to turn the most banal events into heightened drama. This can be great for travel writing. This can also be not so great for situations that call for less drama.

Not long ago, following an exhausting and not-prosperous work trip, my flight home from Bilbao was delayed seven hours by a terrible windstorm that shut down several European airports. I spent five and a half of those seven hours stuck in a line of hundreds, while two overwhelmed workers at the Lufthansa desk ever so slowly attempted to reroute more than 300 passengers. As the line trudged forward, I watched the departures board helplessly as flights left, one by one, for Paris, for London, for Madrid, for Lisbon, all connections that would have gotten me home. I had an important meeting in the morning, and then my son's first soccer game, which I'd committed to coach. As the hours passed, I knew I would miss both. By the time I reached the front of the line, there was no way across the Atlantic until the next day, and I was assigned an evening flight to Frankfurt. I was given a handwritten voucher for a hotel, and another voucher for a free dinner.

In the grand scheme of my travels and travails, this was all relatively small potatoes. I've been a passenger on two planes that nearly crashed, a bystander caught in the midst of political demonstrations that turned into riots, and a victim of several felony crimes during many years of travel. My normal response to this seven-hour delay would include some cursing and a few useless, angry phone calls to the airlines, finally giving way to heavy sighs and then drinking.

When I arrived at Frankfurt airport, it was dark and rainy, and a taxi took me to a hotel in the middle of an industrial park in a suburb called Mörfelden. After checking in and explaining to my son that I would not be home in time for soccer, and hearing my boss's dismay at my absence, I slumped down to the hotel's overlit restaurant and grabbed a menu. I was a wreck. My career had suffered some recent blows and this trip was supposed to help turn things around; but it hadn't. In any case, I badly needed some comfort food, and the first item that called out to me was Wiener schnitzel. Why? I don't know. Maybe I was channeling my mother's old veal parm back in Jersey. Maybe it just felt like the opposite of the tapas, especially the ham, I'd been gorging on for days. Whatever the reason, I said, "Yes, please, may I have some Wiener schnitzel?" and presented my voucher. The stern waiter sneered and pointed over to a pathetic buffet in the corner: some stale rolls, a congealed soup, and a platter of rubbery chicken that had been sitting out for hours. This, apparently, was the Lufthansa Stranded Passenger Special that my voucher covered.

I waved the waiter back over. "Please, sir," I pleaded. "Please. I've had a very long day, and what I really need is to eat this Wiener schnitzel."

"It's twenty-one euros," he said. "That food over there is free."

I had kept mostly cool and Zen all day long, but I suddenly had the urge to scream or cry. "Look, I don't care what I have to pay for it," I said, my voice rising. "I just need you to bring me this Wiener schnitzel. Right now. Please." Something in the stern waiter's demeanor seemed to change; empathy washed over his face. He nodded, wrote my order, and whisked away the menu. A few minutes later, he brought a plate with the schnitzel. And along with it, a bottle of Rheinhessen Riesling.

"Sir," he said. "I am so sorry. I cannot honor the voucher for your meal. But please. I asked my manager, and he said I could pour you this Riesling in exchange for the voucher." I thanked him quietly and averted my eyes, blushing.

I ravenously tucked into that schnitzel and took a long drink from the wineglass. It wasn't the greatest schnitzel or Riesling, but for some reason, my eyes started to well up and tears ran down my cheeks. These were tears of frustration, but also very much of embarrassment. I'd suddenly realized that the heightened travel drama happening in my own head had selfishly put this poor waiter in a tricky professional spot. He'd only wanted to make sure I clearly understood that I was passing up free food. Surely I wasn't the first agitated, stranded passenger he'd faced at this airport hotel, and surely there'd been misunderstandings and complaints in the past. He didn't need any trouble from his manager on this lousy night in Mörfelden. Meanwhile, I'd chosen to turn the moment into some kind of angsty, M. F. K. Fisher-esque epiphany.

Perhaps only someone who reads too many travel stories would think of Ryszard Kapuściński while eating schnitzel alone in an airport hotel. But I was reminded of Kapuściński's masterpiece, *The Soccer War*, when he writes: "There is so much crap in this world and then, suddenly, there is honesty and humanity." This sudden shift, from banal to dramatic, from ugly to beautiful, from tragic to comic, from insignificant to profound, is what travel writing, at its best, does. I believe you'll see the dynamic at work throughout this anthology.

The waiter reappeared and said, "Is everything OK, sir?"

"Yes, yes," I said. "Thank you very much. Everything is quite OK."

The stories included here are, as always, selected from among hundreds of pieces in hundreds of diverse publications—from mainstream and specialty magazines to Sunday newspaper travel sections to literary journals to travel websites. I've done my best to be fair and representative, and in my opinion the best travel stories from 2014 were forwarded to guest editor Andrew McCarthy, who made our final selections.

I'm fascinated by McCarthy's journey from box-office heart-throb (as a teenager, I was insanely jealous that he'd ended up with Molly Ringwald in *Pretty in Pink*) to travel writer. Andrew has come to the travel writing genre humbly, with great respect for the work, and he has admirably paid his dues. His selections have been surprising and unique, and I'm happy to have so many new voices and new publications represented in our collection.

I'd also like to thank Tim Mudie, at Houghton Mifflin Harcourt, for his help in producing this year's outstanding collection.

I now begin anew by reading the hundreds of stories published in 2015. As I have for years, I am asking editors and writers to submit the best of whatever it is they define as travel writing. These submissions must be nonfiction, published in the United

States during the 2015 calendar year. They must not be reprints or excerpts from published books. They must include the author's name, date of publication, and publication name, and must be tear sheets, the complete publication, or a clear photocopy of the piece as it originally appeared. I must receive all submissions by January 1, 2016, in order to ensure full consideration for the next collection.

Further, publications that want to make certain that their contributions will be considered for the next edition should make sure to include this anthology on their subscription list. Submissions or subscriptions should be sent to Jason Wilson, The Best American Travel Writing, 230 Kings Highway East, Suite 192, Haddonfield, NJ 08033.

JASON WILSON

Introduction

FOR SOME TIME NOW I've been sounding like a small child tugging at his father's pant leg, asking again and again, *Why?* In my particular case, the "why" in question pertains to travel writing. Why does it matter? What's the point? Hasn't it all been discovered and chronicled? What can we possibly add to the storehouse of information that has come before?

Back in Sir Richard Burton's day, tales brought back from darkest Africa had real import. Freya Stark's journeys through Persia were a revelation. Ernest Shackleton's escape from Antarctica with every soul intact was the stuff of real heroism. How do we top that? The 10 best beaches in the Caribbean right now(!)?

My own experiences with genre emerged only after a long gestation period, as an outgrowth of my travels, the initiation of which sprang from an unwitting urge to connect more with the world in an attempt to better locate my place in it. A 500-mile walk across the Camino de Santiago in northern Spain revealed a fear that had lurked behind so many of my life's actions, and set in motion a decade of wandering that rewrote how I experienced the world. Travel became not so much about the destination as an end but a means of understanding myself *in* that place. The world became my university campus. I traveled, mostly alone, to Africa and Southeast Asia, Europe and South America. I was often lonely and learned not to fear travel's false power. At times I was shrouded in melancholy and came to appreciate the lucidity it evoked. And of course I had serendipitous encounters that still live inside me.

Sometimes I was simply in the right place at the right time. As a young man working in West Berlin I passed through Checkpoint Charlie one early-winter day under the heavy gaze of Communist soldiers. I spent a memorably dreary afternoon walking the deserted streets of East Berlin, the noticeable absence of advertising helping to leave the city a uniform gray under a dirty sky. I ate soggy food and toured an empty museum. Back in West Berlin that night, for the first time I felt the expansiveness of a freedom I had never previously considered. Two days later the Wall fell and I danced amid exultant and pulsing crowds throughout those frigid November nights. I kept my tiny chip of the Berlin Wall for years before it was lost. By then it didn't matter; my experience in Berlin had become a part of me. I had no need of tokens.

I've also been witness to being in the wrong place at the wrong time. Deep in the Rocky Mountains I saw the frailty of human life and how quickly it can be vanquished—a swollen and rushing river, a bad decision, and a moment's loss of concentration that led to tragic results.

My experiences affected me deeply, yet my meandering had an impulsive, almost random quality. It lacked a galvanizing cord. I knew that where I was going and what happened while there had value, yet I struggled with its context.

Then in Saigon I was walking down a sunbaked street one morning when a young man on a scooter drove up beside me and offered to show me the city. I told him to leave me alone and kept walking. He shadowed my movements, he grew insistent—he would be my guide. There was no shaking the young man in the dirty T-shirt. I hopped on the back of his scooter. The Saigon he showed me couldn't be found in my Lonely Planet guidebook.

He took me to the street corner where his father had been arrested and with real anger told me of the elder man's unfair treatment. We spent an hour amid wilting plants under the oppression of Southeast Asian humidity, trudging through the community garden that his mother had often taken him to as a child. At the one temple we visited, my guide skulked in the doorway without removing his shoes, smoking, waiting for me to finish a perfunctory walk-through. Mostly I remember zipping down the wide boulevards and slashing through roundabouts, holding on amid thousands of others on scooters in the life-threatening jigsaw jumble that is daily traffic in Saigon.

When he deposited me back at my hotel, my guide demanded

more money than we had agreed upon. As I sit writing this more than 20 years later, I can see him before me, his bloodshot left eye adding threat to an already insistent glare as the last rays of daylight cast a fiery glow over the yellow wall of my hotel just past his shoulder. The traffic buzzes behind me, forcing me to lean in to be sure I understand his command correctly. "I show you real Saigon"; his voice is harsh, his already outstretched hand shaking under the strain of his gathering tension.

I can feel the myriad emotions that raced through me at the time—my naive shock at his outburst, my confusion, my sense of powerlessness under his sudden aggression. Surely he needed the money more than I did. Was I really that stingy? Yet there was shame in my acquiescence as I handed over the extra five dollars.

Up in my room I became consumed with anger at being taken advantage of; the sensation of emasculation humiliated me. The indignity at having been overmatched and powerless threatened to consume me.

Travel is often a petri dish for both our character defects and our finer qualities, and in this moment my baser attributes had me in their clutches.

I did something I had never done before. I reached for a pen. I wrote it all down.

I had been walking along the street when a boy, maybe not out of his teens, approached me on a scooter. I wrote how I tried to discourage him and then hopped on behind him. I remembered things he had said and I wrote them down as well. I described the places he took me and what it felt like while I was there. Then I wrote of how our day had ended—with his demand for more money. I wrote of my embarrassment and anger—both at him and at myself for giving precedence to my feelings of inadequacy over his genuine need. When I was done, I stuffed the pages in my bag.

A few weeks later, in Luang Prabang, in northern Laos, I came upon a young American woman berating an elderly Laotian man about the inferior quality of the bicycle he had rented to her. When she left I crossed over to speak with the man and followed him into his home and ate lunch with him. I wrote that down, too.

At Victoria Falls in Zimbabwe on Christmas Eve I danced in a basement club, part of a throbbing, sweating mass, then walked out to a florid sun rising over the cascading falls on Christmas morning. In Machu Picchu, on a starless black night, my flashlight died after I had sneaked into the ancient citadel. I crawled on my hands and knees searching out an exit, for fear of stepping off the edge of the mountain.

I wrote it all down.

In my writing I began to make deeper sense of what I experienced. I started to see connections between seemingly unrelated events and glimpse the import they contained. Insights that had eluded me before rose up in front of me. Things that I had simply forgotten were indelibly recorded.

My writing wasn't a journal. I had tried that and found my jottings indulgent and repetitive. Mostly they bored me. But almost unwittingly, what I was doing was writing stories. Things I wrote about captured a quality of where I was and what I experienced in a way my journaling couldn't approach. Sure, others had been here before me, but no one had seen things exactly from my perspective. Suddenly what I saw mattered. I grew more and more connected to the world I inhabited, more invested. My travels had import.

Upon my return home I would toss the notebooks I had by then begun to carry with me into my top dresser drawer. My travel writings were something I did for myself while on the road. I never thought of them as anything more.

Until I did.

I published first one story, and then more. Underneath every piece I wrote was the unspoken message that travel was important. Travel, I was convinced, was not something frivolous, to be indulged in merely by the idle or the wealthy or the unshowered backpacker. It was something worth fighting for. Travel changed my life; it could change yours. Travel mattered: that was my message.

And if it mattered to me, then perhaps it mattered to others. That bond between writer and reader has been much chronicled, and so it follows that if travel mattered, and connecting with the reader was important, then certainly travel writing must have value. Maybe even urgent value.

I devoured the road and wrote about it all. I hiked to the top of Kilimanjaro and dove with sharks off the Tuamotu Islands. I drank tea in Darjeeling, ate prosciutto in Parma; I slept in the Sahara and occasionally in my own bed. I even published that first story from Saigon nearly 20 years after I wrote it. Yet as we grow proficient at anything it can become more and more difficult to maintain access to that original seed of inspiration and connection to the inner delight that first inspired us. Craft and competence are the rewards of repetition, but a dulling of our senses can be the tradeoff. And as any dinner party guest can tell you, there is no greater bore than the world-weary traveler, the been-there-done-that blowhard spewing pronouncements on the military junta in Burma or Patagonia's vanishing wilderness onto whoever is unfortunate enough to be seated beside him. It ought never to be forgotten that travel can be a revelation, offering the very real possibility of recaptured innocence to our jaded eyes. The paradox of travel's effort is the renewal it affords.

Which is why I owe all the writers in this volume a debt of gratitude. Underscoring every story here I can hear the silent calling out, *Yes, this matters. Follow me!*—serving to remind me again why I first left home.

Nowhere in these pages did I feel as if I was being handed a bill of goods. I've grown weary of skimming glossies extolling the luxurious vacation and branding it as travel. (After a good session of travel I've often found myself in need of a nice vacation.) *Tell me a story, don't sell me a destination,* I've thought more than once as I toss a travel magazine aside. You'll find no selling here, just hard-won experience offered up.

These tales are a testament to the importance of setting out, a call to the open road and its possibilities, lessons, heartbreaks, and occasional joys—a reaffirmation of the value of the investment required to leave the safety of shore. As yet unknown riches await the bold.

In reading many of these stories I'm reminded that in so much of the best travel writing, it is the anonymous and solitary traveler capturing a moment in time and place, giving meaning to his or her travels, that inspires and elucidates. I'll always take the subjective account from the lonely troubadour, with all the traps and fallibility it is prone to, over the detached second- or thirdhand summing up by the scholar who never left home.

The tale that Benjamin Busch tells of his return to Iraq 10 years after his posting as a Marine is among the most dispassionate and affecting reportage I have encountered in the thousands and thousands of words I've digested about that conflict. It is also one of the most engrossing pieces of travel writing I've read in a very long while. I'm thrilled to include it here. And Stephen Connely Benz's recounting of his Fulbright year placed me beside him in a Moldova I will most probably never see.

Still another type of travel writing seems to reside almost entirely out of time. Patricia Marx floats in watery limbo during her transatlantic crossing aboard a freighter. David Farley's elegiac meditation exists in a Varanasi that holds a very long view of time, while Paul Salopek's epic walk across much of the planet endeavors to retrace time from man's first steps. And then there's Gary Shteyngart. His hilarious assessment of hotel sex occupies a time and place all its own.

Despite the cynics' cries to the contrary, the world is still there waiting to be discovered. The globe keeps spinning, sometimes at an alarming rate, reinventing itself almost daily. Timbuktu, once an end-of-the-rainbow ideal, recently plagued by strife, is represented in this volume by two stories. Patrick Symmes and Adriana Páramo give us very different reports of intrepid travel to that desert Oz. While Nick Paumgarten's recounting of wild nights in Berlin tells of a different kind of mettle needed on the road.

Of course there are the rabbit holes of travel. Lauren Groff's discovery of mermaids in central Florida, Iris Smyles's cruise down the Rhone River, and Rachael Maddux's unlikely visit to Dayton, Tennesse, hint at lives many of us might never consider. Here also, Maud Newton offers a candid reexamination of a visit to the Holy Land in her brief treatise, and Lauren Quinn takes us to Cambodia to assess Pol Pot's final resting place.

Motion itself has long been a staple of the travel narrative, and it is represented here as well. Monte Reel transects South America and captures much of the continent's internal contradictions, while Kevin Baker's rail journey across America reminds us what a long strange trip in the wrong direction train travel in this country has become.

And it strikes me as fitting that this volume concludes with a piece by the spiritual godfather of contemporary American travel writers. Forty years ago Paul Theroux, with an immersive style, barbed-wire observations, and sometimes merciless candor, rewrote what a travel narrative could be in *The Great Railway Bazaar*. His exploration here through the American South shows us that this lifelong road warrior has not lost a step.

All these writers have rejuvenated my sometimes flagging travel spirits and inspired me to look again to the horizon. Each has re-invigorated me in a different way. Each has reignited my passion to hit the road, to set out—for it is of course in the leaving that we afford ourselves the opportunity to be found. As the stories here reveal, the world is still eager to receive the solitary sojourner with a hungry spirit who is willing to keep a keen eye out and an attentive ear to the ground in an effort to capture the telling moment, then send it back across the wire—and, perhaps, through the years.

ANDREW McCARTHY

The Sound of Silence

FROM *AFAR*

I WAS ABOUT 20 minutes into the four-hour train ride from Glasgow to Fort William when I realized I couldn't stand the two men seated in front of me. This realization was based on nothing other than what I could overhear—which was every bloody word—of their conversation. They were traveling to a friend's house, but before they arrived they would need to stop at the supermarket for cheese and wine, of course; though white, not red, since the carpets were beige and the host had a policy. One of the men also had a sister of whose parenting skills he disapproved, a nephew who would likely end up in juvenile court, a new backpack whose every compartment required minute explication, and a penchant for a Danish television series whose plot twists he could recall in terrifying detail. Did I mention that the train ride was four hours long?

I know. The problem wasn't Mr. Chatty and his mate. It was me. In the weeks before I went to Scotland, I had found myself increasingly irritated by the constant crush of other people, crowding me in line at the market, checking their phones at movie theaters, coming at me nonstop in tides of e-mails, tweets, and status updates. This happens to me periodically: the deadline pressures and everyday annoyances that normally pass unnoticed accumulate until even benign human interactions begin to feel like too much, and the only thing that helps is radical solitude. I didn't have the time for a trip to Greenland or Mongolia or some other distant, empty place, so when I read a British newspaper story about Inverie, the only town on the Knoydart peninsula, one of the most untouched parts of the Scottish Highlands, I thought it might be just the cure for my misanthropy.

The problem? Getting there. Inverie is accessible only by boat or on foot. In my state of mind, the two-day hike seemed the better choice. I planned to start at the nearest access point—a road that dead-ends at a settlement near a lake called Loch Hourn, about 50 miles from Fort William—follow the trail along the lake's edge to Barisdale Bay, spend the night there, then head over a pass and down to Inverie. It would be a 16-mile trek through steep and rocky terrain, and at hike's end, I would be in a town with a population of roughly 100 people, no cell-phone coverage, and a pub billed as the most remote in mainland Britain.

At last, the train arrived in Fort William. I picked up some granola bars and a map and checked into a hotel for the night. The next morning, a taxi driver named Jamie picked me up, and we set out for the 90-minute drive to Loch Hourn. I had not a minute to contemplate the hills and sheep as we passed, as Jamie and I were too busy chatting. I learned about Scottish independence ("It's the football hoodlums that are for it") and a tiny biting insect, smaller than a mosquito but given to traveling in swarms, that was an annual plague in these parts. "Midgies," Jamie said. "Worse than the independentists."

Unlike the self-absorbed man on the train, Jamie was a charming conversationalist, so I didn't terribly mind the barrage of sound. Still, after he left me at the trailhead, a quiet fell with the abruptness of a tsunami. It wasn't silence. Birds chirped and water ran in small, stony falls down to the loch. But there was no human sound except for the crunch of my feet on the trail. The weather was gorgeous: bright sunshine, a warm-but-not-hot temperature. The view was even better: wildflower-covered hills jutting down to shiny blue water. And when I went to check my phone for the weather forecast, I had no connection. For the first time in months, I felt relaxed and at peace.

The walk that afternoon was easy. There were a few climbs, but mostly the trail hugged the lakeshore. Before I knew it, I had reached the juncture where the lake spills into Barisdale Bay. It was low tide, and across the shimmering flats, a few people dug for cockles. I picked my way through a flock of sheep until I came to a small house where a bare-chested, sunburned man was mowing the grass. He cut the engine, but he wouldn't speak to me until he had run in to put on a shirt. Barisdale, it seemed, was an estate, and it was his job to manage it.

Craig explained that I could stay in the bothy, the first of several adorable Scottish words I would learn. A bothy is a rural shelter, open to walkers, that affords the simplest of accommodations on a first-come, first-served basis. This one looked like it slept about 12, which was 11 possible roommates too many. I paid extra for a private cottage on the property. A very loud rooster with a poor sense of time crowed with equal fervor at five o'clock in the afternoon and at six in the morning, but otherwise my accommodations were quiet. Toward dusk, I found myself drawn, out of habit, to my phone. I went outside in search of a signal, but to no avail. Instead of checking e-mail, I settled into the cottage and read some of the guidebooks near the fireplace.

The books agreed there was a spectacular Munro (adorable Scottishism No. 2: Munro = mountain), the tallest on the Knoydart peninsula, several kilometers off the trail to Inverie. I had no intention of climbing it. I used to do a fair bit of hiking, but that was more than a decade ago, and it left me with enough respect for serious mountains that I wasn't going to waltz up one on a lark. Besides, it would add extra miles to a walk that would already take me the better part of a day.

The next morning I slipped out of the estate without seeing another soul. In minutes, I came to a path that headed to the right and cut vertiginously uphill. I said a prayer of thanks that I didn't have to tackle that ascent right out of the gate. Instead, I went left, where the trail climbed more gently. I thought of Lord Byron and those other Romantics who sought solitude in the woods. Time alone in nature felt restorative for them. And that was before the Internet. Solitude in the outdoors was surely all the more healing for those of us who had not only the physical and moral pollution of industrialized society to escape, but also the incessant chatter of everyone we have ever known running constantly across our screens and phones. It was a relief to turn off all those voices and focus on the path in front of me.

Soon the trail crossed a stream and became so vertical that it wasn't long before I was playing little mental games with myself to keep moving: Walk to that boulder, then you can rest, I told myself. Walk 100 steps, then you can rest. The good thing about

hiking alone, I decided, is that there is no one there to see you
humiliate yourself.

After what seemed like hours but was probably only 45 minutes,
the ascent plateaued. Behind me, Barisdale Bay sparkled through
the folds of the mountains. Ahead, it was just as the guidebooks
had described: I had come through the pass, sharp peaks soared
around me, and down below I could see a lake, its cobalt waters
rimmed with ribbons of sand.

I set off happily toward the distant lake. But the bone-jarring
descent quickly tempered the relief I had felt when I'd reached
the pass. Down I went, my toes slamming into my boots with each
step. At times the trail disappeared altogether in bog, but the lake
gradually got closer. From my reading the night before, I knew
that once I reached it, the trail would turn into flat jeep track, and
I'd be 4 kilometers from Inverie.

When I reached the lake at noon, I felt triumphant, even a bit
smug, despite the ache in my feet. With plenty of time to make it
to Inverie before dark, I took off my boots, ate a sandwich, and
took a nap.

I awoke with a start.

Something—I couldn't say what—made me think I needed
to look at the map. The trail had been so clearly marked that it
hadn't occurred to me to take it out earlier. Now I spread the map
and traced my path. There was the climb up from Barisdale, there
was the pass, there was the descent to the—I stopped. The map
had me coming up to the lake on its right shore. I had arrived on
the left.

I tried turning the paper, to see if I had somehow gotten the
orientation wrong. I walked back up the trail I had come in on, to
make sure that it was indeed a trail. And here is the part that, even
now, I can't explain. Absurd as it sounds, instead of admitting I
had made a mistake and turning around, I convinced myself that
the map was mistaken.

I had no one to ask, no GPS to orient me. A stone path lay
across the shallowest end of the lake and I took it, convinced
it would lead to the jeep track, and hence to Inverie. And sure
enough, I found a trail on the other side. I followed it until it
disappeared at the edge of a fast-moving river, beyond which lay
another loch. The prospect of going back seemed so horrible that

I persuaded myself that if I just kept going, I would soon come across that track.

I followed what I took to be a trail, then lost it again amid the bog and grass and sheep droppings. I walked for another hour, trying to make sense of my location. Finally I came to the far shore of the loch. I saw no trail. It was after 3 p.m.

I gazed at the sun, trying to determine where it would set, but the days were so long in July that it was still straight overhead. Without a mobile connection, I knew the compass on my phone wouldn't work, but I pulled it out and clicked the compass anyway. Amazingly, the needle began to spin. I lay the compass on the map and watched as it hit north—exactly opposite of where I thought it should be.

In that moment, with horrible clarity, I realized that I had taken a wrong turn at the beginning of the trail that morning. The right-hand path I had judged to be the one that led off to the highest mountain was, in fact, the path to Inverie. My current location wasn't even on the map.

In *For Whom the Bell Tolls,* Hemingway famously describes how fear, real fear, eradicates your ability to spit. It turns out to be true. In that moment, as I realized that I was lost, I felt a physical terror I hadn't known before, and my mouth went bone-dry. No one knew where I was. This is how people die in the wilderness, I thought: out of reach, ill prepared, and utterly alone.

I considered my options, and slowly I accepted that I had to quickly retrace my steps, all 10 miles of them, to make it to Barisdale before dark. I managed to overcome my panic enough to hustle back up the devilish incline, my feet again mud-soaked, my muscles aching. I found myself propelled by the thought that each step erased a small piece of my mistake, and I hiked with tunnel vision. I made it to Barisdale just as the sun was going down and knocked on the estate manager's door, embarrassed, but perhaps never in my life so glad to see another person. In the cottage, as I cleaned my bleeding, blistered feet, I wondered whether I could catch a boat to Inverie.

But, motivated mainly by shame, I had my feet bandaged and my pack on at seven the next morning. I walked out along the same trail I had the day before, but this time stayed to the right. The trail turned steeper than the previous day's. I didn't even try for 100 steps; I barely managed 20 at a time. The climb seemed endless. If I hadn't just learned that I could get myself out of a bad situation—even if it meant trekking 20 miles out of my way—I might well have given up. But I kept going.

Finally I reached the summit. There, as promised, was the pass, and down below, on the other side, a loch. I nearly ran down the hill. Sure enough, the trail came in at the right side. Sure enough, it turned into a wide, flat track. Ninety minutes later, I faced another bay surrounded by peaks. To the right, the white houses of Inverie hugged the shore.

I went first to the Gathering, a bed-and-breakfast where the owner, Cara Gray, welcomed me with a glass of wine. This, I remembered as I sank into her sofa, was one of the benefits of humans: frequently they will give you alcohol. Gray told me a bit of the town's tragic history. It was never an easy place to live. "People used to bleed their animals and mix the blood with oatmeal for protein, then sew them back up," Gray said. During the Highland Clearances in the nineteenth century, Knoydart's population was obliterated. Landowners decided it was more profitable to turn the land over to grazing sheep than to let crofters (tenant farmers) continue to work on it. All of the peninsula's nearly 1,000 residents were evicted; some were sent to Canada, and others were left to fend for themselves.

Gray, like most of today's 100 or so Inverie residents, was drawn to the spectacular scenery and found the town's remoteness a lure, not a disadvantage. She saw the lack of cell-phone towers as a good thing.

There isn't a grocery store or a doctor in Inverie. To get to those requires a trip by ferry. But Gray can depend on a hundred other souls when the cupboard gets low. "It's ironic, though, isn't it?" she said. "Here I was drawn to the isolation, and I end up getting a stronger community than I would have had in the city."

Her words resonated with me. Maybe, I thought, what I had been craving wasn't escape from all human contact—only from certain types. I went into town, such as it was, to test the theory.

The center of Inverie, both physically and metaphorically, is the Old Forge pub. J. P. Robinet recently bought the place, having first come to Inverie on a stalking holiday, as a hunting trip is called in these parts.

Determined to maintain the pub's reputation for sociability, he turns off the Wi-Fi every night. "I want people to talk to each other," he says. And talk they do. I spent the early part of my dinner gazing out at the bay, but soon conversation was unavoidable. Locals, for whom the pub is the source of all social life, mixed with a few visitors. They drank pints, laughed loudly, and shared plates of fish and chips and steamed mussels.

A pair in their sixties, a couple of self-proclaimed Munro-baggers (adorable Scottishism No. 3: Munro-bagger = hiker who likes to knock mountains off his/her list), struck up a conversation from the table next to me. "We've been coming since 1983," said Peter. They asked what I was doing there, and, with more than a little embarrassment, I recounted what had happened. They laughed but didn't make fun of me. Instead, they urged me to try one of the pub's dozen or so scotches. I asked for guidance, and Peter suggested Talisker, made on the nearby Isle of Skye.

"Not that one!" his wife, Helen, chided, swatting him. "It's too smoky."

Soon every person within a three-table radius was weighing in on which scotch I should drink. So passionate did the conversation grow that we barely noticed when a few bars of fiddle sawed the air. One by one, diners stood up and assembled at a nearby table. Two guys with guitars joined the fiddle player, and someone else grabbed a banjo off the wall, where the pub keeps instruments for anyone who wants to play. As the musicians picked up speed, a chorus of voices joined them, first on "Irish Rover," then on Simon and Garfunkel's "The Boxer."

It had been three days since I started my trip, three days since the mere presence of others had set me on edge. But my wrong turn in the wilderness had forced me to confront true solitude and, in the process, clarified the source of my previous irritation. It wasn't all human interaction that was the problem; it was the virtual stuff, the kind of running commentary that comes at you every time you turn on your computer or pick up your phone: a constant flood of irony-tinged banality that is always on. Companionship, help, easy cheer—the interaction I found in the pub —was something altogether different, and altogether welcome. I found myself telling a few stories of my own, eager to keep this passing but real engagement going long into the night.

The next morning, I took the first ferry out to the village of Mallaig. There were about 10 others onboard, and all but one of them pulled out their phones as soon as the boat crossed back into range. I wasn't ready for that, however. Spotting the only other person who wasn't busy scrolling through missed text messages, I sidled up. It was nothing but small talk, but I was glad for the conversation.

Lawrence's Arabia

FROM *Smithsonian*

SIPPING TEA and chain-smoking L&M cigarettes in his reception tent in Mudowarra, Sheik Khaled Suleiman al-Atoun waves a hand to the outside, in a generally northern direction. "Lawrence came here, you know?" he says. "Several times. The biggest time was in January of 1918. He and other British soldiers came in armored cars and attacked the Turkish garrison here, but the Turks were too strong and they had to retreat." He pulls on his cigarette before adding with a tinge of civic pride: "Yes, the British had a very hard time here."

While the sheik was quite correct about the resiliency of the Turkish garrison in Mudowarra — the isolated outpost held out until the final days of World War I — the legendary T. E. Lawrence's "biggest time" there was open to debate. In Lawrence's own telling, that incident occurred in September 1917, when he and his Arab followers attacked a troop train just south of town, destroying a locomotive and killing some 70 Turkish soldiers.

The southernmost town in Jordan, Mudowarra was once connected to the outside world by means of that railroad. One of the great civil-engineering projects of the early twentieth century, the Hejaz Railway was an attempt by the Ottoman sultan to propel his empire into modernity and knit together his far-flung realm.

By 1914, the only remaining gap in the line was located in the mountains of southern Turkey. When that tunneling work was finished, it would have been theoretically possible to travel from the Ottoman capital of Constantinople all the way to the Arabian city of Medina, 1,800 miles distant, without ever touching the ground.

Instead, the Hejaz Railway fell victim to World War I. For nearly two years, British demolition teams, working with their Arab rebel allies, methodically attacked its bridges and isolated depots, quite rightly perceiving the railroad as the Achilles' heel of the Ottoman enemy, the supply line linking its isolated garrisons to the Turkish heartland.

One of the most prolific of the British attackers was a young army officer named T. E. Lawrence. By his count, Lawrence personally blew up 79 bridges along the railway, becoming so adept that he perfected a technique of leaving a bridge "scientifically shattered"—ruined but still standing. Turkish crews then faced the time-consuming task of dismantling the wreckage before repairs could begin.

By war's end, damage to the railway was so extensive that much of it was abandoned. In Jordan today, the line runs only from the capital city of Amman to a point 40 miles north of Mudowarra, where a modern spur veers off to the west. Around Mudowarra, all that is left is the raised berm and gravel of the rail bed, along with remnants of culverts and station houses destroyed nearly a century ago. This trail of desolation stretches south 600 miles to the Saudi Arabian city of Medina; in the Arabian Desert there still sit several of the war-mangled train cars, stranded and slowly rusting away.

One who laments the loss is Sheik al-Atoun, Mudowarra's leading citizen and a tribal leader in southern Jordan. As one of his sons, a boy of about 10, constantly refills our teacups in the reception tent, the sheik describes Mudowarra as a poor and remote area. "If the railway still existed," he says, "it would be very different. We would be connected, both economically and politically, to north and south. Instead, there is no development here, and Mudowarra has always stayed a small place."

The sheik was aware of a certain irony in his complaint, given that his grandfather worked alongside T. E. Lawrence in sabotaging the railroad. "Of course, at that time," al-Atoun says ruefully, "my grandfather thought that these destructions were a temporary matter because of the war. But they actually became permanent."

Today, T. E. Lawrence remains one of the most iconic figures of the early twentieth century. His life has been the subject of at least three movies—including one considered a masterpiece—over 70 biographies, several plays, and innumerable articles, monographs, and dissertations. His wartime memoir, *Seven Pillars of Wisdom*, translated into more than a dozen languages, remains in print nearly a full century after its first publication. As General Edmund Allenby, chief British commander in the Middle East during World War I, noted, Lawrence was first among equals: "There is no other man I know," he asserted, "who could have achieved what Lawrence did."

Part of the enduring fascination has to do with the sheer improbability of Lawrence's tale, of an unassuming young Briton who found himself the champion of a downtrodden people, thrust into events that changed the course of history. Added to this is the poignancy of his journey, so masterfully rendered in David Lean's 1962 film, *Lawrence of Arabia,* of a man trapped by divided loyalties, torn between serving the empire whose uniform he wore and being true to those fighting and dying alongside him. It is this struggle that raises the Lawrence saga to the level of Shakespearean tragedy, as it ultimately ended badly for all concerned: for Lawrence, for the Arabs, for Britain, in the slow uncoiling of history, for the Western world at large. Loosely cloaked about the figure of T. E. Lawrence there lingers the wistful specter of what might have been if only he had been listened to.

For the past several years, Sheik al-Atoun has assisted archaeologists from Bristol University in England who are conducting an extensive survey of the war in Jordan, the Great Arab Revolt Project (GARP). One of the Bristol researchers, John Winterburn, recently discovered a forgotten British Army camp in the desert 18 miles from Mudowarra; untouched for nearly a century—Winterburn even collected old gin bottles—the find was touted in the British press as the discovery of "Lawrence's Lost Camp."

"We do know that Lawrence was at that camp," Winterburn says, sitting at a Bristol University café. "But, as best we can tell, he probably stayed only a day or two. But all the men who were there much longer, none of them were Lawrence, so it becomes 'Lawrence's camp.'"

For most travelers, Highway 15, Jordan's main north-south thoroughfare, offers a dull drive through a largely featureless desert connecting Amman to more interesting places: the ruins at Petra, the Red Sea beaches of Aqaba.

To GARP codirector Nicholas Saunders, however, Highway 15 is a treasure trove. "Most people have no idea that they're traveling through one of the best-preserved battlefields in the world," he explains, "that all around them are reminders of the pivotal role this region played in World War I."

Saunders is at his desk in his cluttered office at Bristol, where scattered amid the stacks of papers and books are relics from his own explorations along Highway 15: bullet casings, cast-iron tent rings. Since 2006, Saunders has headed up some 20 GARP digs in southern Jordan, excavating everything from Turkish Army encampments and trenchworks to Arab rebel campsites and old British Royal Flying Corps airstrips. What unites these disparate sites —indeed what led to their creation—is the single-track railway that runs alongside Highway 15 for some 250 miles: the old Hejaz Railway.

As first articulated by T. E. Lawrence, the goal wasn't to permanently sever the Turks' southern lifeline, but rather to keep it barely functioning. The Turks would have to constantly devote resources to its repair, while their garrisons, receiving just enough supplies to survive, would be stranded. Indications of this strategy are everywhere evident along Highway 15; while many of the original small bridges and culverts that the Ottomans constructed to navigate the region's seasonal waterways are still in place—instantly recognizable by their ornate stonework arches—many more are of modern, steel-beam construction, denoting where the originals were blown up during the war.

The GARP expeditions have produced an unintended consequence. Jordan's archaeological sites have long been plundered by looters—and this has now extended to World War I sites. Fueled by the folkloric memory of how Turkish forces and Arab rebels often traveled with large amounts of gold coins—Lawrence himself doled out tens of thousands of English pounds' worth of gold in payments to his followers—locals quickly descend on any newly discovered Arab Revolt site with spades in hand to start digging.

"So of course, we're part of the problem," Saunders says. "The locals see all these rich foreigners digging away," he adds wryly, "on our hands and knees all day in the hot sun, and they think to themselves, 'No way. No way are they doing this for some old bits of metal; they're here to find the gold.'"

As a result, GARP archaeologists remain on a site until satisfied that they've found everything of interest, and then, with the Jordanian government's permission, take everything with them when closing down the site. From past experience, they know they're likely to discover only mounds of turned earth upon their return.

Set amid rolling brown hills given over to groves of orange and pistachio trees, the village of Karkamis has the soporific feel of many rural towns in southern Turkey. On its slightly rundown main street, shopkeepers gaze vacantly out at deserted sidewalks, while in a tiny, tree-shaded plaza, idle men play dominoes or cards.

If this seems a peculiar setting for the place where a young Lawrence first came to his appreciation of the Arab world, the answer actually lies about a mile east of the village. There, on a promontory above a ford of the Euphrates, sits the ruins of the ancient city of Carchemish. While human habitation on that hilltop dates back at least 5,000 years, it was a desire to unlock the secrets of the Hittites, a civilization that reached its apogee in the eleventh century B.C., that first brought a 22-year-old Lawrence here in 1911.

Even before Carchemish, there were signs that the world might well hear of T. E. Lawrence in some capacity. Born in 1888, the second of five boys in an upper-middle-class British family, his almost paralyzing shyness masked a brilliant mind and a ferocious independent streak.

For his history thesis at Oxford, Lawrence resolved to study the Crusader castles of Syria, alone and on foot and at the height of the brutal Middle East summer. It was a 1,200-mile walk that carried him into villages that had never seen a European before—certainly not an unaccompanied European who, at 5-foot-4, looked to be all of 15—and it marked the beginning of his fascination with the East. "I will have such difficulty in becoming English again," Lawrence wrote home amid his journey, sounding much like any modern college student on a junior year abroad; the difference in Lawrence's case was that this appraisal proved quite accurate.

The transformation was confirmed when, after graduating from Oxford, he wheedled his way onto a British Museum–sponsored archaeological expedition decamping for Carchemish. As the junior assistant on that dig, and one of only two Westerners permanently on-site, Lawrence saw to his scientific duties—primarily photographing and inventorying the finds—but developed an even keener interest in understanding how Arab society worked.

Learning Arabic, he took to quizzing members of the local work crew on their family histories, on the region's complex clan and tribal affiliations, and often visited the laborers in their homes to glimpse their lives up close. To the degree that these workmen had dealt with Westerners before, it had been in the master-servant form; to meet someone who took a genuine interest in their culture, joined to Lawrence's very un-Western tolerance for hardship and hard work, drew them to the young Briton as a kindred spirit. "The foreigners come out here always to teach," he wrote his parents from Carchemish, "whereas they had much better learn."

The dig in northern Syria, originally funded for one year, stretched into four. He wrote a friend in 1913, extolling his comfortable life in Carchemish, that he intended to remain as long as the funding lasted and then go on to "another and another nice thing." That plan abruptly ended with the onset of World War I in August 1914, and Lawrence, back in England on leave, was destined never to see Carchemish again.

From his time in Syria, Lawrence had developed a clear, if simplistic, view of the Ottoman Empire—admiration for the free-spirited Arab, disgust at the corruption and inefficiency of their Turkish overseers—and looked forward to the day when the Ottoman "yoke" might be cast aside. That opportunity, and the chance for Lawrence to play a role, arrived when Turkey entered the war on the side of Germany and Austria-Hungary. Because of his experience in the region, Lawrence was dispatched to Egypt, the British base of operations for the upcoming campaign against the Turks, as a second lieutenant in military intelligence.

Despite the fact that he and other members of the intelligence branch urged that Britain forge alliances with Arab groups ready to revolt against the Turks, the generals in Cairo seemed intent on fighting the same conventional frontal assault war that had already proved so disastrous in Europe. The most immediate result was the Gallipoli fiasco of 1915, in which the British Commonwealth suffered nearly a quarter-million casualties before finally conceding failure. Making it all the more painful for the deskbound Lawrence was the death in quick succession of two of his brothers on the western front. "They were both younger than I am," he wrote a friend, "and it doesn't seem right, somehow, that I should go on living peacefully in Cairo."

It wasn't until October 1916, two years after his arrival in Egypt, that Lawrence would find himself catapulted to his destiny.

*

To approach the Arabian Peninsula by sea is to invite one of the more unsettling of natural phenomena, that moment when the sea-cooled air abruptly collides with that coming off the desert, when the temperature can jump by 20, even 30, degrees in a matter of seconds. Probably no one described this better than T. E. Lawrence, who, when recounting his approach to the Red Sea port city of Jeddah on the morning of October 16, 1916, wrote, "The heat of Arabia came out like a drawn sword and struck us speechless."

His presence there had come about almost by chance. Four months earlier, and after protracted secret negotiations with British authorities in Cairo, Emir Hussein, ruler of the Hejaz region of central Arabia, had launched an Arab revolt against the Turks. Initially matters had gone well. Catching the Turks by surprise, Hussein's rebels seized the holy city of Mecca along with Jeddah, but there the rebellion had foundered. By October, the Turks remained in firm control of the Arabian interior, including the city of Medina, and appeared poised to crush the rebels. When Lawrence learned that a friend in Cairo was being dispatched to Arabia to gauge the crisis, he arranged a temporary leave from his desk job to tag along.

Over the course of that 10-day visit, Lawrence managed to fully insinuate himself in the Arab rebel cause, and to win the confidence of Hussein's chief battlefield commander, his third son, Faisal. In short order, Lawrence was appointed the British Army's temporary liaison to Faisal, a posting that soon became permanent.

Having used his time in Carchemish to study the clan and tribal structure of Arab society, Lawrence intuitively grasped the delicate negotiating process necessary to win tribal leaders over to the rebel cause. What's more, waging war in early-twentieth-century Arabia revolved around the same primal issues—where an army on the move might find water and forage for its animals —as the wars of fourteenth-century Europe that Lawrence had so thoroughly studied at Oxford. Very quickly, Faisal came to regard the young British officer as one of his most trusted advisers, as Lawrence, donning the robes of an Arab sheik, assumed a position of honor in tribal strategy sessions. With British naval help, the Arabs captured a succession of Turkish-held towns along the Red Sea coast, while Lawrence organized guerrilla raids against the inland Hejaz Railway.

But Faisal's young liaison officer also harbored a guilty secret. From his time in Cairo, Lawrence was aware of the extravagant promises the British government had made to Hussein in order to raise the Arab Revolt: full independence for virtually the entire Arab world. What Lawrence also knew was that just months after cementing that deal with Hussein, Britain had entered into a secret compact with its chief ally in the war, France. Under the Sykes-Picot Agreement, the future independent Arab nation was to be relegated to the wastelands of Arabia, while all the regions of value —Iraq, greater Syria—were to be allocated to the imperial spheres of Britain and France. As Lawrence recruited ever more tribes to the cause of future Arab independence, he became increasingly conscience-stricken by the "dead letter" promises he was making, and finally reached a breaking point. His first act of sedition—and by most any standards, a treasonous one—was to inform Faisal of the existence of Sykes-Picot. His second would lead to the greatest triumph of his career: the capture of Aqaba.

By the early spring of 1917, talk of a joint British-French amphibious landing at the small fishing port of Aqaba gained great currency among the Allied leadership in Cairo. Aqaba was both the Turkish enemy's last outpost on the Red Sea and a natural gateway —at least so it appeared on a map—to the southern reaches of Syria, the heartland of the Arab world.

Modern Aqaba is a sprawling city of 140,000, its dense downtown giving way to new subdivisions, shopping malls, and office complexes steadily expanding over its foothills. If King Abdullah II of Jordan has his way, the expansion won't slow any time soon. Reflecting the king's vision for converting his nation's only seaport into a world-class economic and tourist destination, the empty land south of town has been laced with modern roads. But those roads lead to nowhere in particular, while tattered billboards advertise the condominium complexes and industrial parks allegedly to come.

Those in search of "old Aqaba" will be disappointed. This consists of a tiny stone fort near the oceanfront promenade and, next to it, a dusty four-room museum. Dominating the small plaza in front of the museum is perhaps Aqaba's most peculiar landmark, a 430-foot flagpole—the second highest freestanding flagpole in the world, according to the local tourism bureau. It was at just about this spot that, on the morning of July 6, 1917, Lawrence and his exultant rebel followers would sweep through the streets to take a "victory bath" in the sea.

By odd happenstance, Lawrence had visited Aqaba just a few months before the war began. From that firsthand experience, Lawrence knew that the "gateway" into Syria was actually through a winding, 20-mile-long mountain gorge that the Turks had laced with trenchworks and forts designed to annihilate any force advancing up from the coast.

Lawrence also perceived a political trap. If the British and French took control of Aqaba, they could effectively bottle up their Arab allies and contain their rebellion to Arabia. That done, whenever the two European imperial powers did manage to push into Syria—promised to the French under Sykes-Picot—they could renege on the promises made to Hussein with a clearer conscience.

Since any advance inland from Aqaba would be murderous, Lawrence's solution was to first take the gorge and then the port. And to thwart his own nation's imperial designs, he simply kept his plan to himself. On the day he set out from the Arabian coast, embarking on a 600-mile camel trek through the desert to fall on Aqaba from behind, not one of Lawrence's fellow British officers knew where he was headed or what he intended to do when he got there. Accompanying him were a mere 45 rebels. On their journey, a two-month ordeal that would take them across one of the world's harshest landscapes, each of the men started with only water and a 45-pound sack of flour as provisions.

Forming the dramatic centerpiece of Lean's *Lawrence of Arabia* is the moment when Lawrence and his rebel band launch their surprise attack on Aqaba from behind. Led by a triumphant white-robed Peter O'Toole, the rebels bear down on the stunned Turks.

In reality, the crucial battle for Aqaba occurred 40 miles to the north, in the "lost" wadi of Aba el Lissan. It was there, with the hellish two-month trek through the desert completed and Aqaba almost in his grasp, that Lawrence learned a Turkish relief force was marching in his direction. Even if his rebel army—swelled to nearly 1,000 with recruits—continued on to Aqaba, Lawrence reasoned, this enemy column would soon catch up; there was no choice but to destroy it first.

They found the Turks camping in Aba el Lissan on the night of July 1, 1917, and what ensued there was less a battle than a massacre. The Turkish force of 550 soldiers was virtually wiped out at the cost of 2 Arab dead. With the path cleared, Lawrence and his men rushed on for Aqaba, the Turkish garrison there surrendering after barely firing a shot.

Clad in worn sandals and lifting the hem of his robe to avoid the snag of thornbushes, Abu Enad Daraoush picks his way over the hillside. To the untrained eye, the wadi of Aba el Lissan is indistinguishable from a thousand other windswept valleys in southern Jordan, but Daraoush, a 48-year-old farmer and shepherd, knows its secrets. Reaching a rock outcropping, he points out a feature on the level ground below: five or six circles of cleared earth, each about 10 feet across and delineated by rings of large boulders. Resembling oversized fire pits, the circles are the traces of a Turkish Army encampment, where soldiers had cleared the earth and pitched their distinctive round tents. In 2014, that camp is nearly a century old—97 years old, to be precise.

Daraoush and the other villagers of Aba el Lissan have collected military detritus here—bullets, uniform buttons, metal bits from horse harnesses—enough to know that the Turkish force was sizable. They also know it ended badly for the Turks. From the rock outcropping, Daraoush points to the wadi basin, perhaps 200 feet away. "Down there we found the bodies," he says. "Not complete bodies, but bones. When I was a boy, I used to take them to school to show my friends." Daraoush gazes up at the enclosing ridgelines. "This is a place where many, many Turks died."

As Daraoush and I walk across the battlefield, he laughs lightly. "Now that you are here, perhaps you can finally show us where the gold is buried."

It is meant as a joke, but one with a slight edge to it. While a Turkish force often carried a small quantity of gold, during Lawrence's two years at the battlefront, his caravans frequently included several camels used to haul nothing but gold coins to pay his recruits. As a result, the urban—or rather, rural—myth was spawned, holding that sacks of stashed gold are likely to be found wherever the two warring sides collided.

Aba el Lissan has been virtually stripped bare of any remnants of war by scavengers. In this impoverished corner of Jordan, the smallest piece of metal has value for scrap. In over an hour of scouring the land, I found only a Turkish bullet casing and the top of an old British Army rations can stenciled with the words *Punch here*.

Toward the end of our walk, Daraoush leads me to one particular gold-hunter hole set away from the others. With a tinge of embarrassment, he offers that "a neighbor" had dug the hole a year or two earlier in search of booty, but instead had found the skeleton of a buried Turkish soldier. "He had been placed on his side, with his hands folded under his head," Daraoush says. "It was like he was sleeping." He pointed to the hole. "So we just buried him back up. What else was there to do?"

While the Aqaba campaign is considered one of the greatest military feats of the early twentieth century—it is still studied in military colleges today—Lawrence soon followed it with a masterstroke of even greater consequence. Racing to Cairo to inform the British high command of what he had achieved, he discovered that the previous British commander in chief, never a strong supporter of the Arab Revolt, had been dismissed following two failed frontal attacks against the Turks. His replacement, a mere two weeks into the job when an emaciated and barefoot Lawrence was summoned to his office, was a cavalry general named Edmund Allenby.

Rather lost in Lawrence's electrifying news from Aqaba was any thought as to why the junior officer hadn't informed his superiors of his scheme, let alone of its possible political consequences. Instead, with his newfound celebrity, Lawrence saw the opportunity to win over the green Allenby with a tantalizing prospect.

During their slog across the desert, Lawrence had, with only two escorts, conducted a remarkable reconnaissance mission across enemy-held Syria. There, he told Allenby, he had determined that huge numbers of Syrian Arabs were ready to join the rebels. Lawrence also vastly exaggerated both the strength and capability of those rebels already under arms to paint an enticing picture of a military juggernaut—the British advancing up the Palestine coast as the Arabs took the fight to the Syrian interior. As Lawrence recounted in *Seven Pillars:* "Allenby could not make out how much [of me] was genuine performer and how much charlatan. The problem was working behind his eyes, and I left him unhelped to solve it."

But Allenby bought it, promising to give the rebels all the aid he could and consider them equal partners. From now on, in Lawrence's estimation, the British Army and Arab rebels would be joined at the hip, the French relegated to the margins. If the rebels reached Damascus first, they might be able to wrest Syria from the French altogether. Or so Lawrence hoped.

After our tea in his reception tent, Sheik al-Atoun takes me in his old four-wheel-drive Toyota up to a promontory overlooking Mudowarra. Along for the adventure are five of his young sons and nephews, standing in the Toyota's open bed and trying—with limited success—to avoid being pitched about during the bucking ride. Ringing the hilltop are remnants of the trenchworks from which the Turks had repeatedly repelled British attacks on the town. "Even with their armored cars and airplanes, they had great problems," the sheik says. "The Turks here were very brave fighters."

Al-Atoun's words hint at the complicated emotions the legacy of World War I and the Arab Revolt stir in this part of the Arab world: pride at having cast off their Ottoman overseers after 400 years of rule, a lingering sadness at what took its place. The sheik points to a cluster of whitewashed homes perhaps 10 miles away.

"That is Saudi Arabia. I have family and many friends there, but if I wish to visit them—or they to visit me—I must have a visa and go through customs. Why? We are one people, the Arabs, and we should be one nation, but instead we have been divided into—what, twenty-two?—different countries. This is wrong. We should all be together."

Quite understandably, Sheik al-Atoun blames the situation on the peace imposed by the European imperial powers at the end of World War I, a peace that T. E. Lawrence tried mightily to forestall.

Despite punching through the Turkish line in southern Palestine and taking Jerusalem in December 1917, the British Army ground to a halt as Allenby's troops were siphoned off for the western front. Operating from the Arabs' new headquarters in Aqaba, Lawrence continued to lead raids against the railway and into the hill country west of the Dead Sea, but this was hardly the grand, paralyzing offensive he had outlined to Allenby. The desultory nature of the war continued through the summer of 1918.

But something had happened to Lawrence in the interim. In November 1917, while conducting a secret reconnaissance mission into the strategic railway town of Deraa, he was briefly captured by the Turks, then subjected to torture—and, by most all evidence, rape—at the hands of the local Turkish governor. Managing to escape back to rebel lines, a far more hardened, even merciless, Lawrence began to emerge.

While Lean's *Lawrence of Arabia* dealt obliquely with Lawrence's Deraa ordeal, one aspect it captured exquisitely was his gradual unhinging in the field. In some battles, Lawrence ordered his followers to take no prisoners, or administered coups de grâce to men too badly wounded to be carried. In others, he took nearly suicidal risks. He attacked a Turkish troop train despite being so short of weapons that some of his men could only throw rocks at the enemy. If this was rooted in the trauma at Deraa, it seems he was at least as much driven by the desperate belief that if the Arabs could reach Damascus first, then the lies and guilty secrets he had harbored since coming to Arabia might somehow be set right.

On every road leading out of the ramshackle Jordanian border town of Ramtha there occurs a curious phenomenon: three- and four-story mansions set amid manicured and walled gardens. "The smugglers," explains the owner of a tiny refreshment shop on Ramtha's main street. He points down the road to the border crossing with Syria, a half-mile away. "The frontier has been officially closed for a year and a half now, so there's a lot of money to be made. They move everything across—guns, drugs, cooking oil, whatever you can imagine."

Six miles across that border stands the Syrian town of Deraa, the site where today's Syrian civil war started and where Turkish forces briefly imprisoned Lawrence. Now, by all accounts, Deraa is a shattered shell of itself, its streets in ruins, the vast majority of its population gone. Many have ended up in the sprawling Jordanian refugee camp of Zaatari north of Amman—or here, in Ramtha.

"All the shops here are run by the Syrians now," the Ramtha shopkeeper said, gesturing out at the commercial thoroughfare. "They have completely taken over." His complaints about the newcomers echo those one hears about immigrants everywhere in the world: that they take away jobs from the locals, that they have caused rents to skyrocket. "I don't know how much worse it can get," he says with a long-suffering sigh, "but I know it won't get better until the war there ends."

Fifteen miles to the west of Ramtha lie the ancient Greco-Roman ruins of Umm Qays, situated on a rocky promontory. On a clear day it is possible to see as far north as the Golan Heights and the Sea of Galilee. In the closing days of World War I, it was not these distant spots that made Umm Qays vitally strategic, but rather the sinuous Yarmouk Valley lying directly below.

When General Allenby launched his offensive against the Turks in Palestine in late September 1918, the engagement quickly turned into a rout. Virtually the only escape left open to the Turks was up through the Yarmouk, to the railway at Deraa. But awaiting the Turks once they climbed out of the valley were T. E. Lawrence and thousands of Arab rebel soldiers. One year after Deraa, Lawrence returned to the place of his torments and now he would exact a terrible revenge.

At one time, the 2,000-year-old stone fortress of Azraq rose out of the eastern Jordan desert like an apparition, a 60-foot-high monolith. The upper floors and battlements collapsed in a massive earthquake in 1927, but the structure is still impressive enough to draw the occasional tourist bus from Amman, 50 miles to the west. The first place these tourists are led is to a small garret above the still-intact south tower, a space that guides refer to simply as "the Lawrence room."

It is a low-ceilinged chamber, cool and vaguely damp, with stone floors and narrow windows that give a view onto the surrounding desert. It has the feel of a place of refuge, and in fact Lawrence recuperated here after his ordeal in Deraa, 60 miles northwest. It is also where, at the climactic moment of World War I in the Middle East, he plotted the Arab Army's all-out assault on Turkish forces in inland Syria.

That attack was to be coordinated with Allenby's sweep north through Palestine. It was Lawrence's mission to cut off the Turks' retreat at their most vulnerable spot: the railroad juncture of Deraa. Early on the morning of September 19, 1918, Lawrence and his followers began slipping out of Azraq castle, bound for the town where Lawrence had been tortured.

On September 27, after coming upon the village of Tafas, where the fleeing Turks had massacred many residents, Lawrence ordered his men to give "no quarter." Throughout that day, the rebels picked apart a retreating column of 4,000, slaughtering all they found, but as Lawrence doubled back that afternoon, he discovered one unit had missed the command and taken 250 Turks and Germans captive. "We turned our Hotchkiss [machine gun] on the prisoners," he noted in his battlefield report, "and made an end of them." Lawrence was even more explicit about his actions that day in *Seven Pillars.* "In a madness born of the horror of Tafas we killed and killed, even blowing in the heads of the fallen and of the animals, as though their death and running blood could slake our agony."

Racing on to Damascus, Lawrence swiftly set up a provisional Arab government, with Faisal at its head. But when Allenby reached Damascus two days later, he summoned Lawrence and Faisal to the Victoria Hotel to inform them that, as outlined by Sykes-Picot, the city was to be placed under French administration. No sooner had a defeated Faisal left the room than Lawrence begged Allenby to be relieved of his command.

But Lawrence wasn't finished fighting just yet. With the war in Europe drawing to a close, he hurried to London to begin lining up support for the Arab cause at the upcoming Paris Peace Conference. Acting as Faisal's personal agent, he frantically lobbied prime ministers and presidents to uphold the promises made to the Arabs and to prevent a peace imposed along the lines laid out in Sykes-Picot. By that scheme, "Greater" Syria was to be divided into four political entities—Palestine, Transjordan, Lebanon, and Syria—with the British taking the first two, the French the latter. As for Iraq, Britain had planned to annex only the oil-rich southern section, but with more oil discovered in the north, they now wanted the whole thing.

Lawrence sought allies wherever he could find them. Surely the most remarkable was Chaim Weizmann, head of the English Zionist Federation. In January 1919, on the eve of the peace conference, Lawrence had engineered an agreement between Faisal and Weizmann. In return for Zionist support of a Faisal-led Syria, Faisal would support increased Jewish emigration into Palestine, tacitly recognizing a future Jewish state in the region. The pact was soon scuttled by the French.

But the most poignant what-might-have-been involved the Americans. Suspicious of the imperialist schemes of his European partners in Paris, President Woodrow Wilson sent a fact-finding commission to the Middle East. For three months, the King-Crane Commission toured Syria, Lebanon, and Palestine, and what they heard was unequivocal: the vast majority of every ethnic and religious group wanted independence or, barring that, American administration. Wilson, however, had far more interest in telling other nations how they should behave than in adding to American responsibilities. When the commission returned to Paris with its inconvenient finding, the report was simply locked away in a vault.

Lawrence's efforts produced a cruel irony. At the same time that he was becoming a matinee idol in Britain, courtesy of a fanciful lecture show of his exploits delivered by American journalist Lowell Thomas, he was increasingly regarded by senior British officials as the enemy within, the malcontent who stood in the way of victorious Britain and France dividing the spoils of war. In the end, the obstreperous lieutenant colonel was effectively barred from the peace conference and prevented any further contact with Faisal. That accomplished, the path to imperial concord—and betrayal —was clear.

The repercussions were swift in coming. Within the year, most all of the Middle East was aflame as the Arab world, enraged at seeing their Ottoman masters replaced by European ones, rebelled. Lawrence was particularly prescient about Iraq. In 1919, he had predicted full-scale revolt against British rule there by March 1920 —"if we don't mend our ways." The result of the uprising in May 1920 was some 10,000 dead, including 1,000 British soldiers and administrators.

Tasked to clean up the debacle was the new British colonial secretary, Winston Churchill, who turned for help to the man whose warnings had been spurned: T. E. Lawrence. At the Cairo Conference in 1921, Lawrence helped to redress some of the wrongs. In the near future, Faisal, deposed by the French in Syria, would be placed on a new throne in British-controlled Iraq. Out of the British buffer state of Transjordan, the nation of Jordan would be created, with Faisal's brother, Abdullah, at its head.

Gone forever, though, was the notion of a unified Arab nation. Vanished also was Lawrence's spirit for the fight, or desire for leadership. As his collaboration with Churchill drew to an end, he legally changed his name and petitioned to reenlist in the British military as a private. As he explained to a friend, he never wanted to be in a position of responsibility again.

On a country lane in the southwestern English county of Dorset sits a two-story cottage surrounded by rhododendron bushes. It is a tiny place, less than 700 square feet, consisting of two small rooms on each floor connected by a steep and rickety staircase, redolent with the smell of leather and old books. Curiously, it has neither a kitchen nor a toilet. Known as Clouds Hill, it was the last home of T. E. Lawrence. Not that this was how he was known to his neighbors; he was Private T. E. Shaw, a reclusive serviceman rarely seen except when riding his beloved Brough motorcycle through the countryside.

After rejoining the British military in 1921, Lawrence spent most of the next 14 years in lowly military positions in bases scattered about Britain. While stationed in Dorset in 1929, he bought Clouds Hill as a place to go in refuge, to read and listen to music. In walking through the claustrophobic cottage, however, it is hard to escape the image of a broken and lonely man.

Along with the disappointment of seeing his dream for the Arab world slip away, the postwar Lawrence clearly suffered from what is known today as post-traumatic stress disorder; throughout the 1920s and early 1930s, he suffered bouts of depression, cutting off contact with all but a handful of old friends. In 1935, at the age of 46, he decided to retire from the military—the only "family" he had known for 20 years—but this was a decision that also filled him with a certain dread, unsure of how he would fill his unregimented days. As he wrote to a friend on May 6, 1935, as he was settling into Clouds Hill permanently: "At present the feeling is mere bewilderment. I imagine leaves must feel this after they have fallen from their tree and until they die. Let's hope that will not be my continuing state."

It would not be. Precisely a week later, Lawrence had a fatal motorcycle accident near Clouds Hill. At his passing, Winston Churchill eulogized, "I deem him one of the greatest beings alive in our time. I do not see his like elsewhere. I fear whatever our need we shall never see his like again."

In the Arab world, memory of Lawrence is far more mixed; indeed, the changing view of him there underscores the lingering bitterness still felt over the peace imposed nearly a century ago. That becomes clear when I ask Sheik al-Atoun in his reception tent in Mudowarra how Lawrence is regarded today. At first, he tries to tactfully skirt the question.

"Some people think he was really trying to help the Arabs," he replies, "but others think it was all a trick, that Lawrence was actually working for the British Empire all along." When I press for his opinion, the sheik grows slightly discomfited. "May I speak frankly? Maybe some of the very old ones still believe he was a friend of the Arabs, but almost everyone else, we know the truth. Even my grandfather, before he died, he believed he had been tricked."

It was a comment that seemed to encapsulate the ultimate tragedy of both Lawrence and the Middle East—but there is a far more graphic illustration of that tragedy. It is to be found at Carchemish.

It was at Carchemish that Lawrence first came to despise the despotism of Ottoman Turkey and to imagine an independent Arab nation with Syria at its heart; today, of course, Turkey is a democracy while Syria is in the grips of an unspeakably savage civil war. Karkamis, where the town's sleepiness gives way to a tinge of menace, sits at the very dividing line between those two realities.

The hilltop sprawl of Hittite ruins is now a Turkish police post, off-limits to visitors, while at the base of that hill a 15-foot-high concrete wall topped with concertina wire has recently been erected. On the other side of that wall, in the Syrian town of Jarabulus, fly the black-and-white war flags of a rebel group known as the Islamic State of Iraq and the Levant, or ISIS, an Islamic fundamentalist faction so murderous and extreme it has been disavowed by its former umbrella organization, al-Qaeda. In Karkamis's grim little park, idle Syrian men who managed to escape tell of family and friends being butchered at the hands of ISIS, of how Jarabulus has become a ghost town.

A Syrian refugee in his mid-forties, unwilling even to disclose his name, tells me that he had planned to escape with his family six months earlier when, on the eve of their departure, ISIS had grabbed his teenage son. "I sent my wife and younger children on to Lebanon," he says, "but I stayed behind to try and get my son back."

He points to a teenager in blue jeans and a red T-shirt sitting on a brick wall a few feet away, gazing up at the canopy of trees with a placid, faraway smile. "That's him," he says. "After six days, I managed to get him back, but the terrorists had already destroyed him." The father taps a forefinger against his own temple, the universal gesture to indicate a person gone mad. "That's all he does now, smile that way."

From the Turkish side could be heard the call to jihad wafting from ISIS's loudspeakers. Somewhere over that wall, a half-mile from the Carchemish ruins, sits Lawrence's old research station, a former licorice storehouse that he lovingly repaired and converted into a comfortable home. Now it is a place that no Westerner will likely see for a very long time to come.

21st Century Limited

FROM *Harper's Magazine*

WE START IN DARKNESS. After fighting our way through the dingy, low-ceilinged, crowded waiting room that serves as New York City's current Pennsylvania Station, we pull out through a graffitied tunnel that follows one of the oldest roadbeds in America. Freight trains once clattered along open tracks here, spewing smoke within a few dozen yards of the mansions along Riverside Drive and attracting one of the most dangerous hobo encampments in the country, before it was finally all buried beneath a graceful park in the 1930s. Today we emerge into sunlight for the first time in Harlem, following a route up the glorious Hudson River, past Bear and Storm King Mountains and the old ruined Bannerman castle on Pollepel Island.

A dining car is attached at Albany—a delay that takes an hour. For that matter, we are not actually in Albany but in Rensselaer, across the river, where in 2002 Amtrak completed the largest train station built in this country since 1939—a structure that has all the individuality of a shopping-mall Barnes & Noble. But we gladly seize the opportunity to stand on the open platform and stare across the Hudson at the capital. It's a splendid early-fall evening, and we're at the start of an adventure. We smoke and stretch our legs, and I chat with Derrick, our sleeping-car porter, who is in charge of providing for all the passengers in his five compartments and ten "roomettes." He tells me he emigrated from Uganda and has been working for the railroad for the past two and a half years.

Amtrak's long-distance dining and sleeper-car crews tend to be efficient and almost indefatigably friendly, despite the long trips and the relentless demands of their jobs. A high percentage of them are people of color, an old railroad tradition. (George Pullman, searching for an uncomplaining workforce to service his new cars, began the practice of recruiting former slaves to work as porters soon after the Civil War. Yet they did not prove as pliable as Pullman would have liked; though it took them decades, they organized their own union, the Brotherhood of Sleeping Car Porters, under slogans such as "Fight or Be Slaves," and hired a socialist firebrand named A. Philip Randolph to run it.)

By the time we step back on the train in Rensselaer, we can hear the dining-car crew setting up for the evening meal. Once, railroad-dining-car chefs produced some of the best food in America at almost any time of the day or night, serving up regional specialties on real china, with glass, silver, and fine linen napkins. Today the food is prepackaged and warmed up, airline-style meals served mostly on hardened paper or plastic dishes. All across America the menus are the same: a choice of reasonably edible steak, hamburger, chicken, salmon, or pasta, accompanied by a couple of dinner rolls and an anemic salad. But the real attraction is the strangers you're seated with.

My first night I sit with a merry retired couple, Mark and Linda, a former middle-school teacher and an accountant from Hyde Park, New York, who love train travel. They constitute, I will discover, one of the three leading categories of long-distance train passengers: train enthusiasts, derisively called foamers by Amtrak crew members. (The others are tourists from Britain and those who, for one reason or another—physical or psychological—cannot tolerate the many inconveniences of air travel.)

Mark and Linda are foamers. They buy everything on their Amtrak credit cards in order to run up rewards points, as do many of the enthusiasts I encountered. Mark is also a model-train buff. They are New Deal liberals, and though outright politics is almost religiously avoided around the close quarters of an Amtrak dining table, most sleeping-car passengers will let on quietly, almost conspiratorially, that they believe in things like public investment, and not just for trains.

Mark can reel off the names of the towns we are passing in upstate New York even in the darkness—"Amsterdam, Utica,

Syracuse!"—from his time spent camping in the area with his two sons. But he and Linda are disheartened by the economic disaster that has hit much of upstate, and wonder what is to become of the region where they've spent so much of their lives.

We are following the route of the New York Central's most famous train, the 20th Century Limited, which once rivaled Europe's Orient Express in extravagance. At five o'clock every evening, porters used to roll a red carpet to the train across the platform of Grand Central Terminal's Track 34. The women passengers were given bouquets of flowers and bottles of perfume; the men, carnations for their buttonholes. The train had its own barbershop, post office, manicurists and masseuses, secretaries, typists, and stenographers. In 1938, its beautiful blue-gray-and-aluminum-edged cars and its "streamline" locomotives—finned, bullet-nosed, art deco masterpieces of fluted steel—took just 16 hours to reach Chicago, faster than any train running today.

The 20th Century Limited became a cultural icon. It was a luxury train, but middle-class people rode it, too. In the heyday of American train travel after World War II, they also rode the Broadway Limited, the Super Chief from Chicago to Los Angeles, and the California Zephyr, which were nearly as celebrated and beloved.

Some 20 years later, it was all over. Virtually every privately owned passenger rail line had died by 1970, done in by cheap gas and jet engines. The pathetic mishmash of decaying stock that remained was lumped together into a Nixonian experiment: a publicly funded, for-profit corporation dubbed Amtrak. It was widely believed that this arrangement was set up to fail, because saving trains seemed pointless. Americans wishing to travel long distances could drive their cars on the interstates or take a plane or intercity bus. Railroads seemed as archaic a mode of transportation as the wagon train.

But unexpectedly, ridership began to creep up—from fewer than 16 million in 1972 to more than 21 million in 1980. After 9/11, when air travel turned into unmitigated misery, it shot up to 30 million. Along the northeast corridor, between Washington and Boston, which generates 80 percent of Amtrak's revenue, the train's share of all combined plane and rail traffic has more than doubled, from 37 percent in 2000 to 75 percent today.

Barack Obama, during his 2011 State of the Union address, promised to lead America into a green industrial economy, and he committed his administration to a vision of giving "eighty percent of Americans access to high-speed rail within twenty-five years." In 2009, invoking our history—Lincoln starting the transcontinental railroad while the Civil War raged, Eisenhower building the interstates during the Cold War—and challenging our national honor ("There's no reason why we can't do this: this is America"), the president made the argument that "building a new system of high-speed rail in America will be faster, cheaper, and easier than building more freeways or adding to an already overburdened aviation system—and everybody stands to benefit."

Trains would help end our dependence on oil as well as our rapid transformation of the earth's climate and allow us to recreate sustainable communities. Now we would have new trains, fast trains, magnetic-levitation trains that never touch the ground. Not just between nearby cities but across entire states and regions, eliminating the need for new airports and highways, replacing countless barrels of oil with electricity, or maybe using no traditional power source at all!

Yet by the fall of 2013, plans for any new high-speed national rail system—plans even for seriously upgrading our existing rail system—had been delayed for the foreseeable future. How had this come to pass? We used to value trains, used to imbue them and their stations with all the grace, beauty, and efficiency we were capable of as a people and a democracy.

To cross the continent by train in the fall of 2013, just as the organized right was about to shut down the national government, was an opportunity to trace our country's entire fantastical boom-and-bust progress. It was also a chance to glimpse an American treasure that if squandered might never be regained.

The Lake Shore Limited is not, strictly speaking, a limited train, since it makes 18 stops on its way to Chicago. The name is due mostly to Amtrak's effort to evoke the great trains of the past, but it does follow the old water-level route around the Great Lakes, advertised as superior for sleeping because it does not climb and descend the mountain grades of the Alleghenies.

Nonetheless, I'm awakened repeatedly by the banging of cars and the grinding and wrenching of metal wheels along the track.

The Lake Shore Limited pulls into stations or onto sidings to let other trains pass, then sprints to make up the time—a constant slowing and accelerating that is characteristic of long-distance Amtrak trains and that makes sustained sleep difficult.

At half past three in the morning we stop again, and I peer outside into the darkness. There is only a flat little box of a train station visible, and a small parking lot surrounded by a chain-link fence. A few figures hurry furtively to their cars. I watch as they drive out past a single, towering wind turbine, a tangle of utility wires, and a looming football arena with a sign proclaiming it First-Energy Stadium. Only by looking at the Lake Shore's timetable can I tell that we are in Cleveland.

"FirstEnergy" is appropriate enough. Cleveland was the hub of America's first real energy boom, in the original oil fields of western Pennsylvania and eastern Ohio. This is where John D. Rockefeller made his fortune, not so much because of any expertise he had in finding or refining oil but because of a deal he cut with the railroads whereby they agreed to charge all his competitors as much as double the rate while providing Rockefeller with a secret discount and kickbacks on his competitors' shipments.

The landscape before me today, a hundred years later, tells a different story of corporate hegemony. The old Cleveland station, where intercity trains stopped until 1977, was an outstanding example of Beaux Arts design constructed in the late 1920s by local brothers named Van Sweringen in imitation of New York's Grand Central.

The station is still gorgeous, but trains don't run there anymore, save for a few local commuter lines. Amtrak couldn't afford the rent, so instead it lets anyone who wants to go to Cleveland off where we are, at Lakefront Station. Lakefront is what foamers call an Amshack—a building that looks as if it might be a storage facility for the files of an accounting firm that went out of business sometime during the Ford administration.

It used to be that private corporations could be relied on to build exquisite public spaces at their own expense, not just slap their names on a finished product. American train stations were once the most magnificent in the world. Even in the smallest towns, they tended to be little jewels of craftsmanship. In bigger cities, they were the first monumental modern buildings erected without reference to God or king, built by the people to move the people.

Most of the leading American architects from the 1890s through the next 40 years tried their hand at a train station, or more than one—Daniel Burnham, Cass Gilbert, Charles Follen McKim, Henry Hobson Richardson, Stanford White. What they produced were predominantly Beaux Arts beauties but also pretty much the entire array of architecture practiced in this country up through the 1930s, including some astonishing amalgams of styles.

Many of the great stations have been ingeniously repurposed and restored as commuter-train stops, shopping malls, museums, restaurants, even movie theaters, thanks to the foamers and the more enlightened city governments stuck with them once the old railroads died. Yet the removal of function from form is an essential societal disconnect. As Ed Breslin and Hugh Van Dusen write in the lavishly illustrated *America's Great Railroad Stations:*

> Each station functioned as did the main gate on a medieval town: it was the welcoming portal to that community, and it was meant to impress, comfort, and reassure the visitor. Each station was a focal point of collective pride, a civic monument large or small. All embodied America's love of, and genius for, commercial excellence. Whether built on the scale of a small chapel, a substantial church, or a monumental cathedral, all of these stations personified and reflected America's secular spirituality fueled by the belief that life could endlessly be enhanced by aesthetic beauty, industrial might, technological know-how, and creature comforts while traveling in style with alacrity from one point on the compass to another.

In Chicago's Union Station, the Metropolitan Lounge is in chaos. The station is one of Daniel Burnham's surviving gems, but for some reason its grand hall lies empty and still, while long-distance passengers and their luggage are jammed into a drab, undersized basement room. Only Amtrak could turn a luxury lounge into a refugee center. Most of the passengers struggle and sway hauling their baggage down to the train, then up the twisting stairs inside the double-decker cars.

Gazing out the window in the dappled afternoon light a few minutes before we leave, I see luggage handlers piling bags atop an ancient, wood-bedded open wagon. I might have witnessed much this same scene, even this same equipment, at Lincoln's first convention, back in 1860, the first in a long line of political conventions of all denominations—Democratic, Republican, Bull

Moose, Socialist, Communist—held in Chicago, because it was the nation's premier train hub.

Over on the next platform are a couple of antique railcars, a charter doubtless ordered up by some of the wealthier foamers. There are entire associations of private-railroad-car owners and renters who still hook up their cars to Amtrak trains. This is a subtler threat to the future of Amtrak and passenger-rail service than are the budget-cutters in Congress—the danger that train travel will be seen as merely a hobbyist's preoccupation. But it's impossible to deny the beauty of the antique observation car I can see from my window: it's another perfect artifact from the height of train design, full of padded leather armchairs and matching art deco side tables.

In the 1930s, America was mad for design, especially when it came to machines. Devastated by the Depression, facing their first serious competition from airlines and automobiles, the major railroads completely overhauled their rolling stock. Many trains were converted from steam to cheaper diesel-electric power. All were put in wind tunnels, tested to see what could make them go faster, use less fuel, take turns more quickly and more safely. The most prominent industrial designers in the country went to work on them. They streamlined trains, lowered their center of gravity, cut their weight, and increased their speeds. The designs alone made the trains *seem* fast. Amtrak's observation cars today are built with no equivalent sense of artistry—or any artistry at all—but they *are* comfortable, maybe the most agreeable means of travel aside from ocean-liner staterooms. One sits up high in the double-decker, at a table or a long row of swivel chairs that run down each side. There are tables and drinks stands at each seat, and the windows provide an almost 360-degree vista as you move through the American countryside. There are no observation cars east of Chicago because of low-hanging wires, but in any case the double-deckers are best served by the West, where you are viscerally reminded of just how vast our country is, how abundant and majestic—where the words of all the old patriotic songs come true.

Traveling through Wisconsin, we spend the rest of that day passing fields of perfect rows of cabbages, pumpkins, beans. By the following morning we are in North Dakota, and the landscape becomes sparser and more monotonous: miles of shallow marshes and fields of high green grass, occasional rows of old trees planted

8o years ago by the youth of the Civilian Conservation Corps to serve as windbreaks. But all of it is punctuated by breathtaking beauty. A pair of eagles swoop and glide low over a golden field of wheat near Williston. A white horse ambles and grazes its way alone through some marshland. A flock of small black birds rise and wheel suddenly through yellowed grassland. Black cattle stand out against a pasture, muzzles up, watching us pass.

The company in the dining and observation cars is so amiable that I was dissuaded from asking people's last names when they weren't offered. The passengers talk quietly and freely with one another. A pair of children march in with their mother, pretending to be a parade. A young man with an enormous Afro sits alone reading. A group of blustery young white men come in, regaling one another with tales of getting arrested.

At my table at lunch there is Kate, an English assistant headmistress, just retired. She tells me about how she taught in New Guinea with her husband for seven years, then raised four children by herself after being widowed very young. Now she is finally on holiday, having sent the last child off to university. Kate is fascinated by America's sheer size, and also by its countless religions: "I think they're related. When people want to, they simply go off and start another one."

The train makes her case for her. In a single afternoon moving through North Dakota, I have conversations with an Amish person and a Mennonite. There are plenty of each traveling on the Empire Builder. Alice, the Mennonite, is a pretty, birdlike woman who owns her own catering business in Canada. Apart from her old-fashioned dress and her hair bun she seems thoroughly modern, showing me a picture on her phone of her congregation's little blue church.

Felty Miller is a young construction worker, part of a large party of Amish bound from western Tennessee to a wedding in Washington State. He does not object to my interrupting his reading of a big illustrated Bible in the observation car. Like the other Amish men, he is dressed in a neat dark-blue shirt, pressed black pants, and a vest, and has light-brown, curling chin whiskers. He dandles Elias, his two-year-old towheaded son, over his knee as he patiently explains to me that, yes, he is used to the speed of the train, having ridden in trucks that the outside contractors the Amish work with drive. He speaks of how bad the economy still is—and offers the opinion that more money needs to be put into the national rail system.

For all the pastoral beauty of the plains states, passenger trains are interlopers here amid the hidden industrial life of the country—hidden, at least, to those of us who live in more crowded places. In Wolf Point, Montana, we watch as a truck heaped with rolls of hay drives by on the cracked two-lane highway. We pass huge grain silos, some abandoned and open to the elements, most still in use, a few houses and barns huddled nearby. Interminable freight trains sweep past us.

Some of the freight trains are made up of boxcars, some of the oil-tank cars now overwhelming our neglected infrastructure in a series of spectacular derailments and fires around the country. On one freight train alone, I counted 104 tank cars, fat and rounded as big black pigs. They slow to pass us, but still we rock in their wake like a small boat on a heavy sea.

Freight is the main economic reason why trains—or any other form of mass transportation—exist. "A passenger train is like a male teat—neither useful nor ornamental," groused James J. Hill, whose nickname, "the Empire Builder," adorns our train, when he was running the Great Northern Railway through these parts more than a century ago.

U.S. passenger trains may be, "quite simply, a global laughingstock," as *Time* magazine put it a few years ago, but American freight trains "are universally recognised in the industry as the best in the world," according to *The Economist,* and they still have an estimated 43 percent share of the freight market in the United States—the highest proportion in any industrialized country, and nearly 10 times the total tonnage moved by freight trains in the entire European Union.

Freight companies also own most of the rails in the United States, which is one reason why U.S. passenger trains lag so far behind high-speed systems in Europe and China, where trains rocket along at more than 150 miles per hour, much less Japan's new Shinkansen bullet, which runs at 200 miles per hour. All these trains travel on dedicated tracks or in sunken, walled corridors, and so can be built light and fast.

Amtrak trains, by contrast, must weigh about twice as much as the average European passenger train in order to have any chance of surviving a potential collision on the rails they share with the freights. Even the Acela—the result of Amtrak's big 1990s effort to build a train that might average 150 miles per hour on the northeast corridor—is so bulky and plodding that the French and Canadian engineers working on it nicknamed it *le cochon,* "the pig." The Acela never actually achieves that speed, save on a couple of very short stretches of track in New England. Overall, it manages just about 69 miles per hour—about the same as Amtrak's regional trains, or the cars on the highways just outside its windows.

At dinner the first night out from Chicago is Jason, returning to his job laying pipe in North Dakota's Bakken oil fields. A trim, big-shouldered man who looks younger than his 40 years, Jason just celebrated his twentieth wedding anniversary in Michigan with his wife. The Bakken job pays well and he likes it, having worked in the past as a firefighter and a die maker for "a big company" at which he saved "a documented two hundred fifty thousand dollars over nine years, but never got a penny raise for it." Now he is part of a 28-man crew in the fields, along with his brother-in-law and his 19-year-old son, whom he says he is glad to have the chance to keep an eye on.

In North Dakota, Jason lives with three other men in an RV, where he cooks and also raises and cans vegetables from his garden plot. Local food prices are at boomtown levels. For everything else he needs, he goes to the Walmart in Williston, though he reports that demand is so high now that the shelves are often empty, which forces him to travel some 125 miles to the better-stocked Walmart in Waterford Township.

At Minot, a small prairie city in North Dakota, the porters bring on stacks of the *Minot Daily News,* which boasts the most risibly far-right editorial page I have ever seen. There are two syndicated columns, one by Rich Lowry arguing that we don't need any more gun-control laws, the other by Brent Bozell arguing that we don't need any more gun-control laws, and a column by George Will mocking President Obama for *not* comparing the civil war in Syria to the Nazi blitz on London.

Will wrote an equally vitriolic diatribe in 2011 for *Newsweek* entitled "Why Liberals Love Trains." In it, he scorned "the president's loopy goal" of giving 80 percent of all Americans access to high-speed trains, citing the contentions of the Cato Institute's Randal

O'Toole that "high-speed rail connects big-city downtowns where only 7 percent of Americans work and 1 percent live," and that the "average intercity auto trip today uses less energy per passenger mile than the average Amtrak train," while "high speed will not displace enough cars to measurably reduce [traffic] congestion" and will in any case be too danged expensive.

All the practical reasons for promoting train travel, which Will sneers at for their "flimsiness," are in fact of vital importance in a world where every day brings a new report from actual scientists that climate change is proceeding at a pace faster than anticipated. An average freight train expends slightly more than one twelfth the BTUs per short-ton mile as a heavy truck, while, as Tom Zoellner puts it in his book *Train*, "one trainload of passengers equals about a hundred city blocks of cars." Amtrak expends an estimated 1,600 BTUs of energy per passenger mile, according to the U.S. Department of Transportation, compared with about 3,300 for buses, 2,500 for airplanes, and a whopping 3,900 for the cars that now besiege most American cities and suburbs in hours-long traffic jams. This is not even to mention plane travel—conspicuous in its omission from Will's rant—in the course of which one is now X-rayed, wanded, patted, groped, deprived of shoes and belt like any other prisoner, then sausaged into an ever more crowded tube, charged for every minor amenity, and dropped at least a good hour and $50 from one of those allegedly desolate downtowns we don't need to reach anymore.

Silliest of all Will's charges, though, is his insistence that trains are "Archimedian levers" designed to make Americans "more amenable to collectivism." Beyond the immense freedom that Amtrak trains in fact provide the individual to read, work, eat, drink, sleep, or stare out at the beauty of America, what stands out about any Amtrak train, at least in the day coaches, is the incredible diversity of the passengers. The usual categories only begin to scratch the surface. To walk through the Empire Builder at night was to pass scenes of incredible sweetness: couples snuggled together under blankets, mothers with babies in their arms, whole families of every possible color and age and creed strewn out over the seats and snoring uninhibitedly.

In the observation car, the Amish wedding-goers sat up together at two tables in the dimmed lighting—lighting perhaps no brighter than the oil lanterns provided when trains first rolled across these plains: the men dressed and bearded like Felty Miller, the women in long black or blue dresses and white bonnets, all of them talking and laughing quietly in their unique German dialect, members of one of the very first religious groups to find refuge in America from persecution. It struck me that Whitman would be right at home on the train, even if Will would not.

What *is* the appeal of train travel? Ask almost any foamer, and he or she will invariably answer, "The romance of it!" But just what this means, they cannot really say. It's tempting to think that we are simply equating romance with pleasure, with the superior comfort of a train, especially seated up high in the observation cars. But having seen a rural train emerge silently through a gap in the New England woods, having seen the long slide of a 1 train's headlights down the rails of a Manhattan subway station, I suspect that the appeal of trains is something more primitive than this. Trains are huge things that come upon us like predators. Almost from the beginning of the machine age, Americans yearned and sought ways for the train to connect their little towns—to connect *them*—to the greater world.

Romance or not, it is this very practical desire that has probably kept Amtrak alive. The Republican right politicized train travel long before George Will and the Tea Party—almost from the moment it failed to expire on cue, in fact. David Stockman, Ronald Reagan's budget director, dedicated himself to terminating Amtrak, denouncing trains as "empty rattletraps" and "mobile money-burning machines."

Over the years, Republicans have pushed the question of Amtrak's continued existence into that same strange sphere of debate in which they have isolated nearly all public institutions save the military: not whether it serves a valuable social and economic function, but whether it makes a profit.

Highway advocates point to tolls and gas taxes as evidence that pavement is self-sustaining; rail's supporters object that train riders are forced to pay such subsidies, too. Federal highway subsidies came to some $41.5 billion in 2013; federal aviation subsidies, to $16 billion. Amtrak, by contrast, received only $1.6 billion. *All* Amtrak's subsidies for *the past 40 years*—almost its entire existence—do not equal what the U.S. Treasury transfers from its General Fund to the Highway Trust Fund in a single year. To put it another way, each American citizen pays $4.07 a year to keep Amtrak running.

Whether even this amount will be forthcoming in the future is open to conjecture. Rail service has many friends but a limited constituency. There are just over 20,000 Amtrak workers; by comparison, New York City's MTA system employs more than 70,000 people. Only 2 percent of Americans say they've ever set foot on an Amtrak train, and only 3 percent of American workers commute by local train. A cursory swing through the nation's capital confirms what an uneven struggle the politics of trains really is. Amtrak's leading defenders are only the rail service itself, ensconced in Washington's Union Station, and the National Association of Railroad Passengers, a plucky nonprofit advocacy group with a membership of only 23,000, tucked away in a few rooms of a town house in an old neighborhood not far from the station.

And yet, so far at least, this uneven struggle has not worked out the way anyone expected, thanks not just to the fervor of trains' defenders but also to the votes of Republican congressmen and senators, often from the region of the country I am passing through now. Amtrak is the only public-transportation link to the outside world for more than 300 of its stops—many of them in small communities scattered over the Empire Builder's route through North Dakota, Montana, Idaho, and eastern Washington State. For years, Stockman's desire to defund Amtrak was thwarted by Mark Andrews, an otherwise undistinguished one-term North Dakota senator who came to Washington on the coattails of Reagan's sweep in 1980 but was determined to keep train service available to his constituents.

In recent years, Republicans have mostly confined themselves to their trivial if mean-spirited proposals for paring down train costs—what is perhaps intended to be a death by a thousand cuts. While Amtrak workers actually make less than private-sector employees in similar positions, the GOP objects to their health-care and benefit plans. Other Republican congressmen have pushed the bold idea of replacing the café cars with vending machines, and there have been the frequent suggestions that our national passenger-rail service should simply be privatized and returned to the states.

How this might in fact work was demonstrated by Amtrak's recent request that Colorado, Kansas, and New Mexico each chip in

$40 million annually over the next 20 years—$2 million per state per year—to help keep the Southwest Chief line running along its current route. Even this small request for additional state funding has set off extended bickering and created a deadlock between the states involved—along with outcries from many of the small communities the Southwest Chief now serves.

An object lesson in what the train means to the small towns of the West is Shelby, Montana, hard by the Canadian border. The Empire Builder reaches it around ten-thirty at night, running five hours behind schedule thanks to the freight traffic. Shelby was where the craziest of all western booms took place, back in 1923 —boom and bust, all in one day. After an oil strike that drove the town's population from 500 into the thousands overnight, Shelby's leading citizens decided they might parlay their good fortune into becoming a permanent resort destination, provided they could host a fight for the heavyweight boxing championship of the world on the Fourth of July.

It was a typical western dream: audacious, patriotic, idiotic, and quickly exploited by a grifter from back east. But Shelby's town fathers were on to something. Theoretically, at least, it didn't matter now how small their town was, or how far it was from any other population center. The railroad could magically alter time and space.

"There was good railroad service into Shelby along the tracks of [the] Great Northern [Railway]," Roger Kahn wrote in his 1999 biography of boxing legend Jack Dempsey, *A Flame of Pure Fire.* "Fight fans could come in on coaches and Pullman cars from Spokane and Seattle and San Francisco, or from Grand Forks and Minneapolis and St. Paul, even Chicago and New York."

The trouble was that the railroads, never quite believing the town could pull off the big fight, declined to run any special trains. Just under 8,000 paying customers showed up, in an age when heavyweight-title bouts routinely attracted 100,000 spectators. By the time it was all over, every bank in the area had gone bust, and Dempsey's nefarious manager, Doc Kearns, was stuffing the last of the town's money into a suitcase and running for his train while the locals discussed whether to string him up from some nearby cottonwoods. "Lonely-looking trees they were, at that," Kearns would remember.

Seen from the train, Shelby today is little more than a gas-station sign looming out of the darkness. But it's a working town of more than 3,000 citizens, out here in the illimitable western prairie, still served twice a day by the Empire Builder.

The next morning breaks bright but turns appropriately overcast as we snake our way down along the bank of the Columbia River and into the rain shadow of the Rockies. This is ominous-looking, barren country, studded with desolate gray and brown hills. It is another industrial landscape, with enormous machinery scattered here and there, but the only sign of human activity to be seen is another train, making its way along the south bank of the wide, slow river. The clouds hang lower, but the hills grow steadily more steep and wooded, each passing scene more dramatic as we approach the Pacific.

I catch the Coast Starlight out of Portland's pretty red-brick-and-stucco Union Station, with its high clock tower and its mural of Lewis and Clark inside. The Coast Starlight is the closest thing Amtrak has to a 20th Century Limited—to an elite carrier—even if the differences from its other long-distance lines are trivial. A voice purrs quietly over the public-address system, urging us not to bother our fellow passengers too much by using cell phones. A complimentary split of champagne and a wine-and-cheese tasting are on offer in the "parlor car."

There are "wine tastings" on many long-distance Amtrak trains, but this usually means a few plastic cups of table red. On the Starlight, local vintages and artisanal cheeses are served in actual glasses and on real plates, and they are presented with copious guides to what we are about to devour and which bottles will be available for purchase. It's all wittily moderated by a train steward with a steady comic patter, much to the delight of a small English tour group and an Australian family of three, who are reduced to almost nonstop laughing and snorting by the wine and japes.

The parlor car was built for the Atchison, Topeka, and Santa Fe Railway in 1955, during the last gasp of opulent train design. It has cut-glass booth dividers with the name and logo of the legendary, long-vanished railroad it was intended for, and well-crafted corner cabinet bookcases that hold a few musty books, magazines, and board games. Downstairs is a tiny movie theater that shows a

children's film during our imbibing and, later on, the most recent
Great Gatsby for the adults.

The Coast Starlight does not really travel along the coast until
San Francisco, but we do pass through lush river valleys and alongside well-heeled small towns, suburbs, and country homes.

California was supposed to be where President Obama's vision
for the future of rail was to become reality. In theory, his plan
was a good one. It called for immediate upgrades on "existing
infrastructure to increase speeds on some [Amtrak] routes from
seventy . . . to over a hundred miles per hour." This would be followed by longer projects to create true high-speed-rail systems on
13 major corridors throughout the United States, each of them
100 to 600 miles in length and running between multiple urban
centers. It was, in short, a plan to replicate what already works
—Amtrak's northeast corridor—all over the country and make it
better, maybe building a permanent ridership for trains in the bargain.

The trouble came, as it so often does with Mr. Obama, on the
follow-through. The $9.3 billion he requested for railroads in the
first stimulus proposal was a ridiculously small amount for the project at hand—one that signaled through its size alone what a low
priority rails really are for this administration. Of that $9.3 billion,
a mere $1.3 billion went to upgrading existing Amtrak operations,
partially through the purchase of 70 new, badly needed electric locomotives. The remaining $8 billion was allocated to the planned
high-speed-rail corridors. This was barely enough to build a hundred miles of track. The original 13 proposed corridors were narrowed down to 4, in California, Florida, Ohio, and Wisconsin. But
none of these plans was put into place before the 2010 elections
swept Democratic governors and legislatures out of power in Florida, Ohio, and Wisconsin. Their Tea Party replacements gleefully
renounced federal money for the train corridors as "high-speed
boondoggles."

The one exception was California, where Jerry Brown was back
as governor and where voters had already approved a referendum
authorizing the state to spend $9.95 billion to build new trains
that could travel from Los Angeles to both San Francisco and Sacramento, and do it in no more than two hours and forty minutes.
The federal government has now pledged some $6.4 billion of the

original $8 billion designated for fast trains to the California project, with the hope that it will be completed sometime in or around . . . 2033.

It has been determined that at least 40 percent of the new rail will be elevated, with an estimated 22,000 enormous concrete pillars carrying the train through earthquake-prone California and replicating the very sort of hated elevated urban highway that so many cities have just spent decades tearing down at enormous cost and trouble. Even in the depressed farming communities of California's Central Valley, where the first leg of this monstrosity is supposed to take shape, opposition has been intense. Governor Brown, however, has remained committed, ridiculing the plan's opponents as "fraidy cats" and "fearful men—declinists who want to put their head in a hole and hope reality changes." But the changing reality proved to be the system's projected costs, which started at an estimated $42 billion, then rose to $68 billion—or $190 million a mile, enough to run two public high schools for a year. By the end of 2013, Brown was in China, still seeking additional funding for this El to nowhere—now estimated to cost more than $91 billion.

If, as Zoellner writes, the American rail system today is an example of "technological regress," the Obama fast-train project is political regress. A large and immediate commitment of money to upgrade successful existing Amtrak trains—increasing their speeds and frequency, making their service and safety better, reducing their price—might have bolstered a growing constituency for mass transit while providing jobs, improving the environment, and supporting smarter growth. Instead, the Obama administration's failure to move with alacrity, clarity of purpose, or even basic competence has probably doomed not only its own efforts but a critical national project.

Whether or not California's fast rail will ever reach San Francisco, no Amtrak train goes there today. Now a trip back across the continent starts with a predawn bus pickup along Fisherman's Wharf, for delivery to another Amshack, in Emeryville, a generic northern California suburb where there is not a hint of, say, a hotel. An electronic board lists all of two local trains; a sign next to it announces that the two long-distance lines here, the Coast Starlight and the California Zephyr, will *not* be listed on the board.

The Zephyr runs across both the Sierra Nevada and the Rockies, back through the heart of empire. By the afternoon, we are climbing steadily through the foothills of the Sierra, passing just north of where gold was discovered at Sutter's Mill in 1848, setting off the daddy of all western booms. Soon we are between 1,500 and 1,800 feet above the American River, then the Bear River, revealed to us in one stunning vista after another through the mountain woods, territory so absolutely beautiful that all we can do in the observation car is snap away with our cameras or phones, or sit helplessly mumbling superlatives.

At 7,000 feet, we reach the pass where the Donner party came to grief, resorting to murder and cannibalism when their wagon train was caught by the first mountain snows, though their fate was exceptional. Planning their trips with incredible care, almost every other wagon train made it through. Even so, only about 200,000 pioneers had followed the Overland Trail to California by the time the Civil War began. The journey took five to six months, and the only alternatives—traveling around Cape Horn or across the fever-ridden Isthmus of Panama—were full of worse perils.

A young railroad man from Connecticut had another idea. Theodore Judah talked so obsessively about the idea of building a railroad across the continent that people began to call him Crazy Judah. By 1860, after four years of searching, he was sure he had found his route—the one we are taking now through the Donner Pass.

The transcontinental railroad proved a remarkably easy sell, even with the country about to lurch into civil war. In part, the Union wanted it as a way of keeping California and Oregon attached to the country. Yet well before the war, America was sold on the idea of a continental road—its leaders and opinion makers remarkably prescient about the prospects of global trade. For John C. Frémont, the transcontinental meant that "America will be between Asia and Europe—the golden vein which runs through the history of the world will follow the track to San Francisco, and the Asiatic trade will finally fall into its last and permanent road." Asa Whitney, a New York dry-goods merchant, wrote in 1845:

> You will see that it will change the whole world ... It will bring the world together as one nation, allow us to traverse the globe in thirty days, civilize and Christianize mankind, and place us in the center of the world, compelling Europe on one side and Asia and Africa on the other to pass through us.

In reality, the transcontinental railroad was not merely ill conceived but actively destructive, according to historian Richard White, who makes the case in his 2011 book, *Railroaded,* that all the rail lines eventually built through North America were run by "inefficient, costly, dysfunctional corporations" and should not have even been attempted. In their immaturity, White maintains, they were "failures as businesses" that started repeated financial panics; "helped both to corrupt and to transform the political system by creating the modern corporate lobby"; "flooded markets with wheat, silver, cattle, and coal for which there was little or no need"; wrecked communities, including many Native American nations, as well as individuals; crushed their own workers; and "yielded great environmental and social harm."

White's criticisms are inescapable, but they seem more an indictment of the nation and the age than of the railroad itself. Certainly the Native American peoples *east* of the Mississippi fared no better than those to the west, even if it took white settlers—without trains—centuries longer to overrun them. Booms and busts had roiled America from the time of the Jamestown Colony, as had financial chicanery since at least the moment the first government bonds set Wall Street in motion. The railroad was not so much a cause as a symptom or a tool.

What remained, though, was that prophetic nineteenth-century vision of America at the center of the world, strategically situated between the economic powerhouses of Europe and a resurgent Asia. And, of course, the physical reality of the railroad itself.

Abraham Lincoln enthusiastically signed the Pacific Railway Act of 1862 into law with almost no opposition from Congress. His government chartered both a Union Pacific Railroad company, to build west from the Missouri River, and the Central Pacific Railroad, to build east from Sacramento. Both companies would be granted 10 square miles of land for every mile of track laid—an enormous government giveaway. Government bonds would raise $16,000 a mile for construction over flat land, $32,000 a mile in the high plains, $48,000 a mile for the passage through the Sierra and the Rockies.

Despite this subsidy, nobody was sure the job could be done. The Donner Pass route that Judah proposed might be compared to a great ramp up the mountains from Sacramento. Climbing it today, we can still appreciate how gradual it is, perfect for a means of conveyance clamped around two metal rails. But just past Donner Lake was a 1,000-foot rock wall, and all along the route were granite ridges, liable to sudden rockslides and 30-foot snowfalls.

The work required 13,500 men to hack away at the Donner Pass with the most primitive of tools—picks and shovels, wheelbarrows, and one-horse dump carts. Progress slowed sometimes to as little as 2 or 3 inches a day. The solution was nitroglycerine and Chinese immigrants. The former had to be concocted on-site, after a shipment annihilated a San Francisco dock and killed 15 people. But the largely Irish immigrant workforce still wouldn't touch the stuff, and the Central Pacific resorted to the almost entirely male population of Chinese laborers who had come to California chasing the *Gum Sham*, "the Mountain of Gold," only to be ostracized, persecuted, and frequently lynched by local whites.

The Central Pacific loved them, eventually hiring some 12,000 Chinese men—who would work for lower wages than white laborers demanded and made up about 80 percent of the workforce— to bring the road through the mountains. Lowered along the rock walls in gigantic baskets, they drilled holes 15 to 18 inches deep, poured in the nitroglycerine, capped the hole, then set the nitro off with a slow match. They worked carefully and well, but the real benefit to the Central Pacific was that nobody much cared how many of them got blown up. Estimates vary widely as to how many died cutting their way through the Sierra, obliterated by the nitro or crushed under the rockslides it set off. It was carnage enough to provoke even these desperate men to go on strike, though they won a raise of only $5 a month.

The California Zephyr climbs steadily along Judah's great ramp, moving all the while past what remains of the rustic mountain towns founded to help build the railroad and support its operations. At 4,700 feet, we pass Blue Canyon, once a town of more than 3,000 people, with water so pure and delicious it was considered the best in the West and was served on all South Pacific Coast trains. Today the town consists of a few scattered houses, half hidden in the woods. We pass Gold Run, where hydraulic engines lifted millions of dollars' worth of gold out of the ground before the mines gave out and the town was abandoned, and Cisco, a supply depot 5,938 feet above sea level where more than 7,000 people once made their home—now no more than a few houses and some rusting sheds next to Interstate 70.

After Lake Spaulding, we move into a long snow shed, built to protect passing trains in the event of an avalanche. Once there were 37 miles of them, snaking their way through the mountains. Sparks from the old engines routinely set them on fire, but the railroad work crews kept rebuilding them. Supposedly, one third of all the forest in California was chopped down to provide the timber for them, and for all the bridges and the work sheds and the ties needed to build the railroad and keep it running. Near Norden, another tiny community, we pass the Summit Tunnel, the peak of the railroad in the Sierra, where the Chinese blasted their way through 1,649 feet of solid rock, making a way that passenger trains and freights used continuously until 1993.

After Norden, we descend in a series of dazzling, miles-long switchbacks, the end of our train visible on the mountain plateaus above us, and pass Truckee, a flourishing resort town that in the late nineteenth century held 14 lumber mills and countless saloons and burned down six times in its first 11 years; then Verdi, a tiny community with a large trailer park; and Boca, a once-thriving lumber and ice-harvesting town that went bust when the sawmill shut down and the hydroelectric dams brought electricity, and now all that remains is the ruins of its vaunted brewery and a few crumbling bridges over pretty little trout streams.

This mountain scenery is so infectious that it makes us giddy in the observation car, where we continue to chatter and take pictures. At dinner I sit with two of the friendliest people from our long afternoon over the mountains, Lilly and Jackie, a mother and daughter from California. Lilly lives in Sacramento, her daughter in Stockton, which she staunchly defends, claiming the media has it in for her town.

They are traveling together now on a sort of grand tour, going to see friends and relatives in Chicago, Washington, D.C., Virginia, and Atlanta. Lilly was married for many years to an air force man, and they had seven children and lived all over the world. Jackie remembers being most impressed by the cherry blossoms and the 1964 Tokyo Olympics when their family was stationed in Japan.

Jackie relates stories from her 20 years as a federal corrections officer. She tells us about drug couriers who tried to smuggle their contraband into the country inside dead babies, and about the racketeer Michael Milken, whom she calls a rascal, and Heidi Fleiss, whom she calls ugly and says was stoned when she first reported to prison. She is afraid that she became too paranoid during her years as a guard. She is proud of her knowledge of guns and self-defense, but found that for months after she retired she would catch herself searching her home for places where someone might conceal a weapon.

The scenery changes the moment we get out of the mountains, the way it does so often across America. From the train, most of Nevada looks like exactly what it is, the bed of an ancient sea, a landscape broken only by the remnants of more bridges, tiny clusters of houses, and distant highways on each side of the tracks. The exposed desert rock glows softly in the dusk, a drowsy, pastel sunset after the dramatic landscapes of the Sierra.

The headlines on the bundles of *USA Today*s brought aboard read "House, Senate Parry on 'ObamaCare' as Shutdown Looms." It's not of much concern on the California Zephyr. At breakfast, I reminisce with Gene—a devout Nebraska Cornhuskers fan wearing a bright red team jacket, on his way back to Lincoln, where he has been teaching mathematics for 53 years—over Johnny Rodgers's greatest game. At lunch, I talk to Leah and John, both of whom have their pilot's license and have lived and worked all over the world in public health, about Mayor Dick Lee and his struggle with the Model Cities program in New Haven, Connecticut. We speculate about a middle-aged couple who hold hands everywhere they go on the Zephyr, and whom everyone wonders about until we realize that the man is blind. I marvel anew at the range of conversations you can have on the train even as you're being Archimedied into collectivism.

As it happens, the Zephyr is unable to take its usual scenic route through the Rockies because torrential rains have washed out the track near the Moffat Tunnel—the second washout due to extreme weather I've encountered within a week of travel. Suddenly we are in a tale foretold. Ayn Rand—the devoutly atheist cult leader who has somehow become the prophet of fundamentalist Republicans —loved trains. In her major opus, *Atlas Shrugged,* one of her great heroes of capitalism—her "prime movers"—runs a railroad. In doing research for the book, Rand supposedly rode in locomotives of the New York Central and even operated the engine of the

20th Century Limited, later claiming, "Nobody touched a lever except me."

When the prime movers of *Atlas Shrugged* decide to go on strike until they are properly appreciated, trains are transformed into tools of almost biblical retribution. They plunge off a bridge into the Mississippi, or asphyxiate all aboard in a badly ventilated mountain tunnel, or simply stop in an Arizona desert, leaving passengers and crew to be rescued by a passing wagon train(!).

Here, then, is Rand's prophecy, much echoed in recent years by Republicans from Mitt Romney on down, though usually with reference to Europe. It is finally happening! Our indulgent, unaffordable welfare state has caused our entire civilization to collapse!

Except the employees of Amtrak have made provisions for this contingency. It turns out that somehow we are not to be choked to death in our compartments or turned out to wander the prairie like so many buffalo, just rerouted through Wyoming, where we will be following the rail bed of the original transcontinental railroad.

We are hustled through the state like Lenin being carted across Germany to Russia in his sealed railway carriage during World War I. No one is allowed off the train at the brief stops, even to stretch their legs, lest we contaminate the good citizens of Cheneyland with our collectivist ways. The only exceptions are a couple of passengers who have brought dogs. We watch enviously from the windows as they cavort through the high prairie grass with their pets during a stop.

Wyoming is almost unbelievably empty, even compared with the rest of the West. Mile after mile, there is nothing: no visible water, no sign of human habitation beyond the snow fences along the tracks, just two steel lines moving across the land. An army topographic engineer once called the high plains west of the Mississippi the Great American Desert. The region averaged less than 20 inches of rain a year, and much less during its years-long dry spells. Blizzards and long cycles of drought killed off the settlers' cattle. Locusts devoured their crops. Even in the good years, they often lived in sod houses infested with spiders, snakes, and centipedes, and burned buffalo chips as their only source of fuel.

Against this dispiriting reality, the railroads took up with land speculators to turn the Great American Desert into the Great Plains and "the Garden of the World." Posters and pamphlets promised "riches in the soil, prosperity in the air, progress everywhere. An Empire in the making!" A booster invented that dangerous absurdity, "Rain follows the plough!" The more the settlers churned up the earth, they were promised, the more moisture would be absorbed into the soil and circulated back into the atmosphere. The Atchison, Topeka, and Santa Fe insisted that the "rain line" moved west with its tracks, the steam from its engines condensing into clouds. Pseudoscientific properties were attributed to the steel rails themselves, or to the electrical impulses leaping along the new telegraph wires, or even to loud noises. If all that failed, farmers were urged to embrace "dry farming"—plowing furrows 12 to 14 inches deep, then harrowing their fields after each rainfall.

When it was finally conceded that the West could not be the East, the area was reconceived as a sort of colossal factory. Almost anything that could be extracted was cut down, torn up, dug out, shipped east by rail, then processed and shipped on again. Between the Civil War and the Great Depression, new industrial booms followed one after the other, in cattle, in timber, in coal and other minerals—even in bison meat. The railroad was, once again, its conveyor.

When World War I disrupted wheat exports from Russia, farmers on the high plains found a bonanza selling their wheat to Europe. They poured their newfound cash into mechanized plows and reapers and tractors and got rid of many of their work animals, freeing up another 32 million arable acres formerly dedicated to pasture. Wheat production grew 300 percent in the 1920s—but all this succeeded in doing was driving down the price of wheat. Desperate farmers responded by plowing up increasingly marginal land. The buffalo grass that had stitched the western plains together for 35,000 years was gone overnight.

The end was an ecological as well as an economic catastrophe. With the next, entirely predictable cycle of drought, the dust started blowing, in 1932, and didn't stop for a decade. A huge oval of land on the plains, roughly 100 million acres, 400 by 300 miles in size, soon lay desolate. The dust was everywhere, covering farm machinery and entire houses, piled up against barns like Saharan sand drifts. One third of the Dust Bowl's inhabitants—250,000 people—ended up leaving. In a generation, as the historian Donald Worster points out in his book *Dust Bowl*, much of the region had gone "from a spirited home on the range where no discouraging words were heard, to a Santa Fe Chief carrying bounteous heaps of grain to Chicago, and, finally, to an empty shack where the dust had drifted as high as the eaves."

No traces of that devastation can be seen today. The discovery of aquifers (now rapidly being depleted) and the creation of farm subsidies and government conservation and resettlement programs allowed for the land to be restored—at least for the time being.

The trains, too, got taken in hand, by private enterprise and government alike. J. P. Morgan and others snapped up as many lines as they could. Populist and progressive revolts gave the Interstate Commerce Commission unprecedented powers to regulate rates and conditions. With our entry into World War I, every train in the country was nationalized under the U.S. Railroad Administration. This practice proved so efficacious that after the war the ICC proposed a comprehensive national plan to consolidate the rails, though it was never implemented. In the 1920s, the United States still had 1,085 railroad companies. But the mergers of many rail lines during the 1930s and more forced consolidation by the government during World War II succeeded in creating by the 1940s a more rational system.

The dining car on the Zephyr loses its air-conditioning when its electrical board malfunctions, and the kitchen becomes unbearably overheated. The menu is limited, but the staff remains remarkably helpful, and we are not asphyxiated. We move south, into Colorado, and actually reach Denver early, because of the detour. Dinner is served while we are halted on the tracks just past the center field of the Colorado Rockies' park, Coors Field, finished in 1995 at a cost of $300 million.

The next morning, we push through into the farm country of Nebraska, then Iowa. The kitchen stays down all the way to Chicago. For a day and a half and a dozen stops, no one has the wherewithal to fix the malfunction. Onboard, the bloom is off the rose, thanks to the sheer length of the trip. We resort more and more to the subterranean café car, run this time by Carol, a perpetually angry attendant, who treats any efforts at empathy with marked hostility. When someone remarks that she will surely be glad to see Chicago at the end of the sweaty, 53-hour voyage of the Zephyr, Carol snaps, "Why? I *hate* the city!"

I skip the Metropolitan Lounge on the trip back to New York, preferring to sit in a dark, beery commuter bar in Chicago's Union Station. But the Lake Shore Limited is cheery and bright, and another helpful steward serves us complimentary wine and cheese.

He gives a leftover half-bottle to a couple in their thirties. They laugh and smile and hold hands in the club car. They speak glowingly about all they have seen on the way out to Spokane, where Lisa had a speaking engagement, and back, the lights of the oil and gas fields at night in North Dakota, the beauty of Glacier National Park by day.

Eric works mostly in Maryland and Washington, but he owns a home and 50 acres in Binghamton, New York. He's hoping that it will attract a fracking company—the great dream of everyone in upstate New York not looking to hook up with one of the four casinos recently promised to the region—and he dismisses any environmental concerns: "If you look at the science, it's perfectly safe."

In the morning, we pass the ruined cities of upstate New York again. By afternoon we are headed back down through the dappled autumn loveliness of the Hudson to New York City and Penn Station. We plunge back under Riverside Park, the sort of structure we used to routinely build above our buried trains, with what was then our endless talent for practical and gracious innovation. But today a journey of more than 7,000 miles, into our greatest city, ends where it began, the disembarking passengers staggering along a drab, dimly lit concrete platform. "One entered the city like a god; one scuttles in now like a rat," wrote the architectural historian Vincent Scully after the original Penn Station was torn down, in 1963.

That building, designed by Stanford White, was a symphony in glass and steel, clad in pink Milton granite and honey-colored travertine, lit through lunette windows, and festooned with clocks and map murals of the great nation it stood in tribute to. It was something "vast enough to hold the sound of time," as Thomas Wolfe wrote in *You Can't Go Home Again*.

But when it was thought that something more profitable might be built in its stead, its vaulted glass roofs were smashed with wrecking balls and its granite and marble walls were jackhammered to pieces. Its graceful Greek columns were sawed through, and its great clocks, its carved-stone eagles, and the maiden sculptures that represented Night and Day were pulled down and taken over to New Jersey, where they were dumped in the swamps of Secaucus, like the body of a murdered Mob stoolie.

"The message was terribly clear," Ada Louise Huxtable wrote in the *New York Times*. "Tossed into that Secaucus graveyard were about 25 centuries of classical culture and the standards of style, elegance and grandeur that it gave to the dreams and constructions of Western man."

In addition to being beautiful, the old station was the pinnacle of an immense technological achievement, a vast network of infrastructure that included two rail tunnels under the Hudson River, four more under the East River, and the Hell Gate Bridge. To build the Hudson tunnels alone, crews of sandhogs dug toward each other beneath the river for three years, under intense heat and pressure, behind 200-ton iron cylinders or shields. Finally "the shields met, coming together rim to rim," in the words of the historian Lorraine Diehl, "like two gargantuan tumblers." For the first time, America was connected by rail from Montauk to San Francisco.

"It was one of those rare architectural masterpieces that are able to touch man's soul," Diehl wrote of the station that so fittingly crowned it. "Built as a landmark, it was a monumental gateway meant to last through centuries."

Instead, it lasted a little more than 53 years. When the decision was announced, in 1962, the only protesters were some 200 people, mostly architects and academics. Few others seemed to care. Officials posed smiling for pictures next to the lowered eagles. "Just another job," said John Rezin, the foreman of the demolition crew. "Fifty years from now, when it's time for our Center to be torn down, there will be a new group of architects who will protest," Irving Felt, president of the Madison Square Garden Corporation, predicted.

It has been another 50 years, and not only architects but many New Yorkers in general would gladly take Madison Square Garden apart by hand if it meant a chance to see a new Penn Station rise. But nothing gets done. The Garden was stuck atop the grave of the old Penn Station back in the 1960s because white commuters were supposedly too afraid to venture very far into the big, bad, black city—about as terrible a perversion of urban planning as has ever been practiced. Ironically, the scariest people around the new Penn Station are the drunken suburban louts in their Rangers jerseys on game night.

Plans for building a twenty-first-century train station in the Beaux Arts central post office across Eighth Avenue from the Garden have been on the books for 20 years now. Architects have churned out any number of wondrous fantasies of what a new station might look like. But the Garden and its teams are owned by a thuggish cable-TV heir who stubbornly holds out against any intrusion on his ugly cash cow. Amtrak, citing money worries, still hasn't fully committed to the proposed new facility, to be dubbed Moynihan Station (in honor of former New York senator Daniel Patrick Moynihan, a leading rail advocate), and all the grand plans aside, it's unclear what passengers would get in the end—maybe just a bigger Amshack.

As one state official told the *New York Times* architecture critic Michael Kimmelman in 2012, the "project aspires to be more like the Frank R. Lautenberg Station in Secaucus, N.J."

We have always been a country of boom and bust, and a rail has always run through our wildest schemes. The train was a wonderful tool that came into being before anyone, even the men who owned it, really knew what to do with it. As with the rest of our democracy, it was the learning, the mastering of these men and their machines, that would eventually provide us with some measure of what this country has always personified.

We did incredible things with trains. We ran them through mountains and deserts and under rivers and swank avenues and beautiful buildings. We turned them into rolling luxury hotels and made them into something so extraordinary that adults as well as children came running just to watch them as they passed. We learned how to coast them into stations without their locomotives and how to string whole cities of commerce around them. We looked 100, 200, 300 years into the future, and built railroads to match our vision. Then we discarded trains as something hopelessly antiquated and unnecessary.

The America we live in today does not even have the political will to connect a train to a platform in many places, much less build a new generation of supertrains. Amtrak and its supporters remain confident that it can endure, even triumph, and they may be right. Trains still have advocates even in the reddest of western states, and unlike so many of the public-sector areas that the right's corporate sponsors would like to fully privatize—education, health care, prisons—no one seems eager to get their hands on a passenger-rail system.

But the odds are just as good that Amtrak will vanish completely. Against the rigid ideology that now drives the Republican Party, the old politics of horse-trading and constituent services may not suffice. The government shutdown ended 12 days after we pulled back into the bowels of Penn Station, a big defeat for the Tea Party movement. But within weeks, its memory was obliterated by the Obama administration's botched rollout of its already woeful health-care plan. The unwillingness of the Democratic leadership to commit to any public good has already disfigured the liberal idea, and its continuing failure may well sweep our national rail service away, along with everything else. For all Amtrak's shortcomings, losing it would be a very bad thing. The train muddles through wonderfully, given all the restrictions we put on it. We are capable of more—or at least we used to be.

Land of the Lost

FROM *JMWW*

MORNINGS IN MOLDOVA: I left the flat, descended six stories in a dark stairwell—bare concrete, pervasive smell of boiled cabbage —and emerged in the tenement courtyard where, every day, stray dogs were plundering the garbage bins. Then I walked along Avenue Kogalniceanu toward the university, a 2-mile trudge on treacherous, muddy sidewalks. A dense fog made everything—buildings, trolleys, pedestrians, mongrels—appear insubstantial. Through the gloom, thousands of shadowy crows watched from tree branches. Moldova's weather was supposed to be mild for Eastern Europe, but during my time in the country it seemed to be perpetually raw and overcast. The chill went to the bones; I never felt warm, despite the high-priced cold-weather gear I had brought with me.

Stepping gingerly down the street, I always started to feel nervous as I approached the university. It was not the classes in American literature and culture that put me on edge—I enjoyed teaching the classes and I liked the students. No, the little spasm of dread I felt as I mounted the steps to the philology building each morning was entirely due to my unavoidable encounter with the gatekeeper, the Matron of the Keys—a short, stout woman about 60 years old who dressed in a starched white outfit reminiscent of a nineteenth-century asylum nurse. It was from her that I had to obtain the key to my classroom—kept with all other classroom keys in a cabinet that she guarded from behind a desk at the entrance to the building. This was her domain, and she ruled over it with an iron will and a suspicious mind.

Each day I had to ask for the key, and she would only acknowledge requests made in Russian—proper Russian. Upon independence from the Soviet Union, Moldova had adopted Romanian as its official language; nevertheless, many Russian-speakers refused to conduct business—even government business—in anything but Russian. The matron did not approve of my Russian pronunciation, and day after day she made me repeat the classroom number—458—many times, correcting each phoneme with a martinet's exactitude and demanding that I try again. She would not accept the individual numbers—*four, five,* and *eight.* Nyet. Only the correct complete number would meet the requirement: *four hundred fifty-eight.* She knew exactly who I was (I stood out as a foreigner, not least because of my burgundy-colored down parka), and she knew exactly which room key I needed, but she would not alter the procedure. No key could be issued until the number was stated correctly.

We went through five, six, seven cycles of "Nyet. Bad. Listen. Repeat. Again." Eventually she would pause after another of my stammered attempts, then grunt a grudging approval: Da. The key was surrendered, and I signed my name in a huge ledger along with thousands upon thousands of other signatures (many of them mine) to acknowledge receipt of the key and acceptance of dire penalties should the key not return. Finally—finally!—I could climb the four flights of stairs (the elevator was always malfunctioning) where my hundred or so students awaited me in the hallway. We opened the door and entered the forlorn lecture hall—a concrete room equipped with broken desks, a cracked chalkboard, and ill-fitting windowpanes that allowed the wind to whistle through. There was no heat. Outside, flurries eddied about, and sparks showered down from trolley wires. With chalk I had bought myself on a weekend trip to neighboring Romania (a relative consumer paradise compared with Moldova), I wrote an American poem on the chalkboard. The students copied it down in their notebooks—most of them managing to memorize it in the process (a skill developed during years of forced memorization in school)—and the lecture began.

This was my Fulbright year, the fulfillment of a longstanding desire. After the collapse of the Soviet Union in 1991, I was eager to revisit Eastern Europe to see what had changed in the years since I had been a university student on a study-abroad tour of the Soviet bloc at the height of the Cold War. I was thinking I would go to Poland, the Czech Republic, or maybe Hungary. But when my chance came, a chance to teach as a Fulbright Scholar, the as-

signment was not for Prague or Bratislava or Budapest or Vilnius.
The call came not from Kiev or Sofia or Bucharest or Warsaw. It
came instead from tiny, remote, unknown Moldova and its capital
city with two names: Kishinev in Russian, Chişinau in Romanian. I
was initially ambivalent, but when I learned more about Moldova
—such as where to locate it on a map—I wholeheartedly embraced
the opportunity to live in such an isolated place still relatively unaffected by the rapid Westernization that had transformed other
countries of the former Soviet bloc.

Moldova became an independent country in 1991 following the
collapse of the USSR. Until then, the area now called Moldova had
never before been truly independent. From 1944 to 1991, it was a
republic of the Soviet Union. Before that, between 1918 and 1944,
it had been a province of Greater Romania. Czarist Russia controlled the territory from 1812 to 1918. And once upon a time, Moldova had languished as a tributary outpost of the Ottoman Empire,
ruled fitfully for several hundred years by the Turks. A tiny wedge of
steppe land between the Prut and Dniester Rivers, known for much
of its history as Bessarabia, Moldova had been traded back and forth
in the various treaties that temporarily resolved disputes and wars
among the regional powers. For centuries, Moldova had never been
more than a pawn in the diplomatic chess match—maybe not even
a pawn, but merely a square on the board waiting to be occupied.
Yet after the breakup of the Soviet Union in 1991, Moldova had suddenly become an independent country left to its own devices and
struggling for survival and identity.

In the years following independence, attempts to dismantle the
Soviet system had been chaotic and inconsistent. Yes, democratic
elections had occurred in Moldova. Yes, the invisible hand of capitalism had tinkered, or rather fumbled, with the economy. But
by the late 1990s, the economic, political, and cultural transformations were still incomplete. Important structural reforms had
not yet taken place, and the IMF and the World Bank were pres-
suring the Moldovan government for more drastic changes. The
economy and the government were still largely in the hands of
Soviet-era apparatchiks who had simply adopted new titles in the
transition. Many were now linked to the emerging Russian mafia.

As the first decade of independence drew to an end, income
distribution in Moldova was widening considerably, with a very
few getting rich—primarily through corrupt capitalist ventures—

while the vast majority grew poorer and poorer. In some cases desperately poor: according to reports, large numbers of Moldovan women were being enticed to work as prostitutes in Western Europe, where many of them had disappeared into the netherworld of sex slavery. There were rumors that traffickers in human organs were buying Moldovan kidneys to sell on the black market. Before my year in the country was over, Moldova would officially become the poorest of the former Soviet republics and the poorest country in Europe, dropping below even woebegone Albania. This was the gist of the situation in Moldova when I arrived.

When I wasn't at the university, I spent much of the day walking in parks and along city streets. Kishinev reveled in its parks, and the parks were without question Kishinev's best feature. There was the Park of the Cathedral, with its flower stalls and diminutive copy of the Arc de Triomphe (not big enough for a street, it straddled a sidewalk). Across the city's main boulevard was a park dedicated to Stefan the Great. A huge statue of Moldova's national hero—sword in one hand, cross in the other—guarded the entrance to the park. In the fifteenth century, Stefan took on the ruling Turkish lords and managed to establish Orthodox Christian hegemony over the region. The brief sovereignty, however, didn't last beyond Stefan's lifetime. Upon his death, the Turks returned with a vengeance, and for the next 300 years Moldova languished on the fringes of the Ottoman Empire.

Near the middle of Stefan the Great's park stood a column dedicated to Alexander Pushkin. It was to Kishinev in 1820 that the Russian poet was banished for his liberal proclivities. Young and unknown, Pushkin spent three long years in the isolated town. At the time, Kishinev was little more than a village of peasants in the far southwestern corner of Russia, a place of unsophisticated culture and few amenities. Fittingly, Kishinev's most celebrated resident lived there involuntarily and spent his three years in the town pining to leave. He referred to the place as "accursed Kishinev." Another city park surrounded an artificial lake dug by the Communist Youth in the 1950s. In a remote corner of this park stood the formerly prominent statues of Marx, Engels, and Lenin. Elsewhere in Eastern Europe similar statues had been destroyed. But the Moldovans had not been so drastic in their treatment of fallen heroes. Removed from their positions of prominence and banished to a copse on the far side of an isolated lake, the trinity watched over the transition to capitalism from afar. The busts of Marx and Engels brooded ineffectually, while Lenin stood full of ferocious energy, one leg forward, as though he were ready to mount a countercharge against the forces that had exiled him.

The city's infrastructure provided further evidence of Moldova's struggles. Walking around, you saw the decaying apartment blocks of the Soviet era, some buildings eroding before your eyes as the wind wore away mortar and sent pellets of concrete eddying down to the sidewalks. One abandoned shopping center had a postapocalyptic look to it: disintegrated stairways, collapsed storefronts, exposed rebar, corroded girders. So it was wherever you looked: decaying buildings, choppy roads, crumbling sidewalks. And unfinished buildings, too: scores of construction projects that had been abandoned in 1991 when Moscow's largesse had dissipated along with the quotas and five-year plans that had put the projects into motion. As a consequence, abandoned projects were everywhere, untouched for years.

My walks also took me past a place that I mistook at first for a nature preserve. From the street, all I could see was a tangle of growth —an unkempt forest—behind a high wall. Eventually I learned that this was the old Jewish cemetery, long abandoned now that there were almost no Jews left in Moldova. Other than being the locale of Pushkin's exile, Kishinev had secured its small place in history as the scene of gruesome pogroms. At the beginning of the twentieth century, nearly half of the city's population was Jewish. Kishinev was under Russian jurisdiction at the time, and Russia in 1900 was a virulently anti-Semitic state. Jews were loathed and feared. The czar's authorities considered them revolutionaries. The peasants envied Jewish business successes. Folk stories of ritual murders—Jews killing Christians for their blood—circulated, and the authorities did little to squelch them. Profit-driven newspapers worked rumors into fully realized reports of atrocities. The tabloids printed accounts of Russian boys and girls falling into the clutches of butcher Jews who were diabolically collecting Christian blood for their Passover feasts. Such a story surfaced in Kishinev just before Easter 1903. Over the Easter weekend, the city's good Christians went on a rampage, exacting their revenge on the Jews by burning and looting Kishinev's ghetto. Hundreds of Jews were seized from their homes, clubbed, and mauled. Some 43 Jews died. The twentieth century had just begun, and remote Kishinev was foreshadowing its major motifs. Indeed, the 1903 pogrom was only a prelude to what was to come in Moldova. When Romania (to which Moldova then belonged) aligned itself with Nazi Germany, 400,000 Bessarabian Jews and 40,000 Gypsies were sent to nearby concentration camps. Many were eventually deported to Auschwitz.

By the end of the twentieth century, very few Jews lived in Kishinev (less than 1 percent of the population), and almost no one I met had heard of this history. A small, unassuming stone slab in a park on the edge of the city was dedicated to the victims of the 1903 pogrom, but the history museum ignored the matter altogether. Most people I spoke to were puzzled by mention of the pogrom. Such a thing had never happened in Kishinev, they were sure. Nor did they believe that the city had once been nearly half Jewish. During their lifetime, the city's Jewish background had been all but obliterated. For example, the official city map did not indicate the location of the Jewish cemetery. To passersby, it was just a large, abandoned tract of land hidden behind deteriorated walls. When I finally learned what was behind the walls, I made several visits and found thousands of uprooted and overturned gravestones entangled in a dense thicket of vines and briars. But according to the maps, the cemetery did not officially exist. Nor was the location of the erstwhile concentration camps marked or memorialized in any way. My Moldovan acquaintances professed surprise that such places had ever existed and questioned my sources of information.

My status as a Fulbright Scholar and my consequent connection to the American Embassy put me in close contact with the expatriate community in Moldova. This community included personnel at the Western embassies and aid workers representing various NGOs. Some of the expatriates had formed a "diners' club," which met once a month at local restaurants, where we were often the only patrons except for perhaps a handful of government officials and Russian mafia functionaries huddled in a corner. Many Moldovans I knew had not been to a restaurant in years; none had been to the fancier establishments (probably mafia-owned) that the diners' club favored.

On a typical outing, 25 or 30 of us were seated at a long table. Musicians played loud Gypsy-style versions of movie and show standards — the themes from *Dr. Zhivago*, *Titanic*, and James Bond were in heavy rotation—meant to entertain us during the long, inexplicable waits between courses. When a break in the music permitted conversation, the expats returned to their favorite themes: the rapid disintegration of the country and their intense desire to get out. Many expressed anxiety about being trapped in Moldova. True, some claimed that "Moldova could get in your blood" and professed to truly love the place, its people, its culture. These were the foreigners who had married Moldovans or who had some ongoing research project, something that tied them to the place. But for most of the foreign community, Moldova was a temporary post in a disagreeable backwater. They spoke longingly of previous assignments or speculated and dreamed about where they would go next, once they had "put in time" in Moldova.

The anxiety that these expats felt led them to carp about the country and its citizens. A long list of complaints was drawn up and reiterated at each gathering. Almost anything could be the subject of complaint—the mud, the cold, the bread, the milk, the hard water, the baffling pattern of one-way streets, the Moldovan custom of hanging rugs on walls. The emblem for their irritation was the typical Moldovan lift, whether in a tenement, a government building, or a store. The grumbling, lurching elevators inspired fear and loathing in expats. "I just won't do it," someone would grouse. "I won't take one of those things. I'd rather walk up ten flights, thank you." Who got stuck in a lift, when, where, and for how long was one of the favorite news items amongst the foreign community.

Despite its incessant disgruntlement, the expat community proved to be a valuable source of information. It was during expat meet-ups that I heard confirmation of the many rumors now circulating about the dark side of Moldova's economic decline. Peace Corps officials, USAID personnel, and staff at some NGOs —people with inside information—confirmed that what we had heard was true: Moldova had become one of the principal countries of origin for the trafficking of women. Criminal gangs had lured or kidnapped thousands of young women and sent them into sex slavery abroad. An official of the Organization for Security and Cooperation in Europe called Moldova the "largest supplier state" of sex slaves in Europe. Members of medical missions told us that the black-market organ stories were true as well. Moldovans were being taken by bus across the Turkish border—sometimes with false promises of a job—where they were pressured into selling a kidney for a few thousand dollars. But what could be done? Most Moldovans earned well under $1,000 a year. When someone showed up offering "jobs" that paid $2,000, of course desperation would lead people to take a chance. And once they found themselves across the border in a hospital room with all their documents taken from them, they probably felt that they had little choice but to go through with it.

That was Moldova at the end of a sad century: a land of poverty, a land of frustration, a land of cynicism, a land of despair, and sometimes a land of depravity. And yet there was always wine—the one thing for which Moldova had won renown—and as long as there was wine, the Moldovans themselves weren't going to go down without a toast. Perhaps because there was so little to celebrate, Moldovans celebrated anything and everything with enthusiasm and aggression. Weddings and religious feasts could last for days. A *sashlik,* or picnic barbecue in the woods, could turn into a bacchanalian marathon lasting the entire weekend. Invitations were easy to come by, as foreigners were prized and honored guests. I received several invites from people I met at the university. The presence of a foreign guest intensified the affair, the toasts coming with furious frequency, the food foisted to the point of nausea. Expats in Moldova referred to it as "terrorist hospitality." Once a celebration began, you simply could not escape. You were held hostage, plied with food and drink, forced into toast after toast, no objection or excuse tolerated.

In my several experiences, terrorist hospitality began at ten in the morning with a quick shot of Moldovan champagne. It was obligatory to drain the glass at once. From champagne you progressed to various homemade wines poured from repurposed plastic soda bottles. Plates of food were brought forth—herring, sausages, cheeses, radishes, pickles, cucumbers, tomatoes. Bottles were lined up on the table: brandy, wine, and vodka. You raised glasses for the first toasts, which were generally microcosmic in theme: to your health, to your mother, to the success of all your endeavors. Then came mamaliga—a cornmeal mush—and then came noodles, then a beet and walnut salad, then spaghetti. At last the main dish appeared, a steaming lamb joint that cost perhaps a month's salary. But first another round of toasts, now advancing to more macrocosmic themes: to America, to Moldova, to world peace, to space exploration.

At this point, you might try a few ploys to stem your intake. You could explain that you had to curtail your drinking because of some ongoing stomach complaint. Or that you were taking medicine that forbade interaction with alcohol. Or that your religion imposed moderation if not teetotalism (a word even the best English-speaking Moldovans could not understand). But no begging off was allowed. Every possible excuse was parried, and a new bottle produced to meet the objection. Stomach complaints? Try this special cognac, known to settle stomachs and cure digestive ills. And try this white wine, too, known to enhance the properties of any prescription drug. As for religion, what could be more spiritual than wine? One by one, the bottles appeared and continued to appear. This one for arthritis. This one for asthma. This one for fever or flu or headache. At several households, the hosts told me with great solemnity that the bottle of wine now proffered could prevent and cure radiation sickness. You had no choice but to acquiesce. All right, you would say, but this is the last round. "Or next to last," your host responded, draining the glass in a gulp and urging you to do the same.

Then it was time for dessert: cheese blintzes, fruit blintzes, cakes, and cookies. All manner of flummery washed down with more champagne and more sickly-sweet wine. The pressure to consume more kept intensifying: Oh, but you must try this. And this. And some of these, too, the host declared. Surely we will have more, for life is short and poor. Toasts now ventured into the realm of the inane. To road repair. To Monica and Hillary. Success to the McDonald's corporation's opening in Moldova. It was impossible to leave. Afternoon became evening, evening became night, and you could scarcely get permission to leave your chair. Any attempt to excuse yourself was preempted when someone in the host family brought out something to show and tell: photos of a trip to Bulgaria, a CD collection of American pop, old internal passports and other mementos of communism.

And in truth it was this sharing that made the visits worthwhile. It took an enormous effort to focus away the haze and the spinning in your head, to shut out the din of music and joke-telling and political argument that turned the room into a whirling Chagall canvas. Some of the stories were incredibly moving; every family seemed to have a *Zhivago*-esque epic somewhere in its recent history. Stalin was a constant presence on these occasions, a ghost haunting the fetes of a people still not free of his legacy. Hushed voices told a tortured history, sometimes barely audible as though afraid the ghost still listened. Everyone in Moldova had at least one relative sent to Siberia after the war. Most of the exiled never returned, and their ghosts, too, lingered in the room alongside that of their persecutor, as samples of their handicrafts or their writings or their photos were brought to you for examination. A university professor told me about finding a pair of wooden boots in the family attic when she was a child. When she asked about them, her mother told her to forget she had ever seen them, to say nothing about them to anyone. The boots were never seen again. Only years later, after the fall of communism, did she learn the truth about those boots: After the war, her father and uncle were sent to a labor camp in Siberia. Eventually they escaped and managed to walk back to Moldova, 3,000 harrowing miles, wearing the wooden boots. Her uncle died of tuberculosis shortly after returning home; her father never told the children the story, fearing that knowledge of it would put them all in danger.

The table talk always included as well reminiscences of the early days of independence, a brief, hopeful interlude in lives long on hardship. Moldovans wistfully recalled the energy and excitement that accompanied the events of 1989–1992, as an inchoate Moldovan nationalism asserted itself and then suddenly the Soviet Union fell apart, leaving Moldova independent and on its own. A carnival atmosphere had presided in those days—rallies, parades, citywide parties late into the night. Everyone was eager to experience this newfound freedom, to know democracy, to taste capitalism.

And it turned out that freedom had a particular taste to it: the taste of bananas. Several Moldovans told me that in Soviet times bananas were unknown, seen perhaps in pictures but never in real life. Bananas had the status of being a forbidden fruit, even if no policy specifically forbade them. They were simply unattainable. Then came independence and suddenly bananas from Iran appeared, expensive but not prohibitively so. People were so curious they stood in long lines to buy bananas from street vendors. Bananas became part of everyone's conversation: Have you tried one? What did you think? They discussed the flavor of bananas like they discussed wines—describing the taste sensations, the sweetness, the texture. The fruit came to symbolize freedom, and Moldovans thronged to consume it.

Then the ruble collapsed. Everyone's money turned worthless almost overnight. Five thousand rubles, enough to buy a car one month, couldn't buy groceries the next. The banana queues dwindled. Few people could afford to indulge. They had to be content with seeing the bananas displayed on sidewalk tables, but buying them? Tasting them? No. Impossible. As one of my Moldovan hosts put it, "What was once unavailable is now merely impossible to attain." For Moldovans, the unattainable banana had transformed from a symbol of freedom to a symbol of discontent and frustration.

During my time in Moldova, I heard that frustration voiced by nearly everyone, young and old alike. For the young in particular hope was wanting. The students in my classes felt vulnerable and uncertain in the new Moldova, and they wanted to leave their homeland as soon as possible. Their future was constricted, they said, with no careers to go into, no opportunities available to them. They badly wanted out, but the possibilities were few. Hoping to win a scholarship to study abroad, they diligently practiced English, French, and German. But even in their studies they were frustrated, for the Moldovan educational system reflected many of the problems in society at large. It was an antiquated system that still followed Soviet procedures in everything from administration to pedagogy. The only textbooks available were out-of-date leftovers from the Soviet era. Rote memorization was still the principal means of instruction. Upon enrollment, students were assigned to a group. They remained part of that group throughout their years of study, and they were never allowed to choose their own classes or schedule. They and their group went where they were told and studied what was chosen for them. Worse, it was a corrupt system with bribery the norm. Gaining entrance into the university might involve greasing the palms of administrators. Teachers often expected payment before permitting a student to sit for an exam. The students I spoke with were clearly disgusted with the status quo, but they were resigned to it and saw little hope for reform. This despair led them to dream of leaving Moldova. And if they had the good fortune to win a scholarship abroad, they had no intention of ever returning to help in building a new Moldova. What for? What "new Moldova"? They were certain that the metastasizing ills were too virulent. Moldova was a terminal country on life support. They were smart, eager, capable students, full of promise. And yet they viewed the future with despair. They were young, but already they believed that their lives were doomed to be wasted. Their eyes pleaded with me: *Do something.* Yet there was no heat to their pleas. They did not believe I could help them. They knew I would not stay long in Moldova. Like shades in the Inferno, they stared as I passed through, hopelessly hoping that someone might rescue them.

Two weeks before the end of the term and the end of my sojourn in Moldova, I approached the Matron of the Keys to ask for the classroom key as usual. She assumed her habitual scowl as I approached. For at least the hundredth time, I attempted to request the key, fully anticipating her draconian reproach. She stared hard at me, and I prepared to try again, re-forming the Russian phonemes in my head.

But this time she merely grunted and said, "Horocho." Good.

"Horocho?" I repeated with astonishment.

"Da. Horocho."

Finally! At long last I had succeeded in winning her approval on the first try. I felt an unexpected joy at this accomplishment. I beamed at her, waiting for the issuance of the grail-key. But she continued to stare at me, now rapping her knuckles on the desk.

"And the key?" I asked tentatively. As usual, I stumbled over the Russian words. In response, she launched into an emphatic, stern-voiced disquisition of some sort—knuckles rapping more vehemently as she spoke—leaving me baffled and cowed, the joy of my triumph now completely drained. Fortunately, one of my students came along just then and listened impassively to an exact repetition of her diatribe.

"Ah," my student said. "It appears this room is no longer operational."

"Not operational?"

"Yes, we are to move to different room. Number six hundred eighty-four."

He said the number in Russian for me. I tried to repeat it for the matron, but, flustered, I botched it. I looked imploringly at my student, but he could not help me now. He was not authorized to request the key. And in fact he, too, was scowling at my bad pronunciation. I tried again.

"Nyet," the matron said. "Bad. Listen. Repeat. Again."

BENJAMIN BUSCH

"Today Is Better Than Tomorrow"

FROM *Harper's Magazine*

> What makes Argia different from other cities is that it has earth
> instead of air. The streets are completely filled with dirt, clay
> packs the rooms to the ceiling . . . From up here, nothing of Ar-
> gia can be seen; some say, "It's down below there," and we can
> only believe them . . . At night, putting your ear to the ground,
> you can sometimes hear a door slam.
>   —Italo Calvino, *Invisible Cities*

IT HAD BEEN 10 years since I had invaded Iraq, armed and
dressed to look like dirt. I pulled out my new map of the country
as a visitor this time. No targets, no units, no routes given code
names as women or beer. I'd spend 10 days working my way from
Baghdad through Wasit Province to Jassan, a town near the Iranian border. I had served as its provisional military mayor in 2003
but hadn't seen a single report on it since I left. My hope was to
return without revealing that I'd been there before, to travel under my first name, concealed by a beard, to the place I was known
only as Major Busch.

On December 9, I boarded a small plane and made the jump
from Amman, Jordan, across the angry Sunni provinces and into
Baghdad. As we glided into the city's variegated glow, I looked for
red tracers, bullets fired into the sky. I looked for the war. But we
didn't dive like military transport planes avoiding rockets; we just
shuddered onto the surface as a voice welcomed us to Iraq. It was
a few months yet before fighters from the Islamic State of Iraq and
the Levant (ISIL) would threaten the capital.

At passport control, there were two signs, in Arabic and in

English: IRAQIS and OTHERS. I stood under my label. We had spent nine years trying to determine which Iraqis we had come to free and which to fight, and we had never really learned the difference.

No traffic from the city is allowed within miles of the terminal, so shuttle vans take arrivals to a meeting area at the far edge of the security perimeter. I sat in the back next to two Syrians and behind four Jordanians, one of whom spoke in a hush while our Iraqi driver examined the currencies and worked the exchange values in his head. He held my $10 bill up to a light before sliding it into a stack of Turkish lira, Iranian rial, and Syrian pounds. I didn't say a word, my cover already blown by Alexander Hamilton.

The road was empty as we drove, fountains lit in the median with colored lights. Everything was in good order there in no man's land, an immense empty space meant to keep the runways out of rocket range. My interpreter, whom I'll call Khalil, was waiting in the sequestered lot at the airport's entrance. He had a cough but, like most Iraqis, continued to smoke. He was dry about it. "If it doesn't kill me, it would have been something." He offered me a cigarette, but I declined. "See. Americans get everyone to smoke . . . and then you all quit."

Khalil always wanted to travel, and it damned him. He worked for the Intelligence Service under Saddam, the only job he could get after school, and was posted to New York City as a United Nations diplomat with the Iraqi Ministry of Foreign Affairs. In 1991 he watched coverage of Desert Storm from his apartment on Manhattan's East Side while, two hours up the Hudson, I watched as a senior at Vassar College. Because of his connection to the Baathists, he can't get a visa to move his family to the United States now, despite many years as an interpreter for American forces during the occupation. He will be left in Baghdad as Iraq falls apart.

Traffic was sparse as we drove into the city's center, where I spent two nights in the Karada district. The storefronts were luminous at the base of dark apartment buildings. There were no police rushing past, no shots fired, just the growl of generators and thump of trucks hitting holes in the road, the cool air thick with exhaust. A radio reported car bombs: 8 killed, 22 wounded.

"The numbers are all lies in Iraq," Khalil said. "How many votes, how many dead."

"How was it here today?" I asked.

He smiled. "Shit." He was numbed by survivor's fatigue. The

country had all the symptoms of collapse, but the lights were on, international flights were landing, and stores were open as bombs went off. "Even if it's bad we say, 'Today is better than tomorrow.'"

Traffic filled the streets, and sunrise lit the haze. Flocks of pigeons turned bright as they beat their way above the shadows cast by buildings. Cigarette smoke hung in the lobbies, the clink of small tea glasses ringing like bells. In the alleys wires were draped loose and tangled from rooftops.

Iraq is a place of prismatic identities, the ancient diluting the present, portraits of Shia martyrs appearing on market walls beside crude paintings of Mickey Mouse. There was a time when, despite ethnic and religious conflict, Iraqis were forcibly nationalized. But our occupation labored to ensure that Baathists were criminalized, erased with the declaration that the country was to be a democracy in which they could not participate. Soon people began to see change not as progress but as a steady decline into dysfunction. Many now feel nostalgic for Saddam's autocratic predictability, and they see their internal conflict as a proxy battle between foreign powers.

A man sweeping the sidewalk said, "Look around. There are only products and politics from other countries here. This is not Iraq anymore."

A salesman who overheard our conversation added, "What is my country? This is my homeland, but I'll be a refugee here all my life. I'm a refugee who can vote."

The street merchants had not yet set up. Congestion and checkpoints delay many motorists for up to three hours, so even at 10:30 most are just getting to their shops. The clothing-stand mannequins are bare, hundreds of plastic torsos hanging on steel bars or wrapped in sacks, legs piled in carts along the curb. Suicide bombers often target crowds in shopping areas like these or cafés where young men gather to watch soccer and play cards, punished for simple pleasures. There were almost no children to be seen out in public areas.

Crews worked jackhammers in the streets for pothole repairs, but the ground underneath was just dirt, sandy concrete shoveled in and leveled, the business of a city sealing its wounds with scabs. Construction was under way everywhere: buildings being chipped down and new ones being poured into rough molds. The quality was so poor it looked like they were erecting ruins. Khalil explained that this part of Baghdad was Jewish until the early 1950s; it is believed the land is still in their names, billions in real estate, but they are gone.

Foreign imports drive the marketplace now. An iPhone 5 is $700, but gas is only 40 cents a liter ($1.51 a gallon). The most popular shirts and jeans come from Turkey; fruits and vegetables come from Egypt, Iran, and Lebanon. China is pumping the stores full of cheap merchandise, and though the lore of American quality still exists, the Chinese have found the bottom dollar. This has wiped out most local shoemakers, carpenters, and textile workers. Unemployment is high. Almost no Iraqis have credit cards, so people can spend only what they have in hand.

Every few blocks there was a corner that glittered with tinsel on artificial evergreens. Ranks of inflated plastic Santas smiled with lunatic glee from patches of cotton snow. I asked Khalil whether there were many Christians in the neighborhood. He said, "No. Everyone here celebrates Christmas."

Billboards showed another world, clean and Edenic. Framed posters of waterfalls were everywhere, fantasies imported along with wide-eyed dolls and stuffed bears. Photo shops covered their windows with studio pictures of children posed on backgrounds that resembled anywhere but here.

The Fourteenth of Ramadan Mosque blared its call to prayer over the whine of police sirens. It stands on one side of Firdos Square, where U.S. Marines pulled down the statue of Saddam in 2003; his bronze feet are still standing on the pedestal. Across the square from the mosque is the Cristal Grand Ishtar, a former Sheraton, where many Western journalists stayed during the war. There were dozens of flags flying in front of it, but the American flag was missing. The absolute absence of Americans anywhere was noticeable. I didn't see us on the streets, at the airport, or even in the hotels. Our diplomats are hidden in the embassy, our largest oil company is divesting from wells outside of Kurdish control, and our military has vanished.

Banners with Husayn ibn Ali's impassive face colored the streets. He was killed in Karbala in 680 and enshrined there. The pilgrimage had begun, Shias walking to his tomb to mourn his death, targeted by Sunni extremists along their route. Traffic was constant, the jabbing of horns continuous. Iraq looked busy but it did not look happy, a concrete hive filled with families grinding out the day just to make it to the next one. As long as I kept moving I stayed inconspicuous. It was when I stopped that I felt out of place. Iraqis moved around me, purposeful like I had been when I was a Marine.

The door of a corner post office opened into a blackened hole, the inside filled with bricks and trash, wild cats slinking over the piles. It had been hit by a car bomb and had never been rebuilt. I asked how people got letters now, and a snack vendor replied, "Who would write?"

Khalil and I stopped at a café on the next street. In October 2007 another car bomb went off here, killing 230 people, Khalil said. (Official estimates put the number of dead at only 25.) Khalil had lived above the café; his apartment was destroyed and his daughter was badly wounded. He was an interpreter for an American army unit based in Baghdad at the time, and the soldiers came to her rescue after Khalil made a desperate phone call to their headquarters.

Baghdad is a city of armed men and bullet-pocked barricades. The ministries are still ringed with our fortification walls and makeshift watchtowers. Wire, soldiers, and up-armored Humvees are placed at regular intervals. The feeling is of an invisible siege, the awaiting of another inevitable defeat. In 2003 the transition from what Iraq had been into what it could be, though in disarray, was colored by potential. We couldn't see that instability was going to replace autocracy so completely—and then Nouri al-Maliki's government brought both. The blast barriers we erected as temporary defenses became permanent fixtures, giant nameless gravestones.

To get to Jassan, we had to go to Kut, the capital of Wasit Province. At a transportation hub on the eastern edge of Baghdad, drivers yelled the names of Iraqi cities as if they were reading from a Shia map: Basra, Najaf, Nasiriyah, Karbala, Kut. The U.S. State Department had been emphatic in trying to dissuade me from independent travel in Iraq, especially so far from Baghdad, but journalists have always come to that city and told the country's story from its point of view. I needed to see what had become of the distant villages I had known. They had remained intact for centuries because of their political insignificance and isolation. It was my hope that those same qualities had preserved them, so far, from the violence and social collapse of the cities.

Khalil got a cab to Kut for 30,000 dinar ($25 at 1,200 dinar per dollar), and we set out on a route that ran east, above the erratic path of the Tigris. The traffic out of Baghdad moved in jerks, passengers expressionless as they stared into other cars, men in the front and women in the back. We passed a former American base, now Iraqi, and it looked rundown, dirt-filled Hesco barriers sagging into piles, soldiers slumping at their posts. We saw hundreds of flatbeds loaded with rebar for new construction, and there were herds of sheep, pens of chickens, and mesh bags of melons pressed up to the road. Baghdad was being fed from its immediate perimeter like a medieval city. It is a medieval city.

We were stopped and questioned at an elaborate new structure on the border between Diyala and Wasit. It had the design of a triumphal arch, the paved passages through it incomplete and the building still empty. It looked just like a border station between countries. These never existed between provinces before. There was no point. Khalil felt it was preparation for the future division of Iraq.

Boys swirled through the stalled traffic selling boxes of cookies and cigarettes. A heavy man in the passenger seat rubbed beads in one hand, smoked with the other, and spoke as if he had grit in his throat. "Half of us are soldiers, the other half are merchants now. All of Iraq is a shop with a war in it." The backs of his hands were dark tan, his palms bleached pink. The driver looked like a bird: long, sharp, drooped nose, small eyes, gray leather jacket. He barely made a sound, eyes fixed on the road.

For a few miles, when the river curled close, there were fields of green grass and young palm trees. New brick houses have replaced huts once built from the silt of the Tigris. It was like another climate, a verdant country winding through an arid one, the two sharing nothing but proximity.

Police checkpoints profiled "foreign" Arabs, men from Saudi Arabia and Qatar especially. Muqtada al Sadr was on billboards promoting his religious rank among Shias, his dark glower no longer adolescent. (His Mahdi Army, raised to expel occupation forces, has been reconstituted as the Peace Brigades and is now fighting ISIL alongside the Iraqi army.) Gigante cigarettes posted their own highway signs, photographs of wealthy men smoking.

They stood above hovels where laborers squatted by fires, the fumes from burning plastics stuck to the air. Mourning flags waved over homes, and donkeys grazed in trash. Traffic surged after each checkpoint, and we sped along the open road, sparse scrub on the desert side, tall reeds and fields irrigated from the Tigris on the other.

Roadside refreshment stands had been set up with rows of chairs for pilgrims to rest on as they made their way to Karbala. Separate tents were nearby for men and women to sleep in. I asked Khalil whether he had ever walked the route, and he said you only walk if you believe.

In 2003 we advanced from Kuwait to Kut with orders to push all the way to the Iranian border afterward. Most of our maps had nothing but a single road drawn through flat space, our pen marks on the route meaningless to the land. We would piece the maps together as we drove north, passing from one rectangle of desert to another. The terrain was open and scarred by tank trenches dug to guard the only highway from the Persian Gulf to Baghdad. The tanks—Soviet imports—were still there, scorched by air strikes, relics of two-dimensional thinking. In these dirt barrens nationhood was impossible to see: a herd of sheep and a single man, a Bedouin tent sometimes afloat on the near horizon. My unit had been brought from the cold, wet coast of North Carolina late, and we hurried into Iraq far behind the fighting. It was a kind of immediate war tourism, the burned wreckage of our own amphibious assault vehicles still on the muddy shore of the Euphrates in Nasiriyah. Torched and hollow, they sat below the bridge as we crossed, heading north in disbelief. The fires had died out, but the buildings along the river looked long forsaken: pitted by bullets, windows chewed open, with bricks spilling from the walls. Marines from Task Force Tarawa were on rooftops and street corners, Iraqi women walking cautiously around rubble and wire with their children, in occupied territory.

The war moved entirely along two highways, both regime and coalition forces ignoring small periphery towns, the vast desert and its villages of no strategic importance to anyone. As we approached Kut, Iraqi army uniforms lined the road near abandoned outposts. No bodies or blood, just helmets, pants, and shirts. There had been a large army garrison waiting for the advancing Marines, but they quickly fled or dissolved into the city dressed as civilians.

Today, as our cab arrived at Kut, Iraqi soldiers at the checkpoint wore U.S. tricolor desert camouflage, the same my unit had been issued for the invasion. It was as if the hidden army of Saddam had reappeared wearing our uniforms. They walked carefully along our cab with a fake bomb detector, purchased from a crooked British contractor who resold $20 American novelty golf-ball locators for $27,000 each. Corrupt Iraqi officials bought $40 million worth of them. The soldier stared intently at the indicator light, three years after their sale had been banned, a keeper of the lie. "Everyone knows it does nothing," the passenger in the front seat said. They scrutinized my passport and visa stamp. "Ameriki?" they kept asking, as if it couldn't be true, and then brought out an officer to verify my papers. He walked from the office with annoyed importance and asked where our weapons were. Khalil explained that we were alone and unarmed. The official looked up from my passport, shook his head, and let us go. Ten years ago I might have done the same to him.

My photographs have been kept in an order absent of chronology: a blindfolded skull, a pile of boots, an English gravestone, a child waving. I never labeled them, just expected I would remember like everyone does. Seven months of circumstantial evidence. Military mobile exchanges only sold 400-speed film, meant to shoot subjects in lower light, so the reduced resolution is noticeable when the pictures are enlarged, their definition becoming increasingly granular, as if composed of pressed dust. The imperfection of vision is at work, the flickering of lines, the involuntary squint to identify exactly what you're seeing, the desert going from vast and static to pulsing and immediate, like memory does.

Kut was familiar but disorienting, the streets swollen with shoppers and thousands of pilgrims. The city made the sounds of collision: sharp honks, truck engines, salesmen calling out, and the constant chirp of police whistles. Goats ate the stiff dead grass in the median. The center of town looked battered.

We stopped in at the Iraqi Journalists Syndicate office. All the government furniture was foreign-made, wood glossy with thick lacquer chipping at the edges. Everyone smoked. They couldn't believe I came by cab from Baghdad with nothing but an unarmed interpreter. A man shook my hand and smiled. He said they have a proverb: "You enter the house from the door, not by the window." The last American journalist anyone could remember came here three years ago in an armored convoy and only stayed for an hour. The manager said, "There is not enough violence for Kut to be news. You look for stories, and the city doesn't exist." Another added, "I would rather not exist than make the news here."

A man named Nassir took us to see a cemetery built by the British for the men lost in the battle for Kut during the First World War, its headstones, like its soldiers, brought from overseas. It was the only place in the region that commemorated the people most responsible for Iraq's creation.

Nassir drove in rushes and jolts, stabbing in between cars, everyone around him doing the same, warning beeps constant, lanes filled like blood vessels, everything somehow pumping through. Traffic intensified as we pushed into the marketplace, the streets channeling a reckless braid of pedestrians, motorcycles, trucks, carts, and cabs.

"It's amazing the roads aren't filled with car accidents," I said. "I can't believe no one gets hit here."

Khalil interpreted and Nassir laughed. He had a joyful face.

"Happens," he said, smiling.

He'd been assigned as our official escort for the next eight days in the province and had been cheerful since we arrived. Tomorrow we would hear that he hit a young boy on his way to pick us up, and a cousin was sent with another car to drive us in his place. The child died in the hospital, and we wouldn't see Nassir again as his life became suspended between tribal atonement and court. But today he was happy to be on a journey with the only American in Wasit.

We went to the souk, which was easily three times the size it had been in 2003. Even then the market had been a kind of neutral space, uninterrupted by invasion or regime, the stalls passed from generation to generation. Trade was conducted in dinar notes stamped with Saddam's victorious image or in dollars stamped with our own Founding Fathers. Under Saddam, an Iraqi soldier made the equivalent of $120 a year. By 2004 the Coalition Provisional Authority desperately rehired them at a salary of $400 a month. There was immediate, irreversible inflation. Corruption in the military bloomed as soon as wages did. An Iraqi soldier makes $1,000 a month now.

When I first walked through the market in 2003, the concrete pillars in the central square were covered with Xeroxed posters of the people "disappeared" by the regime. A week later, near the Iranian border, we would watch as some of them were exhumed from the site of their execution.

Today we passed through groups of women in black, children emerging and retreating beneath their parade of robes, salesmen with handfuls of cash manning caverns of cloth, sandals, and spice. We arrived in the street where the Kut War Cemetery lay. There was a new fence in front, but the rear wall had been pushed down, exposing the site to the city. The concrete cross still stood, but it looked changed, some graffiti spray-painted on it, the U.S. Marine rededication plaque torn off. Children played on a worn dirt clearing where headstones had been, kicking a ball over the soldiers below, one of them digging on the surface with a little toy shovel. Phragmites reeds had overgrown the rest of the lot. The owner of a nearby shop said it had been used as a dump but the Americans cleaned it, and for a while it had flowers and a guard. The guard went unpaid, he added, and "kids" took the headstones and sold them in the market. The cemetery was a dump again.

"Many groups have come to study the cemetery since 2003. The Americans built a new fence to replace the British one. Then the British built one to replace the American one. They all look for the missing stones, but they find nothing. They ask questions, take pictures, and leave. Just like you." Just like me.

Outside Iraq, Kut is a city remembered only as a military disaster. The British had marched a colonial Indian division up the Tigris toward Baghdad but were stopped by the Turks and their Arab allies at Ctesiphon and sent into a retreat that ended here. For five months they were trapped by siege, unable to resupply or escape, pounded by Turkish artillery, finally surrendering at a loss of 12,000 men. Only 420 have graves here; the rest are buried somewhere underneath the city. I waded into the dense stand of reeds and found a few toppled headstones still largely intact.

1525 PRIVATE
W. HOSKINS
SOMERSET LIGHT INFANTRY
24TH NOVEMBER 1915, AGE 20
LORD REMEMBER ME
WHEN THOU COMETH
INTO THY KINGDOM

The reeds stood 10 feet tall and were plumed with clouds of seeds. I watched them sway above me while crouched by a grave in their shade, a cat passing by using the line of fallen stones as a path. It was my birthday, and I thought of all these soldiers, their entire lives marked by nothing but the day they died and now marked by nothing at all. I emerged coated with dust, my hair downy with silky seeds. Khalil had been pacing the perimeter, calling to me every few minutes as if I were lost in the wilderness.

Outside the gate, I noticed some bright fragments tamped into the gutter and recognized the elegant carving of a wreath in marble, the crest of a gravestone sunk into gray drain water. Men watched as I took a photograph. They followed as I went up an alley and found an entire headstone facedown in concrete used as a step into a gated courtyard. It showed no sign of damage or wear, dug up unbroken precisely for this purpose and moved a mere 50 feet from its grave. Another photograph and Khalil suggested we hurry. A small crowd was gathering. As we left I found more stacked as a stoop in front of a shop. Then, embedded in the street itself were five stones used to fill in potholes, carts rattling over them, a carved cross facing up. I kicked aside trash and drew attention from nearby vendors, who wondered why I was so interested in the pavement.

In contrast to the forlorn British cemetery, the Ottoman memorial is proudly guarded by an Iraqi Arab paid by the Turkish Embassy. He is the fourth in an unbroken line since his great-grandfather dug the graves. He greeted me with his young son beside him, the next guard. Polished plaques on the gate say TURKISH MARTYRS, 1914–1917 in Turkish on one side and Arabic on the other. The white concrete markers inside bear no names, just the raised Turkish star and crescent, dabbed red with too much paint. These 50 Turkish soldiers and 7 commanders are all that can be found, representatives of 10,000 lost here. I asked where the rest are buried and the guard swept his arm around the horizon. Iraqis are not interred in Kut. They are carried to the city-sized cemeteries in Najaf and Karbala. Only invaders are buried here. The caretaker showed me the visitors' log, and it was a list of foreigners, mostly Turks. I added my name. On our way back to the car Nassir bought diapers for his new baby. Today is better than tomorrow.

We checked in to one of the two hotels in Kut, and it was unfit for prisoners. They made a copy of my passport visa for the Iraqi

police. The state now tracks all guests in hopes of catching foreign
terrorists who have no family and nowhere to stay. Guests in hotels
are all suspect. Despite the thousands of pilgrims passing through
Kut, the hotel was almost completely empty. We tried to find a
restaurant but failed to please Khalil after two cab rides. He was
suspicious of all the kebabs, since meat is no longer inspected and
regulated like it was under Saddam, and some places will secretly
serve donkey. (If there is anything an Iraqi disrespects more than
a donkey, I'd like to know. I remember a police officer wiping his
hands and saying, "Saddam Donkey," as the highest sign of his disgust.)

I lay awake most of the night, feeling insects real or imagined,
seeds from the cemetery still in my hair, the bed uncomfortable
and heat up too high. The ventilation fan didn't work, pigeons
nesting in it, septic gas seeping out of the bathroom and smearing
the air in the room. Unlike Baghdad there was no security curfew
in Kut, so the sound of horns and police whistles came through
the coo of birds all night. A loose wire kept a long fluorescent
light blinking, the mint-green paint on the walls appearing and
disappearing in flashes. Everything was worn down and dirty like
everything else in the city.

In the morning, after being locked in our room by a broken
latch, we waited to meet Mahmoud Talal, the governor of Wasit,
in a building notable only for a sign in the lobby that Khalil translated as "Don't torture your children." Men waited with papers,
their needs requiring the brief review of government. Some strode
through with an obvious sense of privilege, family of the governor
or officials of note.

We were finally invited into the governor's office, a large empty
space with ornate chairs pushed up against the walls. He reviewed
and signed documents, pausing to speak with us, his attention
often drawn to men bringing messages whispered to him. He
answered questions with the neutrality required of his position,
the room listening carefully. I asked about the British cemetery,
and he said it had been reported to the British Embassy but they
had done nothing. I asked about the arrest warrant issued by Maliki against Sunni members of his Provincial Council, and he regarded his audience. "That is just political propaganda," he said.
I responded, "It is very effective political propaganda." Everyone
laughed.

The area around Kut had become dangerous for tribal sheiks. Notable men were said to be targeted by al-Qaeda now because it was big news and reflected poorly on national security. It was believed that Sunni extremists were attacking their own to frame Shias and encourage sectarian violence. But Kut was rarely the target of bombings. Most of Wasit's own security forces had been sent to the mixed city of Suwayrah, near Baghdad, which had been especially unstable. Governor Talal was trying to preserve the support of his Sunni minority while Maliki was estranging them. I found out later that a sheik sitting in the room was from Asaib Ahl al-Haq, the violent Shia militia allied with Maliki. They had attacked Americans for years. He was a very dangerous man who smiled benignly while I questioned the governor and radiated consequence as he responded. I was the only one who didn't notice that he was silently presiding over the conversation. It must happen all the time. The man who confided this to us said, "We can't make him leave."

After the interview Khalil and I were invited to stay in the governor's guesthouse, a kind of overwrought hostel for officials visiting from out of town, and we were very grateful to leave our miserable hotel. Our new room could have been anywhere in the world. The bedsheets had *Pour les Amoureux du Café* printed on them, and the furnishings still wore plastic wrap as if their newness could be preserved, the desert dust kept off for one more day. An ad for a Saudi falconry contest played on the TV, the only clue that we weren't somewhere in Mexico, and most channels showed American movies.

Back out in the city I traced the edge of the Tigris and came to the souk from a new direction as night fell. The air was damp and smelled of fresh bread.

One shop selling uniforms for security forces displayed the modern U.S. Marine desert digital camouflage, *USMC* in tiny letters embedded in the pattern. They can only be purchased with an official government ID, and the vendor showed me the logbook in which each purchase was recorded. A T-shirt had the misspelled slogan *If Everything Is Exploding Around You. "Thrt's Probably Us."* At a tailor's shop, portions of shirts and pants were pinned to the wall. They looked like men blown apart, clothing for the bare dismembered mannequins piled on the streets of the Karada district.

The American memories of Iraq are largely urban. Drawn into

population centers where people and religion rubbed against each other, our experience became associated most with the names of a few cities. The villages spun away in an expanding orbit, growing more distant from us, and from Baghdad.

The floodplain between Kut and Jassan was covered with winter rainwater, a gray sea reflecting the cloudless atmosphere. As we rode out the next day, the horizon was without distinction, above and below nothing but a singular color, the sky spilled onto the desert. The land here betrayed no proof of an underneath, no outcroppings of bedrock, no hills and no sedimentary layers distinguishable in the dust. It seemed to be of an almost infinite depth, the soil going down for miles, all the way to oil.

Stockpiled aerial bomb fins we once found on an abandoned air force base in Kut were now painted white and used as traffic cones at checkpoints everywhere. We saw buses full of Iranians on their way to Karbala, a sign of tremendous change here. Our cabdriver said that once, a few years after the Iran-Iraq war, "they found a candy wrapper made in Iran and the whole area was swept by the military looking for the Iranian who dropped it. All the way from Kut to the border. There was no border traffic before the U.S. invasion. Control by the Iraqi military was absolute."

The road was lined with blown tires or the rusted steel rings of burned ones. We stopped to visit Bedouins camped along the route. A man from a nearby hut guided us across a ditch to a tent. His wife immediately called his cell phone, afraid that we had taken him. He smiled as he explained her worry. "In Iraq many men have been taken. Walk off like this with unknown people and never come back to the wife."

Sheik Sha-lan Debon invited us in for tea. Inside his tent there were two sitting rugs, a small ring of raised clay for a fire, plastic containers of water, and a pile of dry branches. The camp is moved every five days. The camels they raise sell for between 400,000 and 500,000 dinar in Najaf. There was government land for grazing during the regime, but now it's all privatized and he has to pay rent. His herd is shrinking every year. "The old map should be honored," he said. When I asked if he had a copy of it, he said, "Of course." I asked if I could see it, excited by the discovery of the elusive tribal map of the desert, but he just smiled and pointed to his head. A cousin handed me a cup of tea. They have a saying: "Drink your tea and all will be fine."

Debon said he is in charge of a thousand men. I asked how many women, and he scoffed. "I don't know. Women come and go in the tribe. Men stay." The tribe is spread over hundreds of miles, from Basra to Babylon, and he coordinates all of it by cell phone. He has no radio, television, or Internet. "Everything is by speaking." He takes his flag to funerals or has it taken in his name. A sword and a crescent. He just went to a funeral in Ramadi, where a Sunni rebellion was taking form. I asked whom the tribe sides with now. "We have no enemies," he said.

He was disappointed by the end of reliable food rations. During Saddam there were monthly allotments of flour, sugar, oil, milk, tea, and beans, but now there is only flour. "If the Americans had stayed or had not come it would be better," he said. Six of his family members have recently tried to join the police. No success. They participated heavily in the military and police forces during Saddam's regime. "Without family in government we have no connection to it. We are not represented with anyone we can trust. So we have no government. No state." The Bedouins had always been considered stateless, but now they longed for one. They voted for Governor Talal. He visited them in their tent and in Jassan but they haven't been able to see him since the campaign. "A good man, maybe only for election. Ten years electing people and we get nothing." He said they join no parties. Anyone who does gets fired from the tribe. He's had to fire some.

Criminals are also expelled. If guilty of murder they are exposed to the judicial system, but traditional law runs parallel to state law —tribes meet and blood money is paid or people are forced to move. It is most important for the tribe to go to the person bringing the charges and try to handle it out of court. Just yesterday he had to negotiate such a dispute. "Najaf people's car hit one of our tribe—killed. Ten million dinar if someone kills on purpose, but this was accident. My tribe asked for nothing." I thought of Nassir. The American military generally paid $2,500 to families for civilian deaths caused by military operations in 2003. It was considered a small fortune then.

"Once, everything here moved by camel. Bedouins were first in society. Now we are the poor and soon camels will only be in zoos. Where will we go when all the land is owned?"

One of Debon's family members invited us to his house by the brick factory. Khalif Milbus is married with 15 children, and his elderly mother lives with him, too. No government support, and the area is off the electrical grid. "Since always there has been a problem with power," he said.

"Electrical power or political power?" I asked. He smiled.

"Yes."

Regular blackouts continue throughout Iraq, towns darkening and then flickering back as private generators are tricked on. I heard the same two words everywhere in 2003: *Maqqu kaharlabbah* (We have no power). It is slang born from decades of corruption and savaged or inadequate infrastructure.

Milbus's sons did not see herding as their future. Zaid wanted to be a teacher; Aneed, a doctor. His eldest son left school to work in the brick factory. He didn't mention his daughters. They will marry one day. Milbus served in the military "from 1988 until Bush the Son released us." He was paid no salary, so he had to escape service to earn for his family. If he had money he would buy a tanker, a truck, a tent, and camels. "I would not stay in this prison house." He would "travel Iraq as a true Bedouin" again. I asked whether he fears the Bedouin way will end in Iraq. "Yes. It is almost destroyed. Not much left. Someday men will not know the sun or the land. Only roads."

At the brick factory, a kiln the size of a warehouse was filled with ruined bricks. The fuel supply was inconsistent, and they didn't bake properly. Weeks of labor and 260,000 bricks lost. The tall stack blew smoke in a trail thick enough to cast a shadow on us. I stood on the hot roof of the kiln looking through the heat at the burned land. Boys ran, kicking a soccer ball, their lungs filling with soot.

Beside the factory is a settlement constructed of discarded bricks. There were women there, and I was cautioned not to take any photographs. They were all squatters who worked at the factory, dead poor, a sewage trench the color of oil running past their homes. I asked Milbus whether he had any family living there. He replied with scorn that he would "never allow his women to live like this."

When we got to Jassan it was almost unrecognizable. A new colony of 100 two-story brick homes had been built along the road. In

2003 the entire village was on a hill. It was ovular, organic, interdependent, and defensive in its construction. Its dirt walls had been kept smooth for 1,000 years by the vitality of dense occupation. Now it was beginning to wear down, roofs collapsing and spring rains washing the mud away as families resettled in the brick buildings on the plain. The spreading construction was gridded, edged, and fragmentary, suburban seeds of a new order. They seemed to belong to a different people, the tight rural community broken apart into solitary satellites.

While waiting to meet with the town councilmen on the new central street, I asked a policeman why so many people were moving to Jassan and building houses. "Loans," he said. "Ministry of Financing and Housing gives them now. Thirty million dinar. Free for a while, then monthly payments. No new people moving here. Everyone is from the hill." It seemed improbable that there could be so many, but the population in the old catacomb of homes on the hill had always been impossible to guess from the outside.

We were invited to meet in the city manager's office, recently built across the street from the old city council building and jail my unit had restored in 2003. They looked old and smaller now in comparison with the new buildings, diminished in scale. Mr. El-Timmimy Hawas, district manager, greeted us and then worried how his tie looked when he saw my camera. He said there were no problems with the Americans, just disappointment. "When coalition forces came, Iraqis heard they would get whiskey with the rations, but all they brought were blades." He said the Georgian troops who were last stationed here were all right also. "They stayed to themselves, which was best." Ukrainians before them had caused some trouble when they restored a clinic and painted their flag over the entire exterior. "We didn't want another flag on us."

Their problems were few in comparison with those of the cities. A drought had dropped the level of the Tigris, and the pipe that drew from the river could no longer reach it. The lack of rain had also stressed herds and palm orchards, but the farmers were still keeping them irrigated. They have three clinics but no doctors or surgical wards. Pregnant women and serious injuries must go 31 miles to Kut. They had asked the Provincial Council for aid to expand, but the budgets are based on population, and Jassan, despite administering eight other little desert villages, has only 12,000 people. With an annual budget of about $1.7 million (around $140 a person), they can do only so much. Turkey is contracted to build them a new water pipeline from the Tigris, and a water-purification plant is being built right across the highway from town. They also won a Japanese grant to upgrade the aging Soviet pumping stations.

We headed over to meet Ali Talib Muhammed, a councilman from the original 2003 city council who has kept his post since. He is an exceptionally solemn man. We had met many times while I was stationed in Jassan, but now he didn't recognize me. With a beard, a pen, clothing from the street in Baghdad, and 10 years, I was transformed, detached from their memory of who I had been when I wore a pistol and a rank.

Muhammed recounted the village's response to our invasion. Saed Khalum was the most respected man in Jassan in 2003, and on his own, he had assembled a council before coalition forces had even arrived. I met them on April 29, 13 days after their first town meeting, when my unit moved up from its position farther south along the Iranian border. Two years later, on May 30, 2005, the Provincial Council officially acknowledged them as the city council, and they received their first salary. By then I was on my second deployment fighting Syrians and Sunni extremists in the city of Ramadi on the other side of Iraq. While in Jassan this time, I met 9 of the original 11 councilmen.

Muhammed said the town has been stable: "There are no strangers living among us in Jassan. Everyone is related or known, so troubles are solved by families." I asked whether dividing Iraq into three states—Sunni, Shia, and Kurdish—would bring peace. He said no. "I'm from Zubaidi tribe, all over Iraq. We have seen other countries divided and see how much trouble they have." I asked whether he met with any U.S. forces. "They came to ask some questions, like you do now. Didn't achieve anything."

I asked whether he remembered the night the council voted to close an illegal water pipe that irrigated a farm owned by Saddam's wife Sajida. It was their first recorded vote as a governing body. He said, "Yes. Major Busch." I wrote my name as if it were unknown to me, but I was pleased to hear it. The night of the vote, a child walked up to the front of the room and handed over a note from the Fedayeen Saddam that promised my death. I had driven off after that meeting sick with a high fever. The desert became a hallucinatory space as I struggled to stand, my night-vision goggles creating a claustrophobic depiction of the open land, the darkness shrinking the view, and my pyretic blood throbbing in my eyes. I don't remember falling into my tent a few miles away or being worried about snipers, but I do remember walking out of the building with hundreds of men chanting, "Good Busch." Through my illness it still felt like the only triumph of the war. I thought the new country would be all right. For one night I was sure of it.

Muhammed said Iraq was failing now because state officials are not qualified for their jobs. During the regime, officials had college degrees for their positions. He saw this problem all the way up the Iraqi government. "But Jassan is apart from Iraq." He felt that the village has always governed itself, drifting in the country rather than anchored to it. "We had the first election in Iraq, and we have been working ever since. No one else in Iraq did this," he said.

Saad Kareem Izbar, another original councilman, said, "We never agreed with any ruler. Iraq is always against its government (and all foreigners). There wasn't much of that under Saddam, but he ruled with an iron fist. You can fix anything, but not the man himself. Saddam said that if he was going to turn over Iraq to anyone, he would turn it over as dirt." I looked out at the desert and said, "And so he did."

We visited Muhammed's childhood home on the hill. The house had almost no decoration at all, high ceilings, bare walls of mud and straw painted white. It was cool and felt like an underground chamber. His family were all born here. Now he rents it to a relative and has built a new brick house. He showed me an original door made of slabs cut from a date-palm trunk. It looked ancient, worn, and dust-dried. He opened it with true pride, a museum artifact still at work in a dying town. It was the first time I had been inside a home in Jassan. As a Marine I always stayed outside.

We left the hill and went to meet the new council chairman, Abu Hassan, at a tiny café whose interior was painted a flat pink. We sat with five of the original councilmen on a ledge padded by single sheets of cardboard. I asked what had changed since Saddam. They seemed most upset about the awarding of government posts to Maliki's friends and allies. "Before the new government, the old employees of the ministries worked very hard and serious, not watching our watches. Now they just wait for salary and holiday."

I passed around pictures from the "military records," photographs I had taken myself in 2003, and they were thrilled. They called out the names of people and handed them back and forth. A man smiled at one and said, "Major Busch." The picture he held did not have me in it. I asked him to explain. "Only Major Busch could have taken this picture. He carried a camera and visited my house." "Did he go inside for tea?" I asked. "No. He went inside no homes. He allowed no raids in Jassan." "Did you ever invite him inside?" "No. Our women were there. Only we invited him for tea." At this, a councilman told my story.

"Major Busch had tea with us on the hill and asked why we poured our tea into our saucers. We told him it cools it quicker. Busch asked why we didn't just wait for it to cool off. We all laughed and said if we waited we would never form any agreements." The councilmen all laughed again together. What they remembered so well of me and found so extraordinary, I did not remember at all. I would be told this story again from two other men in Jassan. There was something pleasant in hearing stories about myself, like being present at my own funeral. They did not recall the message declaring my imminent assassination. They recalled only that I was there. Drink your tea and all will be fine.

I asked how they felt about people moving off the hill. "The new houses are better, of course. Life on the hill was harder. But I miss the old way. We were all close. Everyone lived together. The doctor lived beside the herder and the farmer. Now we just pass sometimes."

Abu Hassan took us up the slope again, into old Jassan. The curved passages through the town are all too narrow for cars, so supplies are carried from door to door by donkey. I could hear children playing behind the earthen walls.

The tour followed the same route as the one I had been given in 2003 and Hassan repeated the same anecdotes. He showed us the house that was bombed during the war with Iran—rebuilt by a local Iraqi army commander with his own money. "Two women were killed," he said. I asked whether the soil was contaminated. "Only artillery and air bombs here. Not chemical attack. Soil is fine." He estimated that 80,000 palm trees were destroyed by the Iraqi army during the war. So far they have planted only a few re-placements.

Here in the center of the old village was the original meet-ing house, an empty room with quartered palm trunks as ceiling beams and woven reed mats to hold the clay roof. No one maintained it anymore, and a corner had opened as if hit by a bomb. Sunlight came in through the hole now, but it must have been completely dark when it was intact, everyone inside lit only by fire. It had fallen into use as a manger, the floor spongy with an uneven depth of sheep manure, a few handmade rugs sinking into the filth. An old man wandered up and spoke with reverence in the space, telling of when the British governor met with the village elders in the 1920s. "He had tea right here," he said. "This is a historical site, and the government should preserve it." They have asked, but no one cares. "Soon this will be gone," he said. "All the stories will have no home." It will just be an empty square on the hill, like the British cemetery in Kut.

The exterior wall around the settlement was giving way in places, revealing empty rooms and exposing the town's mysterious interior, so long concealed. "Every year there are more like this," Abu Hassan said. "If the roof is not maintained before the rains, in two years a house will fall." An elder added his suspicion: "This is part of a plan to thin the blood of the village. These loans are chains to the government. Always we lived without debt on the hill. Now we live in brick houses . . . but we don't own them. We leave the place of our fathers and accept a home that can be taken from us. What will our sons have? Not even memories." But he has moved off the hill, too. "We used to watch the sun set on the land. Now we watch the TV."

And then there I was again, in the middle of a sentence about the past, Major Busch drinking tea with the grandson of the man who drank tea here with the British governor in 1920—neither of us remembered as enemies, but neither of us remembered for anything more than having been here once. It could have been centuries ago, the old men telling brief stories of our brief presence. We'll all have to hope there were children in the room to hear them or we will finally, truly be gone.

We headed back down to the market. It was the feast of Ashura, and about 300 people had assembled for qimah, a dish made from ground lamb, chickpeas, tomato sauce, and spices, which was served from large aluminum pots. We spoke with Jabir Surman Daoud, who was captured on May 6, 1982, during the war with Iran, and released nine years later in a prisoner exchange. He said life as a captive was good. He had a job at the post office before the war, when Jassan was peaceful. When he returned, the area was crowded with the Iraqi military. He felt like he was returning home to a prison. He resented being away but didn't blame that on Iran. "We were forced to fight, like against America. We were not volunteers." I asked what he dreamed of when he was young. "Saddam could see our dreams, so we did not have any."

I spoke with Jaoudit Abdul Settar as he waited in line for food. Settar was two days into the six-day walk to Karbala from Kazania, his hometown. He had been a carpenter, but all furniture is imported now. "Kazania is also built on a hill. It's doing the same as Jassan: loans, new houses, everyone leaving the hill. Saddam destroyed our town once before because he accused us of helping Iranian troops. Now we are destroying it."

As we left, Khalil said, "Jassan is a dead town. Tourists bypass and they have no real product except some farming." It was a cold assessment of a place that appeared to be well managed and progressing in a country that was largely broken. But he wasn't wrong.

After three days in Jassan, we drove to the town of Badra, the last Iraqi settlement before the Iranian border. The old section of the village was leveled during the war with Iran and is nothing but low earthen ruins now, a worn maze where rooms had been. Saddam had built some new concrete apartments and government offices there, but, like Jassan, brick houses are rising on the outskirts, making the pre-invasion buildings look dilapidated by comparison. We visited the border with the city manager, Jafar Abdul Jabar Muhammed, who had salt-and-pepper stubble and wore a tidy checked blazer. Like so many government managers, he was gracious with his time and guarded in his answers, but as we traveled with him he began to open up. "Our problem is water," he said. "There is drought, and our farms take from the Badra River." We crossed a bridge over the wide, dry bed. The river flows from Iran, but the Iranians built a dam and cut it off, he said. "I can't imagine my childhood without the river. I tell kids the stories, but they see only stones." The area had been known for its date palms, but we drove past dead orchards, hundreds of tall, bare trunks standing beside living groves that had been kept irrigated. It takes about eight years for a palm to begin producing date crops. It takes one bad year for it to die. It was not only the water, though. Some families have moved away for work in the cities, neglecting their plots of palms. "Before America came, everyone stayed."

On the approach to the border checkpoint, we saw several lifeless miles of empty cargo trucks either returning to Iran or waiting to load Iranian exports. There were no trucks of Iraqi products. We also saw parking lots full of buses for Iranian passengers traveling to Karbala. The government in Kut has allocated billions of dinar to build a welcome center here to encourage more tourism from Iran. Nearby is the new Badra Oil Field, which is being drilled by the Russian energy company Gazprom Neft. It is a joint venture with oil companies from South Korea, Malaysia, and Turkey. The well is now producing 15,000 barrels a day. Half of the jobs are contracted to be local, which Jabar Muhammed believes will solve all of Badra's unemployment problems. There were no American oil companies here, and he said Americans didn't even bother to bid on the project. I was the first one he'd seen in six years. The border follows a rise in the land, and, like most boundaries that aren't defined by a shore, it is an arbitrary division of uninhabited space. In 2003 we were told to keep our distance because the placement of the line was still contested, our maps only an estimation. Now it seemed like the end of nothing and the beginning of nothing else, Wasit Province a territory with customs stations on both sides, one for Iran and one for the other fragments of the former Iraqi state.

("They're trying to change the maps," a merchant in Kut's souk told me. "They are always moving the borders here, since Nebuchadnezzar. All these dead empires from outside. Why here? They're drawing lines in water.")

Now the borders we watched so carefully, a vigilance we inherited from Saddam Hussein himself, have almost dissolved. Sunni militants have captured Iraqi cities and declared the territory part of their caliphate. The government in Baghdad has called out for American military aid while cursing us, and we have begun bombing campaigns again. Two battalions of Iranian troops, known to have been employed in attacks on U.S. forces during the occupation, have been welcomed into Iraq.

On the route back to Kut we passed the site of the mass grave I saw in 2003. The dead were revolutionaries America had encouraged to rise against Saddam during our first invasion of Iraq. Our withdrawal had left the rebellion unsupported, its members identified and executed. After our invasion, families came to take the bodies for proper burial. They dug the bones and lifted them out of the pit; the arms were still bound with wire and the skulls still blindfolded with strips of cloth. For 12 years they had been in the soil here, unmarked, and now their empty graves were filling in like the trenches along the border.

My tactical maps were all lost when I went home. All I have left is an evasion chart I never used. On it is a tiny square representing the former Iraqi army base where my unit had been stationed. Years ago, I stood in the courtyard of a military training school here as Iraqi maps from the war with Iran blew all around me. Nothing but pulverized bricks and a few concrete bunkers were left now. The bunker entrances still had graffiti from Saddam's army scratched into them along the stairs descending underground, the interior now used as a shelter for herds of sheep. It felt like an ancient tomb inside, the floor soft with dung and the dead carried off. In 2003 the footprints of Iraqi soldiers were still fresh in the dried mud.

Back in Kut we watched the news. Cloying coverage of Nelson Mandela's death, riots beginning to push over police barricades in Ukraine, fighting in Syria. Nothing yet about Iraq. As we waited for a cab to Baghdad, there was a brief notice that Peter O'Toole had died, Lawrence of Arabia dead again as the Middle East began to redraw his map. I finally told Khalil that I was Major Busch. "Holy shit!" he said, extending a hand to shake as if I had performed a magic trick. His face was lit up for the first time in our eight days together. "They didn't know you."

We spent our occupation complimenting Iraq on its sovereignty, its bravery, never believing it. What was most surprising, seeing our total disappearance, was that 1.5 million Americans served in Iraq. We were 5 percent of the country's population averaged over a decade; 4,486 of us died there; none of us are buried there.

I have now seen Jassan's old walls falling, its children eternally standing there only in my photographs. Jassan will continue to exist, its name still on maps exactly where it was, but it will not be the place the elders remember. It will not resemble their stories of it. I am already unrecognizable to the people there, part of Jassan's past life and not part of it at all. Why should I have expected us to be real to Iraq, to be lasting, when Iraq is starting over again every day without us?

We sought for years to define the Iraqi people, give their nation one cogent label that would allow us to administer a cure. But Iraq has every disease there is; its mind is deranged with too many voices, its organs corrupted, its limbs only long enough to tear at its own body. "It was religion that did this," one man I met shortly after I arrived told me. "It is religion fighting. Iraqis aren't themselves. They were an invention by the British. Me, I'm Sumerian." I asked how he knew. "I just do." When I asked whether he favored Iraq's division, he said, "No. That won't help. The three parts would be ruled by the outside countries, and they would fight." Several men I met said they were proud to be Shia, but they didn't think Iraq meant anything anymore. "It is just a place. Since Babylon it has just been a place."

The Iraq I knew already seems to be underground, the new situation piling up on top of it, the people lamenting its burial but unwilling to dig. The land around Kut is filled with the unmarked graves of foreigners, the removal of the tombstones in the official graveyard just the natural urge of the desert to be blank. The mass grave we exhumed near Badra is filling in, the loose bones and clothing moved and buried again out of order, mud villages slowly reduced to mounds, images of Saddam destroyed, museums looted and the Americans gone, all the footsteps from all the patrols rubbed off by the wind.

On the way back to Baghdad our cab went 100 miles per hour and smelled of gasoline. The windshield had a crack, and my view of everything was split by a bright line. Unlike the village, where the past was being abandoned, Baghdad looked like a place preserving the war, its wreckage kept on display. How many times has Baghdad fallen? This was the land believed to have been the location of Eden, Adam and Eve expelled for taking the advice of a snake.

The main route to the airport was closed to allow Shia pilgrims to walk without the threat of car bombs, so we had to take the long way around to the south and then head west. As we passed a sign that said RAMADI, FALLUJAH, AND ABU GHRAIB, I was reminded that I was crossing an invisible line between religious sects and into a part of Iraq where most stories about Americans are grim. On the long road to the terminal, a single word appeared in polished silver letters raised on a curve of concrete: GOODBYE. It was in English, without translation into any other language. No one else is bid farewell from Baghdad. We probably paid to have the sign installed, wishing ourselves away.

Back home in the quiet snow of Michigan, I saw a one-line report about an explosion in the Karada district and wrote to check on Khalil. A few days later he wrote back:

Dear Sir,
    Thank you for asking the explosion by booby-trapped car was near my apartment all the window glasses were flown up every were thanks god my both daughters were safe, my wife almost got killed by it, but she is safe.

                              Best regards,
                                  Khalil

Baghdad is preparing for another invasion. ISIL is executing young Shia men from the surrendered Iraqi army, their bodies displayed in bloody ditches, mothers and fathers looking for their children in the grainy videos being posted by terrorists. I imagine families peering into those glowing frames, trying to know for certain that their son is dead. My father used to study the news reports during my deployments, scanning the troops walking behind journalists for men who might be me. The nameless announcements of casualties became his child every day until he had proof that it wasn't. He was far from the war, but Iraq also seems a place far from itself now, its own ruins mostly distant, Iraqis in the east viewing Mosul and Ramadi as foreign places few have ever seen, the desert separating everything with sunlight. ISIL has gotten to within a few miles of the capital. They drive American military vehicles and they carry American weapons. Some now wear our uniforms. We have sent troops to guard our embassy and the Baghdad airport. The embassy is the last piece of ground we own, kept out of touch with Iraq in the International Zone, and the airport is the only way out. We are defending the silver sign that says goodbye.

MADELINE DREXLER

The Happiness Metric

FROM *Tricycle*

ON FRIDAY EVENINGS in Thimphu, the capital of Bhutan, men, women, and children throng the main street, flowing together in a slow dance. Swaggering teenage boys, arms slung over each other's shoulders, speak in surprisingly gentle voices. Stray dogs assertively cohabit the city. One often hears singing—on sidewalks, pouring out of windows, on construction sites. The melodies persist in the undulating countryside, where men engaged in matches of archery or darts break into congratulatory chants when the other side scores.

Article 9 of the Constitution of the Kingdom of Bhutan says, "The State shall strive to promote those circumstances that will enable the successful pursuit of Gross National Happiness." In the fall of 2012, I traveled to this simple, complicated, lavishly lovely place to find out how GNH, as the policy is known, plays out in real life. My intention was to glean what makes for happiness in a fast-changing society where Buddhism is deeply rooted but where the temptations and collateral damage of affluence are rising. Bhutanese have practiced happiness, reflected upon it, debated it, dissected it, and legislated it—and they seemed to me, on the whole, happier than Americans. But if for no other reason than the nature of impermanence, that may soon change.

Sandwiched between the world's two most populous countries, India and China, Bhutan is half the size of Indiana, has a population of about 740,000, and has never been colonized. The land rises from 300 feet in the southern lowlands to more than 24,000 feet in the mountains—some sacred and unclimbed—bordering the Tibet Autonomous Region. Bhutan is the only country in the world where Vajrayana Buddhism—deity-dense, merit-based, karma-focused—is the official religion, the only country in the world where Dzongkha—the soft, sibilant tongue closely related to Tibetan—is the national language. The four most common household assets are a rice cooker, a curry cooker, a water boiler, and a religious altar.

Bhutan's constitution stipulates that 60 percent of the country must remain under forest cover forever; today, despite breakneck urbanization, that figure is 80 percent. The government bans plastic bags. Capital punishment was abolished in 2004. Bhutanese take off 16 public holidays and numerous local festival days. And the country is a global biodiversity hotspot.

Yet Bhutan is also rich in contradictions—paradoxes that undermine the promise of GNH. The country prohibits tobacco advertising, smoking in public places, and the sale or illegal possession of tobacco products, but there was a public outcry in 2011 when a 23-year-old monk received a 3-year jail sentence for smuggling in $2.50 worth of chewing tobacco. Leaders have vowed to grow 100 percent organic crops, but most agricultural products are imported from India. The government strives for economic development, but offers few incentives for small, self-owned businesses, which are culturally perceived as ungenerous toward the collective. Bhutan has strict seat belt and antilitter laws, but most citizens flout them. Homosexuality is illegal, but no one is arrested.

In Bhutan, every conversation about GNH became at some point definitional. Can a nation be happy if individuals are not? Can individuals be happy if others suffer? Will the country's traditional foundations of happiness erode, to be replaced by a surfeit of stuff?

In the capital, many told me, happiness is increasingly being defined as consumerism. "People in Thimphu are getting competitive. If he has a house, I want a house. If he has a car, I want a car," said a young Ministry of Health worker. "The ones who are making money think GNH is good. The ones who aren't think GNH is bad."

But in rural Bhutan, older villagers' definition of happiness is starkly different. On the way to Punakha Dzong, the resplendent seventeenth-century monastery/fortress, I spoke (through a translator) with 79-year-old Sangay Lham, a smiling, gray-haired woman dressed in a checkered *kira* and fine silver brooch, selling fruit by the side of the road. What, I asked, does GNH mean to her? "As long as we have fire when we need it, water when we need it, warm food on the table, tasty curry, what else do we need?" she said. "Happiness is to be good at heart."

"We talk about the economy, but the core Buddhist understanding of GNH, the reality of GNH here, is the realization of compassion," said Lama Ngodup Dorji, a man with a beatific face who is the seventeenth member of his family over 15 generations to head the Shingkhar Dechenling monastery. I met him in Thimphu at the offices of the affiliated Ati Foundation, which gives economic assistance to poor citizens and rural communities. The foundation is housed in a brand-new glass-clad building with polished marble floors and an Italian restaurant on the second floor. The weather had turned chilly, and Dorji was wearing a down vest over his red robes. Happiness, he said, warming his hands around a fresh cup of coffee, is a choice. "You have to brew it in yourself. Even from a lump of food, we choose each grain to suit our need. Likewise, in the philosophical manner, we choose to be who we are."

If the word *materialism* is earnestly bandied about here, much as it was in America during the counterculture half a century ago, it's largely because until quite recently Bhutan was a medieval society.

In 1960, virtually the entire nation was rural. Thimphu, a collection of peasant hamlets situated in a valley on the banks of the Wang Chu River, became the official capital only in 1961. Average life expectancy was 33 years. The gross national product per person was $51. (By contrast, that same year in the United States, a comparable measure—gross domestic product per capita—was $2,935.) There was no centralized government administration. Agriculture was subsistence—people bred animals and cultivated only as much from the land as they needed. There were no roads and no motor vehicles—mules, yaks, and horses were the principal modes of transport. There was no electricity, no telecommunications network, and no postal system. Foreign visitors were not permitted. Bhutan had only four hospitals and two qualified doctors.

Then everything started to change. The first paved road was completed in 1962. Schools and hospitals were built. Citizens gained free health care and free education. Internet and a national

TV station arrived in 1999. Today, life expectancy stands at 67.6 years. Eighty-six percent of people ages 15 to 24 are literate. Per capita income is just under $3,000. More than 100,000 tourists visited the country in 2012. Ninety-three percent of households own a cell phone. About a third of the population is urban, and the government predicts that figure could rise to 70 percent by 2020.

This rapid development has brought new problems and exacerbated old ones. In Thimphu, there are 700 bars and one public library. The long-hidden issue of domestic violence has exploded in public discourse. Urbanization has put a strain on housing and sanitation. The economy is stagnant, the private sector is on the verge of collapse, and inflation is soaring. Youth unemployment is up, and along with it formerly rare violations such as drug abuse and vandalism. The country struggles with a dire shortage of doctors and nurses. When a recent government survey asked respondents how their welfare could be most improved, their top answers registered the stubborn needs of a developing nation, GNH or not: roads, water, commerce, transportation, and communications.

In Bhutan, which is ranked 140 of 186 countries in the 2012 UN Human Development Index, the question is how the nation can become modern without losing its soul.

When first conceived, Gross National Happiness was the enlightened guiding principle of development at a time when Bhutan was starting to emerge from cultural isolation and material deprivation. Since 1907, Bhutan had been ruled by a lineage of progressive monarchs. The most visionary of these was the Fourth Dragon King, a somber-looking man named Jigme Singye Wangchuck, who took the throne at 16 after his father's death in 1972. Two years later, shortly after his coronation, the teenager coined the witty phrase Gross National Happiness. In 2006, as a logical extension of the policy, Wangchuck announced that he was voluntarily giving up the throne to make way for a parliamentary democracy in the form of a constitutional monarchy.

The Fourth King's conception of Gross National Happiness rested on four "pillars": good governance, sustainable socioeconomic development, cultural preservation, and environmental conservation. The humanity of GNH is seen in the roomy definitions of what are known as the policy's nine "domains": good governance; psychological well-being; balanced time use; community vitality; health; education; culture; living standards; and ecological diversity and resilience. "Living standards" refers not merely to per capita income but also to meaningful work. "Environment" includes not only the measured quality of water, air, and soil but also how people perceive the quality of their natural surroundings. "Community vitality" reflects not only crime but also volunteerism.

To learn how these ideas play out in policy, I visited Karma Tshiteem, who at the time was secretary of Bhutan's Gross National Happiness Commission. I had first met Tshiteem at an April 2012 United Nations conference on GNH. He sat at my lunch table and impressed me as a jokester and a sharp observer—the class cutup who was also the smartest student. Now, as we sat over tea in a modestly furnished anteroom to his office, he wore on his right hip an incongruous ceremonial sword, a reminder of his responsibility to the people.

I asked Tshiteem if a GNH society was really possible, and mentioned that though smoking is illegal in Bhutan's public places, I had seen kids lighting up. "That's OK," he said. "There is no one ideal GNH human being. And we are not trying to define a GNH person. We posit GNH, but it doesn't mean we won't have these outliers and we will not have a problem with youth, because youth is a time of exploration and rebellion. GNH doesn't mean that everything has to be picture-perfect all the time."

In Bhutan, major policy proposals go through a GNH screening tool that has real teeth. In 2008, for example, GNH Commission officials were enthusiastic about joining the World Trade Organization. A preliminary vote showed 19–5 in favor of joining, based solely on economic criteria. But when the proposal was fed through the GNH policy-screening tool, which assesses draft policies based on their impact on GNH's nine domains, the downsides far outweighed the benefits. Among other things, WTO membership would have compelled the green-centric and health-conscious country to open its economy to a phalanx of junk food franchises such as McDonald's and Domino's Pizza. A second vote was taken, and the proposal lost 19–5. Bhutan did not join the WTO.

"What this tells us is that the decisions we make are very much influenced by the frameworks we use," said Tshiteem. "When you use the same framework that every other government uses, even Bhutanese arrive at the same conclusions. But when we brought in the GNH framework, which made them think deeply about all the other aspects that are important, suddenly they did not see this as such a great idea. One of the results from the screening tool was that WTO membership would raise the level of stress. That's something that would never be measured in the United States in anything having to do with economics."

Every two years, Bhutan conducts a fine-grained survey that captures the texture of citizens' lives and their sense of rootedness in the traditional culture. Among the questions: Do you consider karma in the course of your daily life? Is lying justifiable? Do you feel like a stranger in your family? How much do you trust your neighbor? The survey asks respondents if they know the names of their great-grandparents; if men make better leaders than women (gender equality is preached but not achieved); if they planted trees in the past year; how they rate their total household income (in 2010, 71 percent said "just enough" and 20.3 percent said "more than enough"); if they think Bhutanese have become more concerned about material wealth (87.8 percent said yes); if they feel safe from ghosts ("rarely," 20 percent said).

Respondents are considered "happy" if they achieve "sufficiency" in at least six of the nine domains, not outsized achievement in one domain at the expense of another. As Tshiteem reminded me, in Buddhism happiness is balance. "You can't make up for lack of personal time with community vitality—you cannot. Because each domain, in itself, is a necessary condition," he explained.

In the 2010 survey, 40.8 percent of survey respondents in the land of Gross National Happiness tested happy.

The Centre for Bhutan Studies has devised a formula that purports to boil down national happiness into a single number:

$$GNH = 1 - (H_n \times A_n)$$

where

H_n = percent of not-yet-happy people

= $1 - H_h$ or (100 – percent of happy people)

and

A_n = percentage of domains in which not-yet-happy people lack sufficiency

In 2010, the most recent survey, that calculation turned out to be 0.743—which means . . . well, I don't know. It did seem to contravene what one Bhutanese friend remarked: "Isn't it the simplest thing that makes you happy? Isn't it the most complex thing that doesn't make you happy?"

Around the world, happiness indexes are proliferating, but in Bhutan, the question of measuring happiness is divisive. Even the GNH Commission's Karma Tshiteem disagreed with the idea of boiling down population-wide happiness into a number. "There is this misconception that, with our clever index and indicators, we are trying to measure happiness." Rather, he said, Bhutan's GNH parameters should be used like the gauges on a car's dashboard, alerting leaders to problems. Others say that Bhutan wasn't interested in measurement until the UN and World Bank caught wind of the idea, and the country faced international pressure to come up with hard numbers.

Former prime minister Jigme Y. Thinley conceded that Bhutan's hand was initially forced by outsiders. In an election upset in 2013, he and his ruling Peace and Prosperity Party were voted out, in part because of the country's decline in that second *P.* "What the modern world wanted was a system of measures, indicators quantifying everything," he told me. "At first, yes, I was not very happy with this, because the pressure was on Bhutan to adopt . . . the attitude of the material world: anything that is good must be measurable. And what is measurable and quantifiable has a price to it.

"I thought it was demeaning the sublime value that human society should be pursuing. And I also worried that developing metrics could lead to pursuing what is measurable and what is quantifiable, thereby risking the possibility of leaving out what is not quantifiable—but may be far more meaningful and far more important to creating the conditions for happiness."

Thinley changed his mind and acceded to the data-driven West, partly because he felt Bhutan's evolving instruments to assess well-being did, in fact, extract the essence of GNH. But, he added, "Bhutan has achieved what it has, not because we had the facility of metrics. We simply believed in the idea of happiness being the meaning and purpose of life."

*

Tshering Tobgay was Bhutan's opposition leader in parliament when I visited him. Today he is prime minister. A tall, strapping man with a shaved head, his physical energy is barely contained. Soft-spoken, Harvard-educated, Tobgay at times answered each of my queries with a broader question. At other times, he was bracingly candid.

In American politics, Tobgay would probably be slotted as a libertarian brain with a communitarian heart. He heads the People's Democratic Party, which believes in smaller government, decentralized power, and a strong business sector—another seeming contradiction in the land of Gross National Happiness, where the governing policy stresses nonmaterial values.

Outside Bhutan, GNH enjoys great cachet in liberal circles, as dozens of cities and countries dip their toes in the philosophy. Bhutan's tourist logo,"Happiness Is a Place," makes it a prized destination for spiritual-minded vacationers. But Tobgay is skeptical about the Western left's glorification of Bhutan—"the people who tout and market Bhutan as a living Shangri-la."

As he put it, "Bhutan is small, nonthreatening. This can be very cute. And people who are frustrated are desperately looking for alternate paradigms . . . I want to tell them: Don't misuse our philosophy for your own political agenda." To illustrate, he mentioned an American working for a corporation in Bhutan who writes a blog about the country. "He recently took a picture of the only baggage carousel in the airport—and he is shocked. He is mortified to find that it's packed with flat-screen LCD television sets. About three years ago, a whole team from Brazil—Brazil is very enamored of GNH—came here. They called me for an interview. And the anchor immediately pounced on me. She said, 'We were disappointed. The airport was packed with television sets.' My answer to that lady, my answer to the American, and my answer to you is, Who on earth said Bhutan is a monastery?"

Each of Buddhism's Four Immeasurables—loving-kindness, compassion, sympathetic joy, and equanimity—has a "far enemy" and a "near enemy." The far enemy is the virtuous mind's polar opposite—cruelty is the far enemy of compassion, for example. But the near enemy is trickier to root out, because while it seems wholesome, it is tinged with "mental poisons," or destructive emotions. The near enemy of compassion, for instance, is pity.

Traveling through Bhutan, I kept thinking that the near enemy of the country's generosity and pride and abundant sense of time is complacency. Many of my contacts there also seemed disquieted by this shadow side of their benign culture. As a reader observed in *The Bhutanese,* "The truth is that GNH or no GNH we still struggle with our daily problems of corruption, indifference, and our general tendency to slack away at everything we do and give it the name of GNH."

Until recently, the Royal Civil Service was the largest employer of the educated, and these undemanding office jobs were coveted. Despite a religion steeped in the idea of impermanence, citified Bhutanese had come to rely on permanent government employment and benefits. Now, however, government payrolls can no longer accommodate new college graduates. "We have been spoiled," one official told me. Or as a long-term expatriate here explained, "The people have been infantilized. There is a sense of entitlement that is a time bomb for society."

Bhutanese proudly abjure blue-collar work. In the construction sites that dominate the urban landscape, it is almost entirely Indians who hammer and saw, pour cement and lug rebar. And it is mostly Indians and Nepalese who make up the road crews that labor in broiling sun and biting cold with crude hand tools, repairing the damage from landslides. (The Bhutanese Citizenship Act of 1985—which raised the threshold for citizenship and erected bureaucratic hurdles for naturalization—hurt the Nepali-speaking residents of southern Bhutan, tens of thousands of whom were forced to move to refugee camps in Nepal. Oddly, the controversy is more conversationally alive in the West than in Bhutan itself, where people have been kept in the dark about the painful events of that time.)

"There are plenty of jobs, but the graduates don't want to take them because they think the job is low for them," a teenage boy told me. "They want to achieve greatness at a single step. They want to go to office carrying briefcases and laptops. They see people carrying iPhones and they want to carry them, too."

In 2000 there was one newspaper in Bhutan—the government-run *Kuensel.* Today there are 11, though nearly all are struggling to survive on low ad revenue. More than 84,000 Bhutanese are on Facebook and 5,000 on Twitter. Lively blogs command thousands of followers. And GNH is jokingly said to stand for Gross National Haranguing or Gross National Harassment.

Democracy has helped the Bhutanese find their voices. As a result, some have conceived an admiration—perhaps reverse idealism—for the United States, which they perceive as culturally more upfront and politically more transparent. This is especially true of those who have lived in the States. "What I liked about people there is they don't have a double standard," said Chimi Wangmo, the feminist who directs the anti–domestic violence group RE-NEW, which stands for Respect, Educate, Nurture, and Empower Women.

As Wangmo knows well, domestic violence has been shrouded in silence. Bhutan's 2010 Multiple Indicator Survey found that 68.4 percent of women ages 15 to 49 "believed that a man was justified in hitting or beating his wife if the woman was not respecting the 'family norms' such as going out without telling a husband, neglecting a child, burning the food or refusing to have sex with him." When she began lobbying lawmakers for a bill banning domestic violence, Wangmo was met with incredulity. Opponents insisted that there couldn't be domestic violence in Bhutan, because "Bhutan is a GNH nation." She countered their tautologies with facts, inviting legislators to RENEW's headquarters to view photographs and videos of battered women. (In February 2013, the National Council passed the Domestic Violence Prevention Bill.)

"Bhutan must come out of self-denial: It is not a Shangri-la," said Wangmo. "No matter how much we flaunt GNH, no matter how much we picture ourselves as a happiness country, the hard reality remains that we are among the most backward, poorest countries in the world. GNH is a beautiful concept. But we could do better than this—not just talking about GNH, but living it. It's basically fundamental human rights, which the Western countries have done much, much better than us."

With Gross National Happiness, Bhutan has turned the metrics of the material into the metrics of the spirit. At the moment, however, the country is poised between centuries-long traditions and an understandable rush toward the security and comforts that the affluent West takes for granted. Will these ambitions subvert the poetic possibilities of GNH?

While preparing for my trip, I had read a number of blogs from

Bhutan. One in particular struck me as smart and eloquent, authored by someone who deeply understood this cultural turning point. *Land of the Thunder Dragon* is written by Yeshey Dorji, a government bureaucrat turned entrepreneur turned nature photographer.

I met Dorji on the street in front of my hotel in Thimphu. Tall and bespectacled, dressed in jeans and a black quilted Patagonia jacket, he was gracious, impatient, cantankerous, and funny as hell. Everyone seemed to know and respect him. Wherever we went in Thimphu, people greeted him with a smile or came up to talk politics or gossip, and I thought of him as the unofficial mayor.

Dorji is highly attuned to the poignancy of impending loss. "We have jumped from one very strange period to another very strange period," he explained. "Today, people have all the time in the world to talk to you. It's not productive, but it's the human side of life. Soon, development will change all that. Bhutanese people will be abrupt, fast-moving. They will no longer be Bhutanese."

Yet he also believes that Bhutan could learn from the American example. "Times have changed. We have to change ourselves. But we aren't willing to do that. I am convinced the Bhutanese mentality needs a makeover—total. We keep complaining about how fast your life is in New York. But without the development of that culture, you wouldn't be where you are." What he admires about American culture is its energy, innovation, drive, curiosity, cosmopolitanism, ambition—qualities, in fact, that are conspicuous in Dorji himself and have enabled him to be a shrewd observer/participant in his homeland.

Like many people I met here, Dorji feels caught between two ideals: the past perfect and the future perfect—that is, the Bhutan that was serenely remote and the Bhutan that somehow will negotiate modernity. "Development changes the way people move, talk, think, the way they look at value. If you keep the same old habits, then you can't change the Bhutanese," he said. "But the moment you change the Bhutanese, you've probably lost GNH."

DAVID FARLEY

Ashes to Ashes

FROM *AFAR*

"YOU PEOPLE COME to Varanasi from the West because you're so unprepared for death," said the 85-year-old who opened the door. His voice was bullish and loud. "But what you're all missing is this: You need to be a *see*-er." Now he was screaming. "A *see*-er! You understand me?"

I wasn't sure I did. I had come to Varanasi, a city of some 1.5 million people in northeastern India, on a mission: to engage with death (a strange quest I'll explain shortly). So there I was at a place called Moksha Bhavan, a gated housing compound about a 10-minute auto-rickshaw ride from the Ganges River that could best be compared to a convalescent hospital. Except no one there was necessarily sick or needing care. The place was more like a waiting room for death, for the people who come to Varanasi to die. According to Hindu belief, succumbing in this holy city gives people more good karma to achieve *moksha*, or liberation.

Seatia Nararyna, as the man who screamed at me was called, had been there for 22 years. "Your eyes are covered, and the only way to uncover them is to really know yourself. Meditate. Think about yourself. And do this until you find *ananda*," he said. When I asked what *ananda* was, he leaned forward and looked deep into my eyes. I felt myself starting to shake.

"Bliss!" he screamed. "You need to do this until you have found bliss! Now go back to the ghats, think about yourself and death, and dedicate your life to *ananda*." With that, he slammed the door in my face. So I went back to the ghats, the multipurpose stone riverbank steps that give access to the Ganges at various points.

Varanasi, it turns out, is a great place to die. People—alive and dead—have been gravitating to the city for millennia. The living come as pilgrims and tourists, visiting the plethora of temples that hug the riverbank; the dead arrive to have their bodies burned to ashes on a pile of banyan or sandalwood at one of two cremation grounds—Manikarnika ghat and Harishchandra ghat—and then scattered in the Ganges. To be cremated in Varanasi is to achieve *moksha*—a reprieve from the cycle of life and death: You don't have to endure rebirth in the world, you don't collect 200 rupees, you go directly to nirvana.

Which, given that I'm still alive, wasn't *exactly* why I was there.

When a good friend was killed in a car accident in high school, I felt profoundly unprepared. For the first time in my life, I found myself asking why such things happen. I didn't have any answers. What really disturbed me was the way many friends of the family reacted—by quickly and quietly drifting away. I decided that no matter how difficult it might be, I wouldn't turn away from the face of grief and death.

A few years later, I volunteered at a hospice in Los Angeles. As a "friendly visitor," I'd turn up at the homes of the dying and chat about whatever they wanted to discuss. Often they would tell me how much they appreciated my presence, and that many of their friends, out of discomfort with pain and death, had already disappeared from their lives. Making these visits for about six months was a deep plunge into the way Western culture deals—or doesn't deal—with death.

The first person I visited after going through the three-week training program, a 67-year-old accountant, took his last breath as I sat beside him holding his hand. Being around the dying, and talking to them, helped demystify death for me. At least enough so that the questions of existence and mortality didn't haunt me as they had before.

That is, until about a couple years ago. I was going through the toughest time of my life. The end of a marriage, an unexpected rift with my parents, and the loss of a few friendships left me feeling like I was stuck in a deep pit, one that I could not, for the life of me, claw my way out of. At one particularly low point, during the holidays (isn't it always during the holidays?), I felt defeated. I was ready to give up.

To paraphrase a passage from David Foster Wallace's *Infinite Jest,* I was standing on the ledge of a burning building, and jumping seemed a lot more attractive than facing the fire. Fortunately, at the last moment, and for reasons I'm still not sure of, I stepped away from that metaphorical ledge. In the days that followed, Varanasi kept popping up: there it was in a magazine; there it was on TV; there it was on someone's Facebook profile. The city, I realized, was a place defined by life and death, where loss is viewed in a completely different way. If I was going to walk through the fire, I needed to go to Varanasi, where darkness is nothing to fear. And I'd be showing up with a lot of darkness.

"Welcome to the center of the universe, my friend. You're standing at the beginning and end of all life, the epicenter of creation, the spot of ultimate transformation, the passageway through which souls achieve *moksha.*" The man delivering this spiel, his face barely peeking out of a brown scarf that was wrapped over his head, had accosted me the second my foot landed on this supposedly most holy ground, Manikarnika ghat. And he wasn't just making this up as he went along. On my flight from New York, as I was reading a scholarly book on Varanasi, one line particularly struck me: "Just as India is the navel of the world, and Varanasi is the navel of India, so Manikarnika ghat is the navel of Varanasi." I was standing in what was, for the 1 billion Hindus on the planet, the core of all creation.

The guy who had become my impromptu tour guide was one of the *doms,* the people who work at the cremation grounds. They're among the untouchable caste, the lowest of the low, and are more or less condemned, as were their ancestors, to exercise this profession all their lives.

"Look around," he added, fanning his arm at what could have been a postapocalyptic landscape, a panorama dotted with bonfires, stacks of wood the size of a small house, the odd leaning temple spire in the distance, and a riverside sprinkled with bathers ritually immersing themselves in polluted Ganges River water. Impossible to ignore were the groups of a half-dozen men jogging lightly and carrying shroud-wrapped dead bodies on bamboo litters above their heads. They chanted, *"Rama nama satya hai!"* (Only the name of God is truth) and were headed right toward where we were standing, the main cremation ground in Varanasi.

"This spot, this ghat," said the *dom*, "was not made by human hands. It was made by Lord Shiva 3,500 years ago."

I followed him as he scurried up the ghat's muddy, irregular steps, past sleeping canines and garbage-grazing bovines that seemed unfazed by all the activity. Inside a portico overlooking the ghat, a flame, no bigger than what you'd see in an average fireplace, flickered. "This is the sacred fire," he said, adding that it has been burning constantly for 3,500 years and had been lit, naturally, by Lord Shiva. "This is the flame with which all bodies are ignited," he said. "This is the flame that sends people to *moksha*."

Traditionally, that flame is controlled by the Dom Raja, the lord of the dead. He rules over the *doms* and is one of the richest people in town (despite his low caste). If you want to use the flame to cremate a loved one, you have to negotiate with him. As with royalty, the position is hereditary. When the Dom Raja dies, his title is handed down to the eldest son. But when the Dom Raja Kailash Choudhary passed away in 1985, something interesting happened: there was a power struggle in the family, and eventually his five sons decided to split the Dom Raja duties.

There's more to Varanasi than just death. Though nothing as compelling. Also called Benares, Kashi, City of Light, and Forest of Bliss, this city on the Ganges is not, despite the implied tranquillity of some of its nicknames, a peaceful haven. It's a cacophony of auto-rickshaw horns and buzzing motorbikes, a maelstrom of swirls of dust and more dust. The smell of exhaust fumes, chai, and curry, plus the occasional waft of incense, intermingle to create the olfactory imprint of this ancient city, said to be one of the oldest continually inhabited spots on the planet. Just up from the riverbank is a warren of narrow, twisting, dank, excrement-dolloped lanes where every second storefront seems to be a yoga or meditation school. To the first-time visitor, the walkways go on forever.

This is not the India of techie call-center employees and upwardly mobile professionals. Varanasi exists far removed from that India. One finds few trappings of globalization and almost no cosmopolitan culture here. There are no kitschy souvenir shops in Varanasi. No racks of postcards. No stands selling *My Uncle Went to Varanasi for Enlightenment and All I Got Was This Lousy Good Karma*

T-Shirt T-shirts. Mumbai might have its Bollywood stars and Delhi its politicians, but Varanasi has its crumbling riverside palaces and temples, the dead, and the Dom Raja.

Still, besides gawking at the cremation grounds, one of the main things visitors to Varanasi do is stroll the 3-mile waterfront, which is lined with 84 ghats. Here, between the river and the mishmash of dilapidated palaces, one will be accosted every seven seconds by teenagers selling hash or wanting to take you out in a rowboat —"Boat? Boat, sir?"—and men befriending you so you'll pay a visit to their silk shops. Near the river, holy men meditate and children play cricket with tattered, taped-up balls. In the river, locals bathe and women wash bedsheets.

Each ghat has its own distinct personality and function. Gaya ghat, for example, near the northern end, is a place where pilgrims board boats to sail down the river, making stops at ghats that contain important temples. Dashashvamedha ghat, the "main ghat," is the busiest, with holy men, or sadhus, planted under mushroomlike wooden umbrellas, some beckoning tourists over to receive a bit of wisdom, maybe in exchange for a few rupees. At the opposite end from Gaya ghat is Assi ghat, which has become a backpackers' ghetto, chock-a-block with Western-friendly vegetarian restaurants and cheap hotels. In stark contrast, the other side of the wide river is a gloomy nothingness of brown dirt and haze.

Around the cremation ghats, Manikarnika and Harishchandra, the activity is relentless. For the denizens of Varanasi, it's all very commonplace. But as a newcomer I was paralyzed with morbid curiosity, my attention inexorably drawn to the transformation of bodies from flesh to ash in a theater of death played out 24/7 for all to watch. More than 30,000 bodies are burned annually here. Harishchandra ghat even has an audience platform, allowing onlookers, along with family members, to get a better view of the flaming spectacle. It may seem like a serious taboo for Westerners with eyes blanketed from death, but this sort of experience is exactly why we travel—to witness the "unreal," to take in the extraordinary ordinariness of a way of life we could never have imagined.

The day after my haphazard introduction to Manikarnika ghat, I returned for a deeper exposure to its rituals and protocols. Flames from the pyres punctuated the smoky landscape. The *doms* quietly went about their business, poking at the fires with bamboo sticks.

Human ashes rained down on my head and shoulders as I watched a body being laid upon a stack of wood. The corpse was wrapped in a gold shroud, which I was later told indicated that the deceased was an elderly man who had died a good death. Red flecked with yellow is for high-caste women who die before their husbands, and white is for most men. Five men from the deceased's family stood around the pyre. (Women aren't typically allowed here, for fear widows will throw themselves on the blaze.) One man, the chief mourner (according to tradition, the dead man's eldest son), held a thick sheaf of straw on which he balanced an ember from the sacred fire. The men circled the pyre five times, one circumnaviga-tion for each element: fire, water, earth, air, and ether. They walked counterclockwise, because, as one *dom* said, "in death everything is reversed." The chief mourner placed the hay and the smoldering ember upon shavings of sandalwood that had been sprinkled atop the body. Thus ignited, the body began to burn. The rituals, while no doubt profoundly spiritual, were performed in such a routine manner that it put me at ease.

Around the cremation grounds, I talked to several *doms* about their jobs. They seemed largely unaffected by living and working in the constant presence of death. "It's just a job," said Gautam Choudhary, 22, when I asked about his work. Loulou Choudhary (all *doms* share the same last name, even if they're not related), 31, who has been doing the job since he was 16, wandered over a few minutes later and echoed Gautam's sentiments. "It's not a matter of like or dislike," he said of his job. "This is what I do. This is what my ancestors have done"—he's a seventh-generation *dom*—"and it's what my children will do. After all," he added, "we're untouch-ables."

A body can take anywhere from 2 to 12 hours to burn. "It de-pends on one's karma," another *dom* told me. "The better the karma earned in life, the faster you burn." He then told me about the five types of people who can't be cremated: pregnant women, children, sadhus, lepers, and people who died from a cobra bite. These people get a rock tied to their bodies and are dropped into the Ganges.

About an hour after the elderly man's corpse had been lit, the chief mourner approached the pyre, carrying a bamboo pole. He raised the 4-foot stick over his head and then thwacked the corpse's skull. It split open. This, Loulou Choudhary told me, is the moment when the soul is officially freed from the body and travels to the afterlife. Calmly, the mourner walked away. He showed little emotion.

I showed plenty. The enormous difference between the American and Indian outlooks on death hit me like a lead pipe, or a bamboo stick. The idea of having to split open your father's and mother's skulls so that they can successfully achieve heavenly liberation was something that I had a hard time wrapping my own head around. I had to remind myself why I was here—to better understand some of the unfortunate choices I'd made (or almost made). But I was still having a hard time making sense of what was taking place in front of me. I didn't yet fully grasp the power of Varanasi, how the people here could be so accepting of death.

Then I met S. B. Patel. A 25-year-old college student in a nearby town, S.B. happened to sit next to me on the viewing platform at Harishchandra ghat the next day. We began chatting while an older man and a middle-aged woman were being cremated in separate pyres. The man's head was burned to a blackened crisp. The woman was almost all ashes. A man who had been swimming in the Ganges walked over to one of the pyres and held up his wet towel to dry a bit in the heat. A dog was sniffing around the other pyre.

"So what are you doing here?" I asked.

"You see that woman burning over there," S.B. said. I looked over and nodded. "That's my sister."

"Are you sad?" I asked, realizing this was about the dumbest question of all time.

"Yes," he said. "But I can't show it. It's bad karma for the soul of the dead if mourners show grief during the cremation." Forty-four years old and married, his sister had died of a heart attack. This was her funeral. I asked if it was strange that I and other people who didn't know his sister were watching this.

"No," he said, shaking his head from side to side. "In Hinduism we try to let go of our ego. I'm appreciative that you're taking an interest. My sister would have liked it."

Just then, someone crashed our death party. He was introduced to me as Nehna. He was one of the five Dom Raja brothers.

This Dom Raja of Varanasi was wearing gold chains and a tank top. His beach ball–sized belly protruded from under his shirt.

Nehna Choudhary, 32 years old, said he worked at Harishchan-dra ghat. (His brothers controlled Manikarnika.) He couldn't stay to talk; he had business to do, but he asked me to meet him here tomorrow.

The following day I met Dom Raja Nehna along the river at Harishchandra ghat. "We take a boat," he said. Minutes later we were in the middle of the Ganges River. Smoke from three differ-ent cremations wafted toward the sky. Nehna explained the intri-cacies of splitting what had been one job several ways. He works about 105 days a year, he told me, as he rowed the boat toward the other side of the river. "I'm no longer fazed by what I see," he said.

When Nehna spoke, he did so through his lower teeth, because he always had a chunk of betel nut stuffed in his lower lip. It made him sound like a subcontinental version of Marlon Brando's *Godfa-ther* character. Which was fitting, since Nehna was pretty much an analogous godfather to the dead and their mourners.

"My idea of life and death hasn't changed," Nehna said, inter-rupting my thoughts. "But I do get a sense of happiness when I'm on the cremation grounds."

My ears pricked up when he said this. What would I learn from the Dom Raja, who has been around death all his life, where the acceptance of mortality is probably deep in his genes? "Because of *moksha*?" I asked. "Because it has made you see the important things in life, or it makes you feel redeemed about life on a daily basis? Because it reminds you of the impermanence of all things and that you have to live in the moment?"

In my excitement I was speaking too quickly for Nehna, who I suspected wasn't even listening to me anyway.

"I feel happiness when I'm there," he said, "because I can see all the money I'm making."

I sighed and focused on a nearby pilgrim who was leaning down from his boat, throwing water over his head and repeating, "Shiva, Mother Ganges."

We bumped up to the riverbank, and Nehna pulled in the oars. I'd been looking across to this side of the Ganges, and its empti-ness, ever since I arrived. This side of the river is completely un-inhabited, with absolutely no signs of human handiwork—Vara-nasi's antipode, a barren yin landscape to Varanasi's baroque yang. It makes the habitable side of the river, the one crammed with crumbling palaces and crawling with living beings, feel like the beginning of the world, the place where civilization starts, the spot that, five days earlier, I was told is the epicenter of creation. Or, depending on how you look at it, the place where civilization ends, and thus begins all over again. Which was suddenly all starting to make sense, since a sadhu or a pilgrim or even an auto-rickshaw driver will remind you, as they did me, that in Varanasi there are no beginnings and endings, only passages and transformations.

Here I was, being rowed across the Ganges by the Dom Raja himself. It almost felt like I was physically making the postcremation journey to *moksha*. Perhaps I was nearing *ananda*, just as Seatia Nararyna, the 85-year-old man I met at Moksha Bhavan on my first day in town, had advised me: bliss through nothingness, the kind of state a Hindu (or a Buddhist) tries to attain during meditation. Symbolically, the far side of the Ganges is devoid of desire and ego and grasping, because, well, there's *really* nothing there.

I'm a long way from the bliss that Mr. Nararyna charged me to go and seek. But this I learned in Varanasi: I had walked through the fire during those unlit days a couple of years ago. I did it just after stepping away from that ledge. But it took coming here, talking to the *doms* and the mourners about death, feeling the vast blankness across the most holy river in Hinduism, to see that I only needed to let go, to realize that in nothingness is clarity and in clarity is peace. For nothingness isn't empty; it is the beginning of a hitherto unknown spirit we have the ability to tap into.

If we just choose to.

Once we rowed back to the habitable side of the river and got off the boat, the Dom Raja invited me over to his house for dinner that night. I said thank you, but no. I think, until my own time comes, I'm done with death for a while. I shook his hand and walked away, ready to make my exit, fully alive, from Varanasi.

LAUREN GROFF

Daughters of the Springs

FROM *Oxford American*

A FEW MILES southwest of Gainesville, the arching oaks of central Florida loosen into long fields full of beef steer. They tighten up again into the Goethe State Forest (pronounced, hereabouts, as *Go-thee*), and finally peter out into US 19, a soulless and endless miracle mile of corporate chains from Applebee's to Zaxby's, hitting nearly every letter in between. In the town of Homosassa, I saw a smiling gray manatee the size of a VW van on the side of the road, surrounded by a sea of yard-sign valentines that someone had left to fade in the March sun. Homosassa is famous for being one of the best places in Florida to view West Indian manatees, those gentle thousand-pound sea cows that are routinely torn up by Jet Skis and motorboats. Skeptics believe that sailors mistook sea mammals like manatees and dugongs for women, giving rise to the myth of the mermaid. After a few months at sea, one starts to see what one expects to see, and long ago, sirens were a matter of fact, not myth. Henry Hudson reported a sighting of a mermaid, and Christopher Columbus saw a manatee surfacing somewhere near the Dominican Republic on January 9, 1493, and noted in his diary that mermaids were not nearly as beautiful as they were painted. True. Manatees are pewter-colored and have faintly hound-doggish heads and platters for fins; they don't look much like Daryl Hannah. Still, the word *manatee* comes from the Taíno word for "breast," and a manatee on her back, with her forefins folded on her chest, can appear to have a goodly bosom. It's not hard to see how, after months of male company, the sight of one rising from the waves like a massive and fleshy woman could evoke intense erotic yearnings.

Mermaids—which I'm using here as shorthand for uncanny female water spirits—are common wherever human beings rub up against bodies of water. In Japan, there are *ningyo*, strange woman-faced semi-immortal fish figures; in ancient Syria, the goddess Derceto was described by Diodorus Siculus in his *Bibliotheca historica* as having a fish tail. There are *margyr* in Scandinavia and *sabawaelnu* in the Mi'kmaq culture of North America. There are Celtic *morgens*, aboriginal Australian *yawkyawks*, Russian *rusalki*. The Greeks had whole taxonomies of water spirits, from the Oceanids of the salt water and the Nereids of the Mediterranean to the Naiads, the spirits of fresh water. The most famous mermaids in myth—Odysseus's singing sirens, whom he resisted by stoppering his sailors' ears with wax and tying himself to the mast—were not mermaids at all but immortal bird-women, with wings, who once sang against the Muses in a competition (they lost and in punishment were plucked). That these creatures have slid from avian to piscine over the years speaks to the sexual appeal of mermaids. The sirens call men with their voices and bodies, water is voluptuous, and there's nothing sexy about a woman with a chicken's netherparts.

I think the widespread ubiquity of these dangerous, capricious female figures has less to do with lust and mistaken sea creatures than with a stunning human capacity for metaphor. Water is necessary, urgent, everywhere; it gives rise to life. It is also perilous, subject to its own laws, and contains dark and hidden depths. The makers of myths are the victors, the ones allowed the leisure and education to write (men, in other words, for most of human history). The myth of mermaids both explains and distances woman, that great and confounding mystery. And the appeal isn't just for men; girls are drawn to mermaids' wildness and beauty and power. After all, the sea creatures are the ones who get to decide if people who fall overboard will swim or sink.

I grew up as a very serious competitive swimmer on a boys' swim team and dreamed at night of being a mermaid, of flying in water and breathing as if it were air, and of luxuriating among the sea grasses and seeing the boats pass overhead like clouds over the sun. There was something about mermaids' ferocity, their danger, their uncompromising strangeness and power, that spoke to a truth deep in me. Every once in a while, even decades later, I still hear an echo of their song and feel compelled to listen.

During my drive to Weeki Wachee, I held the Starbucks siren hot in my hand. The coffee company's logo is a smirker. (I'll cop to my dislike.) She's bicaudal and holds her split tail beside her head with both fists in a frankly pornographic manner, teasing us with the answer to the age-old mystery of how all those seamen and fish-bottomed women were physiologically able to get it on.

No matter; I was on the hunt for far better mermaids, for high-grade Americana. Weeki Wachee is one of many natural springs that run through the state of Florida. They are its best-kept secret: people think of swampland when they think of Florida, or oranges or theme parks or skittery dance music in some Miami nightclub, not cold, clear rivers on which you can float for miles and never come across a single alligator. From underwater, Weeki Wachee appears to be a cragged mountainside, astonishingly steep. Once the site of Timucua, or aboriginal, burial grounds, it served as a swimming and laundry pool for locals in the 1930s and early 1940s as well as their trash heap.

Walton Hall Smith was a writer (coauthoring a book titled *Liquor, Servant of Man*) and founder of the Syfo beverage company, and he had long dreamed of developing Weeki Wachee into an underground theater. In June 1946, he paired up with Newt Perry, who was famous for wrestling alligators at Silver Springs, training Navy SEALs, and pioneering the underwater film industry in Florida; Grantland Rice called him "The Human Fish." With a group of investors, they purchased the site from the city of St. Petersburg and began constructing the theater sunk deep into the side of the springs.

The park was first opened to the public on October 12, 1947. The theater was a low building with twinned ramps that led underground, where a curved auditorium looked out into the springs from 16 feet below the surface, so that one could see much of the chasm and all attendant wildlife: turtles, ducks, alligators, and sometimes even a stray manatee. By the time of the opening, Perry had come up with the idea of bringing in young women in bathing suits to do an underwater ballet for the tourists. In the beginning, the Weeki Wachee mermaids were local teenagers, paid in hot dogs and hamburgers and bathing suits. There were so few cars on Route 19 that every time they heard one coming, the mermaids scampered to the side of the road to lure the drivers in for a show. How startling it must have been to be driving along the scrubby brown fields in the bright and sleepy sunlight, and then, out of nowhere, a line of young beauties in bathing suits. I wonder if anyone resisted them.

At last, Weeki Wachee hove up on the west side of the highway, a strange repository for such an ancient and resonant myth. Even at nine in the morning on a chilly March day, the parking lot was filled with cars and buses. The park itself was half hidden like an afterthought, low-set in the lot's northeast corner. The overall aesthetic was one of midcentury painted concrete, graced here and there with nippleless female busts. Before the entrance there's a huge fountain, and in the middle of the fountain there's an erect pillar topped by female swimmers engaged in a move I'd come to learn is called an adagio. Picture one swimmer vertical, fist extended, lifting another swimmer who is arched on her back toward the surface of the water. I was a little surprised by the statue's lack of tails. It turns out tails on the Weeki Wachee mermaids didn't appear until 1962: the earliest prototype was a very heavy rubber tail made for movie star Ann Blythe in the 1948 movie *Mr. Peabody and the Mermaid*. It wasn't practical: it cost $20,000 and was nearly impossible to squeeze into. These days, park employees or the mermaids themselves make the swimming tails out of stretchy fabric, with zippers on the side. There are also posing tails, with sequins and with zippers on the back, for verisimilitude, I suppose.

John Athanason, the park's genial, ruddy public relations manager, met me at the gate. John told me he'd been an employee at Weeki Wachee during its lowest moment, before it became a state park, when the private owners neglected the place to the point where there were serious safety issues, some involving fire exits and sewage. The mermaids had to launch a campaign, Save Our Tails, to keep the park from closing down. The small park is bare-bones, though there is evidence of recent sprucing: new plantings of sago palm and bougainvillea, new paint. We walked through a clump of high-schoolers to view the springs from above. Sapphire blue in places, the source is fairly small, the hole itself not especially impressive from our vantage and angle. It looked not unlike a pond, with a wee water park called Buccaneer Bay at its far end. John told me some fascinating information—Weeki Wachee was a first-magnitude spring directly fed from the Florida aquifer; divers know that it goes at least 413 feet deep; 117 million gallons pump out of it every day; the current in the water is 5 miles per hour, the temperature a constant 74.2 degrees—but I was also distracted by the teenage boy surreptitiously copping a feel of the tiny teenage girl on my other side. There was a man blowing leaves off the far bank. There were indolent fish.

John led me down a ramp and into the underwater theater, a large curved space with acoustic tiles and a cement floor. It was dark and empty and smelled a little of moldering eelgrass and feet. The audience sits on battered wooden benches. There is a curtain that automatically slides up to show the strange green subaqueous world where the mermaids perform, emerging from underneath shells that flip up on the large flat stage. The distant domed airlock on the far side of the chasm looks like a 1940s dream of the future. Over everything is a layer of green-brown lyngbya algae, even though, once upon a time, Weeki Wachee water was so clear people assumed a trick—that the mermaids were suspended on wires. This is Florida. People here gleefully cake their lawns and golf courses in nitrogen, then wax nostalgic for a time when the springs weren't clouded over.

In the dim blue theater with only fish and turtles sliding by, I heard the weariness in John's voice. Surely he has answered the same inane questions over and over for years, and it must be difficult to maintain a high-burn enthusiasm for a place that's equally worn down and kitschy. Still, he seemed to regard the park and the mermaids with avuncular pride. I asked if he'd ever considered inviting in a reality television show to bring some money to Weeki Wachee. He said he's had dozens of proposals, but reality television feeds on interpersonal drama, and the mermaids are employees of the State of Florida, which is not delighted about employees' interpersonal drama being sprayed about on national television. "And girls are . . . complicated," he said knowingly. I nodded and smiled, but because I'm complicated, I winced every time John called the performers *girls*. I'm a product of the politically correct '90s. When I was a belligerent 14-year-old *actual* girl, with a copy of *The Second Sex* in hand, I was taught to insist on being called a woman. Some of the mermaids may be very young, true, but many are in their twenties. Some are teachers, some are mothers; all are women. We were rousted from the theater by a white-blond woman in a tracksuit, whom I'd later discover is a mermaid, who came into the theater and lowered the curtains over the windows to the springs. It was almost time for the first show of the day: *Hans Christian Andersen's "The Little Mermaid."*

John led me into a small room so hot I nearly fell down. This was the tube room, named for the dark 64-foot underwater pipe that the mermaids have to swim through to make their way to and from the theater. The tube room has to be boiling hot because spending half an hour in 74-degree water can make one rapidly hypothermic. The mermaids came down the spiral staircase from their dressing rooms to finish their preparations for the show. The women wore cake makeup and bikini tops, tights and bloomers. They sat at the edge of a 14-foot well to put on water shoes and flippers and roll their tails on over it all, then zipped the tails up the side. Dry and off, the tails were a little dingy and looked like T-shirts; when they were on the tails looked pretty realistic, if I squinted. The mermaids chatted and answered my questions when I dared to say something, but after a while it was clear that they were being painfully polite so I let them be. Here is what I learned: Karri is a crabber on her off-days and has a one-year-old daughter. Stayce, who was playing the sea witch, is a bartender at Applebee's. Tara, who was managing the safety of the mermaids from the tube, is a chipper, very beautiful mother with the kind of wavy blond hair you think mermaids should have. One by one, they put on facemasks to see their way through the tube, which they'd take off before the performance. Then they fell into the water, took the last sip of air that wasn't going to come from a hose or airlock, did a little half flip with their tails, and disappeared into the tube. There are air hoses every few feet, but the mere thought of having to swim down an enclosed space with no scuba equipment gave me a case of the sympathetic horripilations.

Out in the theater, the audience had arrived, as if by magic. I don't know what I was expecting of a mermaid show on a cold weekday morning in March, but the place was packed with retirees in matching visors and tiny children in mermaid costumes. I suppose I'd been afraid of being the only person in the audience. I'd felt a preemptive fear for the future of this weird place; half an hour in the park, and I was already protective of it. The voiceover was careful to be sure we knew we were about to watch *Hans Christian Andersen's "The Little Mermaid,"* as that other theme park in Florida with claims to *The Little Mermaid* is notoriously litigious and superpowered and humorlessly grasping when it comes to copyright. There was a big blast of recorded music. The curtains went up. Tears stole into my eyes.

Because, god, the show was stunning. A huge curtain of air went up in front of the windows, like giant silver jellyfish bubbles. They cleared to show mermaid Sativa in full tail, reclining on a log, smiling and relaxed, her hand discreetly holding a pellet of bread so fish swarmed around her. The sun shot through the top of the water and set it all to shimmering with a blue and eerie light. In slow motion, other mermaids emerged, moving dreamily through the water, their hair licking in every direction. Women who are beautiful in ordinary ways become full-out gorgeous underwater. Flesh, particularly of the female sort, has an underlying lipid layer that buoys what might have sagged on land: breasts perk to hillocks, jowls lift, hair riffles and sways like its own living thing. The mermaids are impressively athletic. When they move underwater, they must take into consideration how much air they have in their lungs: too much and they float too high, too little and they sink. They have to time their breaths in and out to the music, dropping and picking up their air hoses in accordance with the choreography. They contort their bodies primarily with the use of their arms, their legs constrained in a tail. That they do all this with a smile and holding their breath, in a 5-mile-an-hour current, almost seems like too much to fathom.

I was so overwhelmed with admiration that at first I wasn't paying attention to the story. Then a creeping dismay stole in and the story began to shadow what I was seeing. Did the voiceover say, "Do you believe in love at first sight?" Was that a calypso song, complete with a cutesy sidekick (in this version a turtle named Chester)? Is the theme here really that love conquers all? And oh my *god*, is the *prince* fighting the *sea witch* to protect the *mermaid*?

I'm a tremendous fan of Hans Christian Andersen, that genius masochist, and as much as it troubles me, I love his story "The Little Mermaid." His world is seductive, all blue and gold and red. The imagery is astonishing: from the bottom of the ocean, "when the sea was perfectly calm, you could catch sight of the sun, which looked like a purple flower with light streaming from its calyx."

I read the story to be an allegory for the plight of the Victorian woman, who was asked to give up her voice in order to lure a man to marry her. It's about sexual awakening: when the mermaid drinks the potion and her tail turns to legs, "it felt to her as if a double-edged sword was passing through her delicate body." She sleeps on a cushion at the prince's door, rides on horseback with him, and the prince kisses the mermaid's red lips and plays with her hair and lays his head on her chest, which, in a world that Andersen describes as having slave girls, seems baldly unchaste. The Disney version diverges wildly from the text by allowing the love story to prevail; the prince sees the error of his ways and marries the little mermaid in the end. Andersen's is far more interesting. It's not about love, not really, but rather the mermaid's yearning to attain an immortal soul by getting a human to fall in love with her. In Andersen's tale, the mermaid watches the prince get married to someone else and knows that in the morning she'll turn to sea foam and that will be it. That night, her sisters rise out of the ocean and give her a knife to murder the prince in his sleep. If she does so, she can be a mermaid again; like all mermaids, she won't have a soul, but she will live for 300 years. She considers, but chooses to spare the prince. At dawn, she dives into the ocean and turns to sea foam, but because she showed mercy to the human, she rises out of the water to become a daughter of the air, an ephemeral creature who is allowed to earn a soul through good deeds done over the course of 300 years. There is hope here, but it is a hope deferred and bittersweet, not an easy love of sappy marriage bells and singing crabs. To have the prince—who is deeply unworthy of the little mermaid in all ways—be the one to fight the sea witch takes all the magic out of the story as well as all of the little mermaid's ferocious autonomy, booting it headlong into the banal.

Now, in the springs, as the prince in knee breeches and the sea witch fought to very loud and dramatic theme music, a little boy in a camouflage T-shirt stood and screamed with a bloody light in his eye, "Do it!" As in: Kill her!

For what? For having a huge amount of power? For wanting the mermaid to uphold her bargain, as one who strikes a bargain should do? For not being as young and pretty as the mermaid? I'm getting old. I've begun identifying with the sea witch.

Even as I was watching, I knew that I was expecting too much;

there were kids in the audience, after all. But the heart wants what the head calls unlikely.

We applauded. The lights came on. We shuffled up into the sunlight and chill air and stood like heifers at the salt lick, blinking. I ate a formerly frozen pizza at the Mermaid Galley and wondered at the albino peahens wandering around, then John brought me in to meet the mermaids while they ate lunch. I'll admit that my hands were shaking; I was meeting the mermaids of my dreams! But they were mermaids in tracksuits and wet hair, eating fried foods from fast-food joints down the miracle mile, smiling at me with mildly overdrawn patience. The prince devoured a whole pepperoni pizza by himself. On land, in sunlight, in their puffy clothes, their hair slicked to their heads, it was eerie how much the mermaids resembled a women's college rugby team after a match. On dry land, the mermaids were all very pretty, but some of their glamour had been left in the shimmering water.

I wanted to suss out the mystery of the mythical mermaids, find some of their bone-deep danger, but John wouldn't let me talk one-on-one with any of the performers. "It's not that I don't trust the girls, but . . . ," he said, shrugging, fiddling with his e-cigarette. So I spoke with the lot of them. They answered my questions but did not find them very good. They sighed. They love being mermaids because it is like a sorority; they love each other and are always delighted when former mermaids come back to do shows (in John's terminology, retired mermaids graduated from "girls" to "ladies"). There was no danger, really, they said: they all looked out for one another down there. They had to go through extensive physical testing, be certified in scuba diving, and have a year's worth of training before they were allowed to perform in major roles. There were air hoses and airlocks nearly everywhere in the deep; there was no real worry about running out of air. John peered at me with increasing suspicion every time I asked another question about danger, sex, or myth. In desperation, having come to the end of my questions, I asked if they believe in mermaids. There was an embarrassed silence; they looked at their food as if hoping it would speak for them. One woman threw me a bone. "I mean, I do," she said. "We kind of have to. Like, we *are* mermaids. Right?" Right.

They are mermaids. They're also extremely hardworking hourly

employees of the State of Florida. The state publishes its employees' wages online; it was easy to discover that one of the senior
mermaids makes $13 an hour, and none of them receive benefits.
They work long days, responsible for training newer mermaids,
running various mermaid camps, scrubbing the algae, which they
call "scrunge," off the spring side of the windows, making sure
the theater is clean and the costumes are in order, ensuring the
other performers' safety, choreographing routines, and directing
the shows and in-water practices from a little podlike booth off
the theater. They get to dolphin-kick and smile and make pretty
shapes with their bodies underwater, but the rest of the time it's a
job, and it's a job that requires freezing in icy water multiple times
a day. It's far more difficult than it looks. Their magic is in making
it all look easy.

I went back, face burning, to the theater where the afternoon
crowd poured in. The children had been replaced by late-middle-
aged tourists with sunburned shins and ball caps and bewildered
looks on their faces. The next show was called *Fish Tails*. It began
with a video on high-mounted televisions that showed the history
of Weeki Wachee, with still photographs from the past; all very
informative and clear. I believe the prince from Hans Christian Andersen's "The Little Mermaid" was the announcer for this one, but I
could be wrong. There was a calypso version of "Red Red Wine."
There was an Enya song I hadn't heard since middle school, when
I was going through a crystals-and-Arthurian-legends phase. Some
man behind me complained about his psoriasis acting up. The
curtain rose.

And there, again, was the frisson of joy: how beautiful they were,
those women in the blue light with their shining tails. My disbelief
suspended itself, floated off to the stained acoustic tiles overhead.
The mermaids ate bananas underwater; they drank some brown-
ish drink from a glass bottle. They showed us the human elevator
move, where they can regulate how high they rise or how low they
sink by how much air they take in or let out from the air hoses. A
yellow-bellied slider turtle the size of a steering wheel mimicked
the mermaids' ballet moves and tried to nibble on their undulating hair. The mermaids bent themselves into a circle, grasping one
another's tails, and spun. They shimmied and lip-synched.

During the *Little Mermaid* show, they had lip-synched a song
called "We've Got the World by the Tail." It goes:

> We're not like other women
> We don't have to clean an oven.
> And we never will grow old,
> We've got the world by the tail.

And all I could think was, well, Christ, *I* don't have to clean the oven. I resisted the song when they sang it that morning, but the old-timey feel of *Fish Tails* made me think harder about the young women in 1940s Florida who had few career options beyond marriage and low-level service jobs. How glorious it must have been to be given the chance to shake their stuff in the water and live independently and hobnob with bona fide movie stars like Johnny Weissmuller (who played Tarzan) and Esther Williams, to become celebrities *themselves,* even though they were from the middle of Podunk nowhere and had little more than beauty and youth and willingness on their side. How seductive such a life would have been; it must have threatened men unused to women living independently. It must have been infuriating to see such lissome, smiling exemplars of feminine beauty through the glass—and to be unable to touch them. The women, knowing they were watched, would have felt their own terrific power. I was falling for the history of the show, for all the many mermaids who'd swum here and made it look glamorous.

The penultimate act in *Fish Tails* was advertised as a deep dive of about 120 feet into the mouth of the chasm. Water pours out of the spring at such a speed that one former mermaid described the dive as trying to swim up a waterfall. There used to be enormous catfish that lived down there and an eel that would threaten the mermaids when they hooked their heels into the bar that held them in place. The mermaid disappeared below the lip of the stage; the announcer cannily built suspense by describing what she was feeling as she dove deeper and deeper; at one point she sent up a breath that expanded hugely as it rose, from shower cap to bread loaf to pillowcase. Time ticked and ticked. I nearly passed out by the time she came up, grinning and waving. I'd been holding my breath with her the whole time.

And then it was the final act. A super-patriotic country song boomed loud and the mermaids wore red-white-and-blue costumes and held an American flag between them. My patriotism is manifested in finding it a privilege to pay taxes, in voting, and in turning a critical eye on my government. Nationalistic bombast makes me ill. I closed my eyes to this last part of the show until the audience erupted in roars, and we all filed out, glad to be aboveground in the sunlight again. I thanked John for his real kindness and fled.

I came to Weeki Wachee to sound the mystery of the mermaid, to find danger and sex and darkness and maybe hear my own deeps echoed back. Instead I found a polite performance and excellent work ethic and real people who do what they do out of sisterhood and love for the cold springs. This is what happens when you are given a plateful of hot Americana à la mode and expect to taste profundity; my disappointment was a result of my failure of expectations, not their show. I'd brought a bathing suit, but it sat dry at the bottom of my purse. I think I'd hoped the mermaids would recognize me as one of their own and invite me in for a swim. Oh well. I did spend a day looking at beautiful women, a spectacular way to pass the time.

As I drove back to Gainesville, I thought of the Rhinemaidens. The freshwater Weeki Wachee mermaids are closer to nixies than actual mermaids, who supposedly live in the ocean; the saltwater Gulf, the *mer* of the maids, is miles away from the springs. In Richard Wagner's Ring cycle, the Rhinemaidens are nixies of the River Rhine and keepers of the gold that, when seized, leads to world power. They're seductive and morally ambiguous and elusive and playful. The gold is stolen from them in the first opera of the three, and at one point later they sing angrily:

> Traulich und treu
> ist's nur in der Tiefe:
> falsch und feig
> ist, was dort oben sich freut!

According to my dictionary and my shaky memory of college German, this means: Only the deeps hold intimacy and truth; false and cowardly is the surface's rejoicing.

But the surface is often beautiful; it is often good enough. I drove home in silence, letting my brain decompress. Two weeks later, I'd spend a week at Crescent Beach on the Atlantic coast of Florida, where high-school students rent condos and pack them with dozens of hormonal bodies. I'd watch these teenage girls in their bikinis braving the cold March wind, perhaps—probably —drunk in the middle of the day, delighting in their new, gorgeous, dangerous bodies, flirting with the boys who eyed them with shielded delight, and I'd think, *Aha.* Here *be sirens.* But on the drive home from Weeki Wachee, the long brown fields were tender in the early-afternoon light. The blue sky appeared out of the tunnels of water oak and palmetto scrub, the air calm and cool in these last months before the heat descends like a solid fabric. I cracked the window to let in the wind. The daughters of the air were doing one good deed to earn their souls that afternoon. Sometimes it's lovely to float on the surface of things.

Tales of the Trash

FROM *The New Yorker*

IN CAIRO, my family lives on the ground floor of an old building, in a sprawling, high-ceilinged apartment with three doors to the outside. One door opens onto the building's lobby, another leads to a small garden, and the third is solely for the use of the *zabal,* or garbageman, who is named Sayyid Ahmed. It's in the kitchen, and when we first moved to the apartment, at the beginning of 2012, the landlady told me to deposit my trash on the fire escape outside the door at any time. There was no pickup schedule, and no preferred container; I could use bags or boxes, or I could simply toss loose garbage outside. Sayyid's services had no set fee. He wasn't a government employee, and he had no contract or formal job. I was instructed to pay him whatever I believed to be fair, and if I pleased I could pay him nothing at all.

Many things in Egypt don't work very well. Traffic is bad, and trains get canceled; during the summer, it's not unusual to have five electricity blackouts in a single day. One year, we couldn't buy bottled water for months, because the plant that produced the water somehow caught fire. Since we moved into the apartment, the country has cycled through three constitutions, three presidents, four prime ministers, and more than 700 members of parliament. But there hasn't been a single day when the trash wasn't cleared outside my kitchen door. As a whole, Cairo's waste-collection system is surprisingly functional, considering that it's largely informal. In a sprawling, chaotic city of more than 17 million, *zabaleen* like Sayyid have managed to develop one of the most efficient municipal recycling networks in the world.

At first, I never saw Sayyid working, because he cleared my fire escape before dawn. After three months of this invisible service, he approached me one day on the street and asked if I had previously lived in China. I wasn't sure how he knew this—we had chatted a few times, but never for long. He said that he had an important question about Chinese medicine.

That evening, he arrived at eight o'clock sharp, dressed in his work clothes. He's not much taller than 5 feet, but his shoulders are broad and his legs are bowed from hauling weight. Usually his clothes are several sizes too large, and his shoes flap like those of a clown, because he harvests them from the garbage of bigger men. At my apartment, he produced a small red box decorated with gold calligraphy. The Chinese labeling was elegant but evasive: the pills were described as "health protection products" that "promoted development and power." Inside the box, a sheet of instructions reminded me how sometimes the Chinese can be much more expressive when they use English badly:

2 pills at a time whenever nece necessary
Before fucking make love 20minutes

"Where did you get this?" I asked.

"In the trash," Sayyid said. "From a man who died." He told me that the man was elderly, and had lived down the street. After his death, his sons threw away the pills and other possessions. "Many of these things were *mish kuaissa*," Sayyid said. "Not good."

I asked what he meant by that.

"Things like this": he sketched with a finger in the air, and then he pointed below his belt. "It's electric. It uses batteries. It's for women. This kind of thing isn't good." But talking about it seemed to make Sayyid happy. He told me that the trash had also contained Egyptian sex pills and a large collection of pornographic magazines. He didn't say what he had done with those things. I asked where the dead man used to work.

"He was an ambassador."

I had been studying Arabic for less than a year, and Sayyid's tone was so matter-of-fact that I asked him to repeat this. "He was in embassies overseas," Sayyid explained. "He was very rich; he had millions of dollars. He had four million and forty-four dollars in his bank account."

The precision of this figure caught my attention, and I asked Sayyid how he knew.

"Because it was on letters from the bank."

I made a mental note to be careful about what I threw away. Sayyid asked for details about the Chinese medicine, and I did my best to translate the part about waiting 20 minutes before fucking make love. He was vague about what he intended to do with the drugs. I checked the ingredients—white ginseng, deer antler—and decided that there probably wasn't any risk. I had a feeling that it wouldn't be the first time he'd taken a pill out of the garbage.

After that, Sayyid began stopping by regularly with questions. Over time, I realized that there are a number of people he's recruited as informal consultants. He's illiterate, like more than a quarter of adult Egyptians, so if he wants to read something that he pulls from the trash he goes to the proprietor of H Freedom, a small corner kiosk. If he finds himself involved in a neighborhood dispute, he calls on the man who distributes government-subsidized bread. My own field of expertise ranges from foreign things to sex products and alcohol. If somebody throws away a half-finished bottle, Sayyid checks with me to see if it's imported and thus might have resale value. He's Muslim, but not particularly devout; when he stops by at night, he often asks for a beer. He's the only guest I've ever had who carries away his empties, because he knows he'll end up collecting them anyway.

In part because he can't read, he's skilled at picking up on subtle clues. He hand-sorts all the garbage, and at one point he noticed that foreign women often throw away empty packs of pills whose number corresponds to the days of the month. Sayyid concluded that they were an aphrodisiac, and he asked me if they have the effect of making foreign women desire sex on a daily basis. I explained that this isn't exactly correct, although the assumption was understandable, because Sayyid finds a large number of sex drugs and paraphernalia in the trash. A couple of times, he's brought by other forms of Chinese sex medicine, and he shows up with drugs that have names like Virecta. Anything blue catches his eye—recently he appeared with a half-finished foil pack of Aerius, which excited him until I went online and learned that it's an allergy medication that happens to be the same color as Viagra.

I live on Zamalek, the northern part of an island in the Nile that's situated in central Cairo, and Sayyid has become my most reliable guide to the neighborhood. Occasionally I accompany him on his predawn rounds. The first time I did this, in February of 2013, he led me to the top landing of the fire escape of a building on my street.

"This is Madame Heba," he said, grabbing a black plastic garbage bag and tossing it into a huge canvas basket perched atop his back, Quasimodo style. He descended while engaging in a running commentary about residents, whose names I've changed. "This is Dr. Mohammed," he said at the next landing, and then he climbed down another level. "This one's a priest, Father Mikael. He's very cheap. He gives me only five pounds a month." He heaved two big bags. "He says he doesn't have any money, but I see all the boxes and bags from the gifts that he gets. People give him things all the time, because he's a priest."

On a different floor, we picked our way across a landing covered with rotting food; a pile of trash bags had been ripped apart by stray cats. "This one's a foreigner," Sayyid explained. "I'm not supposed to touch her garbage. The landlord isn't happy with her; there's some kind of fight. He told me not to remove her trash." Sayyid said that this isn't unusual: people can tip him to remove trash, but they can also tip him to allow somebody else's garbage to accumulate. We descended to the next floor, where he remarked that the resident was a Muslim with a drinking problem. "There are always bottles in her trash," he said in a low voice. By way of illustration, he ripped open the bag on her doorstep and showed me the empties: Auld Stag whiskey and Casper wine. He did the same thing with a bag at a building across the street. "This is Mr. Hassan," he said. "He's sick." Sayyid tore open the plastic, rooted around inside, and pulled out a pair of used syringes. "I think he has diabetes," he said. "Every day there are two syringes in the garbage. He takes one in the morning and one at night."

Sayyid's route twisted through a maze of fire escapes that climbed through narrow, chimneylike atria. Periodically a stairway led to the roof of a building, where the gray streak of the Nile was visible two blocks away. Zamalek is a relatively prosperous part of Cairo, and it has always attracted foreign residents, but there are also many middle-class and even poor people, because rent-control laws keep the price of some apartments as low as a few dollars a month. As a result, landlords rarely make improvements, and old buildings have a kind of fading glory. On my street, many structures were built in the art deco style, with marble lobbies and beautifully patterned wrought-iron grillwork along the balconies. It's common for apartments to have a kitchen door that leads to the fire escape, like mine.

Sometimes an early riser will hear Sayyid working, and she'll open the kitchen door to greet him and offer a cup of tea. One morning I was with Sayyid when an elderly woman handed him four hamburger patties that she had carefully prepared in a plastic bag for his lunch. In Cairo, where many basic services have developed informally, and where there's a strong culture of tipping, people tend to be generous when somebody is working hard. This is one reason that Sayyid dresses so poorly—he knows that dirty, ill-fitting clothes are more likely to inspire generosity.

And the information that he gathers from the trash helps him interact with residents. In addition to the door-to-door collection, he sorts garbage in the street, collecting it into piles that are hauled away by trucks. He greets everybody who passes, asking about spouses and children, and he's particularly attentive to details of health. On his early-morning rounds, he comments on whether a resident is receiving injections, or taking medicine, or wearing diapers. If something seems particularly interesting, he'll open the bag for my benefit. Once Sayyid stopped at a landing and whispered that the resident was a sex-crazed Lebanese man. Then he ripped open the trash, found a discarded bottle, and asked me to read the label: "Durex Play Feel Intimate Lube."

Sayyid's conversations revolve around the three fundamental forces in his world, which are women, money, and garbage. Often these things are closely connected. In the beginning, it was Sayyid's father's unquenchable passion for women that led to his son becoming a *zabal*. Sayyid's father worked as a watchman on the outskirts of Cairo, where he embarked on a rapid series of marriages and divorces. All told, he went through nine wives, or ten if you count the Christian woman he married briefly before Sayyid's mother. Nobody seems to know how many children he fathered, but it was too many to support, and he died when Sayyid was six. As a boy, Sayyid never attended a single day of school, and by the age of 11 he was working full-time as an assistant to *zabaleen*.

Despite this difficult childhood, Sayyid speaks fondly of his parents. And in his ancestral village in Upper Egypt residents remember his father in almost mythical terms. They say that at heart he was a true Arab, a Bedouin, a man of the Sahara; and thus he was fated to restlessness. The villagers also make it clear that they don't count the Christian wife.

Sayyid eventually found work as an assistant to a *zabal* named Salama, whose life in garbage was also inspired by an abundance of women. In Salama's case, there was only a single wife, but she gave birth to eight daughters and no sons. "He didn't do anything his whole life other than prepare his daughters for marriage," Aiman, the husband of Salama's oldest daughter, told me once. Aiman runs a small recycling business, and like many *zabaleen* he has a nickname: Aiman the Cat. "Other people build buildings," Aiman the Cat said of his father-in-law. "He built daughters." When Salama died and there was no son to pick up his route, it was loaned to Sayyid. He's allowed to collect the trash, but he has to pick out all paper, plastic, glass, and other resellable commodities and give them to Aiman the Cat.

They have no formal contract, but it doesn't matter, because Cairo's waste collection is shaped by tradition, not by laws and planning. The system began in the early 1900s, when a group of migrants arrived from Dakhla, a remote oasis in Egypt's Western Desert. They became known as *wahiya*—"people of the oasis"— and they paid Cairo building owners for the right to pick up garbage and charge fees to tenants. In those days, much of the garbage was flammable, and the *wahiya* used it as fuel for street carts that made *ful*, the fried beans that are a staple in Egypt.

Inevitably, Cairo's population grew at a rate that upset the delicate balance between trash and beans. In the thirties and forties, a new wave of migrants began to come from Asyut, in Upper Egypt. They were Coptic Christians, which meant that they could raise pigs that ate organic garbage. The Christians subcontracted from the Muslim *wahiya*, who evolved into middlemen, managing access and collecting fees. The actual hauling and sorting was done by the Christians, who became known as *zabaleen*, and who made much of their income by selling pork, mostly to tourist hotels. The government played no role in establishing this system, which worked remarkably well. Social scientists often cite it as a success story among developing-world megacities, and in 2006 an article

in *Habitat International* described it as "one of the world's most efficient resource recovery" systems. It was estimated that the *zabaleen*
recycled roughly 80 percent of the waste that they collected.

But the system became a victim of dysfunctional national politics under the regime of Hosni Mubarak. In 2009, during the
worldwide epidemic of H1N1 swine flu, the Ministry of Agriculture decreed that all Egyptian pigs had to be killed. There was no
evidence that pigs were spreading the disease, but the government
went ahead and slaughtered as many as 300,000 animals. Some
Egyptians believe that the decision was driven by a desire to appease Islamists, who had become outspoken critics of the regime,
and supposedly hated pigs even more than they hated Mubarak.
But the policy backfired, with hundreds of furious *zabaleen* taking
part in protests. They also started tossing organic waste into the
streets, because it had no value without pigs. The declining hy-
giene of the capital and the unrest of the *zabaleen* were part of the
general unhappiness that culminated in the revolution, in January
2011.

For Sayyid, none of this—the people of the oasis, the wandering pig-raisers, the Exodus-style slaughter carried out by a dying
regime—is exotic or unusual. He doesn't believe that there's anything particularly complex about the relationships he has to negotiate in order to gain access to trash. In Zamalek, he collects from
27 buildings, which are subcontracted from 7 individuals. One is
Aiman the Cat, the *zabal*, who is Christian, and the others are Muslim *wahiya* who are known by nicknames like the Beast and the
Fox. The Fox allows Sayyid to handle seven buildings; the Beast
grants him one. Another *wahi* has been dead for a decade, but
his son, a government clerk, retains rights to the trash, so he sub-
contracts to Sayyid. There's also a dead *wahi* who left a widow, so
Sayyid is obligated to send her £E100—about $14—a month. Peri-
odically he checks to see if the widow is still alive, but he wouldn't
dream of cutting her off, out of respect for the sacred link between
women and garbage.

He keeps track of all this, and the monthly tips of more than
400 residents, by memory. And he's constantly acquiring periph-
eral information that can be leveraged into baksheesh. A few years
ago, Sayyid was hauling trash late at night when he saw the daughter of a doorman returning from university with a boy. Believing
that they were alone, they kissed. "Since I've eaten with her father

and mother, I didn't like what I saw," Sayyid told me. "So I told the father." Undoubtedly Sayyid thought that the doorman's gratitude would be of some benefit to him, but this was a miscalculation. The daughter denied everything, and the doorman barred Sayyid from collecting the building's trash. At that point, Sayyid called upon the owner of H Freedom and the man at the local bread kiosk for help, but their intercession only convinced the doorman that the story was spreading. He gave the garbage rights to another *zabal,* and now Sayyid says that he should have minded his own business.

It's rare for *zabaleen* to do hard labor into middle age, and Sayyid, who is 40, has chronic pain in his back and his knees. He expects that within the next decade he'll be unable to continue, but he doesn't know what to do next—he often describes himself as stupid, and fit only for the work of a donkey. But in truth his job requires him to be observant and perceptive, and he must interact with the full range of Egyptian society. In particular, he has to be sensitive toward Christians, who dominate the industry. The first time I accompanied him to his neighborhood to watch a soccer match at another *zabal*'s home, Sayyid prepped me with a list of things that I should and shouldn't say, so that I wouldn't offend his Christian sensibilities.

One evening Sayyid stopped by my apartment to chat, and my wife, Leslie, and I began talking about a rich and notoriously stingy woman in the neighborhood. She's middle-aged and well educated, but she never married, and I asked Sayyid why.

"There's a proverb," he said. "'If you befriend a monkey for his money, then tomorrow the money will be gone, but the monkey will still be a monkey.' That's what it was like with her. Nobody wanted to marry her."

I remarked that the woman is also obese, but Sayyid shook his head. "She used to be pretty," he said. "I've seen pictures of her from fifteen or twenty years ago. She looked so different. Beautiful!"

"Where did you see the pictures?"

"In the garbage," he said. "She threw them away."

I asked why he thought she had done that.

"Maybe she didn't want to remember those times," he said quietly. "Maybe the pictures made her sad."

*

Sayyid himself married late by Egyptian standards. When he was 29, he arranged with some neighbors to marry their cousin, an 18-year-old named Wahiba. She came from a village outside Aswan, in Upper Egypt, and she was educated, having attended a trade school after high school. She moved to Cairo to be with Sayyid, and they soon had two sons and then a daughter.

On the seventh day after the daughter's birth, Sayyid invited Leslie and me to his home for the traditional celebration that's called the *sebou*. We took a cab and then a microbus out to Ard al-Liwa, an area in northern Cairo that includes a number of *ashwa'iyat*, or "informal" settlements—illegally built slums. Sayyid's *ashwa'iyat* is dominated by garbage collectors, and we walked through narrow alleyways full of trash that was in the process of being hand-sorted. There were bags of glass bottles, stacks of old rags, pallets of crushed plastic, and piles of rotting vegetables that would be used as goat feed. In one spot, a man had picked dozens of pieces of bread from the garbage and laid them out to dry; eventually they would be fed to water buffalo. Everywhere we walked, we could hear rats rustling through trash. But the homes were made of concrete and brick, and were relatively well constructed. This is generally true of Cairo, where about two thirds of the population lives in *ashwa'iyat*. David Sims, an urban planner who is the author of *Understanding Cairo,* has pointed out that the capital's slums have a functionality and permanence that's rare in many parts of the developing world.

Before visiting Sayyid's home, I had had the notion that it would be furnished largely with things from the garbage. In Zamalek, he's always showing me discarded objects that still have value, and once he told me that the bread I'd tossed out a day earlier had been perfectly good—he'd taken it out of my trash and used it to make sandwiches for some friends at H Freedom. So I was surprised to find that virtually everything in his two-story apartment was new, and for the first time I realized how effective Sayyid had been at inspiring tips. He usually earned nearly $500 a month, which was about twice the average household income in Cairo, and his apartment had cost more than $30,000. He had two televisions, and his couches were still wrapped in factory plastic. A computer was being installed for the eldest son, Zizou.

When we entered, we were greeted by Wahiba, who was another surprise. She was strikingly pretty, with fair skin and a heart-shaped face, and she wore blue eye shadow and dark eyeliner. She was slender, and dressed in a long white gown embroidered with beads; it was hard to believe that she had given birth to her third child only a week earlier. She greeted us warmly, and we chatted for a few minutes, and then she politely excused herself. A few minutes later, she returned in a niqab, the full head covering that is worn by conservative Muslims.

And after that I never saw her face again. In the next couple of years, I visited Sayyid's home on a number of occasions, but Wahiba usually stayed out of sight. She would remain in the kitchen, behind a closed door, making tea or dinner, which would be served to me by Sayyid or one of the children. The few times that I caught a glimpse of Wahiba, she was wearing the niqab, and we never had another conversation. I realized that I had caught her unaware at our initial meeting, and it felt strange to remember that first and only glimpse. The more I got to know Sayyid, the less I felt I knew his wife, and the more mysterious she became.

Not long after the *sebou*, tensions appeared in the marriage. Sayyid had always worked long hours in Zamalek, but now he seemed to delay going home, often returning as late as midnight. He complained that he was fighting with Wahiba, usually about money. Sometimes he mentioned the possibility of divorce, which has little stigma for male Muslims in Egypt. One of Sayyid's older brothers had recently divorced for the second time and now was searching for a third wife. "You keep one for a while and then you change," the brother had told me when we met at the *sebou*. "It's like changing a tire on a car."

Sayyid and most of his siblings were born in Cairo, but like many residents of the capital they maintain strong links to their ancestral village, which is the source of most ideas about family. In Sayyid's extended family, most women wear the niqab, but the reason seems to be more cultural than strictly religious. It's a point of pride and possession for the men — Sayyid says that his wife wears it because she's beautiful, and if she shows her face in the street she'll be coveted by strangers and harassed. And other traditions serve to control women in more explicit ways. One evening Sayyid and I were watching my twin daughters play in the garden, and he asked casually if I planned to have them circumcised. I looked at the girls — they were all of three years old — and said no, this wasn't something we intended to do. The majority of Egyptian women have undergone the surgery, which opponents describe as genital mutilation. Since 2008 it's been illegal, but many people continue to have it performed on daughters, usually when they're between the ages of nine and twelve. In Egypt, Islamists are the biggest supporters of the procedure, which, among other effects, makes intercourse less pleasurable for a woman. But in fact this tradition is not mentioned in the Koran, and Muslims in most parts of the world don't practice it. Originally it was a tribal custom native to many parts of Africa.

I asked Sayyid if he planned to have the surgery performed on his daughter, and he nodded. "Otherwise, women are crazy for *dakar*," he said, using a word that means "male." "They'll be running around outside the house, chasing men."

For traditionally minded Egyptians, this is a common view: desire should be limited to males, who do what they can to heighten it. All those sex drugs in the garbage of Zamalek aren't an anomaly — in Egypt, I've had a number of casual conversations in which the topic turns to sex, and a man reaches into his pocket and pulls out a pill, to show that he's prepared. Usually it's some version of Viagra, but for Sayyid's class the drug of choice is often tramadol, a prescription painkiller. Cheap versions are manufactured in China and India, and in 2012 the United Nations Office on Drugs and Crime estimated that there were 5 billion tramadol pills in Egypt, a staggering number in a country of 84 million.

Many of the *zabaleen* I know use the stuff. The pills are available on the street for 30 or 40 cents, and they take the edge off the fatigue and pain of a hard day's work. They are also addictive; in America, where the abuse of tramadol is growing, its status has recently been upgraded to that of a controlled substance. Last year, a *zabal* I know asked me for advice about how to quit. He looked awful: he was sweating heavily and his eyes were darting here and there. I knew that he was a devout Christian, so I did my best and came up with two recommendations: pray very hard, and drink a lot of caffeine. I suppose I wasn't a total hypocrite — I do one of these things religiously — but I felt helpless. I was relieved when, a month later, the *zabal* told me he'd been able to kick the habit.

In January, I accompanied Sayyid on a visit to his mother's village, outside Beni Suef, in Upper Egypt, and he carefully prepared a foil pack of five tramadol pills as a gift for his uncle. He was a farmer who hadn't yet tried the drug; Sayyid wanted to give him a taste of city life. But Sayyid has never seemed at risk of addiction, because he uses tramadol primarily for sex. In truth, the drug doesn't function like Viagra, but many Egyptian men seem to believe that it does. And a number of users say that tramadol, which delays orgasm, also intensifies sensation. On Thursdays, Sayyid often grins and shows me his pills for the weekend. Even after he began fighting with his wife, he sometimes took a tramadol before returning home late on Thursday night, which didn't seem like the best strategy for dealing with marital discord. And I found myself wondering about the social dynamics in some Egyptian homes — the combination of men who take sex drugs and women who are circumcised and housebound.

After Sayyid and Wahiba started fighting, she secretly registered their apartment in her own name, at a government bureau. When Sayyid learned about this, their conflicts became angrier, and then one of his sisters, who also lives in Ard al-Liwa, got involved. At one point, Wahiba and some of her relatives confronted Sayyid's sister in the street, and the fight turned physical; the sister's eye was injured so badly that she needed surgery. Then Wahiba kicked Sayyid out of the apartment and changed the locks. For good measure, she filed three court cases against him, including one of nonsupport.

She also sent a steady stream of text messages to Sayyid's phone. At night, he slept on the floor of a garage on my street, where a doorman had allowed him to arrange a pallet. Whenever Sayyid received a text, he had to troop over to H Freedom, where he would stand mortified while the owner read these things aloud:

Yesterday you didn't fight for me. I'll do it myself and you will regret what I'll do.

Oh, you want divorce? I'll take all of my rights, you bitch, and all of the people will see you.

It's not your house, you thief, and you came back to me like a dog, as I wanted you to, and I will send you away as I wish.

As the fight worsened, each relied on one key weapon. For Sayyid, it was money: he stopped giving cash to his wife, who was forced to ask relatives for help. For Wahiba, the weapon was words.

She targeted her husband's illiteracy, sending messages that she knew would become public and damage his reputation in Zamalek. And by filing repeated legal claims, she forced Sayyid into the hostile world of documents and government offices. One morning I went with him to the Real Estate Tax Authority, where he was trying to get the paperwork necessary to fight his wife's claim on the apartment. For more than two hours, he went from floor to floor, office to office, encountering clerks who spoke in phrases that were code for *Pay me a bribe.* "I want to drink tea," one clerk said, and Sayyid gave him £E20. "I have an itch," the next one said, and Sayyid handed him £E5. "I need something to speed it up," the third said, and Sayyid produced another bill.

None of this seemed to surprise or even annoy Sayyid. But the notion of the government as provider of positive service was completely foreign to his experience: he hadn't attended school as a child, he lived in an *ashwa'iyat,* and he had no health insurance or job security. His only significant contact with the state had been when he was drafted into the army, in the nineties. Like all uneducated draftees, he had served for three years instead of the one year that is required of educated males. But this extended service is effectively a punishment, not an opportunity to address Egypt's epidemic of illiteracy. During Sayyid's time as a soldier, the army didn't provide a single class in basic reading. Instead, he spent three long years standing at a guard post in Port Said with a rifle in his arms.

For the leaders of the revolution, who are mostly middle-and upper-class, the experience of a citizen like Sayyid is a perfect example of why radical change is necessary. But there's a point at which somebody is so far removed from the formal system that he has no interest in changing it. Sayyid never cared much about the protests in Tahrir Square, and, like most Egyptians, he tends to support whoever seems to be popular at any given moment. In 2012, he voted for Mohamed Morsi, the Muslim Brotherhood candidate for president, and then, two years later, he voted for Abdel Fattah el-Sisi, the general who had forcibly removed Morsi from office.

With every change in leadership, there have been new promises to reform public services. After Morsi won, he made garbage reform a centerpiece of his "Hundred Days" program, but nothing happened. Since the coup, other proposed changes have failed to accomplish much. The government has been weak and incompetent for so long that people are accustomed to alternatives—the informal services don't always function well, but they function well enough to keep things moving. And when the government does act, its weakness means that it often follows the lead of these informal institutions without adding much value. In the *ashwa'iyat*, officials typically arrive after locals have already tapped illegally into water, sewage, and electricity lines, and then the state installs meters and begins to charge for service.

Waste collection follows a similar pattern. The main flaw with the informal service has always been that it's erratic in poor areas, where *zabaleen* aren't motivated to work, because tips are small and the garbage contains less material of value. In 2003, the Mubarak regime offered 15-year contracts to foreign waste-management companies, which supposedly would cover most neighborhoods, hiring the existing *wahiya* and *zabaleen* and paying them fair salaries. But the plan was underfunded, and the culture of the informal system was too complex and entrenched for foreign companies to navigate. The disastrous culling of the pigs and the instability of the post-revolution period have made things even worse. Hassan Abu Ahmed, a spokesman for the Cairo Cleaning and Beautification Authority, the government department in charge of waste management, told me that the foreign companies are covering only 50 or 60 percent of the services that were promised in the contracts. But he also said that the government owes the companies tens of millions of dollars, because the economy has collapsed in the wake of the revolution.

My part of Cairo is ostensibly cleaned by an Italian-owned firm called AMA Arab Environment Company. At the beginning of the summer, when I met with Ahmed Hassan Ahmed, the project manager at AMA Arab, he seemed exhausted. He said that the government owed his firm almost $30 million, and he had just spent a week dealing with a strike by garbage collectors in northern Cairo. One of his employees had recently been stabbed in the lungs after infringing on a *zabal*'s turf. "If you go to a *zabal*'s neighborhood and ask him for his trash, he's going to slap you in the face," Ahmed told me. His company has instituted regular pickups by truck in some parts of Cairo, but in terms of actual door-to-door collection the main change has been the addition of a new layer of middlemen. On my street, the government subcontracts garbage collection to the Italian company, which in turn subcontracts to a *wahi* called Osama Apricot, who subcontracts to Aiman the Cat, who subcontracts to Sayyid. Bizarrely, payment moves in opposite directions along this chain: from the top, the government pays the Italians in cash, while from the bottom Sayyid pays Aiman the Cat in recyclables. It seems miraculous that so much trash is actually picked up, and that the people on the lowest level participate so energetically in this flawed system. But low expectations, like garbage, are a resource that Egypt has in great abundance. "The beauty is that trash doesn't cost anything," Sayyid once told me happily. "You just pick up the trash and you get paid for it!"

Sayyid spent the winter sleeping on the floor of the garage. A couple of times he used my shower, and periodically a doorman let him warm up in a heated room, but most of the time he looked tired, dirty, and miserable. Finally a neighbor in Ard al-Liwa organized a traditional reconciliation session involving members of Sayyid's and Wahiba's families. At the session, the neighbor gave Sayyid a piece of advice. "If your wife asks for a penny," he said, "give her two."

"Why should I give her two pennies?" Sayyid asked.

"Because the man with three pennies is standing outside your house."

Afterward, Sayyid was optimistic. When I asked how his sister and Wahiba had gotten along at the meeting, Sayyid seemed surprised by the question. "They weren't there," he said. "Women aren't allowed at a reconciliation." He explained that it's impossible to control them in such a situation. "They have long tongues, and they insult people," he said. "There would be a fight."

Soon he was receiving more text messages— *You're going to divorce me with your legs crossed over your head*—and it was clear that the all-male reconciliation had failed to appease this woman's anger. On the last day of January, Sayyid went to see a lawyer he had retained in Ard al-Liwa, and I accompanied him, along with a translator.

The lawyer's office was in one of the dirtiest parts of Ard al-Liwa. As we picked our way through piles of rotting organic material, Sayyid explained that *zabaleen* had been dumping it here since the great pig massacre of '09. But the office itself was neatly appointed. A row of hardbound legal books sat on a shelf behind the lawyer's desk, and he had arranged religious signs throughout the place: PRAY TO THE PROPHET; THERE IS NO GOD BUT GOD. The lawyer was a short, neckless man who leaned forward as he talked, shoulders level with his ears, as if prepared to ram his head into whatever stood in his way. His eyes widened when Sayyid showed him a text on his phone.

"She's calling you a bitch!" the lawyer said. "If she were my wife, I swear to God I would have shot her. *Boom,* I swear!" He shook his head and pointed to some court documents that Wahiba had filed. "The law has no heart," he said. "It has a brain—and the brain is papers. And this paper says that she can't live with you, she can't stand you."

Sayyid said, "Up until now, I still don't want to humiliate her."

"Sayyid, this is love!" The lawyer told him sternly that he was being softhearted, and he held up one of the papers. "Look at this!"

"I can't read," Sayyid said.

"She insults you with nasty words! She writes these things—look at it!"

"I can't read," Sayyid said.

"She insults you!" the lawyer said. "She's filed three cases. Each one is a speed bump. Her goal is to make it so that either you don't go or, if you go, you can't work."

He said that if Sayyid failed to fight the case his wife would get everything. Sayyid appeared overwhelmed—there were bags under his eyes, and he had come straight from work, in his filthy *zabal* clothes. But the lawyer was skillful; he calmly asked questions, drawing details out of his client. Periodically he flourished a document and pushed it in front of Sayyid, who would say the same thing: *I can't read. I can't read.* After a while, Sayyid mentioned that his wife had recently taken a job at a weaving factory. The lawyer's face lit up.

"What's the factory address?" he said. "Tell me and I can have her arrested!" He waved one of the papers: "It says here that she's not working. You see, the law is beautiful!" He continued, "We can send a message to the factory manager: either he can fire her or he can give us proof that she's working."

"She was always asking me to work," Sayyid said. "I told her that when I die she can work."

"So she was asking you to work?"

"Yes, but what am I, a child?" Sayyid said. "I can work. My wife doesn't need to work."

"You won't believe the cases I see," the lawyer said, and he described a client whose mother had been flirting with her own son-in-law. "They get these ideas from watching television," he said.

"Your wife, she's from Upper Egypt, and she's used to being behind a cow." He continued, "She came to Cairo, she got a television, she saw dancing—she wants all of this."

"I have two televisions," Sayyid said proudly.

"It's our duty to teach her," the lawyer said. "When we have a
cow that's aggressive, what do we do? We put a ring through her
nose." He noted that Wahiba had hired a female lawyer, which he
believed was a shrewd strategy for intimidating the judge, who he
expected to be a graduate of Al Azhar University, the most prestigious Islamic institution in the Arab world.

"When this female lawyer talks to the Azhar judge, he'll stare at
the ground," the lawyer said. "He'll be shy; he won't know what to
do. Your wife will say, 'He abused me sexually, he did this, he did
that!' And the judge will say, 'Enough, enough!' Because he's so
shy. But if I go I'll straighten it out."

He explained that by law Wahiba needed her husband's permission to work, because the papers described her as a housewife. "In
Islamic sharia, the woman is like an egg," he said. "Let's say you
have ten eggs. Where would you put them? Would you just leave
them lying around? No, you'd put them in the proper place, in
the refrigerator. Women belong at home. They can go out of the
house with their husband's permission, but that's it."

When Sayyid first entered the office, he seemed near tears. But
the lawyer's confidence was contagious, and by the end of the
meeting Sayyid was smiling. The lawyer told him it was important
not to request the divorce—if Wahiba was forced to initiate it, then
her share of their assets would be much less. He warned Sayyid not
to tell anybody about their strategy. "Keep the secret between your
teeth," he said. "That's why God made your mouth like this!"

Throughout the conflict, I saw Wahiba only once. I went with
Sayyid to Family Court, where both parties made statements to an
official. Sayyid wore particularly filthy clothes, because the lawyer
had told him that appearing poor would improve his odds by exactly 15 percent. Wahiba arrived with her lawyer, her mother, her
sister-in-law, and her three small children in tow; she wore a black
niqab and her hands were gloved. Sayyid and I were asked to go
into the next room while she made her statement. The night before, she had sent a text: *I'm going to go under oath and destroy you.*

I had always liked talking with Sayyid, because of his eye for detail in Zamalek, but I noticed that he rarely said anything specific about his wife. She was crazy, he often told me, and her mind was a lock—a phrase that describes ignorance and stubbornness. But sometimes I wondered if she was almost as mysterious to him as she was to me. In his description, the woman was completely blank, as faceless as a figure in a shroud. And all the skill that Sayyid showed in Zamalek—his insight and flexibility, his ability to interact and negotiate with so many different people—seemed to evaporate when he was dealing with his wife. She was, quite simply, terrifying. And from the male perspective this seemed true of Egyptian women in general, whether they were starting fights, or chasing *dakar*, or intimidating Azhar judges.

I never knew why Wahiba became so angry. Sayyid blamed money, which seemed unlikely. A couple of his neighbors told me the real problem was that Sayyid spent too much time in Zamalek, cultivating his relationships, while Wahiba was stuck with three small kids in the *ashwa'iyat*. But it was impossible to know for certain, just as it was impossible to know why she suddenly dropped her cases. After all the lawyers and statements and all the threatening messages, at the last moment Wahiba backed out. She decided not to file for divorce, and she quit her factory job, and Sayyid went home to Ard al-Liwa as if nothing had happened.

Last year, after Morsi was forcibly removed from office and the military returned to power, a friend of mine remarked that it felt like a revolution "in the circular sense of the word." She explained, "You go back to where you started." The longer I lived in Egypt, the more I sensed the presence of some undefined and undirected frustration that motivated everything from politics to home life. It wasn't limited to a certain class: I was struck by how middle- and upper-class friends also had family fights that were just as intense as Sayyid's. And like him, they almost inevitably returned to whatever was familiar. It felt like a statement, not a demand—people couldn't say what they wanted, but they could say that something felt wrong.

Still, they survived. The circle kept turning. The garbage vanished from the fire escape every morning. At night, Sayyid periodically stopped by my apartment to drink beer and chat. After he was gone, Leslie sometimes asked, "Is it really possible that they're together again?" But he looked so much healthier and happier than he had during the winter. And he was back to taking tramadol on Thursday nights, which had to mean something.

Hail Dayton

FROM *Oxford American*

IN THE BEGINNING, God created the heavens and the earth, or maybe he didn't, but either way vast ribbons of peat came to rest under what became the foothills of Tennessee's Cumberland Plateau, and in time the peat became coal, and later the railroads arrived, along with mines and coke ovens, and near one lazy arc of the Tennessee River workers built homes to return to after their long days of burrowing and burning, and the homes became a town, and the town was called Dayton.

It was here in July 1925 that John T. Scopes was tried and convicted of teaching evolution in a Tennessee public school. And it's here, nearly every July since 1987, that he has been retried and reconvicted as part of the Scopes Trial Play & Festival. Every year the same verdict is read (guilty of violating Tennessee's Butler Act, which made it illegal for state-funded instructors "to teach any theory that denies the Story of the Divine Creation of man as taught in the Bible, and to teach instead that man has descended from a lower order of animals") and the same fine is levied ($100) by a man playing a judge sitting behind the same bench in the same second-floor courtroom at the Rhea County courthouse where the case was first heard nine decades ago.

For much of the outside world—even just 40 miles downriver, in Chattanooga, where I grew up—Dayton has long functioned as both punch line and punching bag, especially in recent years. In 2004, the Rhea County commission briefly approved a measure banning gay people from living in the area. In 2006, a local woman named June Griffin stole a Mexican flag from a downtown grocery store because she felt the proprietors didn't speak sufficient English. Griffin had earned some notoriety the year before when she appeared in a *Daily Show* segment filmed in town. "What's your take on the Scopes trial?" comedian Ed Helms asked her. "Evolution is a total fabrication and a lie," she said. When she announced her candidacy for Tennessee governor, the *Nashville Scene* wrote, "Griffin is creepy, racist and terrifyingly xenophobic. Fittingly, she's a resident of Dayton, Tenn. (of Scopes Monkey Trial fame)."

Dayton is one of thousands of small American towns besot by hyper-conservative goofery, but the residue of the Scopes trial seems to trap and magnify it, even all these years later. Over those two weeks in July 1925, journalists swarmed in from across the country, their baser tendencies prevailing on a new, massive scale — it wasn't the first "trial of the century," but it was the first broadcast live over the radio. Preachers and monkey-souvenir vendors peddled their wares on streets clogged with looky-loos. The defendant lent his name to the production, but the counsel starred: famously agnostic Chicago attorney Clarence Darrow led the defense, with populist statesman turned fundamentalist vanguard William Jennings Bryan a figurehead of the prosecution. Chief among the gawking scribes was H. L. Mencken, whose dispatches for the *Baltimore Sun* and *The Nation* bemoaned Dayton's "forlorn mob" of "rustics" and "gaping primates." Dayton was a "ninth-rate country town," he sneered, a "dung pile" destined to be "a joke town at best, and infamous at worst."

And then came *Inherit the Wind,* on stage in 1955 and on screen in 1960, in which Jerome Lawrence and Robert Edwin Lee interpolated the trial's narrative in service of an anti-McCarthyism parable, à la Arthur Miller's *The Crucible.* The story was presented as fiction but accumulated an honorary factualness, becoming a proxy of the history it dramatized. Its images of the small-minded South were indelible: as a female alto warbles "(Give Me That) Old Time Religion," men in dark suits march to a high school where they find a young teacher, Bertram Cates, lecturing on Darwinism. Cates is dragged from the classroom and jailed. One night, locals mob outside his cell window, carrying torches and itching to lynch him. A bottle thrown at the barred window showers Cates with broken glass.

But the real story of the trial, like Dayton itself, began with the

mines: they were dwindling, the town was suffering, and a group
of local boosters—including drugstore owner and school board
president F. E. Robinson and school superintendent Walter White
—were looking for a pick-me-up. Meanwhile, the fledgling ACLU
was offering pro bono legal representation for any teacher accused of breaking Tennessee's recently passed Butler Act. Soon
as the boosters got a whiff, they pounced. The trial was bound to
be a big to-do somewhere, so why not Dayton? A willing defendant was found in John T. Scopes, a teacher and football coach at
Rhea County Central High School. "I wasn't sure if I had taught
evolution," Scopes wrote in his 1967 memoir. "Robinson and the
others apparently weren't concerned with this technicality. I had
expressed willingness to stand trial. That was enough."

Scopes was served with a warrant but never incarcerated. At the
end of his eight-day trial, Bryan and the prosecution had won. But
in a way, so had the defense—among other maneuvers, Darrow
had angled all along for a guilty verdict, planning to appeal the
ruling to the Tennessee Supreme Court. (He did; they upheld the
ruling, but dismissed Scopes's fine on a technicality.) Both sides
left town nursing a certain sense of bruised victory. The only clear
loser was Dayton.

The twenty-fifth Scopes Trial Play & Festival commenced on a Friday afternoon in mid-July of last year, the sky an unsettling October blue. Dayton had recently made regional headlines after an
anti-gun-control billboard featuring a photograph of Adolf Hitler
appeared on the outskirts of town, but I saw it nowhere along the
stretch of Highway 27 I took up from Chattanooga, just a daisy
chain of old houses and new gas stations, bait shops, gun stores, a
sign for Old Hicks Road. I was ushered into town by a gauntlet of
churches, the largest boasting a strobing LCD marquee and flut-
tering car-lot bunting.

As I approached downtown, I braced myself for the crowds. The
Butler Act was repealed in 1967, but teaching human origins in
Tennessee classrooms remains a touchy subject; in 2012, the state
passed legislation protecting instructors who taught "alternatives"
to accepted scientific theories such as evolution (and, increasingly,
climate change). So a festival celebrating organized religion's gov-
ernment-assisted triumph over science seemed like a sure draw.
But at first the John Deeres gathered on the courthouse's side

lawn for the festival's tractor show were the only indication I had arrived on the right day.

Around the front of the building—three stories and a clock tower, red brick—I found a smattering of vendors lining the sidewalk. Behind one table spread with chunky beaded jewelry, a poster declared GOD KNEW YOUR NAME BEFORE YOU WERE BORN. To one side of the courthouse steps, a vinyl banner said READ YOUR BIBLE. The chalkboard menu of Heavenly Dogs ("Our hotdogs are heavenly") advertised a Scopes Trial Special, two beef franks and a bag of chips for five bucks. On the lawn was an imposing bronze statue of William Jennings Bryan, who popularized the anti-evolution movement that inspired the Butler Act, was conscripted to the prosecution as more of a mascot than a legal mind, and died while napping in Dayton five days after the trial. Bryan College, the fundamentalist Christian school founded here in his memory, originated the festival in the late 1980s, but dropped sponsorship in 2000 to focus on projects illuminating the glorious whole of its namesake's life rather than his fraught final weeks. In 2013, a flier told me, sponsors included the local civic group Main Street Dayton, the Rhea County Historical and Genealogical Society, the Tennessee Arts Commission, and the local Holiday Inn Express, the blandness of which was somehow reassuring.

There were two plays on the festival docket, both staged in the original second-floor courtroom, and I bought tickets from a woman wearing earrings made from Barrel of Monkeys pieces. Friday's matinee, a one-act imagined conversation between Bryan and Darrow staged by a Wisconsin performance troupe, billed itself as historically accurate but showed its hand when its Bryan began pontificating on intelligent design theory, a strain of creationism not codified until the 1980s. I took it as a vote of no confidence that there appeared to be more people watching the rickety bluegrass band outside, where the temperature was sweltering even in the maple-tree shade. But later that night, the courtroom was filled for the festival's main event, the premiere of a new commission called *Front Page News*. With the shaky charm of community theater—poor enunciation buffered by enthusiasm—the play opened and closed with the town boosters mulling over their plot at Robinson's drugstore, the courtroom drama comprising its sticky middle. Between scenes, reporters in boater hats jostled to the front of the newel-post bar. One arched his eyebrow as he quoted *Baltimore Sun* reporter Frank Kent: "A lot has been written since the trial began about what the outside world thinks of Dayton. Nothing has been written about what Dayton thinks of the outside world. It would be interesting to know."

Afterward, the director, Dayton native Morgan Robbins, told me she isn't religious, "can't see any way other than evolution," and almost turned down the gig. But the script, commissioned from Johnson City, Tennessee, playwright Deborah DeGeorge Harbin, won her over. Assembling a largely male cast in a town of 7,200 turned out to be a gnarlier prospect. Only five actors showed up to Robbins's audition, but one was George Miller, portly with a booming drawl—her Bryan, she knew. Still, he needed direction, especially when it came to the trial's climax, when Darrow examines Bryan as an expert witness on the Bible: Did that whale really swallow Jonah? Where did Cain get his wife? How long ago was the Great Flood, exactly?

"I was trying to get him to sweat a little bit when he took the stand," Robbins said. "I was like, 'Can you get a little more nervous? Your religion is being questioned—can you have that in your body, that you're uncomfortable with this?' And he was like, 'I don't think Bryan would have been uncomfortable with this. Bryan's a hero. Do you realize how many people are pro-Bryan? I don't want to be met outside with pitchforks when I'm done.'"

But on opening night, Miller straddled the line between piety and bluster, his face morphing between flustered folds and satisfied grins. Across the aisle, festival veteran Rick Dye, the self-proclaimed "sole agnostic of the group," played Darrow with a wry, crackling energy. Scopes sat in the middle, silent, looking alternately bored and overwhelmed—an unlikely dream role for Bryan theater major Dakota McClellan. "I wanted to play him if I ever got the chance, because he stood up for what he believed in, and that's how I am," he told me later. "I'm on the other side, but as actors we have to get out of our comfort zones, do something different."

The play ended how it always ends: Scopes guilty, Bryan dead. After taking their bows the cast disappeared into a mob of handshakes and bouquets. Outside, no pitchforks—just the lingering scent of Scopes Trial Specials and the stammer of camera flashes as playgoers posed with the stately bronze Bryan in the dark.

*

Saturday morning, the festival's second and final day, I sardined into a first-floor courtroom where signs said PLEASE DO NOT SIT ON THE A/C UNITS OR APPROACH THE BENCH UNLESS DI-RECTED BY THE JUDGE OR PASS TOBACCO PRODUCTS TO THE INMATES. A procession of locals had gathered to talk about their connections to the trial, each taking turns on the witness stand. Ninety-five-year-old Beverly Wilson was the only one who had been alive during the trial, though she didn't remember much about 1925 except her parents arguing—not about theology or science but whether to name her baby brother "Evolution." Jeff Stewart, grandson of Tom Stewart, one of Scopes's prosecutors, confessed that his grandmother went to her grave feeling responsible for Bryan's death; the diabetic had eaten his penultimate meal at her dinner table, including an entire platterful of sliced, salted tomatoes. Pat Guffey, Rhea County's historian, piped up to reas-sure Stewart that Bryan's death probably had more to do with his final meal, taken at the Rogers family home, during which he con-sumed two whole chickens.

Most stories followed this pattern of ramble and swerve; what seemed remarkable was that they were being told at all. When Tom Davis, the Scopes festival's chairman, moved to Dayton for a newspaper job in 1976, he was surprised to find the trial's history languishing. "We just ought to forget that it ever happened," he was told. But over the next decade, the stranglehold loosened, and in the early 1990s, Davis was hired as a Bryan College public infor-mation officer and tasked with organizing the nascent festival—an effort, in part, to coax the town further out of its passive quagmire. "We have not lived down the stigma that came with *Inherit*, and I really do blame us for a lot of that," said Davis, who's now Rhea County's administrator of elections. "We haven't made a real good effort, first of all, to tell the story—just to simply say, 'Look folks, here's what really happened.' We have let the caricature of a nar-row-minded, terribly unthinking fundamentalist mentality ride."

Dayton's tuck-tailed silence has had certain aesthetic repercus-sions, too. Saturday afternoon I boarded a squat school bus for what amounted to a tour of former Scopes-related sites. In place of Robinson's drugstore, there's a postage-stamp park, a swath of asphalt, a cinder-block office building for rent. A different house stands in place of the one where Bryan died. Rhea County Cen-tral High School, where Scopes taught, closed in 1930 and soon reopened as the first location of what was then called William Jennings Bryan University. It was a handsome school, stout dark brick with a mansard roof. Now it's gone, too.

If Bryan hadn't died here and made way for the school, the town might have unraveled completely—the mines closed in 1930, just before the Great Depression rolled in. Dayton eventually came back as a manufacturing town, which it remains today, lately cultivating a sprawl of strip malls and chain stores. Bryan College hosts 1,300 students every year, or retains them—many are local and many more settle in Dayton after graduation to raise their own kids here. There are lakes and hills and woods all around, old coke ovens turned into nature preserves. Niche tourism is on the rise, so there's even a chance the old boosters' scheme might finally pay off. Coal isn't the best source of metaphors for sustainable industry, but some things do need time to sit under great pressure before they can be of use. The Scopes Trial Museum, housed in the courthouse basement, brings in a few thousand visitors each year; in 2013, a few hundred attended the festival. Not quite Disney World, but it's more appealing than blinkered silence. "We're beginning to think, 'OK, everybody along the Tennessee River has a lake and a fishing spot. Not everybody has the Scopes trial courthouse,'" Davis told me. "We don't have to agree that we are ignorant bumpkins just because somebody thinks that—we can show them who we really are and what we're all about if we can get them here."

Saturday evening, taking Highway 27 out of town, I finally saw the Hitler billboard. I pulled into an auto parts store parking lot and stared up. WAKE UP AMERICA, it demanded—the *I* a clip-art shotgun—above the Führer's sour mug. I snapped a photo, posted it online. Soon friends began administering their rueful hearts and stars and thumbs-ups, just like I knew they would. Back at home, I showed my parents the photo and we shook our heads and laughed, just like I knew we would. It was so easy, sinking my fist back into that old punching bag—I didn't even think about it at first, but then I did, and I felt bad. Because I thought I knew better. And I'd come to think maybe Dayton did, too.

PATRICIA MARX

A Tale of a Tub

FROM *The New Yorker*

CALL HIM ISHMAEL. Call *me* Insane. Some time ago, I had a hankering: Wouldn't it be lovely to take a break from the hurly-burly of landlubber life and the oppressive, never-ending connecting with everybody and everything? What could be more restorative than to voyage across the Atlantic aboard a merchant vessel, and, as Melville said, see the watery part of the world? How great would it be to have the time to read *Moby-Dick* instead of just talking about it? Oh, really? Now that I am about to board the *Rickmers Seoul* freighter (Chinese-built, German-managed, Marshall Islands–registered), being a passenger on a cargo ship seems a lot like being an inmate in a prison, except that on a ship you can't tunnel yourself out. Please try to imagine the privations I will brave for three weeks on this 632-foot-long, 30,000-ton hunk of steel as it galumphs across the sea from Philadelphia to Hamburg, with brief stops in Norfolk (Virginia) and Antwerp. There will be no Internet, no e-mail, no telephones, no organized entertainments, no Stewart or Colbert, no doctor, no anyone-I-know, and no Diet Coke. There will be 27 crew members, most from the Philippines, including a captain and a handful of officers from Romania, and, piled high on deck and deep in the holds, an assortment of cargo consignments from the world over that might include yachts, submarines, airplane fuselages, generators, turbines—everything, in short, that would elate a boy of five. There are no freighters that haul vats of sushi or Yonah Schimmel knishes, but somewhere out there is a vessel that carries La Mer face cream, and I hope the *Rickmers Seoul* collides with it.

*

After checking in at the Philadelphia Tioga Marine Terminal with a stevedore named Rhino, I teetered up a steep gangway to the main deck, where I was greeted by a broad-shouldered, doughy Romanian (age 32) with a handsome face and a clipboard. In his orange jumpsuit, he looked like a giant Teletubby. "I am Paul," he said. "I am chief man."

"What does the chief man do?" I asked.

"Chief *mate*," said the Romanian fellow (age 29) by his side, a Sean Penn look-alike with a ponytail and false front teeth, the consequence of tripping on the ship last year, not far from where we were standing. "Chief mate is first mate. I am third mate. I am Raul. You could say I am safety officer."

"Can I look at the cargo sometime?" I asked.

"You must get permission of captain, which is dangerous, of course," Raul said.

"The captain is dangerous, or the cargo?" I said. We laughed, and I still don't know the answer. Before disappearing into one of the many recesses on deck, Raul handed me a list of rules. ("It is absolutely forbidden to bring any weapons on board of the vessel"; "In Islamic countries possession of alcohol and/or sex magazines could lead to heavy fines"; "Do not drink excessively, neither on board nor ashore.") A couple of OSes (ordinary seamen, or entry-level mariners) showed up and wordlessly ushered me and my cumbersome luggage up four flights of stairs to my cabin. In the fluorescent-lit hallway, a merry Filipino AB (able-bodied seaman, one rung up from OS) passed us and enthusiastically informed me, "We are going to have a party with a band and we all dance to Beatles music!"

"OK," I said, because what do you say?

I was pretty sure I had an outfit for the occasion. Here is some of what I brought: a poncho for rain, a down vest for snow, dental putty in case a crown fell out, art supplies in the event that I acquired talent, a shortwave radio for lonely nights, and hair dye for the other nights. Other supplies included 1,000 packets of Splenda, 50 protein bars, an electric kettle, powdered lemonade, tuna fish (which I don't like but was inspired to throw in upon hearing that Mike Tyson subsisted on it in jail), hundreds of books loaded onto two Kindles (one might break—Noah knew what he was doing), a USB drive with more movies than are watchable in a year, a monocular that can serve as a telescope or a microscope, and a box of 100 monitor wipes for my laptop. I ignored the advice of friends who insisted that I could not last without whey powder, incense, Mace (recommended by two people), limes to prevent scurvy, and a shark cage.

Feeling as neglected as a stowed anchor, I surveyed my cabin. It was 14 feet square, including a small bathroom with a tiny shower stall. A college freshman would regard it as a plum room assignment, especially since the metal walls, which were varnished to look like beige oilcloth, seemed indestructible. In an alcove, there was a built-in queen-sized bed on which had been placed a small towel folded into the shape of a peacock. A madras curtain could be drawn to separate this berth from the sitting area (or to put on a marionette play). There was a wooden desk containing a multilingual Bible, a coffee table bolted to the blue floral carpet, an L-shaped sofa in a mauve-and-blue tweed, a nonfunctioning mini-refrigerator, and a clunky TV, which, along with CD and DVD players, was strapped to the credenza—for an understandable reason, but still, it didn't make one feel like family.

From my dirt-speckled porthole, I could see the water and a fire-hose box (location, location, location!). Hanging near a print of Renoir's *Dance at Le Moulin de la Galette* was a placard indicating that the signal for "Abandon ship" is a repeating sequence on the ship's horn of one short blast and one long blast. According to an accompanying chart, in the event of a disaster I was designated to be in Seat 24, next to the steward, in the free-fall boat. This is a neon-orange enclosed lifeboat that looks like a ride at a Soviet-era water park. Lodged on precipitately slanted tracks for easy launch into the water, the boat contains flares, rations, and tools for fishing, but no Netflix streaming.

As I took in the aroma of my room, which can best be described as a base of *l'eau de diesel* and cigarette smoke, with top notes of rotten nectarine and hamster (perhaps a result of Rule No. 4: always keep your windows closed in port and at sea), an alarm sounded— a loud, unbroken tone. "Attention, attention, attention!" a man's voice boomed over the PA. "Crew proceed to the Muster Station. Passengers remain in cabins." I dutifully stayed put for what seemed like hours and then, failing to hear any all-clear signal, ventured out to explore. My cabin was in the Accommodation, a seven-story, elevatorless box that juts up like a billboard from the main deck of the ship's stern. It was the color of provolone cheese, and pockmarked with rust. The Accommodation houses the living quarters, which include not only the cabins but the kitchen, two mess halls (one for the officers and passengers, the other for the crew), laundry facilities, a rec room (with a drum kit, some guitars, a dartboard, and two old Nautilus exercise machines), a passenger lounge containing a lot of Louis L'Amour paperbacks and scratched DVDs, an unfilled swimming pool not roomy enough to satisfy even a trout, and, next to it, a place called the Blue Bar. This pine-planked party room featured a Ping-Pong table, Christmas lights, and a curved wooden bar with sides of sea-foam-green leather. Perched at the very top of the Accommodation is the bridge, a large control room with panoramic windows from which the captain and the officers helm the ship (I hoped).

On a lower deck, there is a "hospital," a white room with a hospital bed and a bathroom worth getting sick for (porcelain tub). The hospital is stocked with everything from prednisone to tetanus immunoglobulin, from oil of cloves (for toothaches) to condoms (don't ask me). Morphine is locked in the captain's room. The second mate, who took a one-week first-aid course in the Philippines, serves as doctor. I didn't see any of this until later, however, because in the stairwell I ran into Raul. "No, you did not ever have to stay in your room, of course," he said with amusement. "Now we have Familiarization in five minutes with other passengers."

You (though not I) can skip Familiarization, unless you care to put on your life preserver, grab your immersion suit, and dash over to the Muster Station—the gathering site in case of emergency —to hear more about the free-fall boat. How about we advance the clock slightly and repair to the officers' dining room, where, on this inaugural night, my three fellow passengers and I became acquainted over a meal of, well, let's call it meat simulacrum camouflaged by mucilaginous faux gravy and accompanied by a hillock of rice and a diced vegetable that was to turn up frequently and which we passengers labeled kohlrabi because we knew it was nothing else. The dining room has green industrial flooring and fake wood paneling, like the other public rooms. Each of two round tables—one reserved for the officers and the other for us passengers—was set for six with Christmas-tree place mats. Intertable chat was generally restricted to this:

OFFICER (*entering*): *Bon appétit.*
US: Thank you.

"Bonne chance" would have been more apt, especially when the dish was Hawaiian Breakfast (pineapple slices and cheese and ham on toast), chile con carne laced with cornflakes (which we surreptitiously flushed down the toilet), or estofado de lengua (hint: this long piece of flesh is found in a cow's mouth). The grub, allegedly Romanian, was prepared by a sweet Filipino man with no culinary training and a fervent attachment to salt and his new deep fryer. The food budget, he told me, was about $7 per person per day.

I paid $2,010 for my passage. For $399 I could have booked a last-minute discounted luxury cruise from Copenhagen to Miami on the *Norwegian Star,* which has 10 restaurants, a shopping center, a video arcade, and an outdoor beer garden.

"You have to be slightly bonkers to go on a freighter," Andrew Neaums, an Anglican priest, one of my fellow travelers, told me at dinner. He was accompanied by his wife, Diana Neaums, a landscape architect. The couple, in their sixties, were wrapping up a two-month freighter expedition ("Wouldn't touch a commercial cruise!" Andrew said) from their home in Australia to their new one in England, where Andrew was to begin work in a country parish. Born in England but brought up in Rhodesia (now Zimbabwe), he is lanky and hale, tan and partly bald, and looks like someone who once won the America's Cup. She, originally from England, has a cordial, puckish face and an outstanding white bob. Roland Gueffroy, 58, a Swiss travel writer with tousled hair and a perpetual stubble, was en route from Zurich to Bern, but not the ho-hum, 80-mile westbound way. He headed east and, two and a half months later, was on the final arc of a circle around the globe that involved trains, boats, buses, and trucks. Roland is laconic, with a dry wit that lapsed only when he insisted on trotting out one of his poop-deck jokes. (A poop deck, from the Latin word *puppis,* meaning "stern," was originally intended as a buffer at the rear of a ship to protect it from waves, but today it refers to the aft deck above the main deck.)

We four were the first passengers who had crossed the ocean on the *Rickmers Seoul* in a year and a half. Until the early 1960s, hopping onboard a tramp steamer or hitching a ride on a banana boat was not unlike taking the Bolt bus to Boston. OK, it was not exactly like that, but the point is that it was not so unusual—and it was cheap. Jonnie Greene, a New York dance and opera critic, remembers crossing the Atlantic on a Dutch cargo ship for about $75 in 1952, when a first-class passage on an ocean liner could have cost about 10 times that. Writers used to favor freighters for the price and the solitude. Graham Greene, Somerset Maugham, and Paul Bowles were devotees. In 1958, airlines began to offer regular flights to Europe, which challenged the supremacy of ocean liners. To lure customers, many cruise lines upped their role as impresarios of *fun* (Baked Alaska parades! Miniature golf! Pastel Night!), promoting the cruise as the vacation rather than the way to get to the vacation. Unable to compete, freighter lines by and large got out of the house guest racket.

Why would shipping lines even consider taking passengers nowadays? At the Rickmers headquarters, in Hamburg, Sabina Pech, the general manager of corporate communications, told me, "It is a matter of entertainment for our crews." Perhaps. Although many crew members were gregarious, they were mainly busy with the operation of the ship. When keeping company with the crew, therefore, I often felt as if I'd shown up at the wrong office for Take Your Daughter to Work Day.

At dusk on the first evening, we peered over the rail of an upper deck, watching two tugboats, the *Reid McAllister* on our starboard and the *Teresa McAllister* on our port (such a pushy family!), maneuver us into takeoff position in Philadelphia harbor, readying us to motor down the Delaware River. We were on our way to Virginia to pick up six locomotives and, for me, a box of gingersnaps. From there we would mosey across the Atlantic at an average speed of 13 knots—14.96 miles an hour—reaching Antwerp in about 12 days. This is the pace that a not-so-schlumpy bicyclist can pedal on flat terra firma. If pirates were chasing us, the ship could hightail itself to safety at 20 or 21 knots, but that kind of velocity would tax the engine, squander fuel, and increase pollution.

I remarked to my companions that 115 years earlier, my paternal grandfather had made almost the reverse trip at approximately the same speed, except that he traveled steerage, from Antwerp to Philadelphia, whereas my cabin was next to the laundry room on the officers' floor (KILO OF WASHING POWDER INSIDE IS

NOT MEANING OF VERY CLEAN CLOTHES, a sign on the machine
stated). Also, my grandfather was seven years old and accompanied
by his mother and five brothers and sisters. His younger brother
Jack was absent because he'd fallen off the train from Romania
while the kids were horsing around on the platform between two
cars. ("Don't tell Mother," my grandfather instructed his siblings
after the accident.) My disaster? I electrocuted my hair dryer later
that night by neglecting to switch it from 120 volts to 220. Luckily,
my cabin was across the corridor from the electrician's.

Somewhere between Philadelphia and Norfolk, I visited the
bridge, where night and day you could bother whichever two crew
members were on duty monitoring the ship's vital signs. This involves various gauges and electronic charts and apparently can be
performed while kicking back in what looks like a dentist's chair.
(The ship runs largely on autopilot, except when it must be navi-
gated through narrow passageways.) It's like playing a very boring
video game, I said to Raul, who covers the eight-to-twelve shift,
both a.m. and p.m. "Yes, except you have to stay *away* from target," he responded. A woman's voice was heard fuzzily over the
radio. "All ships, all ships, all ships," she said, adding, "*Smeterljdrt
fifillsgfdter tere* twenty-four *oik.*" Raul translated: she was from the
U.S. military, and there was a warship conducting exercises in the
vicinity. (We never saw so much as a smoke signal on the horizon.)
Also on the bridge are several pairs of binoculars that afford one
superb views of nothing. The seven seas are, I discovered, as interesting to look at as an unplugged lava lamp. No fish in sight, no
birds overhead, not even the briny tang you associate with a beach.
The ocean becomes oceany only as you approach the shoreline,
where seaweed, plankton, and other things that appear to have
escaped from a Japanese restaurant attract larger marine creatures
and stink up the place as they decay.

At about six the next night, we pulled into Norfolk, the prow
of our high-rise ship aligned with a tiny sign on the quay that said
STOP SHIP HERE. Crew members tossed tag lines down to a team of
stevedores onshore, who lassoed turquoise ropes around four bol-
lards. There were anchors aboard, but they remained tucked away.
Now the loading began—and continued until the wee hours of the
morning. Transferring a locomotive from land to ship is as simple
as depositing luggage into the trunk of a car, except that instead
of oomph you need a few winches, cranes, and lashing slings. Your

job might be to attach the harnesses to the cargo, maneuver one of the four deck-mounted cranes from inside the operator's cab, or figure out where each piece of cargo should be placed so that the ship doesn't tip over. (This is the responsibility of the chief officer.) Or, if you are a crane instead of a person, you will work in tandem, knitting-needle style, with another crane, one of you hooking the harness at the front of the locomotive, the other handling the back end, and then both synchronously lifting your haul 50 feet in the air, swanning it over the open hatch, and lowering it into a capacious hold. The locomotives were stacked in two layers, three to a layer. "This is the most excitement we're going to have for a while," Roland said as we watched the goings-on from the deck. "After this, it's just another day and another day and another day."

Crew members on cargo ships like to say, "It's always Monday or Saturday," to describe their binary schedule. If you are a seaman, for most of the year you are schlepping cargo on and off the boat, painting the crane, derusting the crane, repainting the crane, overhauling the generator, and, after dinner (chicken and rice again), watching *Fast & Furious 6* on your laptop (unless you are Leo Rubio, a 35-year-old able-bodied seaman who has no laptop and thus passes the time at night by weaving rope hammocks). Finally, after a nine-month stint, you hang up your hard hat and go home and sit on your La-Z-Boy until you find another assignment.

"What's the appeal?" I asked some fellows gathered in the crew's mess, smoking cigarettes (nearly everyone smokes) during their morning break. Felito Balde, the bosun, a brawny 56-year-old from the Philippines, whose arm is tattooed with a clipper ship, said, "It's simple: money." For supervising the deck crew, he earns $2,000 a month, four times what he says he could make on land and enough to support his five children. (He has a BS in marine transportation and has been a sailor for 29 years.) According to Balde, an ordinary seaman makes $1,400 a month, an able-bodied seaman $1,760. "To give you an idea about how much this is," the ship's fitter, Valentino Ramos, told me, "a manager in a bank in the Philippines earns a thousand dollars a month, and he must pay room and board. A teller gets five hundred dollars." Nevertheless, this is not a career with high job satisfaction. OS Mark Ryan Miranda Bautista told me, "It's a hard life. You go away and your kid is a baby. Come home, he's working."

"They're not paying us for the work," OS Emerson Tibayan said. "They're paying us for the homesick."

At night, the rocking of the ship made me feel as if I were on a water bed, which I suppose I was—big-time. In my cabin, every hinge and lock rattled, and I could hear what sounded like the rhythmic wheeze of an emphysema sufferer. Some sleuthing revealed it to be the shower curtain sliding back and forth on its rod.

After a few days at sea, when the North Atlantic swells measured 4 to 5 meters, I had assorted lacerations, contusions, and boo-boos on my arms and legs from being hurled willy-nilly into things. My balancing abilities had been reduced to those of a drunk wearing reading glasses while descending a staircase during an earthquake. I spent a lot of time in my cabin, occasionally venturing into the cold and windy outdoors to pass time on the deck, which was furnished with four old plastic chairs roped to a pole. From there, if I was lucky, I could observe a handful of crewmen throwing scrap wood overboard. A chart posted in the bridge states what can and can't be dumped. If you are at least 12 nautical miles from shore, you can toss any sort of food waste except animal carcasses. You must refrain from dumping synthetic ropes, fishing gear, incinerator ashes, and clinkers.

I also sometimes strolled along the ship's flank, past bins of orange chains and green ratchets, spools of thick aqua nylon rope, large burlap sacks brimming with cast-iron thingamajigs, barrels of lubricant, nooks begging for stowaways, a miscellany of green-painted steel structures with names like Void Vent and Cargo Hose Drench Connection, and the four mighty cranes, the winches, and the other things you pray to Neptune don't fall on top of you, until I reached the bow, where—holy moly, could this be?—only a 42-inch-high rail separated me from Davy Jones's locker. I visited the bow of the ship regularly, even though Paul, the chief mate, told me that nobody goes there—"only the passengers, to recreate the scene in *Titanic*."

I haven't introduced you to our captain, Florin Copae, or is it Copae Florin? To be safe, I'll call him captain. Originally I'd been booked on a different voyage, but I jumped ship when my travel agent told me it would be helmed by a man classified "not passenger-friendly." The captain of the *Rickmers Seoul*, a 61-year-old Romanian with a beard, waxy silver hair, a missing tooth, and a convex midriff, is not passenger-unfriendly, but neither would anyone place him in the "palsy-walsy" category. He, like the other officers, usually sat alone at the dining-room table and ate with dispatch. When we were dockside, he wore a khaki shirt with epaulettes and matching shorts or a pressed orange jumpsuit embroidered with the word *Master*. He is all business—in Antwerp, where we were loading 260-ton friction winches, I said hello to him in the stairwell, to which he replied, curtly and justifiably, "I am fully busy."

On the open sea, he wore a T-shirt, shorts, socks, and sandals. From 7:30 in the morning until 1 or 2 a.m., he is bogged down with administrative concerns and e-mails (yes, he had an Internet connection and I did not), but, if you are lucky, you can catch him with time to talk, and here is what you might learn: that he'd had his heart set on being a captain since he was a little boy ("I was reading too many books about Magellan when the teacher asked us what we wanted to be") but didn't see the ocean until his twenties, when he was a student at the naval academy; that he rarely gets seasick but when he does he likes to eat greasy food; that he hasn't read a newspaper for five or six years ("fed up with politics"); that he is on the ship four months and then at home four months; that his wife is a doctor and his daughter is in medical school; and that, with regard to the few females in the business, he has "nothing against women captains and pilots but when the situation is getting hard they are getting lost."

Does he like his job? "I wouldn't do it if I was starting now. Now it's a dog life. I am always doing accounting and paperwork." The combination of the Internet and scads of new environmental regulations, such as a rule that requires vessels to change from high-sulfur fuel to low-sulfur fuel when they are within certain distances of U.S. shores, has made it dreary work. What cheers up the captain? Plants. When we reached Hamburg, a friend delivered a cutting from the captain's garden in Romania, along with a package of soil, so that he could transfer his Red Lucky magnolia to a larger pot.

On Day 5—or was it Day 500?—I found, tucked in a niche, four life-sized wooden dummies standing at attention and looking like G.I. Joes, or perhaps Safety Patrol Kens. They wore orange nylon vests over blue down jackets and had handcrafted Elmer Fuddish toy shotguns tied diagonally across their chests. The faces of these inaction figures, partly obscured by cinched hoods and ski caps, were drawn on with Magic Marker, except for the noses, which were plywood wedges nailed on by someone who clearly was heavily influenced by cubism.

Is this the juncture at which our story takes a kinky turn? No. Pirates, please don't read this: when the *Rickmers Seoul* traverses treacherous zones, such as the Gulf of Aden, the Strait of Malacca, or the Indian Ocean, the mannequins are propped up on the bow like scarecrows. In the event that the bad guys are not stupid enough to fall for this ruse and try to climb aboard, they might be thwarted by the razor wire and electric fencing that surround the ship, not to mention crew members spraying them with fire hoses. If these defenses fail, the plan is for everyone but the captain and one able-bodied seaman to hide out in the Citadel, a panic room in the nether region of the vessel that contains a couple of mattresses, two benches, a primitive toilet, and rations. Passengers need not worry about this contingency, because since 2011 they have not been allowed on any Rickmers ships sailing between Genoa and Singapore. This ban was put in place because certain travelers, according to Cruise People, an agency specializing in sea travel, "ignored officers' instructions to stay off the decks in areas where pirates are active." Partly because so many vessels now carry armed security guards when traversing treacherous waters, the worldwide incidence of pirate attacks is on the decrease (439 in 2011; 297 in 2012; 264 in 2013, which does not include the Tom Hanks movie). Benjie Monana, the messman, told me that the previous ship he was on was fired upon in the Gulf of Aden by pirates in three small boats, satellites of a mother ship. "The captain was going crazy," Monana said, "so the chief mate took over. We escaped, but they found a few bullets on the bridge."

Before long—I mean, after long—it was Saturday night. Everyone not on duty was whooping it up in the Blue Bar. The crew had been preparing for the bash all afternoon. Jell-O molds were jelled, sheet cakes baked, fruit cup dumped into a punch bowl of condensed milk to make a dessert that looked like a polluted pond, Romanian sausage concocted according to a special recipe from the captain, and chicken legs grilled over a fire while, nearby, a pig spent hours being turned on a spit as if it were taking a Pilates class. Throughout the night, the Seoul Mate band—second officer on drums, AB on lead guitar, and bosun playing rhythm guitar and singing—performed "I Saw Her Standing There," "Yellow Submarine," and "Jamaica Farewell," among other songs. The captain, sitting well apart from the crew, drank and smoked and smiled at the musicians as if he were a father at his child's recital. The passengers occasionally danced, one of them because she had given her word that she would.

A week later, we were in Antwerp, where I said hello to some more steel products and goodbye to the Neaums and Roland Gueffroy. Three days after that, I disembarked in Hamburg. This is the part where I'm supposed to tell you that, after an inauspicious beginning to my aqueous venture, ultimately I became one with the universe and also finished *Moby-Dick* (don't tell me how it ends). Unfortunately, when there is very little to do in a day —and you have no Wikipedia—you get very little done. When I set foot on land again, I was reminded of Robert Louis Stevenson's line. "Old and young," he wrote, "we are all on our last cruise." I couldn't have said it better.

TIM NEVILLE

The Great Pleasure Project

FROM *Ski Magazine*

To GET TO the world's most exotic ski resort you must first get
to Pyongyang, the capital of North Korea, where, after the People's Army checks your papers and records your smartphone's se-
rial number, you will end up at the Yanggakdo, one of perhaps
eight hotels in this city of 2.5 million people where foreigners are
allowed to stay. The hotel is grayish blue and lords over a horn-
shaped island. It has 47 floors and 1,000 outdated rooms. About
30 of those rooms are occupied today.

It is mid-February, the year Juche 103. The frozen Taedong
River that flows around the hotel is corpse-gray, stiff and riddled
with abandoned ice-fishing holes that look like bullet wounds. Few
lights burn anywhere, only a billboard flickering in the distance
with images of the country's dictator, Kim Jong-un. He's the reason
I'm here.

But first, breakfast. The elevator snaps shut with crushing authority. It's 38 floors down from my room to Restaurant 1, which
sits next to Restaurant 2, which sits next to a glass-walled gift shop
that sells severed baby bear paws to cure indigestion.

At Floor 35 the doors jerk open. The hallway is a coal mine. No
one is there.

"Hello?" I call. No reply.

The same happens again four floors later, and again three floors
after that. It happens at Floor 25 and Floor 23 and Floor 19. Each
time the scene is spookier than the last. No lights. No people. Only
Floor 5 doesn't open. This is because there is no button for Floor

5, and the stairwells at Floors 4 and 6 are barricaded and locked. Floor 5, I'll later learn, holds all the bugging devices.

There isn't so much eavesdropping to do. Some say fewer than 2,500 Americans have visited the country since the Korean War ended in 1953, although official numbers are impossible to come by. Up until 2010 the regime refused to allow its bloodiest enemy into the country at all save for brief visits to Pyongyang's summer mass games, a highly choreographed display of gymnastics and dances designed to demonstrate the power of the collective over the individual. Visa rules have relaxed since then, but foolish Westerners still get detained from time to time. My friend Dan Patitucci and I are among fewer than a handful of American civilians ever to witness the world's bleakest country in its bleakest month, and our reason is absurd: to be among the first people ever to ski North Korea's first, best, newest, and only luxury ski resort.

Dan and I are spending five nights in and around Pyongyang first to get a feel for the country. When we arrive the entire nation is celebrating what would have been the seventy-third birthday of Kim Jong-il with dances, synchronized-swimming shows, and garish exhibitions of giant genetically engineered begonias called kimjongilias. We must do as we're told. We bow before statues in unison. We may not take pictures of anything "dirty" or "poor" but "only beautiful, please." We may not even leave the Yanggakdo without a minder. Make that two minders—one to watch us and another to watch the watcher.

Back in the elevator the doors crash open into darkness again. This time the air rushes out as a herd of shriveled people rushes in. They are elderly Koreans, barely 4 feet high, their bodies gnarled by a lifetime of hunger, disease, and deprivation. I have no idea who they are or why they are here. They move in such a tight, protective pack that their heads bash together like livestock in a chute. Their eyes—Jesus. I can't stop looking at their eyes. They are gray and so gooey they look like they could drip out of their skulls and stain the floor.

A foreigner is not supposed to see this. This is a glitch in the Matrix that reveals the colossal failures happening inside North Korea. When we reach the lobby everyone scurries out. The bellhop looks at them, then at us. He sees our cameras and reports us to a guide.

"You took photos," the guide says.

"No, we didn't."

"Hmm," he says suspiciously, but he lets us go.

Terrible things can happen if you don't play the game that every North Korean must play. You feign reverence and you swallow lies. You fold your newspaper gingerly to leave no creases on Kim Jong-un's face. Mar his visage with a coffee ring and off to the gulag you go. The worst part is how you must be thankful for this misery. "We owe everything to our glorious leaders," a North Korean flight attendant named Miss Rhee told me with zero emotion. "They love us and we love them."

The first leader, regime founder Kim Il-sung, ruled the Democratic People's Republic of Korea for 50 years after the Korean War killed at least 2 million people and left the peninsula divided into a Communist north and a capitalist south. The oldest of his four legitimate sons, Kim Jong-il, came next, in 1994. He immortalized his father by anointing him the country's Eternal President and resetting the calendar to mark the years since Kim Il-sung's birth and his adherence to *juche*, a belief in Korean self-reliance from the rest of the world.

Psychologists working in conjunction with the Society for Terrorism Research would later show Kim Jong-il to be more sadistic than Saddam Hussein and Hitler. The "Highest Incarnation of the Revolutionary Comradely Love," as he was sometimes called, kidnapped foreign movie stars and spent billions on a nuclear bomb while executing peasants for distributing rice during a famine. He died in a plush train car in 2011 and his youngest son, Kim Jong-un, took over. The boy-faced dictator was such a mystery to intelligence agencies that no one was even sure of his age. Was he 29? 30? 31? What was certain was that the oldest son and heir apparent, Kim Jong-nam, had forever fouled his chances of furthering the dynasty after Japanese authorities arrested him in 2001 for trying to slip into their country on a fake passport. It was no cloak-and-dagger mission. He was on his way to Disneyland.

"These guys have never had to go around kissing babies," says Simon Cockerell, manager of Beijing-based Koryo Tours, who has led at least 140 trips into North Korea since 1993. "They almost never speak. You never see them arriving or leaving or doing anything humans do."

This divinelike mystique allows the Kims to be experts on

everything. When he wasn't murdering his rivals, Kim Il-sung supposedly penned operas with titles like *Sea of Blood*. Kim Jong-il had a "profound knowledge of poultry," shot 11 holes in one on his first game of golf, and apparently never pooed. Kim Jong-un, it turns out, is a pretty great skier.

That last bit might actually be true. Unknown to virtually everyone inside North Korea, Kim Jong-un attended private school in Bern, Switzerland, where he almost certainly went skiing. After all, that entire country takes off for a week every winter to pursue the sport, and the Alps are within easy reach of town. So far his time in power has been characterized in part by the creation of a raft of new leisure facilities. You can now slide around at a water park in Pyongyang, watch dolphins at a dolphinarium, or ride roller coasters at a place called the People's Pleasure Ground.

"Since he's come into power there are so many changes happening," says Amanda Carr, a British guide who has made at least 44 trips to North Korea. "Every year more places are opening up."

A few weeks before my visit, Kim Jong-un unveiled his greatest pleasure project yet: the $100 million Masik Ryong Ski Resort. Located in the Ryongjo Workers' District of Kangwon Province, some 110 miles east of Pyongyang, the resort opened on New Year's Day 2014 with 10 north-facing runs, 6 lifts, and 2,300 vertical feet of cold northeast Asian powder. The army's shock brigades had built it all in just 18 months. Bands played, people cheered. Even Kim Jong-un's good pal Dennis Rodman was on hand, reportedly drunk and roaring around on a Ski-Doo. Then the portly dictator himself donned a dashing black hat and spent a few hours skiing with such perfect poise that he didn't even need his poles. That was the rumor anyway, because no one actually saw it.

Most remarkable of all, Americans could ski there, too. All I had to do was sign up with a North Korean–approved tour company and buy medical evacuation insurance. "I really have to insist that you get it," Rich Beal, a polite Koryo Tours manager told me when we met in China. "The treatment for a compound fracture there is amputation."

Our five days of context in and around Pyongyang creep by. Speakers blast propaganda from rooftops. Bright red signs at intersections scream slogans like DEFENDING THE LEADER AT THE COST

OF OUR LIFE IS OUR BEST LIFE! We go bowling as if nothing is wrong and visit a war museum so full of misinformation that even the East Germans ridiculed it in a 1961 memo. One day we put on ties and bow before the waxy remains of Kim Jong-il, who lies in a glass box like Lenin with his big, glorious head on a white bolster pillow. An Australian in another group gets detained for trying to distribute Christianity pamphlets, a crime against the state.

At last the skiing can begin. It's a four-hour trip to Masik Ryong on roads long and straight enough to land military jets because military jets do land on them. The landscape is severe, indifferent, beautiful: sharp hills, frosty streams, and flat, concrete town houses with rows of doors that look like harmonica chambers. We pass a truck that runs on wood and a soldier on a bike with a rifle bouncing in a handlebar basket. If North Korea were *The Hunger Games*, Pyongyang would be the Capitol: a place reserved for the elite to enjoy good food, nice clothes, and electricity. Out in the districts, the people have nothing.

Dark falls and even the stars seem too spooked to shine. Then, suddenly, Masik: the resort burns away the night like an atomic blast. Lights blaze from the top of two trapezoidal hotels, dubbed Hotel 1 and Hotel 2. Before we enter, a guard checks everyone's permits. Inside, the lobbies twinkle with recessed spotlights and flat-screen monitors. The woodwork is elegant. The tiles sparkle under our heels. Kim Jong-un has good taste. Even the urinals have that new-urinal smell.

The whole thing is sickening, really. A United Nations report lists a prison camp not so far away, a place called Kyohwaso No. 8, where escapees say they expected to die. You can't see it but you know it's there. The cognitive dissonance is so loud I make a deal with myself: see Masik for what it is, not whose it is.

The next morning a light snow falls and a dozen men with witch's brooms line up in ranks to clear the pathways and parking lots, all of which are empty. I wander downstairs to a breakfast of pickled fern and then to the gear-rental room beneath Hotel 2. Unlike South Korea, which will host the Winter Games in 2018, North Korea has virtually no ski culture at all. I expect no line.

The room is packed. Scores of Koreans try on rental ski suits, rental gloves, and rental helmets and jockey for new rental skis and Italian-made ski boots. I have no idea how they can afford any of this, but their excitement is unmistakable. They're laughing, speaking loudly, and brimming with the same anticipation I feel every season. Why shouldn't they have a little fiscally senseless joy?

Outside, 20 or so ski instructors in fluorescent orange and yellow uniforms line up for calisthenics. I get the feeling they're military men now assigned to Masik. Behind them, a giant digital monitor blasts tinny folk tunes to images of swaying flowers, crashing waves, and the occasional missile launch.

"Hoan-young-ham-ni-da!" squawks an electronic voice, "Welcome!" in formal Korean, as Dan and I scan our passes and slip through the first lift gate. The reality of the place soon hits again.

On opening day, Kim Jong-un rode this lift without his skis. All of the lifts are slow and rickety. The footrests hit the ground in spots and you can feel the whole cable shudder. The towers are really far apart, like the recipe called for 12 but only 8 arrived. As we ascend I look down: two workers are tightening some tower bolts with a really big wrench.

It takes 43 minutes and 3 rides to reach the summit of 4,468-foot Taehwa Peak, but we get there in one piece. Two lift attendants in fuzzy white hats bow and spring into action. There is no exit slope to whisk you away—just a flat landing—so Lift Attendant 1 seizes the chair from behind while Lift Attendant 2 helps me shuffle out of the way without getting bulldozed. Lift Attendant 3, the one with a finger on the emergency shutoff switch, doesn't exist.

"Well, let's go ski North Korea," Dan says, and we push off down the slope.

After five days of constant anxiety, we are back in a familiar world of snow and gravity. The storm builds and so does a sense of camaraderie. A skier from Pyongyang poses for a picture with me. Another shakes my hand. Our guides can't ski and have let us roam —alone.

Masik's two groomers made only one pass up the middle of Slopes 1 through 9, all of which fall back to the base, leaving 30-foot-wide sideburns of untracked snow on each side of the pistes. Kim Jong-il could allegedly control the weather with his mind, but I doubt conditions were ever this good for his son. We have virgin powder all day long.

Dan and I race down Slopes 7, 8, and 9. They feel like intermediate runs but the signs don't say. The birch trees to either side are as tight as toothpicks in a shot glass, so we stick to the runs. I imagine Kim Jong-un doing lonely giant-slalom turns with the angulation of Ted Ligety. We bounce past a midmountain pavilion where he probably did some tricks just as his GoPro failed. We settle for views of the brown valleys below, then leapfrog each other, high-fiving our powder eights.

Most of the North Koreans here have never been on skis before. They stick to the bunny hill below but attack it with gusto. Some crash into an orange safety fence. Others can only go right. One lady steams toward a table-filled patio, then diverts to port with the turning radius of a cargo ship.

"I told you you would see lots of local people here," says a guide taking lessons. "This is very new for us."

So new, in fact, that a lot of people don't even bother with skis. Instead they cuddle up and ride the lifts around and around, up and down, thrilled just to be there. Each time our paths cross they wave and smile as if to confirm that this is no dream. These are not the brainwashed marcher-bots we tend to envision, but lovers, maybe my wife and me, content to snuggle on a dawdling loop where "only beautiful, please" plays on repeat.

That evening I go to a karaoke bar in Hotel 1 with a few of the Westerners. The place is empty, just two Korean guys shucking a dried mackerel for a snack. The two barmaids wear maroon skirts and vests. One of them hands me a full bottle of soju, a rice spirit. The other flicks on some disco lights and together they sing sassy duets for hours to a crowd of five. They seem a bit over-enthusiastic. Maybe this is the greatest job ever. Maybe they're being watched.

Our last day dawns cold and clear, but the deal with myself collapses. I feel guilty for enjoying a place where the construction costs would have fed the hungry for years and there's still this air of suspicion that lingers everywhere we go. The instructors ignore me when I ask to warm up with them. Dan and I do runs on Slopes 4 and 5, where the crystals hiss and ricochet off my knees, but the long rides up are becoming unpleasant. There's a camera in the trees.

By the time we leave I still have no idea who in North Korea can really ski here. Our guides say anyone, but I'm skeptical. Lift tickets cost roughly $40 a day. A good job pays $10 a month. You need police permission just to leave your town, and who has any free time anyway? Fridays are manual-labor days. Saturdays are time to study ideological texts. Sundays could work—those are personal-betterment days—but unless you're in good standing with the regime you're probably too busy surviving.

Things are slowly changing, though. You see more cell phones, more cars, more people with watches. Some Koreans may ski for free with their work units. Ski clubs could build the ranks. We in the West can't imagine that people in a place ruled by such darkness and death could ever find joy. But sometimes they do.

It is dark again by the time we pull into Pyongyang for one last night at the Yanggakdo. The city is quiet; we roll down Youth Street, but it is empty. There's a battered streetcar parked on the rails ahead, motionless and dark in the middle of a wide, carless road. When the minibus's lights brush across its windows I see dozens of people pressed against the foggy glass. They don't look sick. They don't look scared. They're just waiting for the lights to come on.

A Doubter in the Holy Land

FROM *The New York Times Magazine*

A FRIEND AND I were beginning that strange dance of making plans to make plans when I mentioned that I'd be traveling to Jerusalem soon. "We should get together right away," he joked, "before you come down with Messiah syndrome." It was the kind of precision-targeted crack only an old friend can manage. I can't remember whether I laughed or winced first.

When I was young, my mother had a feverish conversion and started a church in our living room. I'd always been a tiny bit anxious that I might one day follow suit, hear the calling myself, start roaming the streets, preaching salvation. A committed but fearful agnostic, I'd never intended to tempt fate by visiting the Holy Land. But I was going to the Jerusalem Book Fair, and my husband, Max, who grew up in the comparatively staid Eastern Orthodox tradition, was joining me.

When we arrived, at dusk, the sky was a pale, glowing blue—eerily biblical, which, I had to keep reminding myself, made sense. As we sped into the city, past rocky white hills and almond trees bursting with blooms, we were overwhelmed by incongruous feelings of intense foreignness and intimate familiarity. This was a landscape we knew, from Sunday-school lessons and iconography and bad Old Testament movies, and a place we did not know at all.

Even the mundane became extraordinary. The almonds were soft and sweet, delicate as fruit. When I caught an olive as it fell from a tree and crushed it between my fingers, it stained my skin a brilliant red I couldn't scrub away.

At the Church of the Holy Sepulchre, priests of different sects

tried to pray more loudly than one another. The chambers reverberated with their chanting. As pilgrims knelt to kiss Christ's tomb,
we climbed a staircase to the area said to be Calvary, site of the
Crucifixion. It was not particularly hill-like, that dark and crowded
little platform, and when the woman next to me cried, I felt as if I
were intruding on a wake for someone I didn't know.

Back on the street, the doors to a nearby mosque were tightly
guarded, preventing even a peek to us congregating infidels. We
walked on to the Western Wall, where I stopped, spellbound, despite that same feeling of separateness from someone else's passion. Max pointed out that the men had about three times more
room than the women to pray. We decided against writing prayers
to tuck into the cracks and left the Old City on foot. Above us roil-
ing tufts of gray clouds swept across the pallid sky, out over the wall
of separation.

Inside the gates of the Temple Mount, not far from the gleam-
ing golden Dome of the Rock, stood a group of column capitals,
some chiseled in intricate florals, some in delicate curlicues, others in a sturdy basket weave, all jumbled together, like rubble, at
the mercy of the weather. Throughout the city, walls rested on
other, older walls, often of disputed provenance. Among these ruins of failed occupiers and kings, I kept thinking of the stories of
my childhood: Moses leading the Israelites out of Egypt, Esther
supplicating herself before the Persian king, Daniel interpreting
the dreams of Babylon's Nebuchadnezzar, the Roman prefect Pon-
tius Pilate declaring Jesus the king of the Jews and then washing
his hands of the matter. At times the past seemed so immediate, I
could hardly breathe.

On our last day, we visited the Garden of Gethsemane. The
gnarled olive trees, ghostly in their cragginess, are said to date to
Jesus's time. It was in this place, according to the Gospels, that he
passed his last night praying, willing to die because he believed
that in doing so he could redeem the sins of the world. As we
looked out from that tiny plot of land, contemplating the divisions
of modern Jerusalem, the afterlife (by which I mean the legacy) of
this man seemed both enormous and tenuous.

I'd been warned that visiting the Holy Land intensifies your
deepest religious beliefs. That was unexpectedly true for even this
ardent doubter. Seeing the remains of all the regimes and the

people who had tried to infuse their faiths and customs and architecture into the place and then receded across the millennia, I couldn't understand how anyone could feel sure of any belief, any way of being, in a place that is so constantly shifting. Like Jerusalem, I remained my own stubbornly uncertain self.

My Timbuktu

FROM *The Georgia Review*

I WAS IN elementary school when my dad—a frustrated world traveler—showed me a picture of the Djenné mosque in Mali, the largest mud-brick building in the world. I remember looking at the photograph, running my fingers along the mosque's mud outlines, and asking my father when we could go visit this "church." He smiled, shook his head, and told me it was very unlikely we would ever see it. "You have to make it first to Timbuktu," he said, "and that, my girl, is the end of the world." My father also told me that a long time ago lots of wise, tenderhearted men had lived in this uttermost-end-of-the-earth place, and that's why it was known as the City of 333 Saints. I couldn't take my eyes off the picture. Seeing my fascination with the place, my father added that the people of Timbuktu were blue. Blue.

I grew up thinking of Timbuktu as a mythical place, another legendary Atlantis, until a few years ago when I heard on the radio about Mali's Festival in the Desert, a Woodstock-style concert deemed the most remote music festival in the world. Having inherited from my father an unquenchable thirst for travel, I immediately started to make inquiries. As soon as I found out that the concert, which had showcased African and non-African musicians since 2001, was only 45 miles west of Timbuktu, I made up my mind.

In 2006, my husband and I traveled to the Malian Sahara to attend the sixth edition of the Festival in the Desert near Essakane, the poorest village in a country considered one of the poorest in western Africa. We went for the same reason some mountaineers say they climb Mount Everest, and because three years earlier the Malian singer Ali Farka Touré had shared the stage with Robert Plant and Tinariwen—a band of desert nomads who in 1991 had traded in their rifles for electric guitars. We wanted to experience that medley of distant cultures firsthand. We threw into the mix a bit of musical adventurism/sangfroid/derring-do—all of which we wanted to put to the test—sprinkled our plans with a personal lifelong dream to see Timbuktu, added historical accounts of the Caravan of White Gold—so called because salt from the remote Taoudenni mines, 400 miles north of Timbuktu, was once literally worth its weight in gold—and we were ready to go.

We knew very little about Mali, and the fact that every time we mentioned our impending trip to friends they mistook our destination for Bali didn't help. All we knew was that the area where we were about to camp out for a few days was a godforsaken land known for harboring "desert bandoleers" in the past and terrorists in the present, and for being home to the Tuareg, the nomadic people whose indigo-dyed skin had fueled my imagination with fantastic images for decades. Little did we know as we prepared for our trip that our faces and hands would also be dyed blue from the *cheche*—the several yards of muslin cloth the Tuareg wear around their heads and faces. We were, in fact, about to become temporary members of the clan of the Blue People of the Desert.

We left Florida for Mali—a long and logistically challenging trip through France and Algeria—and more than 24 hours later we were met at Mopti airport by Mahmoud, our tour operator, a handsome Tuareg man with a killer smile and a pink turban. He introduced us to the rest of the travelers under his care, a group that was part of a small convoy of 500 tourists from all over the world attending the festival. Then came the real trip. First from Mopti to Timbuktu—a trek that required an unexpected overnight on the banks of the Niger River after we missed our ferry to traverse it—and later, a jeep ride from Timbuktu to the festival site in the desert near Essakane—a trip fraught with flat tires, malfunctioning brakes, and sandstorms.

The site of the concert appeared on the horizon behind a cloud of haze, like a mirage. The drivers parked the caravan of 4x4s atop the highest dune around, from where we could take in the amazing feat of ingenuity before our eyes. The concert was in the middle of nowhere. There were no sources of electricity or running water nearby, either before or after the concert. The generators, the portable toilets, and the personal allocation of bottled water and goat mutton were short-lived luxuries meant to last only for the duration of the festival. I found it hard not to be awestruck and humbled by the whole endeavor: a group of rugged Tuareg with few resources and a limited budget had planned and were about to run a multicultural festival without sponsors, vendors, or the sale of alcohol.

The high dune provided an excellent vantage point from which Mahmoud proceeded to allot the tents already pitched down below. Walking in the Sahara desert is a treacherous affair. Its powdery sand and the constantly shape-changing peach-colored dunes give the place a dreamlike air . . . until you try to walk on it. Taking a step is hard work. You sink no matter how fast or how slowly you walk. And you sink fast. The soft sand swallows your feet, your ankles, your calves. It's like quicksand without the danger of drowning. My husband and I had to lean on each other as we laboriously made our way from our 4x4 to the tent. Exhausted from the journey, the sun, and the sand, we collapsed on our thin twin mattresses, the only items inside the tent.

We woke up to the voice of a little boy shouting in French, "The Tuareg are coming!" A full moon was already out and an orange dusk enveloped the desert when my husband and I took another short but arduous walk from our primitive tent site to the amphitheater, a flat valley of soft sand surrounded by sloping dunes.

The amphitheater filled up as Malians interspersed with Western faces. At first we couldn't see anything other than the cheering crowd of tourists and locals scattered across the open desert and a few Tuareg working the lights and sound system powered by electrical generators. Then I felt their presence before I could see them. The sand trembled under my feet and the dunes reverberated and changed form as the Tuareg approached. It was like the millions of wildebeest I had seen migrate across the Maasai Mara in Kenya. Like the sound of a cavalry charge. Like thunder. Then, in the distance, a cloud of dust billowed in a manmade dust devil. *The Tuareg are coming.* They arrived on the backs of camels running at full speed, the beasts' four feet coming off the ground simultaneously, making them look as though they were flying, pushing their way toward the arena in front of the stage. *The Tuareg are coming.* They had their faces and heads wrapped in dark indigo *cheche;* they rode barefoot, their legs wrapped around the colorful wooden pommels of their saddles. They raced each other—wielding their swords in the air, waving their daggers, shouting their Tamasheq war calls. They were terrifying and regal and handsome. Some of them dismounted their camels and sat on the sand; a few others stayed atop their animals and gathered to one side of the stage in an improvised camel-parking spot. We sat on the Saharan sand, among the Tuareg and under a savage sky bursting with stars. We tapped and cheered and clapped along with the music delivered by each of the artists. Their bluesy music filtered up into the night. I was high at the concert. High on Mali, on desert, on music.

Khaira Arby, Timbuktu's reigning queen of Malian soul, sang. It was easy to feel small where everything seemed bigger: the vastness of the desert, the infinity of that starry firmament, the stone-cold-sober crowd of Tuareg revelers, all under the spell of Khaira's supernatural, high-pitched voice. Maybe it was the fact that there were no seats and the audience was sitting on the bare sand; maybe it was the constant physical contact with the Tuareg around me, but by the time the concert was in full swing, I was filled with a borrowed, if not clichéd, sense of belonging like no other. We hummed to the same tunes, we exchanged pleasantries in French, we applauded enthusiastically the performers we liked best and we shouted *encore, encore* in unison. By midnight, a few of the revelers started to doze off. Sitting on the sand, they leaned on each other as the night wore on; a few propped their heads on a neighbor's shoulders, some were collapsed on one another's laps. After the closing act, the valley around the stage was dotted with Tuareg men sleeping in the fetal position, with nothing above them but yards of *cheche* shining under the full moon.

Six years later, in 2012, another loud rumble would be heard in northern Mali, not from a group of enthusiastic Tuareg marking the beginning of the Festival in the Desert, but from the Islamic Mujahideen, an al-Qaeda offshoot determined to impose a strict sharia law. My heart sank as CNN aired footage of these Islamists, armed with pickaxes and hoes, demolishing the cultural heritage of the fabled city so dear to my heart. I had to remind myself that these machine gun–wielding fighters were zealots, unlike the gentle Malians I had met in 2006 who were artists using music as their way to extricate themselves from their region's history of rebellion, hunger, isolation, and underdevelopment. The jihadists marched into small villages first, and later into bigger towns like Timbuktu. From my own living room I followed the destruction of Mali on TV: images of robed and turbaned men destroying half of Timbuktu's legendary Sufi mausoleums and shrines, along with sections of the town's grand mosques, Sidi Yahya, Djingareyber, and Sankore. I heard news broadcasters and friends alike use the words *Islamist, al-Qaeda,* and *Tuareg* interchangeably, committing a gross semantic error that tormented me beyond words.

By the time I opened my eyes the morning after the festival's opening, he was already inside my tent. I was still giddy from the concert. He sat on the floor cross-legged and hummed a high-pitched tune under his breath. For a moment I couldn't decide whether I was still asleep, though the Sahara sun was already out and hitting the sand hard, sending a blinding light pouring into the tent.

My husband wasn't lying next to me; he must have gone looking for water so we could brush our teeth. I pulled the sleeping bag up to my chin and stared at the man as he caressed the leather handle of his *tellak*—the short dagger Tuareg men keep in a sheath attached to the left forearm. Now I was fully awake.

"Bonjour, mon amie," he said, smiling. He had dark lips, teeth white like the flesh of a coconut, a prominent nose, and sad squinty eyes. I looked at the dagger, at this turbaned man sitting a mere foot from my mattress, back at the dagger, and at the cloth bag he carried across his chest. His brown fingers were stained with hues of blue dye. I waited for my fight-or-flight instinct to kick in, while outside the desert wind picked up a bit and a camel—presumably this man's—made whistling noises by grinding its teeth. Someone from another tent played traditional music.

"Ahh, Salif Keïta," the man said, referring to the albino singer known as "the Golden Voice of Africa." And I'll never know if it was the music, his camel fussing outside, or the cool January wind that soothed me, but I curled up inside my bag and watched him rock his head softly to the beats of Salif Keïta's song as he absentmindedly emptied the contents of his bag on a piece of cloth over the sand and proceeded to polish an array of Tuareg jewelry as if my tent were his workshop.

I dozed off.

The chaos that follows the coup d'état in Mali puts this war-ravaged country on the map. Everyone with a TV knows now where Mali is, including my Afrikaner neighbor who stops by for coffee and finds me reminiscing about my time there. I have pictures, notes, maps, routes, and a few pieces of Tuareg jewelry spread over my dining table. She finds me trying to reconcile the splendor of this African country before my eyes with the pictures of destruction diffused on the news. My neighbor can't understand why Mali is so dear to me. I tell her about the demolished historic buildings and the loss of ancient manuscripts. She gives me a sideways look that I can't decipher. So I tell her about the current human suffering in Mali and how much I fear for the fate of those Tuareg whose lives we shared in 2006.

I tell her about Oosman, a little boy who pestered us in Mopti as soon as we arrived in Mali until we agreed to use him as a guide. The three of us took a taxi from outside our modest hostel and drove downtown. Minutes into our ride, after my asking Oosman in rudimentary French what this or that building was, it became apparent that he had never been there before and was simply trying to make some money. We decided to rely on our Lonely Planet book, and instead of using Oosman as a guide we saw the trip as an opportunity to get to know him better, to let him be what he was: a Tuareg boy pretending to be a man. In one corner of the market —a vibrant shantytown of dusty stalls where salt slabs competed for space with dried fish, shea butter soap, secondhand clothes, goat meat, and calabash containers—we found the *cheche* section and we asked Oosman to choose one for himself. Immediately wrapping the long indigo-dyed cotton around his head, he looked uncannily mannish.

The following morning he was waiting for us outside our bedroom, sitting with legs spread wide apart on a rickety chair, both hands crossed over his lap. He was visibly upset. We owed him money, he said, for the services he had rendered the day before as a tour guide. Hadn't he been the best guide we could have asked for?

Oosman managed to catch a ride on one of the 4x4s from the convoy driving our group from Mopti to Timbuktu. At our first stop, I noticed the soles and tips of Oosman's shoes were in shreds, his cracked feet pelted with cram-cram desert barbs. I gave him an extra pair of trainers I had. In exchange he gave me one of his splendid little smiles. We were friends again. I also noticed he wasn't wearing the *cheche*.

"Where is your *cheche*?" I asked him.

He shrugged his shoulders. He didn't know. *"Je l'ai perdu."* He had lost it.

"We'll get you another one in Timbuktu, OK?" He smiled coyly, as if he had known all along that we'd buy him a new *cheche*. He had been wearing the same pair of tattered red jeans since the day we arrived in Mopti. By the time we reached Timbuktu, Oosman was wearing my shoes, my trousers, and my husband's fleece jacket. An English woman in our group was wearing a brand-new *cheche*, which she said Oosman had sold her for a very good price.

My neighbor makes a *tsk-tsk* noise. Her husband was a cop in South Africa during the apartheid. She's seen too many Oosmans, she tells me. After an awkward silence I tell my neighbor about Baba Ali, the old Tuareg who invited us to his home for tea the first day in Mopti. We sat on thin mattresses laid on the dirt floor, exchanged pleasantries, and talked about family and country, the concert, and the ways tourism had changed his Tuareg culture. Then came teatime.

Following tradition, we had three cups of black tea: for the first cup, bitter as life, we were considered strangers. Fifteen minutes and many awkward silences later, Baba Ali added sugar to the teapot and poured the second cup, not quite as bitter as the first one but smooth, smooth as death, he explained—and with that one we became friends, true friends. Baba Ali's hospitality was heartfelt and sincere. He was extremely delighted that we had traveled from so far away just to have tea with him—a statement I was not about to debate. And so he added a good helping of sugar to the teapot and poured the third cup, sweet as love, and with this cup we joined his family, and for his family Baba Ali was prepared to do anything. "Even die," he said with a grin that I couldn't quite understand.

He looked noble in his Tuareg regalia: the tagelmust, which he refused to call *cheche*—a word he considered too hip for his old age—concealed his entire head and face excluding a set of scrutinizing eyes and the top of his prominent nose. "I die for you, my friend, yes?" he asked.

"Yes, thank you," I said, moved.

"And you?" he asked.

No, I thought. *I like you, Baba Ali, I really do, but I would not die for you. I barely know you.* I was about to spill a courteous lie when Baba Ali finished his question. "And you? You buy nice silver from an old friend that die for you? Look, nice silver," he said as he displayed before our eyes an array of cheap Tuareg knickknacks made out of tin for which our friend wanted every penny we had ever worked for. We refused politely. Baba Ali seemed offended or hurt, mostly offended, and he whispered something in Tamasheq that sounded like a desert curse. "I die for you. You buy silver from me. Not fair, but OK with this old man. No problem."

"Typical," my Afrikaner neighbor says, and the word comes out with enough sand for me to discover that she carries scars and grudges from the apartheid. So I tell her about Mohammed, the handsome teenager who traveled with us to the festival and who wanted to become the first Tuareg physician, but more than anything wanted to sell me his own stash of Tuareg jewelry, each piece carved with symbols whose meanings and histories varied with his mood. A little squiggle meant a desert dune one minute, and the next it meant the hump of a camel, or the Niger delta, or the vast sky, or the branches of a baobab. Mohammed was a relentless salesman and on Day 1—after he had offered me morning specials, afternoon bargains, and evening deals—I caved in and bought a pair of splendidly blue earrings. They were lapis lazuli. Or opal. Or malachite. Mohammed couldn't make up his mind. We settled for Very Nice Blue Tuareg Gem.

From then on, whenever we ran into each other, he greeted me with, "Necklace for you?"

"No, Mohammed, I'm not buying anything else from you," I said every time, feeling slightly offended that this boy was not interested in me, only my money.

"You buy earrings. Very good, *mon amie.* Now you buy necklace. *Oui?*"

At dinnertime I offered him the dry mutton on my plate. He ate it with gusto.

"You give me food, I give you necklace. *Oui?*" he said as he reached over to fasten the necklace around my neck. I moved away and gave him a hard "No." He seemed to understand, sat cross-legged on the sand next to me, patted my hand, and after a long pause said, "Good price for you."

I tell her about the children of Timbuktu, how throngs of half-naked kids followed us around, chanting *"Toubab, Toubab"* (Foreigner, Foreigner), *"donnez-nous un Bic."* They were barefoot and covered in desert dust, had discolored hair matted in dry kinks, and their clothes were in shreds. If they were sad, hungry, or sick, they didn't show it. They were delighted to follow us around, giggling, pushing each other to be close to us. Instead of begging for money or food, they wanted a Bic pen, a token of Western culture introduced by a missionary a few decades ago when he handed out box upon box of Bics all around the fabled city. A few of them asked for a *cadeau,* a gift, while some others asked for our empty water bottles they could use to store goat's milk.

My Afrikaner friend shakes her head when I show her the picture I took of the children in Timbuktu. She feels sorry for me. I had been used, but I was too much of a romantic to realize it. Based on my accounts, she concludes that the Tuareg are underdeveloped people prone to trickery, thievery, and deceit, just like other black Africans. An awkward pause follows, and then she gives it all to me: How Africa is a mess (present Africa, that is, because colonial Africa was fantastic). How the blacks, *the blacks* and their shenanigans, ruined South Africa, whose golden years were under the apartheid. And how everything in Mali would be all dandy had it stayed under French rule instead of under a bunch of inept black Tuareg. I repress an urge to tell her that actually the Tuareg are not black, they are lighter than the other ethnic groups in Mali because they are descendants of the Berber people, much fairer than their Mandé counterparts from the south, who are truly black. She carries on about how the Tuareg are destroying Timbuktu. Those Arabs are savages. Am I not watching the news? I am about to tell her that the Tuareg are not Arab, that she is mixing apples with pears, but she goes for my jugular and tells me that she is sure my sweet Mohammed is not a doctor but probably one of those turbaned loonies wielding an AK-47 for the BBC cameras. And she goes on and on about fundamentalist Muslims and Tuareg and al-Qaeda, all of them meaning the same to her. To try to educate or persuade this Afrikaner would be a waste of my time, and hers. After she leaves, I cry; I don't know why or over whom. But I cry.

For centuries, the Empire of Mali was a powerful state and one of the world's chief gold suppliers. During the 1500s, when the empire was at its peak, Timbuktu and Djenné were the main African centers of commerce, scholarship, and culture. Mali also controlled all the trade in West and North Africa and regulated the commercial routes along the Niger River. The empire remained intact until the Berlin Conference of 1884, when the European powers got together and agreed on a systematic invasion, occupation, colonization, and annexation of African territory. That plan was like a birthday party for Europe, and Africa was the cake they sliced into unequal but satisfying parts. Britain claimed roughly 30 percent of Africa's population under its control; 15 percent went to France, 11 percent to Portugal, 9 percent to Germany, 7 percent to Belgium, and 1 percent to Italy. By the end of the nineteenth century, Europe had colonized the entire African continent except for Ethiopia, Liberia (an American colony), and Spanish Sahara. Africa, the second largest continent in area and population, had 90 percent of its area and population partitioned and given away to European conquistadors. The Empire of Mali was renamed French Sudan after it fell under French control in 1892. A few years later, the French merged Mali with present-day Senegal and parts of Mauritania, Niger, and Burkina Faso, and called this new territory Senegambie et Niger. Some other chunks of Mali were transferred to French Guinea. In 1904, after a few retouches to its borders, Mali—or rather, the territory known as Senegambie et Niger—was renamed Upper Senegal and Niger. But the name didn't stick, and in 1920 Mali was again called French Sudan. Unfortunately for the Malians, in 1947 the French altered their borders once more after giving away some districts to Burkina Faso and Mauritania. Twelve years later French Sudan became known as the Sudanese Republic, after again changing its borders by annexing Senegal. In 1959, the territory was known as the Fédération du Mali, taking its name from the ancient empire. The federation broke apart a year later and the Sudanese Republic declared itself independent and took the name République du Mali, with its capital Bamako.

Surely, somewhere, due to all of this, someone was bound to revolt.

The Tuareg. The indigenous people of the Sahara. The blue-veiled people of the desert. An animal-herding people in a dying world of relentless droughts. One of the poorest, most isolated, and most militarized peoples of the world. The Tuareg, an ethnic group divided by colonialism among Mali, Algeria, Libya, Niger, and Burkina Faso. An ethnicity whose homeland straddles the largest energy deposits in Africa. Yet the Tuareg in northern Mali remain a neglected group of Berber-descendant nomads fighting for independence from the south of the country.

The ongoing armed conflict in northern Mali is the fourth Tuareg rebellion, or the fifth, or the seventh, depending on whom you talk with. It's hard to tell, really, because the Tuareg have not stopped fighting for autonomy since the Berlin Conference of 1884.

Malian diaspora is confusing. During the 1970s, after a devastating drought that killed livestock and starved northern Malians, a massive Tuareg exodus to neighboring Libya took place. Colonel Qaddafi offered these starved immigrants more than they had ever had: housing with electricity and running water, food, salaries, clothes, and all the other commodities his country had to offer. In exchange, he asked for their military service. He armed them, trained them to be his mercenaries, turned them and their sons into fierce fighters, demanded their undivided loyalty to his regime, and got it. But many years later, following the start of the Arab uprising in 2011 and after the fall of Qaddafi's regime, his mercenary army was forced out of Libya. Hundreds of the deposed dictator's soldiers escaped across the desert, with antiaircraft weapons and heavy machine guns mounted on the backs of their pickups.

Having lost access to the country that was their only source of livelihood, they drove into Mali and found the same crushing poverty, hunger, and drought that had forced them to migrate in the first place three decades earlier. Barely able to feed their children amid total state neglect, the men launched a rebellion to found their own country, an independent Tuareg state in northern Mali called Azawad. They joined forces with local Tuareg and called themselves the National Movement for the Liberation of Azawad (MNLA).

Following the 2012 coup d'état in Bamako, the Malian capital, the MNLA allied themselves with jihadist rebels, including al-Qaeda in the Maghreb, and together they became a force to be reckoned with. But the MNLA were ill disciplined, internally divided, inexperienced in statesmanship, and too dominated by self-serving clan elites to make an independent state viable. Naturally, the jihadists—who were stern and organized, had concrete self-governing plans, and perceived the Tuareg as too secular—seized the moment, fighting and crushing the MNLA. Once again the Tuareg found themselves fleeing, this time to southern Mali, where they were blamed for causing unrest and chaos, and for allowing the Islamists to take control. With nowhere else to go, the Tuareg fled to Burkina Faso, Niger, and Mauritania. And with them went the Festival in the Desert.

I didn't doubt for a second that Abou was a dancer, but it was hard to look at the way he danced and not think of him as an athlete. He was the leader of Tamnana, an extended family of dancers vastly popular with revelers at the six editions of the festival. There was no limit to what he could do as soon as the music started. He could jump, fall, rebound, curtsy, throw in some Cossack-like squats, and then stop instantly, all to the beat of the drums, the vigorous clapping, and the chords of the *amzad*, a one-string violin. I saw him go into the air without warning, defying gravity, then land on his two feet as if the moment of imbalance had been a mirage. Tamnana's dance was half sheer energy, half pure fluidity —a concoction of athleticism, grace, and joie de vivre. Every time the dancers jumped, their indigo boubous billowed in the air, and when the vocalists sang, they moved their hands with a grace that was almost Hawaiian hula, almost Thai fingernail dance. I couldn't imagine them doing anything else but singing and dancing. They were the happiest and, based on their physical strength, the best-fed Malians in the whole country.

After accepting Abou's invitation to visit his village—a short camel ride away—I imagined this place as a colorful and festive little settlement where the music never stops, block parties are mandatory, and people die primarily of dance-induced exhaustion. But the reality was different. Abou's village was a small group of tents made of discolored animal hide, tattered yards of sand-beaten cotton, and dry grass. The enclave looked like an old campsite that had been beaten to its knees, a place last used a long time ago and then abandoned.

The women, some of whom were still breastfeeding, modestly covered their heads with colorful scarves that matched their *pagne*, brought their tatty drums out of the tents, and with the babies still suckling their leathery breasts, performed a set of languid songs for us. Their high-pitched voices, tinged with a lamentation tone, seemed to travel far in the dry Sahel air. Their dissonant chants crawled slow and determined under my skin.

It wasn't a happy performance. There were no smiles or joyful interjections halfway through their songs as we had seen and heard onstage at the concert. No one ululated. This was a group of starving women who were called to perform while they were inside their tents fighting for survival. They all looked wounded beyond repair. I felt vulgar and intrusive. But there I was, sitting on the sand, in a dystopian world where it seemed every woman of reproductive age had already reproduced; malnourished children were raising their own malnourished children; scrawny camels had soft humps; and men looked haggard. And only then did I see Tamnana for what they really were: local artists, born in abject poverty, who each January emerged from raggedy tents to dance, make music, and turn dented pots and discarded tin cans into jewelry and trinkets to sell to tourists. They didn't beg and they didn't ask for handouts. Hungry, thirsty, and with basic needs unfulfilled, they went onstage to dance as if their lives depended on each move, which they did. That's who they were underneath their impressive headdresses and their majestic indigo boubous. What else did they have at the end of the night after performing with such vigor and fortitude but protruding ribs, famished livestock, and dreams of rain and rice?

Then again, maybe the secret of their resilience lies in the lack of rain and rice. Maybe, by some cruel happenstance, the Tuareg chose music in the face of drought and starvation. Maybe, when their future as an ethnic group was pushed too close to the edge, they picked a stage over a grave. Sing or die. Or die singing, as the women of Essakane seemed to be doing. And who better to host the most remote music festival in the world than the Tuareg, a nomadic group of people ethnically, geographically, and administratively dislocated from central Mali and the rest of the world?

Truth be told, the festival is not a modern phenomenon. The Blue Men of the Desert have had these traditional gatherings and celebrations of their way of life for centuries. Generation after generation, they have gathered annually to commemorate the end of the nomadic season, celebrate their culture, resolve conflicts, exchange ideas, and discuss challenges facing their traditions. The festival brought families and clans together, and under a spirit of mutual reliance and harmony they celebrated with traditional songs, dances, and demonstrations of manly prowess and female beauty. They gathered to arrange marriages, swap news, race camels, and make music. The difference between then and now is that now the festival has an international audience. Tinariwen was made known to the world in 2007 when they performed alongside the Rolling Stones at Slane Castle in Dublin. Festival guests such as Damon Albarn of Blur, Robert Plant, and Bono, among other Western artists, made the event so popular that its organizers had to put a cap on the number of non-African revelers at 500.

When the Islamist rebels took over northern Mali, they issued a ban on all music, effectively sealing the fate of the festival in Timbuktu—a devastating blow to a country where music is akin to wealth. The Islamists sent death threats to local musicians, forcing them into exile. Live music and cultural venues were shut down; musical instruments and recordings were set ablaze in public bonfires. The Festival in the Desert was relocated to Burkina Faso but later had to be postponed because of the security risk. In 2014, the concert remains in exile from Timbuktu.

The Tuareg haven't lost hope of hosting the festival in Essakane or Timbuktu again. To them, music is the thread that keeps the fabric of their history together. These musicians are storytellers, history-tellers, truth-tellers. They are present at weddings, birth ceremonies, and funerals. They are griots, and as such they perpetuate oral traditions of families and entire villages, conveying with their music what Malians—who are mostly illiterate—cannot always read or say in words.

When I think of Mali, not only do I see the powdery Sahara desert separating Essakane from Timbuktu, dusty children chanting *"Un Bic, donnez-moi un Bic,"* Baba Ali's dark fingers pouring three cups of tea, hungry women, and sly traders, among other memories, I also hear it: the *djembe* drums, the *kora* harps, the *ngoni*, the talking drum, the tales of the griots on- and offstage. I don't hear the savage sound of Kalashnikovs or the war cries of the jihadists. When I think of Timbuktu, I think of the Flame of Peace monument, erected in 1996 to memorialize the ceremonial burning of

3,000 weapons and to celebrate what was supposed to be the end of the last Tuareg rebellion. I see the memorial: white and blue arches and columns supporting the heavy flame of peace, seven steps leading up to the base of the monument where many of the old guns are embedded in cement.

But the Timbuktu I knew in 2006 is not the same ravaged town of 2014. Recently I saw a picture of the monument taken soon after the jihadists gained control of the town: the flame is missing, the white and blue paint of the columns and arches has peeled off to reveal chunks of red bricks, and where the guns are embedded someone had left the black flag of the jihadists.

NICK PAUMGARTEN

Berlin Nights

FROM *The New Yorker*

THE FIRST PERSON I met in Berlin was a boar-hunting friend of
a friend, who agreed to talk to me only if I didn't print his name.
He was in his early forties, six and a half feet tall, muscular, lean,
and fair, with shaggy reddish brown hair, some stubble, and a great
deal of self-confidence. He had on worn jeans, biker boots, a loose
faded black T-shirt, and a scarf, and yet I'll confess I found myself
picturing him trim and tidy in Heidelberg dueling garb. Precon-
ceptions can be hard to shake when you're fresh in town.

It was a Sunday night in the dregs of December, sleety and dark.
We were at a bar in Mitte, the formerly bombed-out and abandoned East Berlin district that was reclaimed by squatters, clubbers, and artists after the Wall came down and is now agleam with
fancy restaurants, galleries, and shops. Transplants often describe
Berlin's neighborhoods as analogues of New York's, to assess
where they fit along the gentrification continuum. Mitte, they say,
is SoHo. Like SoHo, it is often full of tourists. But this bar, an early
post-Wall pioneer, had a gruff, local air.

The boar hunter stirred an espresso at arm's length and regarded me with martial skepticism. He was a veteran of the city's
after-hours party scene, but he seemed weary of it. "Everyone
knows about this," he said. "You should write instead about black
rhinos." He'd recently bought 15,000 acres in Namibia, in a rhi-
noceros preserve, to help support a conservation program. He
said, "I once shot an elephant."

He had moved to Berlin from Düsseldorf in 1993. He was a
philosopher by training (his business card had him as a "Dr.")

but an industrialist by trade: he'd inherited a manufacturing firm from his father, and had done well enough with it to pursue a life of pleasure and ease, though without ostentation, in keeping with the ethos of Berlin. He'd recently returned from a four-week surfing trip to the Basque coast, where he and a girlfriend—two, actually: one for the first half of the trip, and one for the second—had lived out of a VW bus. There were other women in his life, among them a physician's wife, whom he'd met online. ("He gave her fake tits—thank you, mister!") He described his plans for the following weekend: a day hunting wild boar in a forest on the city's outskirts, then a "sex party" (which should never be said without a German accent) at an acquaintance's apartment, where he'd arrive with one woman but pair up with others ("It's a seedy thing"), and finally, perhaps, just before Sunday dawn, Berghain.

Berghain is a nightclub that opened in 2004 in an abandoned power plant in what used to be East Berlin. The name is a mashup of the last syllable of its neighborhood, Friedrichshain, and the one across the Spree, Kreuzberg, on what was once the other side of the Wall. It is the most famous techno club in the world—to Berlin what Fenway is to Boston—and yet still kind of underground and, as such, a microcosm of Berlin. The people I'd talked to who had been to Berghain—and there were many—conjured ecstatic evenings, Boschian contortions, and a dusky Arcadia that an American hockey dad like me had never even imagined wanting to experience.

Berghain's renown rests on many attributes: the quality of the music, and of the DJs who present it; the power and clarity of the sound system; the eyeball-bending decadence of the weekend parties, which often spill into Monday morning; the stringent and mysterious door policy, and the menacing head doorman, with a tattoo on his face; the majesty and complexity of the interior; and the tolerant and indulgent atmosphere, most infamously in its so-called dark rooms, where patrons, gay and straight, can get it on with friends or strangers in an anonymous murk. For some Berliners, Berghain is an elemental part of their weekly existence, a perfectly pitched and carefully conceived apotheosis of Berlin's post-Wall club culture. To pilgrims and many expats, it is a temple of techno, a consecrated space, a source of enchantment and wonder.

"It's half art project, half social experiment," a friend in New

York had told me. "It's the vampire nightclub to end all vampire nightclubs. People want something like it here, but New York could never metabolize it."

"It's a social-political-economic achievement," another friend said. "It's such a fucking unicorn."

"It's dystopian and utopian," a third said. "Prepare yourself."

The boar hunter had been going to Berghain for years, mainly for the music and the sex. He said he preferred it to, say, the KitKatClub. "The sex clubs have bad music," he explained. He avoided drugs, mostly. He drank alcohol and occasionally smoked damiana, a mild herbal stimulant that is thought to have some aphrodisiac effects. "It's like pot, except it doesn't make you stupid," he said. Perhaps it was for this reason that he had a more prosaic affection for the place. He didn't seem to see it in transcendental terms. He had a Teutonic bluntness with regard to sex. Typically he'd dance and then go to the dark room. He explained that straight couples, in deference to the predominantly gay clientele in the dark rooms, often preferred the toilet stalls, but, for whatever reason, he didn't like the idea of screwing on a toilet. He'd noticed in recent visits to the dark room that, to judge by wandering hands, the patrons were less interested in him than in the woman he was with. Also, he'd had two cell phones stolen. All this was a symptom of gentrification. "Berghain's not as kinky as it used to be, not as eccentric," he said. "There are the easyJet people—Spanish people, Italians. The black-leather homosexuals are gone." Apparently they patronized the club downstairs—Lab .oratory, which has a separate entrance and a more single-minded clientele. In Berlin, offhand references to instances of excess at Lab.oratory—oh, the things that men will do to each other!—are as commonplace as best-burger recommendations in New York.

After a moment, the boar hunter said, "We could go to Berghain now. Would you like to go?"

"Now?" I was jet-lagged. It was Sunday. He looked me up and down, the way Germans do when you walk into a restaurant. He didn't think I'd get in. We made a plan to meet there in a week.

The next morning, the sidewalks in Mitte teemed with citizens on their way to work. Through the windows of an office building across the street from my hotel, you could see young people busy in their cubicles. Somehow, I'd assumed that on Monday mornings everyone in Berlin would be lurking in a club somewhere or else sleeping it off. But it turns out there is a Berlin of museums and gallery openings, of the Bundestag and the Chancellery, of Holocaust remembrance and Naziphilia, of Turkish immigrants and academics on sabbatical, and even of ordinary middle-class families going about their lives and escaping to Wannsee on weekends. It's just that if you are on techno time, you hardly see any of it. You can't fathom that a few U-Bahn stops away, Angela Merkel is busy presiding over the affairs of Europe.

This particular Berlin—cradle of techno culture, hotbed of lost weekends and lost minds—has been an object of international yearning and fascination for more than 20 years. Berlin is to electronic music what Florence was to Renaissance art: crucible, arbiter, patron. Credit for this could go as far back as Bismarck; the city owes its peculiar fertility as much to the follies of statesmen and generals as to any generation of ardent youth. Citizens have spoken and sung for many years of the *"Berliner Luft"*—"the nervous, endlessly quivering Berlin air," as Conrad Alberti wrote in 1889, "which works upon people like alcohol, morphine, cocaine, exciting, inspiring, relaxing, deadly."

The First World War was a bracing infusion. Defeat, poverty, inflation, desperation: the celebrated cultural efflorescence and social tolerance of the Weimar years arose out of, or in spite of, a perhaps equally celebrated atmosphere of perversion and abandon. Berlin was the whorehouse of Europe. War widows, or their children, would do anything for a mark, even as a mark came to be worth practically nothing (4 trillion to a dollar at one point in 1923). The kaiser's censors and police were gone. In came the Continent's decadentsia, with their strong currencies and peculiar fetishes. Sally Bowles at the Lady Windermere, transvestites at the Eldorado, "sugar-lickers" (pederasts), *Münzis* (pregnant whores). Mel Gordon, in *Voluptuous Panic: The Erotic World of Weimar Berlin*, cites the journalist Luigi Barzini: "The story went around that a male goose of which one cut the neck at the ecstatic moment would give you the most delicious, economical, and time-saving frisson of all, as it allowed you to enjoy sodomy, bestiality, homosexuality, necrophilia, and sadism at one stroke. Gastronomy too, as one could eat the goose afterward."

Apocryphal, one hopes, but such was the rep. In some respects, the notion of decadence was as integral as decadence itself. So people, in those Weimar years, also came to gawk, or to get close enough at least for the "mystery-magic of foreignness," as Christopher Isherwood wrote, to rub off. A commodified, self-conscious version of the real thing existed even then. Isherwood cited Berlin's "dens of pseudo-vice": "Here screaming boys in drag and monocled, Eton-cropped girls in dinner jackets play-acted the high jinks of Sodom and Gomorrah, horrifying the onlookers and reassuring them that Berlin was still the most decadent city in Europe." Berlin was already a brand.

The Nazis closed the clubs, hounded and exterminated the homosexuals, and, in the end, brought ruin on the city. Bombed and desolate, traumatized by street fighting, starvation, and mass rape, and ultimately carved up, Berlin, after the war, barely heaved back to life. West Berlin, surrounded on all sides by East Germany, survived primarily as a political gesture, a flagpole in the sand and a thumb in the Politburo's eye. There was very little industry, turnover, or travel in or out. No corporation could take the political risk or tolerate the barriers to commerce. To encourage people to move there, the West German government gave out stipends and exemptions from military service, so the city tended to attract the West's mavericks and oddballs—hippies, homosexuals, political renegades—who shared the town with the elderly and the soldiers watching over them. In such hothouse isolation, a small but fervid club scene took root.

In 1988, the founders of a small record label, Interfisch, started throwing illegal all-night parties in their office. The space, in a Kreuzberg basement reached via ladder, had 6-foot ceilings. It took on the name UFO. The year before, Dimitri Hegemann, one of the founders, had traveled to Chicago to arrange a licensing deal with another label. While there, he had idly browsed through its so-called white labels—rough demos, not ready for sale—and picked out something strange. It was techno from Detroit. Hegemann, a Westphalian who had moved to Berlin in 1978, was a musicologist, a producer of British electronic music, a fan of American punk (especially the Dead Kennedys), and the founder of an experimental electronic-music festival called Berlin Atonal, but he had never heard music quite like this. He brought a stack of Detroit techno records back to Berlin.

*

Electronic music spans many genres, from the experimental bleeps and blurts that you might hear at the fringes of Berlin's CTM Festival to the mega-popular sets performed by famous DJs like Skrillex and Avicii—which you won't really find in Berlin. The genres for which Berlin is best known, house and, especially, techno, are mostly, as manifested there, noncommercial, rigorous, esoteric, and both experimental and orthodox. The music isn't pop, although many elements of it derive from and inform pop. It isn't punk, although it owes something to punk, in spirit and scene. It isn't high art, either. It is, fundamentally, *Gebrauchsmusik*—"utility music," as Paul Nettl, the Bohemian musicologist, described dance music in 1921. The utility, in this case, is mostly that of providing succor and pleasure, a sense of direction and purpose, to addled bodies and minds. The most characteristic subgenre, which peaked in popularity about a decade ago and has been explored to the edges of tolerability ever since, is minimal techno, a spare distillation that people have sometimes likened to the knocking of spoons on pots but which others parse as though it were Brahms.

Techno is repetitive, relying on subtle changes over time to intrigue the ear. It eschews lyrics, melody, and, arguably, harmonics. It doesn't resolve. You don't get crowd-pleasing drops. Its essential element is a basic four-on-the-floor beat—a 4/4 dictatorship in which the bass drum, or its proxy, is struck on every beat, with a snare on each *and*. It sounds like "boots and pants, boots and pants." Say it. Say it again. The pleasure comes in repetition, in sly referents, and in the nature of the sound—the depth and texture of the low frequencies or, in the case of acid house, the squelchy bass of the Roland TB-303 synthesizer. House, which originated in the gay dance clubs of Chicago and (less so) New York in the eighties, often features a snare on the two and the four. "It's to give people with no rhythm a way to hold on to it," a DJ friend, my techno rabbi, told me. "It's the grandma handle in the shower."

Purists object when you call this music EDM, though it is indisputably electronic music made for dancing. "Electronic dance music," lowercase, used to be an acceptable catchall term for the entire range of genres (house, deep house, acid house, trance, techno, industrial, drum and bass, dubstep, brostep, hardcore, happy hardcore, jungle, garage, etc.) created and performed on computers and synthesizers. Shortened to EDM, however, the term has come to signify the party-crowd DJ music that has been the biggest pop phenomenon of the past half decade—Skrillex in Vegas, bros in the house. "EDM took all the gayness and blackness out of it," my techno rabbi explained. "It's fascistic, with the DJ on a stage." Some prefer to call it commercial electronic music. It doesn't have much to do with Berlin, except to the extent that Berlin defines itself in opposition to it. The nomenclature is convoluted. To the dabbler, it can seem that there are more genres than there are differences between them.

Techno emerged in the early to mideighties in and around Detroit, at the hands of black middle-class DJs who for some reason idealized the glamour and suavity of European electronic pop and Italo disco, as it reached them via *GQ* and the radio DJ who called himself the Electrifying Mojo. They brought some rigor and a hint of Motown to it and created an industrial-sounding music that was funky, futuristic, and kind of arch—evoking the auto plants that were putting these kids' parents out of work.

Techno was also developing on its own in West Germany, in the underground clubs of Frankfurt, as a logical extension of the early electronic music of Kraftwerk and of the rhythms and sounds to be mined from the records of synthpop acts like Depeche Mode. Juan Atkins, one of the godfathers of Detroit techno, says he lifted the term from the futurist Alvin Toffler, but it may have been in use in Europe before anyone in Detroit took it up, in record stores, as a designation for synthpop or for the sound that would come to be called electro. The debate goes on. The techno that would flourish in Berlin was the Detroit strand that Hegemann brought back.

As the pent-up underground energy of the West spilled into the empty wastes of the East, Hegemann and his partners, amid the rush to colonize derelict spaces, discovered a hidden depository in a Mitte basement beneath a former Wertheim department store near what had been the Wall. It had been vacant since 1945. They set up in the vault and called it Tresor. The space was symbolic of reconciliation: straddling East and West, packed with reunified Berliners—skinheads and soccer hooligans from the East in frenzied harmony with the gays and the hippies. The soundtrack was techno. In Detroit, techno had hardly left a mark, but in Berlin the music, and the Detroit DJs who made it, found a home. Hegemann has called techno "the most important musical movement of the last century." In Europe, anyway, this statement does not necessarily seem hyperbolic. In some respects, techno—and its variants and relatives—represents a kind of post–Cold War folk music, endlessly adaptable, performable by anyone. As Hegemann has said, "We knew that the concept of the artist who drew all the attention from the audience was dead. Techno was all about anonymity. The artist became part of the public." Not long ago, the Berlin DJ Boys Noize tweeted, "If you see a DJ that uses a mic and screams 'put your hands up' throw a banana at him."

Most Berlin nightclubs aren't like the American kind. Security is light, rules are lax. Generally there is no bottle service, no VIP section, and, Berghain aside, no velvet rope. In this respect, they bear little resemblance to, say, Studio 54, which, glorious as it may have been, begat a stratified style that metastasized into the models-and-bankers Maybach-and-Cristal rat race that deflected a generation away from the clubbing life in the U.S.

Low-density neighborhoods make for lenient noise enforcement and therefore endless nights and powerful subwoofers; a liberal civic spirit means no blue laws or last calls. In Berlin, the authorities don't especially mind your drinking on the street or on the subway. Actually, you can do pretty much anything on the street except jaywalk. It's not a hierarchy town. There's little compunction to network or to strive for entry into more elite social circles. "It doesn't matter who you are here—or it matters less here, anyway, than elsewhere," Robert Henke, a composer of electronic music who performs occasionally at Berghain, said.

Wednesday has always been a big night in Berlin, especially for resident DJs trying new things before a sympathetic crowd. Someone had told me to go to Farbfernseher, a small club in an old television store under the S-Bahn tracks on Skalitzer Strasse. To kill time beforehand, I wandered the streets of Kreuzberg, expecting to find bars and crowds, but on this bitter, windy night—I'd heard this weather system called the Siberian Whip—there was no one around. What bars I passed were all but empty. On my last visit to Berlin, in the spring of 1990, just after the Wall fell, a friend and I had driven from southern Poland, expecting a kind of punk paradise. Instead, we found a desolate sprawling half city with no center and no discernible scene. In other words, a punk paradise, but we didn't have eyes to see it. Here I was in Berlin again, a generation later, still wondering where Berlin was.

Farbfernseher was a shuttered storefront on the ground floor of a graffitied apartment house with building sites on either side. I got there early, at around midnight, and claimed a spot along the wall by the bar, overlooking a small dance floor. The drink prices were listed in a Pong-era font on the screen of an old black-and-white TV. A few people sat on high benches along the walls, and a handful stood on the dance floor, watching the DJ. To my left, a stocky guy in a salmon-colored hoodie was bobbing and bouncing with great enthusiasm. His name was Ash. He and a friend, a DJ and producer named J.P., were from Cambridge and were in town for four nights of clubbing. "Our main objective is to listen to lots of techno and get blasted," Ash said. They were 24 and 23. Mates, not dates. "This is what you might call introspective dancing," Ash said, looking down at the floor. "This room needs some psyche-delics." They pointed out, with approval, the analog Atari mixing deck that the DJ was using: old school. The display brought to mind an abacus. "It's stuff like this that makes me question people who say electronic music is divorced from instrumentalism," J.P. said. "That's a keyboard, basically."

At around 2:30 a.m., I left for Tresor. The walk was about a mile along deserted streets, past giant apartment blocks. It was like a zombie movie set in the outskirts of Helsinki. I tacked toward a pair of giant smokestacks, red lights blinking slow. The original Tresor closed in 2005, and eventually the land was sold to a developer. In 2007, Hegemann and his partners opened a new Tresor in a gigantic decommissioned power plant on Köpenicker Strasse, on the Spree. I had no trouble getting in. Inside, an assault of pounding primal techno lured me down a corridor of smoke and strobes, into a smoky basement, figures appearing and disappearing in it like ships in fog. It didn't seem crowded, but everyone looked to be in a world of his own, some speedy, others half catatonic. The music was muscular, unrelenting. The DJ stood behind steel bars, as though in a cell, and pressed buttons on two laptops. I got a beer from a stern bartender and went to stand in front of a wall of old blackened safe-deposit boxes from Wertheim. One could admire this music—the rigor, the noise, the industrial badassness of it—but after a while it began to seem absurd. Ash and J.P. appeared out of the fog, and we stood together awhile, watching. Scattered about were men in tight T-shirts making severe moves.

"This is the solitary-rave, demolish-your-own-personality school!"
Ash shouted. Later, he remarked, with something approaching ad-
miration, "That was the single most oppressive club atmosphere
I've ever encountered." I lasted 84 minutes.

I returned the next day, in the late afternoon, having all but
missed whatever daylight the Siberian Whip would permit. The
offices were upstairs, shabby and pleasant, with a backstage vibe.
Some gaunt young dudes skulked about. Hegemann, in a faded
hoodie, was at his desk, nibbling from a bag of licorice and talking
in German with a colleague over photos of the ruins of Detroit.

"I'm a space pioneer," he said. "My mission is to transform industrial ruins into cultural spaces. I have ideas. We save cities, you
know? We are like a consulting firm. I could save Detroit."

Hegemann went on, "The music came to us from Detroit. We
got the milk when the milk was fresh. Now I'm older, the music's
older. It's not fresh. We have competition. Techno is known. It is
nearly pop. But it has not lost the intensity."

Downstairs, the techno vault, now without smoke, strobes, or au-
ral assault, seemed no more remarkable than a fraternity taproom.
The bank-vault boxes had been salvaged from the original Tresor.
Their reincarnation here hinted at the creep of affectation and
nostalgia in the techno culture of Berlin. We went up a stairwell
and emerged into the main power plant—an old East German dis-
tance-heating facility that had served Mitte until 1996. It was now
a vast empty cathedral of concrete, with towering pillars and vaults,
arcane markings, and a trace of dusky natural light. Hegemann
and his partners were calling this space Kraftwerk (*natürlich*) and
didn't know quite what to do with it. To get it up to code, for safety
and fire, they'd need to invest millions of dollars that they didn't
have but hoped to pry from the City of Berlin, under the rationale
of government support for an essential cultural industry and tourism draw. In the gloom, you could imagine the rhythmic clamor of
the old turbines and pumps—the rudiments of techno.

The post-Wall abundance of derelict buildings and excess housing
was decisive. "Empty spaces allowed there to be a club culture,"
Robert Henke said. "With no empty space, you get a closed-at-2-
a.m., restrictive-alcohol culture." At first the reclamation seemed
slapdash, improvisational, anarchic, as squatters took over build-

ings and neighborhoods and set off a period of cultural ferment. But the powers that be had been dreaming up developments for years before the Wall came down, and now—amid a boom in real-estate speculation and investment (everyone spoke of the Swedes) —empty space, and the sense of wildness that comes with it, has become harder to come by. "Flats are getting more expensive," Hegemann said. "But we still have many free spaces. This is the secret for why Berlin is still alive."

Some empty spaces have completed their life cycles. One afternoon, I visited the old Reichsbahnbunker, a five-story fortress of reinforced concrete built by the Nazis in 1942 as an air-raid shelter. The Soviets turned it into a jail for POWs. Then it was used to store bananas and other tropical fruit. It was abandoned. In the nineties, it became an infamous techno nightclub, the Bunker. No ventilation, no fire exits. The government eventually shut it down. In 2003, an advertising executive and his wife bought the building and converted it into a museum to house their collection of contemporary art. They also built a glass-and-steel penthouse on the roof, to house themselves. Now the collection is open to the public, by appointment only. I joined a tour one afternoon. The guide, a young art student with a sweet monotone, took us into a cell-like space featuring giant manipulated photographs of the night sky, by Thomas Ruff, and explained that it had been the original dark room of Berlin. "It was very extreme," she said. "It was hot, damp, loud, and dark. It was said to be the hardest club in the world. I'm sure you can imagine the things." She gave a coy smile.

Except for Lisbon, Berlin is the cheapest capital in Western Europe. This despite being the capital of the Continent's richest country. Its population is still lower than it was at the outset of the Second World War. It's a little like a mountain town with ski bums and trustafarians cycling through. The kids come to play, not to stay. Crammed into their WGs (*Wohngemeinschaften,* or "shared flats"), they luxuriate in cheap rents, idle hours, and a capricious and creative cohort. What had been a very German scene became, a decade ago, pan-European, with the rise of cheap air travel and subsidized unemployment. Then came the Americans. It can be hard to find young people willing to work more than three days a week. And yet it can also be hard for someone who is working three days a week, and who is earning the low wages that are typical of

Berlin, to salt away enough money to leave—to afford, say, the first month's rent in London or New York. So it favors those who have some money to spare or who don't care. One ex-Berliner said, "It's spring break for RISD kids."

In recent years, there has been more in the way of regular employment. There are tech startups, which attract engineers. Berlin is Europe's mobile-gaming hub, with the headquarters of Wooga. There are call centers, staffed by legions of young people pulling relatively arduous shifts, and a number of successful startups grounded in the electronic-music scene: SoundCloud, Ableton, Native Instruments. Techno has quietly been professionalized, attracting private and government capital.

Ewan Pearson, a DJ and producer, made his bones in the U.K. rave scene in the nineties and moved to Berlin in 2003, for a clubbing culture he found to be unpretentious and, if not temperate, then at least benign. "I'm from the West Midlands," he told me. "Every time you went out, you were primed for danger."

He and his wife, Caroline Drucker, a Bryn Mawr graduate who came to Berlin in 2003 to pursue a master's in architectural theory, have what passes in Berlin for a bourgeois life. Most weekends, he travels around Europe for DJ gigs. She helped to launch Vice Media in Germany, then moved to SoundCloud, and now she is an executive in the Berlin office of Etsy, the online retailer of vintage and handmade stuff.

Pearson was featured in *Feiern* (*Party*), a 2006 documentary about the Berlin club scene. After describing the vortex into which one can disappear on a strong night, Pearson, wry and already going a little gray (he's 41 now), remarks, "Don't forget to go home." The line gave the film its English title and became a catchphrase among the clubbers of his generation, a click of the slippers in this particular Oz. In a way, it's an accidental mantra for the scene's survivors, those who have fashioned a daytime life out of all those nights, and who have found a way to mellow a bit with age, without quitting entirely.

I'd been warned by a few adherents about what they called "the Berlin jade," the cynicism of the locals, native or adopted, toward the naive enthusiasms of outsiders. Nearly everyone I talked to considered Berlin's peak—its finest, purest, most interesting, authentic, blissful period—to have occurred a year or two before he or she arrived. Newcomers perpetually catch the tail end and stake their claim to the remnants. Any time an article comes out about what you might call the *Berlingeist*—how hip the city is, or no longer is—Berliners stick their fingers down their throats.

The writer Gideon Lewis-Kraus observed, in the Berlin chapter of *A Sense of Direction*, his 2012 pilgrimage memoir, "What the word 'over' really means is that your expectations of a place, your fantasies of who you might have become there, have been confounded by the persistence of you."

Each generation finds a Berlin to test that persistence. One night, I had a drink with two sisters from the suburbs of Chicago, Arielle and Adina Bier, formerly performance artists of a kind, who had recently settled in Berlin, which their grandparents were forced out of in the late thirties. Adina was interested in queer Berlin and liked to go to Homopatik—an all-weekend gay party at a club called Aboutblank—and the Sunday-night Pork party at Ficken 3000. (Its website: "Drink—Dance—Strip—Fuck. Music for prostitutes, indie anti-hits, pink noise, raw static, synth cherry pop, spunk rock, cock 'n' hole, artcore + lo-fi 4 low lifes.")

Arielle mentioned, with some disdain, an advertisement for Coca-Cola that had been making the rounds, in which a karaoke vendor on a bicycle sets up his karaoke machine in Mauerpark, in Prenzlauer Berg, which is known for its flea market, and before long has an amphitheater full of hipsters joyfully taking part. Later that night, I watched the ad a few times and wondered how the jaded Berliners had been persuaded to carry on like that for the Coca-Cola Company. The next day, I had coffee with Tilman Brembs, a very early visitor to Tresor. He worked for a casting agency, DeeBeePhunky, one of the biggest in Berlin; it had a portfolio of a thousand young Berliners as models and actors for hire, and had done ads for Microsoft, IKEA, and McDonald's. It turned out that he had cast that Coca-Cola campaign. He told me that the kids who appeared on camera were well paid. Goodbye, jade.

Brembs had come to Berlin in 1982—military-service avoidance. "The techno movement was like a second puberty for me," he said. When he arrived at Tresor, he helped tend bar and clean up after the parties. "In the early years, there was no running water. We had buckets of water to wash with. It was a crazy time. It was magic. Everything was possible. There were not so many tourists. We had a lot of English from the Allied forces. They got out of their bases at night and they were full of drugs. Then they came

no more. Probably they were arrested. They brought a different
style, the ravers, the Ecstasy, the big printed T-shirts." At the clubs,
he went on, "we had the hooligans, all these rough guys, together
with the gays. There was no violence. Maybe it was the Ecstasy.
There was a Wild East atmosphere. People robbed shops. The police, they drove Trabants and were not fast enough for all the Golf
GTEs. We preferred to take speed. It was the speed users versus
the coke users. The coke people were arrogant. But the drugs were
not the motor of the movement."

He's been finding ways to capitalize on techno ever since. In the
nineties, he was a sanctioned photographer at Tresor ("The Bunker was too hard for me"). He put 10,000 photos online in 2007,
under the heading "Zeitmaschine" (Time Machine). He'd started
a company with D. J. Tanith, an early techno pioneer in Berlin,
selling camouflage fabrics and party gear. For a while, Brembs
worked for the Love Parade, the street jubilee that was canceled in
2010, after 21 people were killed in a stampede—the Altamont of
techno. He is married to a woman from New Hampshire and living
in Prenzlauer Berg (Park Slope), and for the most part no longer
spends much time in the clubs.

In the nineties, two Bunker regulars, Michael Teufele and Norbert
Thormann, began throwing their own gay sex parties, called Snax,
at various sites around the city. Around 1999, they opened a dance
club in a train-repair depot in Friedrichshain, which they called
Ostgut. It was essentially a gay club devoted to techno music, but
it was mixed-friendly—open to women and straight men. Two
years later, they started Panorama Bar, a separate space upstairs,
which was straighter, and played house music and lighter techno.
Downstairs were the burly, bare-chested men in camo pants and
leather boots. Upstairs you had all kinds. The techno clubs of
Mitte didn't yet rely so much on the gay scene, and the gay clubs
were less attentive to the quality of the music. Ostgut was a marriage of the two, and as such created something new—a gay club
with mainstream appeal. It became a kind of distillation of the
nineties scene. In many respects, Berlin's queer culture is the city's
most essential and distinguishing element—the coagulant and the
zest. It was thus in the twenties and in pre-1989 West Berlin, and
remains so today. The clubs are its public face. No one in Berlin is
made nervous or embarrassed by the idea of going to a gay club.

Ostgut closed in 2003, and the building was torn down to make way for a sports arena. A year later, Teufele and Thormann opened Berghain. Not much is known about them. Thormann is a former fashion photographer. They like ballet. They never give interviews or pose for pictures, in part because they value their privacy and in part because of a kind of underground code of silence, exile, and cunning—a combination, perhaps, of vestigial Stasi-era paranoia, punkish disdain for the media, and an embrace of the techno-culture virtue of anonymity. Whatever the case, it has added to the club's mystique, and so one could understand their not wanting to change. By all accounts, they make a lot of money. It is remarkable, in a high-turnover town, that the place has been able to sustain the spell for so long.

People strain to explain Berghain's appeal. The effort is widely deemed futile (to say nothing of blasphemous). This may be a by-product of psychotropic drugs and the ineffability of chemical transcendence. Tales of nights out are like other people's recounted dreams.

You are not allowed to take photographs inside the club. If you so much as hold a smartphone up, you will likely be thrown out. The philosophy is that whatever happens here is for the moment and doesn't exist outside of that moment or outside the club—a righteous stand, perhaps, in a social-media world. There aren't any mirrors. The European press for years has obsessed over the difficulty of getting in. Blogs, and even apps, have tried to decode it: "Don't look too glamorous; look queer; don't act like a tourist; don't look too young; don't show up as a group of straight men or women; dress eccentrically; go alone." Don't speak English, don't stand out, don't act drunk or tweaked. The abiding idea seems to be don't be a jerk.

No one dances to be watched. Fighting and aggression aren't tolerated. Drug use must be discreet. If you're wasted, they'll kick you out. Generally, though, the security presence is subtle. Henke, the composer, told me, "There are lots of things you *can* do there, but there are things that you are not *obliged* to do. You don't go to a fetish party and think, Maybe I'll just have a drink and listen to some music. At Berghain, the architecture, and the social architecture, doesn't force me into a ritual human behavior."

I talked to a promoter who had had a lot of trouble getting into Berghain. Maybe he was too young. ("Older is better," he said.

"Kids are idiots.") He was afraid of being quoted by name, because
of the power that the Berghain owners have in Berlin. Playing
there is such a privilege—not only for professional reputation but
also for the sheer pleasure of playing extra-long sets in a wild and
tasteful place—that no one wants to be subject to a *Hausverbot*. "A
huge ingredient in their secret sauce is control," he said. Henke,
who knows the owners well, said, "They're still not sure how to
handle how this place became so popular."

One way they'd handled it was by keeping journalists and other
squares like me out. But my techno rabbi had got me onto the
guest list of a DJ.

On wide, empty streets, I rehearsed my pidgin-Deutsch greeting
— *"Ich bin auf der Hausliste"*—and walked past superstores that had
sprung up in recent years on vacant lots. Before long, I fell in with
a few other cloaked figures and came upon a line of taxis, then
followed a muddy path along a metal grate toward the old power
station, an industrial-deco block of stone and concrete. Berghain.
Through the windows you could hear the kick drum and see flashing colored lights. The line wasn't long: a few dozen bundled and
murmuring souls. I circumvented it, as instructed, and waited by
the entrance while the bouncer, a big square-jawed crewcut man
in an overcoat, dealt with some supplicants. He was in intense but
quiet conversation, as though about a medical condition, with two
young men with the sides of their heads shaved. Turks, perhaps.

"In spite of this, we say no because we can say no," he told them.
"It's just bad luck."

For some reason, they were holding out their passports, open to
their photos. "Please," one said. "Please," the other said.

"You're not getting in," the bouncer said gently. He ignored
the passports and turned his back. They looked crestfallen. Next
up was a group of five British men, probably in their early thirties,
with a City of London polish about them. The bouncer explained
that there wouldn't be a place inside for them tonight, and one of
them said something cheeky about Berlin being a backwater. The
bouncer shrugged.

"I'm just joking," the Brit said.

"I got it," the bouncer said. He waited for them to go away and
then he turned to face me.

"Ich bin . . ." The bouncer disappeared inside. I'd been told that

the list was no guarantee. I also knew that they didn't want me in their club. ("You're an American," I'd been told, "and to them that makes you a puritan.") After a moment, he came back out with two other bouncers. They looked me up and down, then motioned me in. Another man patted me down. Nearby, Sven Marquardt, the infamously intimidating tattooed bouncer, was talking and laughing with a group. He didn't look so scary, at least compared with the others. At a ticket window, a man stamped my wrist and said, "See? Easy."

Through a door was a big concrete hall. Coat check: the operation was brisk. For a chit, you got a dog tag to wear around your neck, so you wouldn't lose it. I tried some doors and found them to be locked, and realized that Berghain proper wasn't open until the following night. Tonight was just Panorama Bar, an evening billed as "Get Perlonized!," a celebration of the music of Perlon, a small but beloved Berlin techno and house record label. I walked up some side stairs decorated with giant photo portraits of the resident DJs, who were all, it seemed, forbiddingly handsome, and, at a small bar half hidden behind a grate, ordered a Club-Mate—an herbal energy drink—into which, as is the custom, I poured a shot of vodka, and then went Carrawaying around.

A seasoned crowd: diverse in age, appearance, sexual preference, condition of mind. The vibe was laid-back, the look disheveled, wild-eyed, attractive, louche. Bedhead, shaved head —intentional hair. Dark clothing, layers, leather, natural fibers, boots, scarves, piercings. The smell of tobacco and weed and sweat. Groups lounged on benches and in comfy chairs and on the floor. The bathrooms were buzzing with cokey conversation. Couples entered hand in hand and found stalls. While using one for its intended purpose, I heard laughter to one side and rustling to the other, and felt the embarrassment of my puritanical roots. The main bar, three-sided and occupying the back half of the main space, was cleverly lit, with attentive bartenders and no risk of being overlooked. The prices were low. I walked behind the bar area, along a dark corridor of cubbies in which people were fooling around or spacing out, and tacked back toward the DJ, who was working at the front of the room. The DJ table hung from the ceiling on chains. You couldn't get very close, but there was space along the wall, where the floor was strewn with empty bottles—beer, water, Club-Mate—which people generally just toss on the floor. Now and then, a man came through with a crate and unobtrusively gathered some up, but as the night wore on the floor pooled up with broken glass—Berghain jetsam. The sound was loud and yet clean enough to allow conversation. A friend had told me, with regard to the evolution of minimal techno, "If you amplify it really loud, you need less music."

Nothing to photograph here. I stayed until 7 a.m.

Saturday night, or really Sunday morning, is *Klubnacht* at Berghain. I was back at 3 a.m., this time in the main club, approaching peak tourist hour. Past the coat check, there was a giant concrete atrium, pretty much empty, with a bar in the corner. A few glass bottles rained down from above and shattered at my feet. A steel staircase led up to a big dance floor surrounded by various bars and nooks. The left side of the dance floor was dominated by muscular men, many shirtless, and a few doing a dance that I'd heard called, jokingly, Pressing the Dwarf. The straight crowd was to the right, but it seemed that most were up at Panorama Bar. Here and there were concrete plinths, upon which pretty people danced. Groups lounged on beds hanging from chains, gently swinging back and forth.

The dark rooms were around somewhere, but I didn't go looking for them. Perhaps I'd wait for the boar hunter. Here and there stuff was going on, in plainish sight, yet I saw little to upset or titillate. The Caligula mystique, the stories of men defecating on each other or using frozen turds as dildos, seemed disproportionate. No one offered me so much as a glance, to say nothing of an Icy Mike. I had a shot of Jägermeister and an espresso and went out onto the dance floor and stood in front of one of the speakers. There were six of them, each about the size of a Trabant. The sound was revelatory, the deep bass tones like a drug. A DJ named Mathew Jonson, from Vancouver, had taken over the booth for an improvisational turn with two others, who performed under the name Minilogue. The three men hunched over laptops and mixers as though herding tiny animals with their hands. Jonson had a curly mop of hair and a beard, and looked like some wild ape-man of electronica. The music was churning, hypnotic, almost psychedelic, and I abandoned myself to it.

The hours passed. During a weekend, the clubbers come and go, as if to a tidal rhythm. A friend had likened the scene to a

coral reef: various schools of multicolored fish, stubborn crusta-
ceans, the occasional ray or eel gliding by, swimming in an ocean
of techno. In the eddies, there were people who, though all but
motionless, seemed caught up in something intense—you could
see it in their eyes. "You are touched by the different frequencies,"
the DJ Ricardo Villalobos says in *Feiern*. "You start to think about
your childhood." Transcendence and transgression lurked just out
of sight.

At one point, I went up to Panorama Bar, where a DJ from
Windsor, Ontario, was playing a set of Chicago house and Detroit techno. Her name was Heidi—Heidi Van den Amstel. She
had curly peroxided hair, a white T-shirt, tattoos on her arms, and
leather pants. She'd arrived from London shortly before her set,
amid flight delays across Europe—an entire continent of revelers
vexed by a disruption to the techno supply chain. She was part of
the generation of Windsorites who'd fallen hard for the dance music across the river, in Detroit. She moved to Europe a dozen years
ago, living in London and Berlin. This was the first time she had
played Panorama Bar in almost four years. She had been nervous,
but now she was in the thick of it, dancing and tossing her hair as
she worked the mixing console. She flipped through a binder of
CDs and manipulated knobs, her pinkie out, as though she were
drinking tea. Her agent brought her a shot of tequila, which she
chased with a lemon wedge, and she shuddered. A voice in the
music intoned, as though from a *Zeitmaschine*, "Can you feel it acid
house acid house I was there." People were jammed up in front of
her dancing, some with Avalon Ballroom abandon. "I want you,
I need you." This was fun music, joyous music, not the austere
minimal techno of downstairs, or the jazzy techno of Jonson and
Minilogue, or the hardcore techno that would inspire one to press
the dwarf. The bass rattled the empty tin record bins behind the
DJ. I sent a text to the boar hunter, wondering if he was around.
He replied, "KitKatClub."

After a few hours, Heidi stretched her back and leaned into the
climax of her set. Downstairs, the techno—and the crowd—had
turned hard. Upstairs, the dingy gray light of another Baltic morning leaked past the edges of the louvered shutters at the windows.
Soon the shades would flash open in synch with the music, to as-
tonish the congregation with the insult of daylight.

Two DJs who go by the name Bicep took over. Heidi checked

her face in her compact, gave herself over to the adulation of the
dancers down in front, and then, after a moment, made her way
to the bar with her boyfriend and her agent. I joined them for tequila shots and beers. Breakfast in Berlin. This went on for a while.
Heidi had had a marvelous time—too much for words, really—but
she didn't want to talk about Berghain. She was afraid that if she
did, she'd never get to play there again.

Made in China

FROM *The Wall Street Journal Magazine*

ON A RARE clear day, Grace Vineyard, 310 miles southwest of Beijing, might be mistaken for a winery in Tuscany. The balcony of the Italianate mansion overlooks lush rows of grapevines stretching to the horizon, where low mountains hover in the haze. Picnic tables sit scattered in a garden beneath slender trees that rustle in the dry wind. But take a stroll outside the winery gates, and you instantly step into the heart of provincial China. The unpaved lanes lead to farming villages whose crumbling facades are daubed with old Communist Party slogans and hung with tattered red flags. The motorbikes rattling past are beaten-up relics from Mao's day; the grape pickers moving through the fields wear traditional broad peasant hats. Beyond them sit the half-forgotten byways of Shanxi Province, a region renowned in the Imperial era as a center of trade and banking but more notorious in recent decades for its polluted cities devoted to the coal industry. Only a short drive away lie remnants of China's ancient glory, such as the enormous Chang Family Manor, once the luxurious abode of tea merchants, its interior lined with exquisitely carved wood.

Grace Vineyard is focused more on China's future. In the elegant dining room adorned with contemporary artwork, a small army of servers glides around me. While the kitchen prepares a banquet of delectable Shanxi treats, including scissor-cut noodles, sautéed river fish, and fried *bing* pastries, a fastidious wine steward creeps up at regular intervals to refill my glass with Grace's flagship Cabernet blend, the rich and velvety 2008 Chairman's Reserve, rated 85 by Robert Parker's website for its subtle blackberry flavors and hints of bay leaf, pepper, and cedar.

Grace is at the forefront of one of China's more improbable trends, as the most successful of a new wave of boutique wineries. Most have cropped up in the dry terrain of Ningxia in the north. But winemakers are also venturing into China's more varied landscapes, laying vines from the deserts of the old Silk Road to the foothills of the Himalayas. There are now around 400 wineries in the country. Wine consultants from France, Greece, California, and Australia are becoming as common as foreign IT experts in Shanghai, and the local product is being marketed not only to expats but to an increasingly sophisticated Chinese clientele.

The results are beginning to startle critics. In 2011, the Cabernet blend Jia Bei Lan, from the Helan Quingxue vineyard, became the first Chinese wine to take the prestigious international trophy at the Decanter World Wine Awards (judges praised its "supple, graceful and ripe" flavors and its "excellent length and four-square tannins"), and in 2011, four Chinese reds, led by Grace's Chairman's Reserve, beat French Bordeaux in a blind taste test in Beijing with international judges. Although some cried foul—wines had to be under $100, including the 48 percent mainland tax on imported wines—more vocal Chinese patriots hailed the result as heralding the arrival of an industry, evoking the famous blind tasting in 1976 when California wines outshone the Gauls for the first time.

As they advance, China's boutique-wine pioneers may also help upend one of the many myths about the country. The conventional wisdom—or cliché—is that China can reproduce Western manufacturing or technology overnight, but European artisanal culinary delicacies that have evolved over generations are all but impossible to replicate. And yet, even apart from wine, there are dozens of small producers in China who are now attempting to do just that, with surprising success. Truffles, burrata cheese, prosciutto, feta, Roquefort, baguettes, foie gras—almost every Western gourmet item has been tackled by Chinese entrepreneurs for a new audience of adventurous diners. The Temple Restaurant Beijing, a contemporary enclave that is part of a 600-year-old temple near the Forbidden City, offers excellent French-style cheeses crafted by Le Fromager de Pekin, founded by a local producer named Liu Yang. His specialties include Beijing Blue and Beijing

Gray, whose consistency falls between a Camembert and Saint Mar-cellin. At Sir Elly's Restaurant at the five-star Peninsula Shanghai, if you order the selection of caviars, three will be Chinese. For a decade already, a Chinese caviar industry in the rivers bordering Russia has been winning accolades and is exporting to the U.S. and Europe.

The main hurdle is convincing consumers to give Chinese prod-ucts a chance—a problem that is particularly acute with wine. An affinity for grape wine seems culturally far removed from the Mid-dle Kingdom. For some 4,000 years, the Chinese have preferred grain-based wine (typically rice), a dark, fortified brew that often resembles dry sherry. (It became a state monopoly under the an-cient Tang dynasty, when the government ran taverns that doubled as brothels, featuring female musicians outside to lure customers.) And like many uninformed outsiders, when I was first offered a glass of Chinese grape wine in Shanghai's spectacular restaurant M on the Bund, I thought it was a practical joke. The idea tends to provoke remarks about toxic side effects—losing taste buds, for example, or even the sight in one eye. "Five years ago, you might have been right," the owner, Michelle Garnaut, says, handing me a glass of Grace's 2010 Chardonnay as we stand on the balcony facing the skyscrapers of Pudong. The first sip is a surprise—crisp and bright, with subtle nectarine flavors.

In fact, grape wine was first grown commercially in China in 1892, using vines imported from California, when it was marketed to foreign residents and the first rising class of Westernized Chi-nese. It was a strong beginning: in 1915, the winery, Changyu, won a string of gold medals at the Panama-Pacific International Exposi-tion in San Francisco, and in the wild and decadent 1930s, sultry movie star Hu Die ("the Chinese Marilyn Monroe") promoted it in Shanghai. After a long period of stagnation following the Com-munist Revolution, production of wine began expanding after the country's embrace of capitalism in the 1980s. According to Vin-expo, an international wine and spirits trade group, China is now the world's eighth largest wine producer and will be the sixth larg-est by 2016, surpassing Australia and Chile. But the emphasis has long been on quantity rather than quality, with enormous state-owned companies like Great Wall and Dynasty churning out cheap wines for locals with industrial speed, often using grapes imported from Argentina and South Africa.

For a glimpse of an old-school winery, I make the pilgrimage one drizzly afternoon to Chateau Changyu AFIP, located in a rural district an hour-and-a-half drive northeast of Beijing. It's the descendant of China's pioneer 1892 company and now part of a conglomerate whose scale can only send a shudder down the spine of the average oenophile. The winery isn't hard to spot, since it boasts a reproduction French chateau, its turrets rising above the verdant vineyards. The sense of Disney fantasy only increases as I enter part of the winery complex called Foreign Town, a faux European village complete with medieval church, a store where Chinese newlyweds are having their photos printed on wine labels, and a shop mysteriously called the Holy Grail Factory—all utterly deserted but awaiting busloads of tourists.

Accompanying me is the Beijing-based wine blogger Jim Boyce, who has covered the local wine industry for more than eight years and has been a consistent advocate for the boutique wines of Shanxi and Ningxia. Boyce, who has the slightly disheveled appearance and acerbic wit of Newman from *Seinfeld,* is having trouble readjusting his palate to China's pollution after a trip to the bucolic Sonoma Valley. For days after his return to Beijing, he jokes, the bouquet of every wine, good or bad, was vaguely like smog, the first sip rather like lead. ("And the hangovers are worse here," he mourns.)

A guide named Nan Xia leads us into the château to inspect the bunkerlike cellar, where private wine collections are stored behind Arthurian coats of arms inscribed with Chinese calligraphy, and a Wine Culture Museum, which includes a photo of Changyu wines being served to President Obama at a state dinner. ("The closest thing to an assassination attempt yet," Boyce murmurs.) The tour ends up in a cavernous tasting room, where a young sommelier, Wong Fuyue, hesitantly serves a 2008 Chardonnay at room temperature to the Muzak version of the *Titanic* theme song. "I would describe this wine as anemic," Boyce notes. "There's not much nose. But at least it's clean." When told that it sells for more than $100 a bottle, Boyce almost drops his glass. "I can buy a Chilean bottle for $12 at the supermarket—and it's better! Why would I buy this wine?"

Wong Fuyue grins and turns up his palms. "I don't know!" Nan Xia is unperturbed by the bad review. "Can we all take a photo together?"

After visiting Changyu, it is easy to understand why the arrival of smaller producers causes such relief and excitement among China's wine lovers. Some experts believe that the sheer novelty of the situation is leading to overenthusiasm. "A few years ago, Chinese wine was terrible," Boyce says. "Now it's not. But the industry is still in its infancy," he cautions.

The boutique wines are expensive—thanks to their small-scale production and China's high transport costs—retailing from $40 to $80. And production in some vineyards is minuscule. But the quality of the boutique wines is now undeniable—the country has the soil, the climate, and an aptitude for the technical aspects of production—and the range of domestic wines is expanding, like so much in China, at an accelerating pace.

The rise of boutique wineries is just one element turning the wine world on its head; another is the recent boom in international wine imports to China. At the luxury end of the market, the shifting tastes of China's superwealthy are now dictating prices at auction houses around the world. Hong Kong led the way, abolishing the tax on imported wine in 2008 and becoming the world's No. 1 wine auction market by 2011. "People say it's a miracle, but it's not," says Gregory De'eb, general manager of Crown Wine Cellars, a fine-wine storage facility housed in a World War II ammunition depot leased from the Hong Kong government. For decades, Hong Kong's wealthy had been storing their wines in cellars overseas. "In 2008, the floodgates opened," De'eb says. "There was forty years' worth of wine knowledge, forty years' worth of stocks, and a huge amount of capital. All the building blocks were in place."

This wine expertise is now percolating through the mainland. "China started late, but it's catching up quickly," says Simon Tam, head of wine at Christie's in China. "In just a few years, people have reached a very high level of appreciation. Chinese clients used to talk only about prices and vintages, not what was in the bottle. Now the important thing is not how much money you have but how you express it in wine knowledge." Tim Weiland, former general manager of the exclusive Aman at Summer Palace in the emperor's onetime retreat in Beijing, suggests that the image of China's wealthy class as crass nouveau riche—mixing expensive Bordeaux with Coca-Cola, for example—is entirely out of date. "The nouveaux riches of ten years ago are now the old rich," he says. "They have homes in Switzerland and Aspen, they're incredibly sophisticated and well traveled—much more well traveled than I am—and they know their wines."

Foreign importers are eager to expand their foothold far beyond the luxury market, as an estimated 200 million potential consumers in China's growing middle class are exposed to wine for the first time. China is already the world's fifth largest wine-consuming country. At fine restaurants in Beijing and Shanghai, where Chinese diners make up the majority, customers regularly pore over wine lists and discuss options in detail with the sommelier. "Eight years ago, Chinese people were not confident about wine," says Jackie Song, former wine steward at the Mediterranean restaurant Sureño, in Beijing's trendy Opposite House hotel. "All they would drink was French, especially Burgundy. But now they try Spanish wines, Chilean, Greek."

The number of Chinese-born sommeliers has increased exponentially over the past five years, with great career rewards for the most dedicated. Jerry Liao, who won the China National Sommelier Competition in 2013, had barely tasted grape wine a decade ago when he began working in high-end restaurants. "I was basically forced to learn," he says. "Otherwise I would have lost my job." Once he discovered his talent, Liao rose quickly through the ranks and is now hotel sommelier at the new Jing An Shangri-La in Shanghai. Even more meteoric has been the rise of Yang Lu, a gifted young sommelier who became the wine director of the entire Shangri-La hotel empire in 2012. "I'm in the first wave of Chinese sommeliers," he says. "We all realize that we're opinion leaders. We feel a lot of responsibility. And there's a lot of pressure."

Wine is also being offered at more social events in China. When I was invited to a dinner party at the Beijing studio-residence of artist Wang Mai and his wife, Liu Chunfeng, joining poets, pop stars, gallery owners, and curators in a warehouse filled with sculptures and giant oil paintings, the evening began with Prosecco and moved on to Australian Shiraz to complement the Sichuan hot-pot dinner, in which morsels of meat and vegetables are dropped into boiling oil. Wang remembered first trying sweet Chinese white wine at age 10 but has so far been unable to sample the new boutique wines. "The only Chinese wines I can afford are almost undrinkable," he says. "I'll stick with Barossa Valley."

Grace Vineyard is a model for the Chinese wine industry's potential," says Tam of Christie's, pointing to its consistently good results over the past decade. Grace has an annual production of 2 million bottles, specializing in robust reds, with a few fine whites. Next year, Grace is even releasing the first Chinese sparkling wine, a blanc de blanc.

But on China's wild frontier of taste, the artisanal success stories are nothing if not eccentric. Even the birth of Grace Vineyard sounds like the premise of a reality-TV show. "We're considered a miracle in the industry," says Judy Chan, the CEO of the family-owned company, whose father moved from mainland China to Hong Kong in the 1970s after the Cultural Revolution. "We had no experience in wine, no connections, no distribution network." Chan's businessman father, Chun Keung Chan, purchased 150 acres of farmland in Shanxi in 1997 to fulfill a fantasy of owning a winery, and in 2002, as the first vintage was hitting the market, he handed over the reins to his spectacularly unqualified 24-year-old daughter. A psychology graduate who had recently quit Goldman Sachs, Chan had experienced wine only as a teenager on holiday in Burgundy, where she drank two glasses of red and fell asleep on the couch. Her arrival in the backwaters of rural Shanxi was a culture shock, as she was collected from the airport by the surly local vintners, who were suspicious of her youth, gender, and evident inexperience. "When they mentioned Cabernet Sauvignon, I didn't even know what they were talking about," she recalls. "But I BS-ed my way through—a skill I had learned from Goldman Sachs."

She had to learn almost every aspect of the industry from scratch, Chan tells me when we meet at a Michelin-starred Hong Kong restaurant, Bo Innovation, which serves a range of Grace wines with its molecular Chinese cuisine. A local designer created Grace's first label, Chan says, but "it looked like soy sauce. We had to beg people to take it." She hired an Australian consultant, Ken Murchison, and to improve quality, they uprooted half the original vines, which horrified government officials ("In China, everything has to get bigger and bigger!"). Even marketing the unfamiliar product had its comic elements. In 2003, Grace opened its first retail store in Fuzhou, where Chan's family originated. "For sixteen days, not a single person walked in," Chan recalls. When one finally did, the four shopgirls rushed him. "He fled! They scared the poor guy to death."

The breakthrough came when hotels in Hong Kong, Shanghai, and Beijing began to serve Grace wines—the Peninsula chain even commissioned a special label. The initial appeal was to foreigners who enjoyed the novelty, but the new wave of Chinese middle-class diners has now become the majority of the market. "A lot of Chinese people are proud of our wines and want to show them off," says Chan, who admits there is still a deep prejudice against Chinese wine overseas. But if the quality is consistent, China can overcome its poor image, she suggests, as New World wines have. "People forget that when Californian and Australian wines first came out, consumers were very, very skeptical. The French looked down their noses for decades at the Napa Valley."

Wariness of the MADE IN CHINA label is even more severe when it comes to food, thanks to the scandals that have become a staple of international news since 2008, when baby formula tainted with toxic melamine killed 6 infants and sickened 300,000 more. In 2013, tens of thousands of chickens were slaughtered for fear of bird flu, and a crime ring was arrested for passing off rat and mink meat as lamb.

The small producers of artisanal Western delicacies are so far untouched by such scandals. Consider the rise of Chinese caviar. Siberian sturgeon was first imported in 1997 to a research station on the Amur River, on the Russian border. A visiting French scientist suggested harvesting it. Today, China accounts for 20 percent of world output, filling the gap left by overfishing and poaching in the Caspian Sea. The majority is exported to the United States, Europe, Japan, and even Russia, and it's served in first-class air cabins and sold under the esteemed Petrossian label. But it still struggles to overcome the made-in-China stigma.

Swiss-born chef Florian Trento of Hong Kong's Peninsula hotel recalls being deeply apprehensive when his counterpart in Shanghai invited him to try the caviar. "I said, 'Really? Chinese caviar?' He said, 'Trust me!' And it was fantastic." Now two types of Chinese caviar are on the Peninsula menu in Hong Kong. "Often we do blind tastings because Chinese products have such a bad rap," Trento says. "Diners are very, very surprised." He sees it as a template for what is possible in China. "The quality is excellent, the industry is well regulated, the farms are sustainable," he says. "We are very keen to support it." Still, even in Beijing markets, Chinese caviar is sold with Cyrillic labels to look Russian. "In the long term, the Chinese have to fix things. There's been one scandal after another. How much more can you destroy your reputation?"

Because of their size, most top restaurants and luxury hotels import ingredients from overseas—beef from Australia, produce from California, mozzarella from Italy. But in the former French Concession of Shanghai, one upscale restaurant, Madison, has gone to the opposite extreme and makes a point of serving only locally sourced produce. The menu, although technically New American, reads like a lesson in Chinese geography. There's smoked trout from the coastal waters of Fujian, pan-roasted chicken from the mountains of Anhui, Wagyu tenderloin from the fields of Dalian. The truffles for the hollandaise and morels for a *huangjiu* sauce are sourced from the Himalayan foothills of Yunnan, while ingredients for side dishes such as potato puree with garlic scapes are gathered from small farms near Beijing.

"You can't say that China doesn't have great ingredients," says the chef-owner, Austin Hu, who moved with his family to Shanghai when he was eight, studied at the French Culinary Institute in New York City, and apprenticed at Danny Meyer's Gramercy Tavern. "There's a huge amount going on out there. In fact, Chinese produce does not have to be inferior; it can be better." One employee works full-time tracking down produce across the Chinese countryside, meeting farmers and fishermen outside the industrialized food system. "It's a lot of work," Hu admits when we meet at the bar of his softly lit, SoHo-style space, a refuge from the city's chaos. "When you take the extra step to find the little gùys, it can be a revelation." He has discovered small, pesticide-free farms cropping up, with names such as Little Donkey Farm, which sounds as though it was transplanted from Brooklyn. He's met an independent beer maker in Inner Mongolia who sold his brew in 100-crate lots ("We send a guy up there to negotiate and truck it ourselves to Shanghai") and has come across a delectable salt-cured ham from Yunnan. ("I'll put it up against any type of prosciutto.") One small producer near Shanghai was even producing hand-pulled burrata, employing teams of women who once made dumplings by hand. ("Their finger skills are great.")

Hu says that the homegrown concept has been a hard sell. "Some customers, when they discover it's all locally sourced, will stand up and leave the restaurant. I tell them they're being closed-

minded. I say, 'Give it a shot!' But it's hard to break the mindset."
Another problem is the relatively high cost. "Chinese people are
pretty value sensitive," says Hu. "They praise a restaurant that is
xìng jià bi, good value. These local ingredients are not cheap, so
it's a risk for people to break out of their regular eating habits."
But as concern about food quality mounts in China, customers are
becoming more prepared to pay extra to know their food is safe.
"During the bird-flu scare, we sold more chicken than ever," says
Hu's cousin, Garrett, who helps run Madison. "People trust our
sourcing."

It's a strange twist that every new food scandal bolsters the sales
of artisanal Western foods, even in the most difficult gastro frontier, cheese. Many Chinese are lactose intolerant and find the rich
milk product difficult to digest, but Liu Yang, one of the first to
produce French artisanal cheese in China, says that while his first
customers in 2009 were Western expats, they are now outnumbered by locals. "Parents want their kids to have safe, real food," he
says. "When they come to my shop, I explain where my milk comes
from and how the cheese is made." For most, a visit is a totally new
experience. "I give them a tasting platter and talk over tea about
how to appreciate the flavors."

With his close-cropped hair and horn-rimmed spectacles, Yang
looks more like an intellectual from the 1960s than a hipster
gourmand, and his factory, where a half-dozen women in hairnets
work over shiny industrial vats, is improbably located in a row of
shops in an outer Beijing suburb. His own introduction to quality
cheeses began slowly, Yang explains, when he moved to France
to study business management 13 years ago. "Like most Chinese
people, I had only ever tasted processed yellow cheese," he says.
It wasn't until he moved to Corsica in 2005 that he had his conversion, when he learned that his neighbor handcrafted his own
cheese and was willing to share his experience.

On his return to Beijing, Yang tried his hand at cheese-making
using local dairy. Not surprisingly, he could not replicate the exact
flavors: French cows tend to graze on grass in the mountains, so an
herbal flavor infuses their milk, while Chinese cows feed on grain
at industrialized farms. (There is an organic dairy in the region,
but its prices are prohibitive, Yang says.) Even so, he was able to
monitor his milk's quality by buying direct, and he now gets milk
from cows fed with grass in the countryside. Since opening his

shop in 2009, he has expanded from his Roquefort-style Beijing Blue to six cheeses of varying richness and consistency, and he has just begun selling a goat cheese. "Food culture is very important to all Chinese people, and they are open to new tastes," Yang says. "The rich and the poor go to restaurants regularly. Eating is the most enjoyable thing in life." And the cultural leap is not as great as imagined. "We eat fermented tofu, so we can eat fermented cheese."

The speed of change depends largely on the Chinese economy. "We talk about education as a way of developing China's wine culture," says Yang Lu of the Shangri-La chain. "But the most important thing for growth is having a stable middle class, with a disposable income. Unlike in the U.S. or Europe, wine is still a luxury product rather than a daily beverage." Still, many believe that for local winemakers in this near-virgin territory, the prospects can only improve. "It's true that Chinese wine doesn't have a recognizable identity yet, unlike, say, a classic Napa Valley or Clare Valley wine," says David Shoemaker, the American-born head sommelier at Pudong Shangri-La, East Shanghai. "But very soon, I think, we will be able to taste a wine and say, 'Ahhh, that's a classic Shanxi.'"

Mr. Nhem's Genocide Camera

FROM *The Believer*

MR. NHEM'S GOLD-PLATED watch glinted under the fluorescent light. He clasped his hands and smiled at me over his knuckles.

"I can help you," Samithy translated. "I can make you famous."

This was my opportunity to become an investor in Mr. Nhem's museum, and thus a permanent partner. He had everything—the land, the government permits, approval for the development of 14 identified points of interest. Mr. Nhem raised a collection of papers in a plastic book-report cover and flipped through them. He pointed to their stamped official seals. I was in a portable office in a dirt lot in northern Cambodia, and a former Khmer Rouge cadre was offering to make me a partner in the Khmer Rouge Museum.

Mr. Nhem had all the artifacts: over 300 photos from the Khmer Rouge era and the post–Khmer Rouge fighting. He had a pair of Pol Pot's shoes, and part of a statue that was once displayed in Anlong Veng, the town we were in. He even had the camera he'd used when he'd worked as a photographer at the S-21 prison, the infamous detention and torture center where he'd aided in documenting the 14,000 people who came through the facility, only 7 of whom survived. He'd dubbed the relic "the Genocide Camera."

All he needed was investors, he told me. This was my opportunity, he said. They could advertise me as "the American partner Lauren"; I could display my nation's flag, along with a sign that said I had cooperated to support the museum. I asked how much he was looking for. An animated exchange sparked between Mr. Nhem and Samithy, the translator and tour guide who'd brought me to Anlong Veng, who'd tracked down Mr. Nhem and scored me this meeting in his mildewed office.

Samithy wrote down a figure and slid the piece of paper my way: $120,000.

Mr. Nhem had clearly mistaken me for someone other than a preschool teacher living on $800 a month in Phnom Penh. But I decided it was better not to say this.

Anlong Veng is a dusty, sweaty slab of no man's land in northern Cambodia. It's one of those towns you'd pass through on a bus to somewhere better, and nothing about its battered storefronts, rubbled roads, or shabby markets squatting beneath beach umbrellas would make you think it was anything special.

The region had been the last stronghold of the Khmer Rouge, the genocidal regime under which nearly a quarter of the Cambodian population perished between 1975 and 1979. For almost 30 years after the official fall of the Khmer Rouge to Vietnamese forces, the regime remained active in the countryside, attracting devotees and plotting a resurgence that never materialized. The Khmer Rouge had been siphoned into smaller and more isolated parts of the country until, at last, all the diehards holed up in an isolated wedge of land along the Thai border, getting rich off logging and living in relative impunity.

The Khmer Rouge's leader, Pol Pot, was among these men. He spent his final years languishing, bored, inside a mosquito net in Anlong Veng, under a house arrest ordered by a former comrade, Ta Mok. Here, journalist Nate Thayer conducted the famous last interview with Pol Pot, in which the old man with crushed-silk skin declared that his conscience was clear. And here Pol Pot finally died, old and of natural causes; his body was burned beneath a pile of tires.

I'd read in the local newspapers about plans to turn Anlong Veng into a new stop on the temples-and-genocide tour-bus circuit. One article detailed plans to train the area's large number of former Khmer Rouge cadres to become tour guides. Another claimed Nhem En, the spearhead behind the tourism development, had tried to raise money by selling Pol Pot's toilet seat for half a million dollars. (There'd been no takers.)

In the common Cambodian lexicon, the Khmer Rouge era is known as "Pol Pot time," a linguistic reflection of the way in which all the regime's atrocities have become concentrated on one man. It's a way for the living to deflect responsibility, and an important distinction to maintain: while the UN-backed tribunals are painstakingly under way, the current government is composed largely of former Khmer Rouge, including the ironfisted prime minister Hun Sen—men who could, should the tribunals continue, be tried for their role in war crimes. But beyond that, *Khmer Rouge* isn't a cut-and-dried term. Aside from the well-to-do urbanites at the top, the regime was mostly composed of uneducated rural peasants, many of whom were coerced to join as children, under threat of death. Today former victims and perpetrators of Khmer Rouge violence display similar levels of trauma, often living side by side.

Nhem En is one of the former Khmer Rouge occupying this expansive gray area. He isn't one of the big names: he isn't a Brother Number One (Pol Pot) or a Brother Number Two (Nuon Chea), or even any brother, really. He's one of the former midlevel cadres who always have someone above them to point to: "just following orders"; "kill or be killed." He's one of the many who've been folded back into society uneventfully, the way a body most often reabsorbs a blood clot. But while Nhem En's name may not be famous, the work he produced under the Khmer Rouge is. The silent faces in Mr. Nhem's photos from S-21 have become one of the most emblematic relics of the regime. His photographs are prominently displayed at the former prison site in Phnom Penh, now the Tuol Sleng Genocide Museum, one of the top tourist attractions in Cambodia.

Genocide sites are Cambodia's second-ranking tourist attractions, after the temples of Angkor Wat. Foreign tourists seem to have a fascination with the genocide that Cambodians largely don't share. Most often, the only Cambodians one sees at Tuol Sleng or the Killing Fields site are the *tuk-tuk* drivers and acid-burn victims clustered outside the gates, hoping for runoff from the tourist dollars.

The guidebooks and placards inside don't tell you that these sites were created more to influence international opinion than to memorialize the dead. Both were set up by the Vietnamese during their post–Khmer Rouge occupation of Cambodia as a way to justify their occupation and prove that they had not committed the war crimes, as the remaining Khmer Rouge claimed. I'd heard conflicting reports about Cambodians' initial interaction with these sites: expats said that Cambodians were not allowed to visit Tuol Sleng in its first years, but an acquaintance told me of being forced by the Vietnamese to visit Tuol Sleng in the early postwar days—the smell of the blood, she'd said, was awful. What was true was that both of these sites initially featured displays of victims' bones. In fact, the Killing Fields still does—a bone pagoda, a supposed memorial to the victims whose bones lie inside it, is in complete opposition to the Cambodian tradition of cremation. In 2004, the former king Norodom Sihanouk went so far as to claim that the purpose of such a display was "to punish the victims, humiliate them, dishonor them."

Also absent from mention is that the Cambodian government has allowed the Killing Fields to be privatized, selling a 30-year concession to operate the site to the Japanese company JC Royal, which has since raised ticket prices and introduced $3 audio tours that have eliminated the need for local Cambodian tour guides. While Tuol Sleng still employs Cambodian guides, concrete information about who owns and operates the site appears intentionally murky. Thus the only Cambodians one can be sure are engaging with and benefiting from these genocide tourism sites are the *tuk-tuk* drivers and beggars outside the gates.

While genocide tourism is not distinct to Cambodia—Tusafiri Africa Tours and Travels offers a six-day "Rwanda History Will Tell! Safari" for $2,000—the privatization of and profiting from genocide memorials appears to be. Founded by the Polish parliament, Auschwitz-Birkenau Museum is operated by the nonprofit Auschwitz-Birkenau Foundation, whose website offers structural and financial transparency. Rwanda's Kigali Memorial Centre is operated by the local city council, in partnership with United Kingdom–based AEGIS Trust, and maintained by goodwill donations left by its visitors. The Armenian Genocide Museum-Institute, in Yerevan, is a subdivision of the National Academy of the Republic of Armenia and has a similarly donation-based entrance. Bill Clinton headed the founding and fund-raising for the Srebrenica-Potočari Memorial and Cemetery to Genocide Victims, in Bosnia, garnering support from private groups and governments alike. Cambodia's sites, however, are shrouded in opacity, and it is only through careful digging that one can discern who is running and profiting from these sites.

*

"Pol Pot time" isn't often discussed in Cambodian daily life—with so many former Khmer Rouge still in the country, ruling the country, how would the conversation begin? In fact, war history has only recently begun to be taught in the schools, and the silence is so thick that it is not uncommon for youth to believe that the Khmer Rouge didn't actually happen. In high-school-level English classes I'd taught, my students could wearily recite the length of the Khmer Rouge occupation of the country—"three years, eight months, and twenty days"—but they couldn't tell you the difference between Pol Pot and the Khmer Rouge as a whole.

Nhem En was quoted in one of the articles I had read in the local English-language media as wanting to build a museum to preserve the war history for the next generation. It sounded good. But I wondered if a genocide-tourism site developed by a former Khmer Rouge cadre would actually benefit Cambodians and help to end the silence, or if it would be just another exploitation of foreigners' fascination.

The first thing Samithy said to me when I got into the van on our way to Anlong Veng was that both of his parents had died in the Khmer Rouge. His brother and sister, too. I'd been in Cambodia long enough to understand the silence surrounding the war, and to grow suspect of such intensely personal divulgences. It was rarely coworkers, friends, or acquaintances who shared the impact of the Khmer Rouge on their families, I'd noticed, but rather the *tuk-tuk* drivers, shopkeepers, tour guides, and beggars—people with whom my interactions were transactional.

Samithy picked me up from my guesthouse in Siem Reap, the tourist town closest to the Angkor Wat temple complex and the closest accessible city from which to travel to Anlong Veng. I listened to him talk as the van glided through the small city center, its roads lined with the morning bustle of markets and street vendors. Foreigners in sun hats were climbing into *tuk-tuks*, armed with water bottles for a long day spent temple-hopping. Before the Khmer Rouge, Samithy told me, he'd lived in Phnom Penh. His parents had been "high-class people." He'd been separated from them early on in the regime. As a teenager, he'd been sent to a youth camp where he'd slept outside for the first year, even during the monsoon season, working 18-hour days and living on watery gruel. It's a story with which one becomes familiar, living in Cambodia, and one I'd learned well before moving there, growing up with the children of Khmer Rouge survivors in Oakland, California. The majority of these refugees had fled Cambodia by escaping to Thailand following the Khmer Rouge fall to Vietnam. During the actual "Pol Pot time," the country had been on lockdown, with virtually no foreigners coming in or Cambodians going out.

Earlier, on the phone, Samithy had laughed dismissively when I'd asked him about his familiarity with Anlong Veng's history. "I work for the UN for fifteen year. Anything you want to know, I tell you."

"I'm not a big man," he told me now, looking out over the steering wheel. "I don't want a big position. I want to live peaceful in my country. I want to help the people in my country. I want to tell tourists about Cambodia to help my country. In Cambodia, there is no neutrality. The police and military are corrupt. So who will help the people?" He raised his open palm as if offering the landscape to me. We stopped at a security checkpoint; Samithy rolled down the window and exchanged words with the guards. They laughed and waved him through.

"They all know me," he said with a smile. "Because I was a number-one tour guide here. But the government raised the bribe fees to be a tour guide and I could not pay. Now I'm just a taxi driver." He waved his hand and repeated, "I don't want to be a big man."

We passed the Angkor Wat temples, surrounded by tour buses and *tuk-tuks*, saggy-eyed elephants waiting to give rides to tourists. The morning light cut across the crumbly spires. Samithy kept repeating how he didn't want to be a "big man"—so often that it was hard to believe him. We left the temple area, the roadside fruit stands petering out into long, hot expanses of grass and dirt as we moved at a crawl.

We'd been driving for about two hours before Samithy started talking about Anlong Veng. "The people in Anlong Veng—these days they are very isolated, powerless. All the big men from Anlong Veng, the former Khmer Rouge, they are now in Phnom Penh. In 2008, Hun Sen, the prime minister, he said to the big men, 'Come to the government.' And they did." He shrugged. "Now they sit in air-conditioned rooms to make strategy to stop the tribunals."

I asked him what people in Anlong Veng thought about the Khmer Rouge. Samithy was quiet a moment. "In Anlong Veng, they are old people." "Old people" was a term used for rural people during the Khmer Rouge, people seen as loyal to the revolution, whereas "new people" were urban, educated, upper-class, enemies and imperialists—what Samithy's parents had been, and what my California friends' parents had been. "They don't think Pol Pot was so bad, but not so good, either. They think maybe so-so; they live with it but they don't support it." He paused. "They were captured by their leader."

I tried to imagine how the Khmer Rouge would have "captured" the people—through poverty, fear of reprisal, fear of a return to the work camps and violence. Even still, Samithy's casting seemed in direct opposition to my research: I'd read reports of people worshipping Pol Pot in Anlong Veng. I'd seen photos of women burning incense at his cremation site, praying for lucky lottery numbers. "It's like they don't see Pol Pot as a genocidal killer," one former aid worker had told me, "but as a nationalist hero that said 'fuck you' to imperialism." The two depictions of Anlong Veng seemed too polarized to both be true.

"What do the people think now?" I asked.

"Now they are painful," Samithy told me. "When they see Pol Pot die of natural causes, not punishment—they think not good. When they hear the tribunal is slow, they think not good. They don't understand why some people get tried and others don't."

We fell into silence. I looked out the window, the fields giving way to charred stumps and scorched earth: logging territory. During their years in Anlong Veng, the Khmer Rouge's leaders had turned to other means of supporting themselves, namely logging. Ta Mok, a.k.a. "Brother Number Five," a.k.a. "the Butcher," had amassed a small fortune in the semilegal timber industry. By charitably allowing a trickle of the funds to reach the destitute residents of Anlong Veng, Ta Mok had inspired their loyalty and gratitude. Ta Mok remained in Anlong Veng until 1999, when he was brought to Phnom Penh, where he'd die awaiting trial for crimes against humanity. When he left, so did the remaining wealth. Trucks full of logs rumbled past, motorbikes manned by razor-thin boys weaving between them. Women in electric-colored pajama suits covered their heads with *krama* scarves; their black eyes blazed out at us.

We traversed a dusty orbit of bikes and markets and heat, through the center of town and toward a mountain. Ahead of us, a truck heaved forward. I watched a small puppy gallop into the road and disappear beneath the truck bed.

*

At the top of the mountain just before the Thai border, we followed a hand-painted blue sign that read POL POT CREAMATION. We pulled off the highway and onto a pitted dirt road. At the entrance a few meters down, a man lay beneath a tin roof, napping in a hammock. His hand absently clutched the end of a rope strung across the road. We paid him $2, which he slipped into his breast pocket as we pulled into the site. The area was tidy and landscaped, but unelaborate. There were no signs to explain anything, nothing but a simple printed POL POT CREMATED HERE to commemorate the man who'd altered the nation's history and facilitated the deaths of a quarter of its population. There was an altar, but it looked abandoned, bowls empty and ashed incense sticks curled like long fingernails.

We stood in the muggy silence.

Samithy told me how Pol Pot had been cremated under a pile of tires—what the *New York Times* had likened to "a bonfire of garbage."

"Most Cambodians, they're burned beneath wood," Samithy explained. "So this was a punishment." He smiled a little at the words. A few meters off, a group of young men sat in the shade beneath a tree. One sprawled out in a hammock. They craned their necks, regarding me with lethargic half-interest. Samithy motioned to the young men. "They live here. They're construction workers; they build the casino across the road." He pointed to a mammoth gray slab encased in wooden scaffolding.

"Right there," he pointed to the shacks just behind the men, "is their bathroom." He smiled to himself, seeming to take particular pleasure in pointing that out. "See, Pol Pot is behind the bathroom." He chuckled softly.

I asked him if he thought people here wanted tourism. Samithy shrugged. "Maybe it will bring money. But I think mostly they want to forget. You see," he gestured around, "it's not a big or important place. UNESCO wants to preserve, but most people think to forget."

Was it UNESCO or Nhem En that wanted to develop the site, to memorialize and remember? It was another contradiction. I glanced over at the men in the shade, still watching me. The site was gray and drab. Maybe my research into Anlong Veng's Pol Pot–worshipping had been wrong and maybe Samithy was right—maybe people in Anlong Veng did just want to forget. We

continued on to the town's second biggest tourist attraction, Ta
Mok's house: several stilted wooden structures clustered in brown
earth, swept immaculately clean. With childlike murals and thick
tree trunks as doorposts, it wasn't a poor person's house. At an altar near the entrance, bowls brimmed with fruit, stalks of bananas
fanned open, and incense smoldered.

"Who brings that here?" I asked.

Samithy gave a shrug. "Maybe his family."

"It's very nice."

Samithy nodded. "He lived here, in this big nice house"—he
swept his arm across the empty room—"free."

We roamed the grounds for another few moments, more because I felt like I should than out of any real interest. What were
tourists supposed to do in Anlong Veng, with the barren grounds
and minimal sign markings, with hot wind, dust, and abandoned
buildings? We got into the van and pulled away from the grounds,
past a lonesome vendor and a bored security guard. Samithy took
out his cell phone and called Nhem En.

In his fusty office, Nhem En placed two warm water bottles in front
of us. He took three cell phones out of his various pockets and
lined them up on the desk in front of him. He spent a good minute arranging them to his liking. Then he folded his hands and
smiled at me.

"Who is the museum's audience?" I asked.

As I waited for Samithy's translation, I watched Mr. Nhem's face
—dark, pocked skin, smooth comb-over. He looked a little like a
frog, and his voice was high-pitched.

"Of the 2.8 million visitors to Angkor Wat," Samithy said,
"maybe thirty to fifty percent will come to the Genocide Museum."
Mr. Nhem's number was off by nearly a million; there'd been only
2 million visitors to Angkor Wat the previous year. I asked what
he'd based this figure on.

"There are two main objectives of tourists to Cambodia: to see
temples and to know the genocide history. Last year, people from
one hundred and ninety-two countries came to Angkor Wat. And
now we have the new road to Anlong Veng. So they will come."

I asked him if there had been any research into the level of
interest, surveys, even, but the question seemed to get muddled
in translation. I took a sip of my warm water. Mr. Nhem got

more animated as he spoke, focusing on the stats of the proposed museum: he had 13 hectares of land on which to build the museum; there were currently 500 hotel rooms for tourists; there were "many" restaurants. There was "ninety percent security safety" in the area.

All the numbers Mr. Nhem were giving me differed from those he'd reported to the *Phnom Penh Post.* To them, he'd claimed possession of thousands of photographs, not hundreds, and access to over three times the amount of land. It occurred to me that I was in a place where facts were fluid, malleable, open to inflation depending upon who was asking.

In addition to the memorabilia and photographs, Mr. Nhem was also in possession of over 200 Khmer Rouge propaganda songs (to the *Phnom Penh Post,* he'd claimed to have thousands), the kind that would crackle over loudspeakers in the fields as people worked 18-hour days. Would I like to hear one? Before my translated response could reach him, Mr. Nhem lifted one of the cell phones and began pushing buttons. A tinny song blared out, a nasal voice distorted through the small speaker.

Mr. Nhem closed his eyes and listened. A smile spread across his face.

"This song," Samithy said, "would play in the morning."

The comment wasn't a translation.

Of course, there were more artifacts for the museum, Mr. Nhem told me, but he could not discuss further plans with anyone other than his partners.

"I have a great objective," Samithy continued, translating Mr. Nhem's words. "To make a museum for the history. And if you can cooperate as an international partner, it will benefit not only you and your family but the Cambodian people." A pause. "And world history." Another pause. "And it will help develop Anlong Veng."

Samithy shifted slightly in his chair. "And you can meet with an international lawyer to discuss the long-term financial benefits.

"But there is one thing." Mr. Nhem picked his teeth with a toothpick and smacked his lips. "There are many people who have criticisms of the museum plan. They say I have a small heart, that it will preserve a bad history. I know this, but I want to preserve the history for the new generation." Samithy's voice wavered a bit. "I want to keep it for the young people, so they won't follow in my way."

Mr. Nhem placed the toothpick on the table and folded his hands. "So I need a partner who will not listen to that criticism."

We sat there, all three of us quiet.

Mr. Nhem broke the silence by turning on his digital camera. He started showing me pictures of other "potential investors": scruffy-looking white guys wearing cargo shorts and bemused expressions, like they weren't really sure how they'd wandered into the picture. Mr. Nhem continued to scroll through. There were photos from the American War Museum in Ho Chi Minh City—old uniforms and recreated war scenes, an army hammock. This was where he'd gotten the idea for the museum, he told me. Maybe if I became a partner, we could go to Ho Chi Minh together to look at the museum.

Mr. Nhem was getting nowhere with me. Finally he changed tactics and decided that maybe people who weren't investors could see the future museum's artifacts after all—did I want to come to his house to take a look? He put his three cell phones in various pockets and we headed back into the heat. Mr. Nhem hopped onto his motorbike while I followed Samithy to the van. I wanted to ask Samithy if this guy was for real: if he really thought I had $120,000; if he really thought I'd give it to him if I did; if this museum was as much of a scam as it seemed. But before I could ask, Samithy looked at me and said, "He has a very great idea."

Samithy stared over the steering wheel. "He is not a big man. Like I say, all the big men are in Phnom Penh now. But he has a great objective." He looked over at me and nodded. "He would be a good business partner. This is a great opportunity for you."

Mr. Nhem's house was a stifling wooden structure with a makeshift market out front. The air sagged around the boxes piled up —bottles of water and flip-flops and tissues and cell-phone cards, things he sold from beneath the desolate and unmanned beach umbrella. He introduced me to his wife. She pressed her palms together and bowed. By country standards, it was a rich person's house—it had two full stories and furniture. Framed photographs lined the walls, hanging from haphazard nails. Some were Barbie-esque wedding photos; others resembled mug shots of startled-looking relatives, now deceased. There were many photos of Mr. Nhem, posed with various Westerners, standing before podiums and microphones in shabby conference rooms. "This is the old U.S. ambassador."

He pointed my attention to a different photo, an old one of him. He looked young and fresh-faced; he was wearing all black. His cheeks were round and his skin had a healthy glow—not someone suffering from malnutrition or overwork. If it hadn't been for the black pajamas and *krama* scarf, he could have been an upright, eager young peasant from anywhere. In the photo, he held a camera in his hand.

"This is from 1976, when I went to study in China." Samithy's eyes slinked across me as he translated, discreetly scanning my face for some kind of recognition. I knew the significance of the statement. The year 1976 was the middle of the Khmer Rouge reign; no one was going off to study in China unless the regime had sent him there, and unless he'd been deemed valuable. I decided not to reveal that I understood the importance of this. In the home of a former Khmer Rouge cadre in a town without foreigners, with a tour guide who contradicted most of what I'd learned, I instead gave a half smile and nodded.

"The museum will show many photos like this," Samithy translated.

We followed Mr. Nhem upstairs and sat on metal folding chairs. Mr. Nhem fished out a big reel of keys and jangled through them. He cranked open a metal cupboard where objects in large ziplock bags lined the shelves. He took them out, one at a time, tenderly displaying them for me:

"Here are Pol Pot's shoes." They were a pair of rubber sandals not as weathered as they ought to have been.

"Here is the Genocide Camera." It was a vintage-looking box camera.

"Here's Pol Pot's cap." Mr. Nhem flopped it onto his head and smiled.

"Do you want to try on Pol Pot's hat?" Mr. Nhem took it off his head and extended it toward me.

I waved it away: no, thank you; I would not like to try on Pol Pot's hat.

There were other artifacts: Mr. Nhem's notebook from his trip to China, and a rusted old hand-crank radio once used to connect with China. Mr. Nhem wanted me to know that he could certify the authenticity of these artifacts, and it was only when he said that that it occurred to me that there was really no way to prove these artifacts were real.

Then he began to take out photos, plastic sheets without their album covers: freeze-frame glimpses of jungles and soldiers and wooden meeting rooms.

Here was one of Pol Pot's wives, now withered with dementia and awaiting trial in Phnom Penh.

Here was the man who had killed Son Sen, another higher-up. And here was Pol Pot.

He looked elegant in a crisp linen suit. It must have been tailored, the way it hung so perfectly. He was leaning slightly on a railing, a green vista spread out behind him. His salt-and-pepper hair was combed back. His eyes had delicate lines around them. He looked like an aging Hollywood star; he looked like someone's wealthy Asian grandpa. It was the kind of photo that belonged on a mantel.

As I stared, Mr. Nhem interrupted. "He wants to take a picture of you," Samithy told me.

I looked up at Mr. Nhem and something in me buzzed. I thought of all the faces he'd photographed, the thousands of people tortured and executed, their bones later laid out in tourist displays. *The former photographer of S-21 wants to take your picture,* I thought. I'm not sure if I said anything or if I just sat there, shaking my head no. Samithy encouraged me, though, so I dragged myself up and stood by the metal cabinet with Mr. Nhem, sweaty and stiff. I winced a smile. The camera flashed. Mr. Nhem grinned and took the camera from Samithy, examining the viewfinder. He showed it to me—I looked like a strange, ghostly version of myself, wearing the same expression as those other white faces, the other "potential donors" Mr. Nhem had showed me earlier. I considered the fact that I would likely become another face he showed to another foreigner who traipsed through.

I sat back down, now itching to leave, every instinct in my body now screaming that it was now time to go, to get out of this house and this town, to get as far away as possible.

Mr. Nhem pulled out a big bound book and flipped to a bookmarked page. It was a list of donors, a hand-drawn chart with their names, nationalities, and the amounts they'd given. Was this different than leaving donations at a Rwandan or Armenian museum? Was this all just a scrappier version of Bill Clinton raising millions of dollars to open a Bosnian memorial? I didn't know. All I knew was that there was no way to verify where the money was actually going, and no way I was getting out of this, but in that moment I didn't care. I just hoped it would get me out of there faster. I fished $5 out of my purse and handed it to him, hoping it'd help me leave sooner. I tried not to look at Samithy as I did this, but I couldn't help it—I could feel him watching me. But then Samithy took the book from me and began writing his name down. He opened his own wallet and took out $10.

I got up, began to inch my way down the stairs. Mr. Nhem kept wanting to show me things, kept wanting to thank me; he wanted my phone number. His wife gave me another warm bottle of water. I was sick to my stomach. I just wanted to get into the van; I just wanted the air-conditioning to come on; I just wanted to go home. As I climbed into the van, Mr. Nhem called out to me. "He says that maybe you can find a millionaire from your country to become an investor," Samithy told me. "Since there are many there."

Samithy and I were silent for the first part of the ride back. He stared forward at the highway. "That man," he said at last, "he is one of the ones who killed my family."

"Maybe not him," Samithy continued after a pause. "Maybe he didn't do the killing, but someone like him." He paused again. "Maybe he photographed my parents before they died."

"Were your parents at S-21?" I asked at last.

Samithy shrugged. "I don't know," he answered. "We were separated very early on. My parents, they were high-class people. They were the kind of people they killed at S-21. So maybe he met them there."

The silence hummed. I felt the heat blazing in. "He went to China in 1976," Samithy said, scanning my face the way he had back at Mr. Nhem's house.

"I know," I said, looking at my hands.

I asked Samithy if he thought Mr. Nhem was a bad man. He nodded. "Yes, I think he is a bad man. He helped kill many people."

"Then why," I cleared my throat, croaked the words out, "why did you give him money?" *Why did you want me to become an investor?* I wanted to ask.

"I give him because I must forgive." He paused then added, "I am a Buddhist."

"Yes, but aren't you angry? To see that man, like that? Because

I'd—" I stopped myself. I was going to say *I'd be angry*, but I realized that wasn't quite true. I shook my head, corrected myself, "Because *I'm* angry."

"But how can I live if I am angry?" Samithy answered. "How can I work? How can I take care of my family? It's very painful; he is a bad man who did many bad things and he is free. He is not just free; he live a good life. He has a good position and a nice house. Me, I am taxi driver. For me, this is painful."

The sky ahead of us was heavy, the heat pushing against the sealed windows.

"I think the museum is a good idea. I think he should build it, because it is important. I think maybe he use the money I give for drink, for girls." He shrugged. "But I give anyway."

"I don't get it," I finally said, slumping against the seat, my nose twitching with the sting of tears.

"It's because I'm Buddhist."

I shook my head. "I understand that. I understand you're Buddhist. But I'm not. I'm American and I . . . I'm just angry."

"For me," Samithy said, "it's just painful."

We fell into another silence. I considered the fact that after a day of contradictions, this was the first time it felt like Samithy was being truly upfront with me. How was someone, anyone, supposed to move on in a country where the trauma was still so palpable? Where all the same men were still there; where the remnants of the war were that easy to touch and sit next to and give money to? If the wound was still that open, how could tourism do anything but scrape against it?

We fell into another silence. The ruggedly logged landscape passed outside the window. The heat was a hand pushing in on us. Finally it burst and the rain started. It was a real rain, one of those Southeast Asian ones you can't hide from. Umbrellas, ponchos—they don't do anything. There's no fighting it; you just have to surrender.

And that's what people did. Outside the window, I watched the young boys on motorbikes not bothering to cover themselves; I saw women walking slowly alongside the road, their clothes stuck to their bodies. Skeletal cattle blinked placidly in the puddles that had suddenly formed in the fields.

No one looked for shelter.

Camino Real

FROM *The New York Times Magazine*

BEFORE THE PASSENGERS turned on the driver and began plotting a mutiny, the ride was smooth. The bus rolled out of the station in São Paulo at about four o'clock on a Wednesday afternoon last July, and within an hour it had shaken free of the city's clotted tunnels, jammed overpasses, and coded graffiti. By six, we were barreling straight into a lurid sunset that endowed everything with the candied luster of fresh paint. Green hills, silver ponds, golden palms. Two parrots soared in tandem over a sugarcane field, inviting us to drift into a pastoral trance.

Then the engine's fan belt snapped. The bus limped into a roadside service station about 220 miles from São Paulo.

"In a half hour we'll be ready to go," Mauro Yodes, our cheerful driver, assured us. "Go ahead and get something to eat at the café, if you want."

This was the only bus that advertised start-to-finish service on the recently completed Interoceanic Highway, the first paved route to fully cross the big green heart of South America. The breakdown should have been a useful reminder that South American cross-continental travel was still new and many kinks had yet to be worked out. But we were antsy. We had so much ground to cover.

The bus was supposed to cross 3,500 miles of pavement (roughly the same distance as a flight from New York to Paris) in about 96 hours. My plan was to disembark early, about 50 hours into the trip, then I'd cobble together a series of shorter bus routes, which would allow me to spend time in towns and villages, all the way to the Pacific coast. Mauro told us he planned to stop for just 40 minutes a day—enough time, theoretically, for each passenger to wash up and buy food and drinks at a gas station. For the other 23 hours and 20 minutes, as he shared driving duties with his partner, José, we'd be confined to rigid seats—benumbed contortionists sweeping crumbs from our laps.

Among those onboard were more than a dozen unrelated Peruvians who worked in São Paulo and were returning home to visit family; a few Brazilians on vacation; a college professor from Ecuador who said he was studying the continent's "touristic infrastructure"; and a young couple from Cuzco, laboring heroically to entertain their 18-month-old daughter.

The various nationalities rarely mingled. The informal segregation reflected the continent itself, where two of the Western Hemisphere's most isolating geographical features—the Amazon basin and the Andes mountain range—have always gotten in the way of a unified South American culture. Lowland Brazilians and highland Peruvians couldn't be more different—in language, in genetic ancestry, in culinary traditions. But now an unbroken strip of common ground unites them, and every time someone makes the journey from one end of the Interoceanic to the other, the clean divisions between regions blur a little.

By 9 p.m., about three hours into the delay, the independent passengers had become a collective, united by grievance and doubt. Mauro, all smiles, kept ducking back into the cabin to tell us not to worry. But our patience had narrowed to a very sharp point. Passengers began discussing the merits of other South American bus companies—the reliability of their vehicles, the plushiness of their fully reclining seats, their straight-shooting drivers. The Ecuadorian professor, who proved our most enthusiastic mutineer, suggested we present Mauro with a strict ultimatum: either the bus was fixed within an hour, or we got our ticket money back plus return fare to São Paulo.

We marched off the bus and peered through the café windows, watching Mauro settle his dinner bill. Moments later, he walked through the door and straight into our little nest of vipers.

Mauro—a compact 52-year-old who spends an average of 26 days a month driving this highway—calmly illustrated what he would later describe to me as the most important lesson the Interoceanic has taught him: plans rarely match up with reality, and it's almost never immediately obvious whether that's a good or a bad thing.

"Look," Mauro explained to our group, "if we run on schedule, we reach the Peruvian border at about 1 a.m. on the third day." But he said the border-patrol office would be closed at that time. So we would have to sit there and wait until 8 a.m., when the office opened again. He motioned to the café, with its 24-hour food service, its ice-cold drinks, the soccer match on TV. "Waiting here is better, believe me."

Expertly defanged, we offered no rebuttal. About 20 minutes after midnight, more than five hours after the belt snapped, we settled back into our seats—legs stretched, bellies filled, and perspectives altered by a highway that's constantly turning expectations inside out. Many pilgrims have been drawn to the road by dreams of transformation, but those who thrive learn to rewrite their plans on the go.

On my maps, the highway was a thin black line that arched frownwise across the continent. It jagged fitfully, as if drawn by someone with a tremulous hand—an empire-builder in the throes of a fever dream.

In 1970, a cyclical drought scorched the fields of northeastern Brazil and drove president general Emílio Garrastazu Médici to make a promise: no longer would the country's farmers be dependent on a relatively slender tract of arable territory near the eastern seaboard. Médici vowed to open Brazil's vast, forested interior to agricultural and industrial development. Step 1: a road.

The proposed Trans-Amazonian Highway would cross Brazil's western border and connect to Peru's highway system, which itself was mostly hypothetical. A Brazilian government report printed that same year described the continent's core as "an enormous demographic and economic emptiness" where "man continues to be the great absent." The report's authors cast themselves as realists grounded in practicality; the so-called experts who worried about the environmental impacts to the region, on the other hand, were fantasists. "In fact, many of the various scientific missions that have studied [the Amazon region] seem to lose themselves in its immensity, offering reports much more descriptive and full of admiration and astonishment than sound conclusions and objective results," the report declared.

Years passed, and funding evaporated. But the idea of a coast-to-coast road didn't die. In 1984, Brazil finished paving the BR-364, connecting São Paulo to the thickly forested state of Rondônia. Médici's plan for the Trans-Amazonian had envisioned a Peruvian border-crossing hundreds of miles north of the BR-364's trajectory. But by paving an existing dirt road that stretched from the Peruvian border to the terminus of the BR-364 about 500 miles away, Brazil could piece together a more efficient route.

In 2000, the presidents of 12 South American countries identified the completion of an interoceanic route as one of the continent's top infrastructural priorities. A committee of South American leaders approved a financing plan that combined state and private resources with funding from international-development banks. Brazil's government—seduced by the promise of easier access to lucrative Asian markets—agreed to finance much of the work on the Peruvian side. The cost of the new construction has been estimated to be about $2.8 billion.

From Mauro's bus, the highway that emerged after all those years of back-and-forth often looked like a simple country road. For a majority of its length, it was just wide enough for one lane of traffic in each direction. As we motored across the plains of Mato Grosso, I saw drivers choose to travel on the comparatively smooth dirt shoulder instead of slaloming the potholes in the pavement. Tractors and other slow-moving farm vehicles regularly forced Mauro and José to play chicken in the other lane. I never saw a patrol car lying in wait for speeders; the road conditions allowed the highway to police itself.

Back in the 1990s, Brazilian analysts predicted that an interoceanic highway, by shortcutting the Panama Canal, would reduce Brazilian agricultural shipping costs to Asia by as much as $100 per ton. These days, even the highway's most enthusiastic proponents concede that the Asian angle was oversold. "The truth is this hasn't happened yet," said Jorge Barata, who heads the Peruvian offices of Odebrecht, the Brazilian construction firm that built many of the newest stretches of the road and has a 25-year concession to maintain them. The road in its current form, he said, simply isn't suitable for heavy-duty, long-distance shipping. "The cost of river transport ends up being a lot more competitive."

For the first two days, through Mato Grosso and much of Rondônia, the view from the bus was dependably uniform: oceanic fields of sugarcane, soybeans, and corn and flat pastureland studded by rust-colored termite mounds and patrolled by herds of wattle-necked Brahman cattle. No one exposed to more than 50 consecutive hours of it could doubt that Brazil was the world's top beef exporter or that Brazil will most likely produce more soybeans than the United States this year. Similarly, no one treated to so many hours upon this spine-rattling highway could fail to recognize how much more might be possible if Brazil's infrastructure were better. Last year, China's largest soybean-importing firm canceled an order for 2 million metric tons of Brazilian soybeans because of crippling transportation delays in getting those crops to the Santos port.

For several weeks before I boarded the bus, Brazilians were demanding that more of their tax dollars be spent on basic services, particularly transportation infrastructure. Cost overruns related to hosting the 2014 World Cup and the 2016 Olympics enraged a population that was asked to accept a hike in bus fares. Late on the second day, our bus ran into a demonstration in Rondônia. A vendor walking along the side of the road hawking *pamonhas,* a sort of tamale, explained that demonstrators had blocked the highway with metal bars and pieces of wood. "It goes on for kilometers and kilometers," he said. "Traffic has been stopped for six and a half hours."

It came as something of a surprise when the road abruptly came to an end at the Madeira River in western Rondônia. Dozens of bridges had been constructed in Brazil and Peru before South American politicians inaugurated the "completed" Interoceanic almost two years before, but this one was left unbuilt. A barge waited to ferry the bus to the other side.

We began drifting across the inky current at 11:15 p.m. Several of my fellow passengers staggered moon-eyed, mouths agape, conversing in tones that deserved italics and multiple exclamation marks. At first I assumed they'd been drinking, but I had failed to recognize something rare: genuine, unselfconscious wonder. They were staring at the night sky, which shone with enough stars to impart an instant understanding of the infinite. A twenty-something Brazilian tourist named Guilhermo spoke for everyone: "I have never seen anything like that!"

We were leaving the pragmatic monotony of large-scale agribusiness and heading into more improvisational territories. Ahead lay the steamy hollows of the Amazon basin and the stonewashed skies of the Andes, regions where the highway more forcefully influences the enterprises popping up in its path. Guilhermo, doling out high-fives to anyone with a free hand, seemed to sense and embrace the change. Before we got back on the bus, he told me that he'd never in his life been this far from home.

About 62 hours after first boarding the bus, I bid Mauro *adeus* in Rio Branco, capital of the far western state of Acre. It was 4 a.m., and I believe I was the only passenger awake.

I hope the others didn't sleep all the way to the border. *Acre não existe* (Acre doesn't exist) is a Brazilian chestnut that pokes fun at the state's isolation, the gist being that the place is about as real to most Brazilians as is, say, Atlantis. People in Acre tend to shrug off the joke as obvious nonsense, which isn't to say it doesn't bother them a little.

According to government figures, more than 85 percent of the state is jungle; the rest mostly consists of Rio Branco and the string of small villages along the highway. That denuded strip has been filled with people, Toyotas, pizza parlors, and shopping malls, yet the forest's shadow looms over everything. One of Rio Branco's soccer stadiums is called Arena da Floresta (Forest Arena); another is known as Florestão (the Big Forest). The regional government's public Wi-Fi network is called the Digital Forest. A central square is the Plaza of the People of the Forest.

Some people, like Eziquiel Alves da Silva, the manager of the state's first ethanol-producing factory, are pushing for Acre to become more like the regions we'd already passed through. Da Silva told me that he had been visiting local landowners, trying to convince them that sugarcane-based ethanol soon would become a cornerstone of the local economy. He suggested that if exports to Asia took off, market forces could expand the sugarcane industry, now centered in São Paulo, westward.

"We're in a privileged position here," he said of the month-old factory, which perfumed the highway with sweet, pungent notes. "From here, we can go"—he waved his arm with a flourish—"to the world."

But along the highway he seemed outnumbered by people resisting corporate development and experimenting with enterprises that might protect local forest traditions. About 120 miles past Rio

Branco, I passed a government-subsidized company called Natex, which uses latex collected from trees by local rubber tappers to make condoms. A few miles down the highway, I followed a dirt road into a 100-square-mile reserve that's collectively managed by about 80 families, most of whom make their living roaming the forest and harvesting either Brazil nuts or latex. They told me they're trying to carry on the legacy of Chico Mendes, the rubber tapper and activist who was shot in 1988 for defending the rainforest. "This is what he fought for," said Everton Paiva de Oliveira, who manages an ecolodge in the reserve with one of Mendes's nieces.

Trails led into the forest between the flying-buttress roots of enormous tauari and samaúma trees. Dozens of white butterflies erupted upon approach—a handful of tossed confetti. In the tree canopy, Oliveira pointed to an obstacle course of rope bridges and ziplines. Guests can sleep in individual chalets or less-expensive dormitory-style rooms. But when I visited, at a time of year that should have been considered high season, every room was empty.

Over a glass of pale yellow araçá-boi juice, Oliveira admitted that the lodge wasn't turning a profit and depended on state funds to stay afloat. When he mentioned that they didn't have Internet access, I wasn't sure if it was another example of the rustic ambience he was trying to sell or if he was explaining why they were having trouble selling it. The lodge's quandary was Acre's writ small: how much change can tradition absorb before it becomes something else entirely?

On a Saturday night back in Rio Branco, I met Junior Fera, an 18-year-old who doesn't make a habit of worrying about such questions. I first noticed him standing with a small group of friends in the middle of a suspension bridge and embracing a girl. A couple of seconds later, both of them plunged off the side of the bridge toward the current far below, still locked in each other's arms. A harness line, which I hadn't noticed at first, cut their swan dive short. They swung together in a wild arc, a few feet above the water, before their scissoring feet eventually found purchase on the sloping bank. A few minutes later Junior returned to the bridge, alone. "Was that your girlfriend?" I asked, wondering where the other jumper went. He erupted in laughter. "It was just some girl who was walking by!" he said. "I asked her if she wanted to jump, and she actually said yes!"

Once or twice a week he and a group of about 30 friends bring their ropes and harnesses to the bridge. They range in age from 15 to 45 or so, and about the only obvious thing they share is the instinct to embrace the natural world—rivers, forests, mountains, whatever—in the most physical way they can. The group wouldn't exist, they admitted, if the highway didn't; all of their rappelling equipment comes from their periodic road trips into the Andes. "By car, by bus—we go any way we can," said Junior, who told me that he finances his trips by working as a physical therapist. He and his friends were the only people I found in Acre who seemed comfortable honoring both nature and the highway at the same time.

"This is not a big place," Junior said, "so we have to make our own opportunities." He clipped the ropes back into his harness and took another leap into the dark. Acre exists.

About 30 miles from the Brazil-Peru border, in Brasiléia, a man trudged through the 90-plus-degree heat wearing jeans and a heavy denim jacket. One block from the local bus station, he disappeared into a crowd of hundreds of aspiring immigrants. All had journeyed from their homes in Haiti to end up in this makeshift migrant camp. Many arrived overdressed—an attempt to save space in their roller bags.

After the 2010 earthquake, rumors began circulating around Port-au-Prince that Brazil might be a haven for migrants. Human smugglers began offering desperate Haitians travel packages priced anywhere between $2,000 and $4,000 for passage to Brazil, typically via a bus to the Dominican Republic, a flight to Ecuador through Panama, another bus to Lima, and, finally, a ride to the Brazilian border along the Interoceanic Highway.

More than 7,000 Haitians have been granted a visa or permanent residence in the past three years. But the immigration bureaucracy struggles to keep pace. Newcomers were showing up at the pavilion every day, where they generally waited 20 to 30 days for their Brazilian residency papers to come through.

The population of the encampment was around 500 when I was there, but recently it was as high as 1,200, about four times its capacity. Most are men. When I arrived, a mob of about 50 pressed against me on the off chance I was an immigration official. It must have been 100 degrees in the middle of that crowd.

Scores of saggy, stained mattresses lay on the concrete slab under the open pavilion. Many people tried to sleep; others listened to headphones. Few spoke.

"We wait patiently to be able to leave," said Joseph Silas, 34, who left his wife and three children in Haiti. "That's all we do."

The men described conditions that were tolerable, but just barely. A few shower stalls stood nearby, but most said they washed with buckets of water. Their meals never varied—rice, beans, a little chicken. Many complained of stomach problems.

Everyone was focused on getting to São Paulo. They all wanted jobs, the kind of legitimate work they believed they could get only with solid immigration papers. A civil engineer hoped to work in a restaurant, any restaurant; Silas, who was a professional driver, figured he might get a job in construction. Or as an electrician. Or whatever else he could find. They spoke of handing over their life savings, but no one expressed buyer's remorse. "There is no hope in Haiti," Silas explained to me. "That is the difference."

Later that day, I took a minibus to the Peruvian border, sharing the vehicle with two Brazilians and two Peruvians, one of whom avoided Peruvian immigration officials by hiring a motorcycle to take him on dirt paths around the passport station. A couple of miles beyond the office, our driver pulled over to welcome our lawbreaking companion back onboard. I thought of the Haitians waiting in the heat of the pavilion, playing by the rules. Nothing was keeping them in that slice of hell, other than an unwillingness to stop pursuing a rumor of hope.

The jungle town of Puerto Maldonado, about three hours beyond the Peruvian border, seemed clear in its purpose: to squeeze whatever money it could from tourists before they could make it to one of the many riverside ecolodges in the surrounding rainforest. Within the past five years, the population doubled, to some 200,000, and that growth gives the city an every-man-for-himself vibe. The newcomers have included environmental organizations critical of the Interoceanic, and their news releases warn of wildcat gold miners who exploit the opened access to once-pristine rainforests, stripping the landscape of vegetation so they can sift through the soil in search of alluvial gold. Illegal logging is also on the rise, the conservationists say, thanks to many new secondary roads, most unpaved, that branch out from the main highway.

But when I stopped by the offices of the Amazon Conservation Association, the regional director, Juan Loja Alemán, said he tries to be careful not to go overboard with the dire warnings. "There are no comprehensive statistics yet measuring the positive and negative impacts of the highway," Loja, a biologist, said. "But an interesting balance is starting to emerge. Illegal activity has definitely increased, but clearly so has interest in sustainable activities. The Interoceanic is creating a tourist circuit that's getting very interesting."

I rode a motorcycle taxi over one of the secondary roads toward a wildlife rescue center, where staff members and volunteers nursed red howler monkeys, turtles, and white-throated toucans for an eventual return to the wild. Clouds of parrots swirled around the clay banks of the Tambopata River, a short distance from a secluded research center that, according to a sign, was dedicated to reducing human impacts on the forest. Late in the afternoon I stood alone in the middle of a suspension bridge that stretches for nearly a half-mile over the Madre de Dios River. The sky above the glassy water turned orange, then pink, then purplish. The sun dropped so fast I half expected to hear a splash.

The next morning, though, about an hour and a half down the highway, the negative impacts reasserted themselves. The town of Mazuco is the unofficial gold-mining capital of Amazonian Peru, and the Interoceanic is its Main Street. Among the vegetable stands and clothing stores are gold-buying shops, where independent miners can trade their gold dust for cash. The mining boom helped the town's population to grow exponentially, to about 8,000 people, in the past five years, according to the handful of locals I found gathered in a hair salon beside the highway.

"There's so much destruction," said Anthony Andea, who runs the salon with his wife. "There used to be forest. Now it's just sand. A desert." Andea was 29, but like most I spoke to in Mazuco, he sounded like a grumpy senior, wary of more change. "People come here for work," he told me, "but the work is crap. It's exploitation. The wages are terrible, and the conditions are inhuman."

Most of the mining camps are technically illegal, yet some abut the Interoceanic. Environmentalists blame their continued existence on Odebrecht, which maintains most of the highway in Peru. The Brazilian company collects tolls to help finance the upkeep of the road and the land immediately flanking it. The Odebrecht officials I spoke with blamed the Peruvian government for not enforcing the law, and almost everyone bemoaned a collusive atmosphere of corruption that allows the camps to spread without consequence. "Political power in Peru is very centralized, and that power simply doesn't exist here," says César Ascorra, from the local office of Cáritas, a Catholic social service agency, and an outspoken critic of the highway. "The government responds with laws, but that's just paper. The people who come here know this very well."

Before the highway, the only way to get to Mazuco was to hitch a ride on a diesel truck from Cuzco. The trip down the muddy mountain roads usually took a few days, longer if it rained. Nowadays any miner with a few hours to spare can make the journey. All of the old-timers—a group that seemed to include anyone who lived there for more than four or five years—said the miners had brought with them delinquency, crime, and drunkenness.

Actually, not all of the old-timers said that. A man of about 45 interrupted my conversation with a pessimistic clothing-store owner to tell me: "The mining sector has opened things up here, economically." He had lived in town since 1993, he said, when the population was "maybe 150"; anyone who yearned for the good old days had a patchy memory. I asked him his name, but he narrowed his eyes and wagged his index finger at me. "No name," he said, and disappeared down the street.

About a half hour later, I ducked into one of the gold-buying shops. There he was again, manning the scales behind the counter. "Not in here," he said sternly. "This is a place of business." He punctuated the warning with the same wag of his index finger.

Outside, I stumbled upon a taxi driver who said he was going back to Puerto Maldonado and would be stopping to search for additional passengers at a *pueblo de plástico,* villages so named for the plastic structures that pass for homes. These boomtowns were built by gold miners and are occupied for as long as it takes the miners to strip the forest and sift the soil for gold, before they abandon the whole mess in favor of fresher territory. The encampments invariably attract "prostibars", jerry-built bordellos staffed by prostitutes who aren't necessarily adults. I had been warned about stopping at a pueblo. It was too dangerous, said Loja, the biologist from the Amazon Conservation Association. He went twice, once to meet local government officials, and both times he was run off

under the threat of bodily harm. He predicted that as a gringo, I'd
fare worse.

I got out of the taxi and stepped across a wooden plank that
spanned the highway ditch. Brown water ran under the boards
and radiated in channels behind the tents. A young woman, probably in her late teens, carried a case of pisco into a tent labeled
DISCO FONTANA, where another girl in impractical heels swept
trash from the floor. Men in tank tops, athletic shorts, and muddy
wading boots walked between tents. Under a water stall built to
wash motorcycles, a woman scrubbed an infant.

When I walked a short distance into the camp toward what
seemed to be a convenience store, a woman rose from behind
a table, alarmed. Two men, one whose face was hidden behind
the dark shield of a motorcycle helmet, walked toward me. The
woman indicated I wasn't welcome by flashing a sign that I understood perfectly: the wagging finger. I turned and left.

Hairpin turns, screaming tires, near head-on collisions, roadside
crosses, knotting intestines—all come standard on the Andean
stretch of the Interoceanic. I boarded a bus in Puerto Maldonado,
and on my GPS, I monitored its ascent, which topped out at 15,579
feet (imagine three Denvers stacked atop one another). At times it
seemed as if we had been transported back to the sixteenth century
—the terrace farms notched into the mountainsides, the grazing
llamas and alpacas, the mud huts with straw roofs, the stone-walled
gardens, the campesinos bundled in colorful woolen shawls.

I spent one night in Ocongate, the collective name for 33 villages of clustered huts embedded in the mountainside at about
11,500 feet. There I found the first motorist lodge built along the
Andean stretch of the Interoceanic, a 35-bed complex on the banks
of the Mapacho River. A retired Peruvian narcotics-dog trainer
named Rubén Santander built the place in 2010. His clients often
include hikers who trek around the snowcapped Ausangate peak.
In a couple of weeks, he was expecting 25 German hikers, followed
by a group of anthropologists from the University of Minnesota,
but I was alone in the complex.

Santander, like many of Ocongate's residents, had been
schooled in the business of hospitality by Odebrecht. About twice
a month for most of 2011 the construction company held workshops for all locals who might benefit from the expected influx

of highway travelers—grocers, street vendors, even alpaca herders with some wool to sell. Once, the workshop participants took a field trip to Cuzco to visit a five-star hotel. "They wanted us to see how clean it is," Santander said, "and what services they offer."

Santander, who previously helped run a hotel in Arequipa, had nothing but good things to say about the classes. But at the Hostal Flores, about a half-mile up the road, Angelino Flores, the owner, doubted whether the lessons sank in with the citizenry. "These are campesinos who have never gone to a school of any kind, have never sat in a classroom," he said. "It was as if they were speaking another language."

In late December 2012, three American tourists pulled their camper off the highway one night, parking it on a small dirt road in Ocongate. According to an account titled "Nightmare in Peru" on the tourists' blog, they had just popped open beers when villagers approached them and demanded to see their identification. But the Americans, who spoke limited Spanish, refused to surrender their passports and tried to drive away. Rocks were thrown by the villagers, and a can of Mace was deployed by the Americans. "After nearly 11 hours of being attacked, chased, beaten, whipped and held at gunpoint without food, sleep or water, we were led back to the truck," one tourist wrote after getting medical treatment in Cuzco, three hours away. "All of the windows and the windshield of the truck had been broken, and the camper had been broken into."

According to Santander, the villagers who initially approached the tourists were part of a *ronda campesina*—the Andean version of a voluntary police squad. When the Americans refused to show them their IDs, he said, the villagers decided they were thieves. After the melee, local officials convened the members of the *ronda campesina* to try to persuade them that tourists should be welcomed, not chased away. "There were even messages broadcast on television about the importance of treating people well," Santander said.

Most people I spoke with said they were still waiting for the influx of tourists they were promised. Near evening I took a walk for a couple of miles along the highway. I spotted a woman carrying an enormous cloth bundle, which she laid out on the gravel shoulder of the road. Inside the bundle was a load of recently harvested quinoa, which she spread out on her cloth. Then she waited. Within minutes, a large fuel truck whooshed by. The wind from the tires blew over her pile, separating the light chaff from the heavier grain. For centuries, Andean farmers have fanned or hand-tossed their grain to do the same job. The Interoceanic, it seemed, was not wholly without local benefits.

When Cuzco was founded, the wheel was little more than an idea in South America. The Incans called the city "the navel of the world" because an estimated 25,000 miles of footpaths radiated from the city into the known world. Now it's again a hub, the spot where the Interoceanic splits into alternate routes down to the Pacific. At Cuzco's auto expo, an informal event held every Saturday morning for anyone with a new or used car to sell, Haber Enriques, a used-car salesman, praised the increase in business the highway had brought. "Everyone wants a car. You can drive to lots of different places now in a day. That's new for us . . ."

Enriques stood beside two roomy pickup trucks he hoped to move and watched one customer after another pass him by. "Lots of first-time buyers," he complained. "They start off with the little ones, and then they move up to something bigger."

One first-timer was Eudes Ayrampo, 40, trailed by his teenage daughter and son. He quickly eyed a Suzuki Alto, the smallest car in sight. The family huddled together. "It's necessary," his daughter said. "What if there's an emergency and we need to get somewhere fast?" Her brother agreed, and rubbed his fathers shoulders, trying to loosen him up. Eudes conceded that a car would make family trips easier, and with that, another car joined Cuzco's fray.

You can argue that this emerging demographic of car buyers unites one end of the continent to the other. As Roberto Espejo, a 66-year-old cabdriver, told me: "The people believe if you own a car, you are in a different class. It automatically puts you above the lowest." The wave of protests in Brazil didn't reflect an increasing gap between rich and poor, as some articles suggested; it reflected rising expectations of those in the middle. In the past decade, tens of millions of Brazilians climbed over the poverty line to join the middle class, according to government figures. This helps explain why Brazilians bought more than 3.8 million automobiles in 2012, setting a new national sales record for the eighth consecutive year. Peruvians also bought more cars than ever that year—165,427 —eclipsing the previous year's sales total, which had also been a record, by 28.4 percent. Sales in Peru more than quadrupled between 2007 and 2012.

The bus I boarded in Cuzco to get to the Pacific had fully reclining bed seats, silken pillows, and individual touch screens with dozens of movies to choose from. I settled in for a 20-hour ride, planning to enjoy the best leg of the trip, but constant twists and plunges meant sleep was out of the question. Moans issued from the back of the bus, and by dawn, the bathroom had suffered unspeakable indignities. When we finally rolled into Lima on a cloudy afternoon, past Catholic churches, high-rises, and five-star hotels, all I saw was a finish line.

I eventually found my way to the ocean. The words "from sea to shining sea" clanked around in my head. Nothing about that phrase sounded right. That was partly because the idea of interoceanic unity is still too new here to be reduced to cliché, but mostly because the sea in Lima wasn't shining. It was matte gray, leaden. The sky was overcast and drab.

I stood in front of a dark, shaley beach. Six surfers in wetsuits paddled out into the water and disappeared in the blur of sea mist and sky haze. I was staring into the Pacific, but all was fog. It felt very much like the end of a line. There was no horizon to look into or beyond. The only thing to do was to turn around.

The original plans for a transcontinental highway imagined a road that would allow goods to flow outward, from the heart of South America to the world. One day that very well could happen. But for now, the travelers on this road seemed to have reversed the prevailing course. The destinations were right here, inside the very continent that had opened itself up.

When I got back to my hotel room, an e-mail from Joseph Silas, one of the Haitians I met in the migrant camp, was waiting for me. He had received his residency papers, he said, and was ready to hit the road. Based on the date that he sent his message, I calculated that he would be arriving in São Paulo very soon, if he hadn't already. He was traveling every inch of the highway I'd covered, feeling every bump and curve, taking it all in a totally different direction.

Out of Eden Walk

FROM *National Geographic*

I. To Walk the World

WALKING IS FALLING FORWARD.

Each step we take is an arrested plunge, a collapse averted, a disaster braked. In this way, to walk becomes an act of faith. We perform it daily: a two-beat miracle—an iambic teetering, a holding on and letting go. For the next seven years I will plummet across the world.

I am on a journey. I am in pursuit of an idea, a story, a chimera, perhaps a folly. I am chasing ghosts. Starting in humanity's birthplace in the Great Rift Valley of East Africa, I am retracing, on foot, the pathways of the ancestors who first discovered the earth at least 60,000 years ago. This remains by far our greatest voyage. Not because it delivered us the planet. No. But because the early *Homo sapiens* who first roamed beyond the mother continent —these pioneer nomads numbered, in total, as few as a couple of hundred people—also bequeathed us the subtlest qualities we now associate with being fully human: complex language, abstract thinking, a compulsion to make art, a genius for technological innovation, and the continuum of today's many races. We know so little about them. They straddled the strait called Bab el Mandeb —the "gate of grief" that cleaves Africa from Arabia—and then exploded, in just 2,500 generations, a geological heartbeat, to the remotest habitable fringe of the globe.

Millennia behind, I follow.

Using fossil evidence and the burgeoning science of "genography"—a field that sifts the DNA of living populations for mutations useful in tracking ancient diasporas—I will walk north from Africa into the Middle East. From there my antique route leads eastward across the vast gravel plains of Asia to China, then north again into the mint-blue shadows of Siberia. From Russia I will hop a ship to Alaska and inch down the western coast of the New World to wind-smeared Tierra del Fuego, our species' last new continental horizon. I will walk 21,000 miles.

If you ask, I will tell you that I have embarked on this project, which I'm calling the Out of Eden Walk, for many reasons: To relearn the contours of our planet at the human pace of 3 miles an hour. To slow down. To think. To write. To render current events as a form of pilgrimage. I hope to repair certain important connections burned through by artificial speed, by inattentiveness. I walk, as everyone does, to see what lies ahead. I walk to remember.

The trails scuffed through the Ethiopian desert are possibly the oldest human marks in the world. People walk them still: the hungry, the poor, the climate-stricken, men and women sleepwalking away from war. Nearly a billion people are on the move today across the earth. We are living through the greatest mass migration our species has ever known. As always, the final destination remains unclear. In Djibouti city, the African migrants stood waving cell phones on trash-strewed beaches at night. They were capturing a cheap signal from neighboring Somalia. I heard them murmur: Oslo, Melbourne, Minnesota. It was eerie and sad and strangely beautiful. After 600 centuries we were still seeking guidance, even rescue, from those who had walked before.

Herto Bouri, Ethiopia
"Where are you walking?" the Afar pastoralists ask.

"North. To Djibouti." (We do not say Tierra del Fuego. It is much too far—it is meaningless.)

"Are you crazy? Are you sick?"

In reply, Mohamed Elema Hessan—wiry and energetic, the ultimate go-to man, a charming rogue, my guide and protector through the blistering Afar Triangle—doubles over and laughs. He leads our microcaravan: two skinny camels. I have listened to his guffaw many times already. This project is, to him, a punch line —a cosmic joke. To walk for seven years! Across three continents! Enduring hardship, loneliness, uncertainty, fear, exhaustion, confusion—all for a rucksack's worth of ideas, palaver, scientific and literary conceits. He enjoys the absurdity of it. This is fitting. Especially given our ridiculous launch.

I awoke before dawn and saw snow: thick, dense, choking, blinding. Like plankton suspended at the bottom of a sunless sea, swirling white in the beam of my headlamp. It was the dust. Hundreds of animals in Elema's village had churned up a cloud as fine as talc. Goats, sheep, and camels—but, sadly, not our camels.

The cargo animals I had requisitioned months before (a key arrangement in a project that has consumed thousands of hours of planning) were nowhere to be found. Their drivers, two nomads named Mohamed Aidahis and Kader Yarri, were absent, too. They never showed up. So we sat in the dust, waiting. The sun rose. It began to grow hot. Flies buzzed. To the east, across the Rift, our first border, Djibouti, was receding at the rate of three quarters of an inch every year—the speed at which Arabia is drifting away from Africa.

Are you crazy? Are you sick? Yes? No? Maybe?

The Afar Triangle in northeast Ethiopia is dreaded as a waterless moonscape. Temperatures of 120°F. Salt pans so bright they burn out the eyes. Yet today it rained. Elema and I have no waterproof tents. We have an Ethiopian flag, which Elema wraps himself in as he walks. We have found and rented two camels. We plod across an acacia plain darkened to the color of chocolate by the warm raindrops. We tread on a photographic negative: the camels' moccasinlike feet pull up the frail crust of moisture, leaving behind ellipses of pale dust.

After a dozen miles, Elema already asks to turn back.

He forgot his new walking shoes from America. And his flashlight. And his hat—and the cell phone. So he hitches a ride from our first camp to his village to retrieve these vital items. And now he has jogged all the way back to catch up. He complains, laughing, of crotch rash.

This absentmindedness is understandable. It is impossible to remember every detail on a walk of this scope. I have forgotten things myself—nylon stuff sacks, for instance. Because of this, I begin my trek out of Africa with airplane luggage, a city slicker's rig with plastic rollers and collapsible handle, strapped to a camel's back.

It is the scientists of the Middle Awash research project who invited us to begin walking at Herto Bouri, our symbolic mile zero in the Ethiopian Rift—one of the richest human boneyards in the world. This is the famous site where some of the world's oldest human fossils have been found. *Homo sapiens idaltu.* Gone for 160,000 years. A big-boned ancestor—a dawn version of us.

The Middle Awash Project researchers, a team led by Tim White, Berhane Asfaw, and Giday WoldeGabriel, have uncovered in Ethiopia many of the most important hominin fossils of our day, including *Ardipithecus ramidus,* a 4.4-million-year-old biped. My unpredictable Afar guide, Elema, is their veteran fossil hunter.

Raised in a nomad culture feared for its tough warriors, Elema speaks three languages—Afar, Amharic, and a profane English patois gleaned from the Middle Awash scientists. He is a paleontologist in his own right. He exclaims "Wow" and "Crazy, man" and "Jeezus" while identifying the Rift's key geological strata. (Me he calls, not without endearment, White Asshole; I return the compliment with equal fondness, dubbing him and his perennial rash Burned Asshole.) He is the *balabat,* or traditional leader, of the Bouri-Modaitu clan of the Afar. His cell phone holds the numbers of Ethiopian grandees and French academics. Educated to the eighth grade in schools of the Emperor Haile Selassie, he bridges more cultures than a Malinowski. He holds more time warps inside his head than an Einstein. He is a phenomenon.

We are camped at Aduma when the Middle Awash scientists find us. They have come to show us a Middle Stone Age site.

"These tools are still a little early for the people you're following," says Yonatan Sahle, an Ethiopian researcher based in the Human Evolution Research Center at the University of California, Berkeley. "But their technology was basically as advanced. They made throwing weapons that allowed them to outcompete the other hominins they encountered outside Africa."

We lean over a delicate stone point, a work of art that lies where its maker dropped it 80,000 to 100,000 years ago. In the distance we hear screaming. We look up.

An Afar woman strides in from the desert, waving her arms wildly. Where did she come from? Is she warning us off her hill? Is she mad? No. She marches up to a man dozing nearby on the ground. She gives him a sharp kick. She hefts a stone—a Middle Stone Age tool, perhaps—and threatens to brain him. Is it the collection of a debt? A matter of the heart?

I hear the victim laughing. I know this maniacal laugh. It is the man who will guide me to Djibouti, to the Gulf of Aden.

Dalifagi, Ethiopia

Water is gold in the Afar Triangle of Ethiopia.

No surprise. This is one of the hottest deserts in the world. Walking for three days near the western scarp of the Rift, Elema and I find only one miraculous pool of muddy rainwater to ease our camels' thirst. But we stumble across a new type of water hole a day later—a coveted oasis of electrons, the village of Dalifagi.

The immense saltscapes that shroud the borders of Ethiopia, Djibouti, and Eritrea weren't even mapped until the 1920s. For centuries the martial Afar pastoralists who ruled the area resisted all incursions by the outside world. Today, though, besides their usual armament of pointy daggers and Kalashnikov rifles, they carry cell phones. They embrace the tool of instant communication with a vengeance. "It has given them power," says Mulukan Ayalu, 23, an Ethiopian government technician who maintains the tiny power plant at Dalifagi. "They can call different goat traders. They can choose their selling prices."

The diesel generator at Dalifagi chugs out a 220-volt current for six hours a day. Ayalu plugs in the nomads' cell batteries for a few cents each. On Mondays—market day—grizzled Afars line up at his office door. The folds of their saronglike skirts bulge with dead cell phones of faraway neighbors. The nomads are addicted to the devices. "Hallow? *Hallow?*" Elema bellows into his phone on the trail, with an accent that sounds, to my ear, straight out of Brooklyn. But he is asking directions to some ancient well. Or exchanging news of the dreaded Issa, armed raiders from a rival nomad group.

The electronic oasis at Dalifagi would never draw tourists, much less inspire the verse of caravan poets. But it is the real story today in sub-Saharan Africa. Nine hundred million people. A headlong sprint into the digital age. Exploding aspirations. Consequences unknown.

Near the Talalak River, Ethiopia

Footwear is a hallmark of modern identity. How best to glimpse an individual's core values at the start of the twenty-first century? Look down at people's feet—not into their eyes.

In the affluent "global north," where fashion caters to every whim and vanity, shoes announce their wearer's class, hipness, career choice, sexual availability, even politics (the clog versus the cowboy boot). It is disorienting, then, to be walking through a landscape where human beings—millions upon millions of women, men, and children—slip on identical-style footwear every morning: the cheap, democratic, versatile plastic sandal of Ethiopia. Poverty drives demand. The only brand is necessity.

Available in a limited palette of chemical hues—black, red, brown, green, blue—the humble rubbery shoes are a triumph of local invention. They cost a pittance to manufacture. Any pair can be had for the equivalent of a day's field labor. (Perhaps $2.) They are cool—permitting the air to circulate about the feet on the desert's scalding surface. The ubiquitous sandals of rural Ethiopia weigh nothing. They are recyclable. And home repair is universal: owners melt and mend the molded-plastic straps over wood fires.

Our binary camel caravan—our two beasts are named A'urta, or Traded for a Cow, and Suma'atuli, Branded on the Ear—has been joined at last by its two long-lost cameleers, Mohamed Aidahis and Kader Yarri. These men caught up with us from our departure point at Herto Bouri, crossing miles of gravel pans and rumpled badlands during days of quickstep walking. In the manner of life here, no explanation was asked or given regarding the nature of their weeklong delay. They were late. Now they were with us. Each wore a pair of the region's signature plastic sandals. Color: lime green.

The dust of the Rift Valley is a palimpsest stamped by such footwear. Yet if Ethiopia's populist sandals are mass-produced, their wearers are not. One man might drag his left heel. A woman might mar her right shoe's sole by stepping on an ember.

Elema knelt the other day on the trail, examining this endless mutation of impressions.

"La'ad Howeni will be waiting for us in Dalifagi," he said. He pointed to a single sandal track. La'ad was waiting in Dalifagi.

Near Hadar, Ethiopia
We are walking in the direction of Warenso.

The world changes when you are thirsty. It shrinks. It loses depth. The horizon draws close. (In northern Ethiopia the earth butts against the sky, hard and smooth as the surface of a skull.) The desert tightens around you like a noose. This is the thirsty brain compressing the distances of the Rift, sucking in the miles through the eyes, magnifying them, probing them for any hint of water. Little else matters.

Elema and I have trudged more than 20 miles through the crushing heat. We have separated from the cargo camels to visit an archaeological site folded into a wrinkled draw: Gona, the location of the oldest known stone tools in the world. (Age: 2.6 million years.) Our water bottles are empty. We are uncomfortable, anxious. We speak little. (What can be said? Why dry the tongue?) The sun's rays corkscrew into our heads. An Afar proverb: It is best, when you are lost or thirsty, to keep walking under the sun, because eventually someone will see you. To be tempted into shade, to drop under one of 10,000 thornbushes, means death: no one will find you. So we stagger on into the blinding afternoon—until we hear the faint bleating of goats. Then we smile. We can begin to relax. Goats mean people.

Our hosts: an Afar family camped on a hill. Two strong, smiling young women. Eight children in thin rags that once may have been articles of clothing. And a very old woman—she doesn't know her age—who hunches like a gnome in the shade of a reed mat. Her name is Hasna. She has been sitting there, weaving with spidery fingers, since the beginning of time. She invites us to join her, to rest our bones, to remove our shoes. From a battered jerrican she pours us water—chalky and warm, so salty, so alkaline, it oozes down the throat like soap, but precious nonetheless. She offers us a fistful of yellow berries from a wild tree that grows in wadis. She is our mother.

When our ancestors wandered out of Africa 60,000 or more years ago, they encountered other species of hominins. The world was crowded then with strange cousins: *Homo neanderthalensis, Homo floresiensis,* the Denisovans, and perhaps other varieties of people who weren't quite us.

When we met them, perhaps like this, on some remote hilltop, did we share water, or even interbreed peacefully, as some geneticists suggest? (Outside Africa, modern human populations seem to contain as much as 2.5 percent of Neanderthal DNA.) Or did we rape and kill, launching our species' long and terrible history of genocides? (In a cave occupied by modern humans, Fernando

Ramirez Rozzi, of Paris's Centre National de la Recherche Scientifique, has identified a Neanderthal jawbone mutilated by the cut marks of butchery, perhaps cannibalism.) Scientists still debate this puzzle. All that is certain is that we alone survived to claim the earth. We won the planet. But at a cost: We are without close family. We are a species racked by survivor's guilt. We are a lonely ape.

Hasna's gentle voice lulls me to sleep.

When I awake, Elema is hunkered in low conversation with the men of the nomad camp. They have returned from tending their flocks. We shake hands. We thank them. We leave packets of crackers for grinning Hasna, and walk on. We are hurrying to meet the camels, walking toward Warenso. That night, while sipping our gift of salty water around a red fire that saws back and forth in the wind, Elema tells me the men of Hasna's camp had threatened him. He was not of their clan. He nearly hit them over the head with his walking stick.

Dubti, Ethiopia

Moving north and then east, we abandon the desert and stub our toes on the Anthropocene—the age of modern humans.

Asphalt appears: the Djibouti-Ethiopia road, throbbing with trucks. We drift through a series of gritty towns. Dust and diesel. Bars. Shops with raw plank counters. Garlands of tin cups clink in the wind outside their doors.

Then, near Dubti: A sea (no, a wall) of sugarcane. Miles of industrial irrigation. Canals. Diversion dams. Bulldozed fields. Levees crawling with dump trucks. Elema becomes lost. Night envelops us. We end up pulling the weary camels in a gigantic circle. "Wow, man!" Elema says angrily. "No way! Too much change!"

This is the multimillion-dollar Tendaho sugar plantation, an Ethiopian-Indian project that is making the Afar Triangle bloom. Fifty thousand migrant workers will soon toil here, tending 120,000 acres of desert that have been scraped, shaped, molded, and flooded by the Awash River to sweeten the world's coffee, its tea. Eventually it could make Ethiopia the sixth largest sugar producer in the world. It will help break the country's dependence on foreign aid—a good thing.

But the benefits of economic progress are rarely shared equally with all involved. There are winners and losers in every improvement scheme. Here, one of the losers is a bright young Afar woman

—a girl, really, though her poise makes her seem old beyond her years. She is wrapped in a red dress. She stands by a new levee. She is collecting water from what used to be the Awash River.

"The company moved us off our land," she tells us, waving her arm at the sheets of cane. "We get a little work, we Afars, but it is always the lowest work. Watchmen. Shovel work."

A typical sugar plantation salary: $20 a month. The girl says police came to expel the Afar diehards who refused to move. Shots were exchanged. Blood flowed on both sides.

How old is this story? It is one of the oldest stories in the world.

What are the individual names of the Sioux forced from the Black Hills of the Dakota Territory by gold miners? Who remembers this anymore? Who are the millions of people who surrender their livelihoods today—Irish farmers in the European Union, Mexican ranchers shunted aside by highways—for some abstract common cause? It is impossible to keep track. Humanity remakes the world in an accelerating cycle of change that strips away our stories as well as the topsoil. Our era's breathtaking changes flatten collective memory, blur precedence, sever lines of responsibility. (What disconcerts us about suburbia? Not just its sameness, but its absence of time. We crave a past in our landscapes.)

Dubti is a busy green frontier. Ethiopians are flocking there, bringing new hopes, tastes, ambitions, voices, a new future—a new history.

In Dishoto, another truck-stop town, I recharge my laptop at a police station. The officers are all outsiders, non-Afar, from the highlands, from the south. They are friendly, curious, generous. They ply Elema and me with tea. (It is dense with sugar.) Our conversation is interrupted by government ads. The policemen watch these nation-building commercials intently: music played over video loops of strip mining, roadbuilding, workers in medical labs. We thank them. We walk on.

Milan Kundera, the Czech novelist, once wrote that the struggle of man against power is the struggle of memory against forgetting.

The Afar girl's name is Dahara. She is 15.

Near the Ethiopia-Djibouti Border

We camp on the flank of Fatuma mountain, a basalt sentinel overlooking the caravan trails that braid eastward to the old coastal sultanate of Tadjoura. The tiny Republic of Djibouti sprawls below: a scalded plain, hotter and drier than the Ethiopian desert, with dry lake beds of blinding white salt, scarps of gunmetal gray, and doubtless, huddled somewhere in the shade of a doom palm, more Afar nomads—herders cleaved from their Ethiopian brethren by a colonial border, speaking in halting French.

This is where I begin to say goodbye to the Afar camel men from Herto Bouri.

Elema, Yarri, and Aidahis declare themselves ready to push on. They wish to walk with me to the beaches of the Gulf of Aden. But this is impossible. Two of them have no passports, no documents, no scraps of paper attesting to their existence. ("This is all Afar land!" they say.) And besides, Elema is sick. He issues his camel-loading orders lying down, from under his *shire,* his sarong, which he drapes over his head like a sheet. In a few hours we will part ways in the ugly border town of Howle.

What is it like to walk through the world?

It is mornings like these: Opening your eyes to nothing but seamless sky for day after day; a pale, numinous void that for one fleeting instant, when you first awake, seems to suck you upward, out of your body, out of yourself. It is the clarity of hunger, a transparency that seems blown through by the wind, the way a hollow pipe is blown to make it whistle. (We trekked 18 miles yesterday on short rations, on a single bowl of noodles and a handful of biscuits each. My wedding ring, once tight, jiggles loosely along my finger.) It is learning to read landscape with your whole body, your skin, not merely your eyes—sensing camel fodder in a thorn scratch, the coming dust in the smell of the wind, and of course, precious water in the fold of the land: a limbic memory of great power. It is watching the eternity of Africa slip by at a walking pace, and coming to realize dimly that, even at 3 miles an hour, you are still moving too fast. It is the journey shared.

Mohamed Aidahis: a powerful ant-stomping gait. Kader Yarri: the marionette looseness of a skinny man's step. Mohamed Elema: the spring-loaded step of a square dancer. On our best days we four ramblers recognize our immense good luck. We ricochet down steep mountain trails, almost running, with the desert of Ethiopia shining at our feet. We bounce our voices off the walls of black-rock canyons in whooping contests. Then we catch each other's eye, three Afars and a man from the opposite longitude of the earth, and grin like children. The cameleers catch the spark, and sing.

What is it like to walk through the world?
It is like this. It is like serious play. I will miss these men.

Ardoukoba Lava Field, Djibouti
The dead appear on the forty-second day of the walk.

There are five, six, seven of them—women and men sprawled faceup, facedown, on the black lava plain as if dropped from the sky. Most are naked. They have stripped off their clothes in a final spasm of madness. Sandals, trousers, brassieres, cheap nylon backpacks—their belongings lie scattered, faded, washed-out, bleached by the sun to the pale gray of undersea things. The skin of the dead is parched a deep burned yellow. The little wild dogs that come in the night have taken their hands, taken their feet. They might have been Ethiopians. Or Somalis. A few, probably, were Eritreans. They were walking east. This is what unites them now in the mineral silences of the desert: they were making for the Gulf of Aden—for the open boats of the Yemenis who smuggle destitute Africans to peons' jobs in the Middle East. How many such migrants die in the Afar Triangle? Nobody knows. At least 100,000 attempt the crossing to the Arabian Peninsula each year, according to the UN. Police chase them. They become lost. Thirst kills them.

"A crime!" Houssain Mohamed Houssain shouts back at me. "A disgrace!"

Houssain is my guide in Djibouti. He is a decent man. He is angry and perhaps ashamed. He strides far ahead, shaking his walking stick at the stone-white sky. I lag behind. I wipe the sweat from my eye sockets and study the dead.

A demographer calculates that 93 percent of all the human beings who ever existed on Earth—more than 100 billion people —have vanished before us. Most of humanity is gone. The bulk of our heartaches and triumphs lie behind us. We abandon them daily in the wasteland of the past. Rightly so. Because even though I have told you that I am walking to remember, this isn't completely true. As we reenact the discovery of the earth over and over again, to keep going—to endure, to not sit down—we must embark also on journeys of forgetting. Houssain appears to know this. He never looks back.

One day later we reach the Gulf of Aden.

A beach of gray cobbles. Waves of hammered silver. We shake hands. We laugh. Houssain opens a sack of hoarded dates. It is a celebration. We stand on the rim of Africa. The sea is walking —it falls endlessly forward into Africa and then rolls forever back, pulling away to the east . . . toward Yemen and the Tihamah coast, toward the lupine valleys of the Himalaya, toward ice, toward sunrise, toward the hearts of unknown people. I am happy. I write this down in my journal: I am happy.

Brave, foolish, desperate travelers. You almost made it. You fell 3 miles from the coast.

II. The Wells of Memory

There are thousands of wells in the old Hejaz. We walk to them. Sometimes their water is sweet. More often it is salt. It matters little. These wells, which pock the long-disused caravan trails of Arabia, are monuments to human survival. Each concentrates a fine distillation of the landscape. And the same applies to the people who drink from them. In the Hejaz—the fabled realm of a vanished kingdom of the Hashemites, who once ruled the Red Sea coast of Saudi Arabia—there are bustling wells and lonesome wells. There are wells whose waters convey the chemistry of sadness or joy. Each represents a cosmos in a bucket. We take our bearings off them.

Wadi Wasit is a well of forgetting.

We reach it on a fiery day in August. We are halfway through a more than 700-mile foot journey, perhaps the first made in generations, from Jeddah to Jordan. We rest in the dendrites of gray shade thrown by the well's two thorn trees. Here we meet the running man.

He arrives in a pickup truck. Portly, mustachioed, a Bedouin camel herder, he is friendly, curious, talkative, jittery. He mistakes us for treasure seekers. (Why else walk through the scorching desert?) He has come to sell artifacts.

"Look at this!" he says. He displays a tin ring. The iron scabbard of a sword. A well-rubbed coin.

How old are these things?

The running man doesn't know. *"Kadim jidn,"* he says: Very old. He shrugs.

The Hejaz—a crossroads where Arabia, Africa, and Asia meet, and long tied by trade to Europe—is one of the most storied corners of the ancient world. It has seen millennia of wanderers. Stone Age people hunted and fished their way north out of Africa through vanished savannas. People from some of humankind's first civilizations—Assyrians, Egyptians, and Nabataeans—roamed through here, trading slaves for incense and gold. Romans invaded the Hejaz. (Thousands of the legionaries died of disease and thirst.) Islam was born here, in the dark volcanic hills of Mecca and Medina. Pilgrims from Morocco or Constantinople probably drank from the well in Wadi Wasit. Lawrence of Arabia may have gulped its water, too. Nobody knows. *Kadim jidn.*

"Take it!" the running man says. He shoves his orphan finds at us. "Take it for free!" But we decline to buy his curiosities.

Packing our two camels to leave, we spot him once again. He is running now—sprinting around the well. He has removed his white robe. And he is running through the desert in his underwear, circling the well under the ruthless sun. He runs with abandon. Ali al Harbi, my translator, takes a photograph. Awad Omran, our camel handler, guffaws. But I cannot laugh. He is not mad, the running man. Or drugged. Or playing some joke. He is lost, I think. As we all are when we abandon history. We don't know where to go. There is an abundance of pasts in the Hejaz. But I have never been to a place more memoryless.

A small, bottomless well in the Hejaz: a white porcelain cup.

It holds dark, rich coffee. It sits atop a polished wooden table inside an elegant mansion in the port of Jeddah. Three articulate Hejazi women refill the cup endlessly. They take turns talking, wishing to correct misperceptions about Saudi Arabia: that the kingdom is a homogenized society, a culture flattened by its famously austere brand of Islam, a nation rendered dull by escapist consumerism and by petrodollars. No.

Saudi Arabia, they say, is a rich human mosaic. It enfolds many distinctive regions and cultures: a Shiite east, a Yemeni south, a Levantine north, and a tribal Bedouin stronghold in the center—the puritanical redoubt of the Najdis, home of the ruling dynasty, the House of Saud. The women insist, moreover, that no region in Saudi Arabia remains more independent, more proud, than the realm that has guarded the holy cities of Mecca and Medina since the tenth century—the vanished kingdom of the Hejaz. Fully independent by the end of World War I, the Hejaz was annexed by the Al Saud dynasty only in 1925. It remains a place of contradictions, of complexity, of tensions between religion and geography. On the one hand: a sacred landscape, its holy cities long forbidden to non-believers. On the other: the most cosmopolitan and liberal corner of Saudi Arabia, a melting pot, an entrepôt and nexus of migration, brightly checkered with influences from Asia, Africa, the Levant, and a hundred other places—the California of Saudi Arabia.

Laila Abduljawad, a cultural preservationist: "The Hejaz has attracted pilgrims from every corner of the Islamic world. How could this not rub off? Our main dish is Bukhari rice from Central Asia! Our folk textiles are Indian! Our accents are Egyptian! We are more open to the world than the people from the center."

Salma Alireza, a traditional embroiderer: "The traditional dress for women in the Hejaz was not the abaya"—the severe black robe imposed by the ruling Najdis. "Women here used to wear bright red and blue dresses in public. That was traditional. But life changed in the 1960s. The oil money poured in. We modernized too fast. We lost so much in fifty years!"

Rabya Alfadl, a young marketing consultant: "Is the Hejaz still different? Take a look around."

And it's true. The women sit at the table unveiled. They wear casual Western clothing: blouses and trousers. (Such a meeting would be difficult to arrange in the Saudi capital, Riyadh, where gender segregation and tribal ways remain so strict that a man will not utter his mother's name in public.) The house where we chat is sleekly designed, chic, minimalist, global in decor. And outside, in Jeddah's streets, there are art galleries, cafés, promenades, museums—the cultural hub of Saudi Arabia.

"A sense of cultural identity has persisted in the Hejaz for a thousand years. It developed its own music, its cuisine, its own folktales," Abduljawad tells me. She turns her cup in her hands. "We are taking our first baby steps to rescue a small part of this."

These women are daughters of a feminine city. Arab folk tradition holds that the biblical Eve was buried in Jeddah, now a modern, sprawling, industrial port. Eve's tomb—200 yards long, shaped like a reclining figure—was crowned by an "ancient and lofty dome," according to the Moorish traveler Ibn Jubayr. It is gone, marked today by a barren concrete cemetery. Wahhabi clerics, who abhor shrines as idolatrous, likely razed it nearly a century ago. But again, no one can remember.

*

More than 300 miles north of Jeddah, near a dry well called Al Amarah, we stop walking. We look up from our tired feet. A car approaches across a plain of glistening salt. It is a Toyota HiLux, the iron camel of the modern Bedouin.

This is an event. Traversing western Saudi Arabia on foot today is lonelier than it was one or two generations ago when the black tents of Bedouin were still pegged to the brittle hide of the desert. The famous nomads of the Hejaz—the Balawi, the Harb, the Juhayna—have resettled in towns, in suburbs, in offices, in army barracks. Modern Saudi Arabia is heavily urbanized (matching the United States in this respect).

Yet a few diehards remain.

One steps from the truck. He is a graybeard in a stained gray *thobe,* the classic robe of Saudi men. He brings us a gift. "It is our way," says the old man, who calls himself Abu Saleh. He sweeps a callused hand at the surrounding desert. "We welcome all travelers."

No other soul is visible on the horizon. Abu Saleh leaves us with a simple goodbye. His gift: a small well of kindness—a dented steel bowl full of camel's milk.

Built of necessity, the wells in the old Hejaz have faded, softened, eroded into objects of beauty and contemplation.

The earliest of these watering stations were established, precisely one day's walk apart, by the caliph Umar in A.D. 638. "A traveler is the person worthiest of receiving protection," he declared, before pioneering the most sophisticated rest-stop system in the ancient world: waypoints on the pilgrims' trails to Mecca serviced by forts, cisterns, guesthouses, date groves, hospitals, canals, even distance markers.

We trudge the same trails—ribbons of desert burnished by countless shuffling camels, by numberless sandaled feet. Scholars from Timbuktu drank from these wells. So did merchants from Spain seeking frankincense. So did sun-boiled nineteenth-century European explorers who rambled the Hejaz disguised as pilgrims. One who didn't pose was a blustery Englishman named Charles M. Doughty. He announced himself to everyone as a Christian, an infidel, and walked with a knife up his sleeve. (Of one caravan swollen with 10,000 animals and 6,000 people, he wrote: "The length of the slow-footed multitude of men and cattle is near two miles, and the width some hundred yards in the open plains.")

North of the city of Al Wajh we unpack our two camels at a well, utterly ignored by the speeding traffic of a superhighway. This well, called Al Antar, was rendered obsolete a century ago by steamships. It is made absurd today by the pilgrims hurtling overhead in Boeing 777s. I bend over the well's lip. A damp air breathes up from its darkness, cooling my cheeks. I hear from somewhere far below the calls of startled songbirds. I think: *Arabia is like the American West. It is a landscape of terrible absences.*

If the Hejaz still inspires romance in the non-Muslim world, it is due to its long caravan of foreign chroniclers.

There is the nineteenth-century Swiss polymath Johann Ludwig Burckhardt, who traveled to the religious core of Islam as a pauper—a "reduced Egyptian gentleman"—and never made it home. (He died of dysentery and was buried with Muslim rites in Cairo.) There is the brilliant and pompous Englishman Richard Francis Burton, who, if he can be believed, actually touched the Kaaba, the holiest of holies—a massive cube of volcanic stone in Mecca toward which all Muslims must pray. These Europeans witnessed a world locked in time. They found Red Sea towns built of shining white coral blocks, their arched doors and window shutters painted sea green and dazzling nomad blue. They passed through walled cities whose tall gates creaked shut at dusk. They galloped camels between fortified oases with wild-haired men, the Bedouin, whom they found harshly admirable. (Burton: "We had another fight before we got to Mecca, and a splendid camel in front of me was shot through the heart.") This literary Hejaz, if it ever truly existed, has long since disappeared under American-style suburbs and strip malls. Yet outside the old pilgrim's port of Al Wajh, we stumble upon the ghost of one of the most famous of these Orientalists.

Workmen are cleaning out a well.

The well lies within the high rock walls of Al Zurayb fortress, built 400 years ago by the Ottomans. The laborers haul up old explosives: cannon shells that look like rusted pineapples. The ordnance was chucked down the well in panic, probably in January 1917. At that time a camel-back Arab army was approaching fast. The tribes of the Hejaz had risen against their German-allied

Ottoman overlords. And the foreigner who had stoked the revolt —he was barely 5 feet 5 inches tall but possessed a masochistic hardness—whooped along with the attackers. Of the Arab cavalry he wrote: "They wore rusty-red tunics henna-dyed, under black cloaks, and carried swords. Each had a slave crouched behind him on the crupper [of the camel] to help him with rifle and dagger in the fight, and to watch his camel and cook for him on the road."

Thomas Edward Lawrence, more famous as Lawrence of Arabia, is one of our first postmodern heroes: a compromised superman. The young British intelligence officer and Oxford medievalist yearned, subversively, to bring liberty to an Arab world that was then staggering under the corrupt yoke of the Ottoman Turks. Yet he was tormented by the knowledge that the Hejazis who fought alongside him would be betrayed by the European colonial powers that carved up the Middle East after World War I.

"Lorens al Arab," I tell the workmen at the fort. I point to the live shells.

The name means nothing to them. Lawrence is virtually forgotten in Saudi Arabia. He backed the wrong dynasty after the war. His champion, Faisal, the moderate Hashemite prince of the Hejaz, lost a power struggle to the fierce tribes of the interior led by the peninsula's future king, Ibn Saud.

"They were a people of spasms, of upheavals, of ideas, the race of the individual genius," Lawrence wrote of his comrades in the Hejaz. "The desert Arab found no joy like the joy of voluntarily holding back. He found luxury in abnegation, renunciation, self restraint. He made nakedness of the mind as sensuous as nakedness of the body. He saved his own soul, perhaps, and without danger, but in a hard selfishness."

This is what happens when you peer down wells in the Hejaz. You glimpse your own reflection. Lawrence, an ascetic of empire, was describing himself.

Wells of piety: plastic cups of water arranged by the thousands across a stone courtyard in Medina.

It is Ramadan, the fasting month. The holiest month of the Muslim lunar calendar. Just outside Al Masjid al Nabawi, the burial mosque of the Prophet Muhammad, the second holiest site in Islam, at least 60,000 faithful are gathered at sunset to break the day's hunger.

They come from all quadrants of the earth. I see Indians and Africans. I hear French. I am not Muslim. But I have been fasting all month out of respect. Across from me a big pilgrim from Afghanistan—a red-haired Nuristani—kneels in front of one of the prepackaged meals distributed daily at the site. He hands me his orange. I give him mine. We exchange our food like this several times, laughing. On the loudspeakers an imam sings the crowd into prayer. They pray. And beneath a fading yellow sky, we eat in tender silence.

Strange new wells on the roads of the Hejaz: machines humming in the desert.

Their fitted aluminum surfaces shine under the sun. Hallucinations of metal. Of rubber and plastic. They are outdoor electric coolers. They dispense water so icy it numbs the mouth. We encounter hundreds of these mechanical shrines, called *asbila:* public water fountains commissioned by the pious to earn virtue in the eyes of Allah. One day their rusted parts, jutting from the shifting dunes, will puzzle archaeologists. How can any society afford to chill a cup of water in a barrens as gigantic and remote as the Hejaz? It seems impossible. Mystifying. Yet the *asbila* from which we gratefully fill our canteens exist because of other wells—ones drilled in the distant oil fields of eastern Saudi Arabia.

"We've traded away our past for wealth," laments Ibrahim, a water engineer in the port of Al Wajh. "My grandfather's two-hundred-year-old coral-block home? Bulldozed. The docks where dhows from Eritrea brought in camels? Gone. Our city's stone lighthouse that used to be seen from twenty kilometers at sea? Rubble. Nobody cares. It's all old stuff. It has no economic value."

Some Hejazis blame Saudi Arabia's ultra-conservative version of Islam for much of the erasure of their past. In recent years, for example, urban historians have decried the demolition of the old quarters of Mecca and Medina, including the flattening of ancient structures associated with Muhammad himself. Officially this was done to provide services for the 2 million or more pilgrims who swell the cities on hajj. But religious authorities have frequently blessed the destruction of cultural sites. Wahhabis emphasize that all the past before Islam is *jahiliyya:* a time of ignorance. And they fear that even the preservation of Islamic sites may lead to the worship of objects, and not God—thus promoting idolatry, or *shirk*.

It is worth noting that the loudest laments for the disappearing heritage of the old Hejaz come from Muslims outside Saudi
Arabia. "It is difficult to get young Saudis involved in their own
history," says Malak Mohammed Mehmoud Baissa, the mayor of
Jeddah's remnant old town. "It isn't taught seriously in schools."

Breakneck economic change. Modernization. From tents to
Twitter and glass skyscrapers in barely three generations. Europe
must have been this way during the industrial revolution. It is miraculous that Paris survived.

Meanwhile, in the fishing towns along the shore of the Hejaz,
the last local fishermen strain to sing sea shanties into my digital
recorder. Songs from the age of wooden dhows. Songs of warm
Red Sea winds. Of beauties waiting in ports. These Hejazi fishermen, most of whom have hired out their boats to migrant Bangla-
deshis, have earned their own anthropologists. "It is important,"
say researchers from the University of Exeter in England, "to capture the last true remnants of the songs of the sea before they
become mere pastiches."

We inch northward toward Jordan. We guzzle a gallon of water a
day. We seek out wells of memory.

In Jeddah a female artist honors a lost world, displaying on the
old city's walls images of her grandfather sitting with his vanished
majlis, a traditional council once common in the homes of Hejaz
aristocrats. (The art—titled "Where Is My Majlis?"—is mysteriously
removed after a week.)

In Medina a museum director spends seven years of his life constructing a meticulous, 50-foot-square diorama of the holy city's
heart, with its mazy alleys and lemon trees. These timeless features
were scraped away in the 1980s to make way for high-rise hotels.
("Old residents come here to cry.")

The past is fraught territory in every country. Until barely a
generation ago U.S. textbooks rarely acknowledged the complex
universe inhabited by Native Americans. Israel points to biblical
archaeology to cement its right of existence. Yet in Saudi Arabia
this blinkered view is changing.

Riyadh has spent nearly a million dollars on a museum devoted
to the Hejaz Railway—the storied Arabian version of the Orient
Express—terminating in Medina. Jeddah's antique quarter is also
up for review as a UNESCO World Heritage site. (One such global

treasure already exists in the Hejaz: Madain Salih, a colossal ne-
cropolis of the Nabataean empire.) Most extraordinary of all, an
entire Hejazi caravan town of some 800 homes, abandoned and
crumbling for 40 years, has been bought by the government for
renovation.

"This is our greatest experiment," says Mutlaq Suleiman Almut-
laq, an archaeologist with the Saudi Commission for Tourism and
Antiquities, and the curator of the ancient caravansary town of Al
Ula. "We are looking back more. This is good."

Almutlaq is an earnest, friendly man. He scrambles ahead of
me in his white *thobe* through the walled ghost town located south
of Madain Salih. He vaults broken archways and pokes through
covered medieval streets. He shows me courtyards where traders hawked incense, lapis, and silk for eight centuries. Kerosene
lanterns manufactured in Germany rust on the floors of the
empty homes. The legendary Muslim explorer Ibn Battuta passed
through in the fourteenth century, praising the honesty of Al Ula's
populace: pilgrims stored their luggage here en route to Mecca.
Almutlaq takes pride in this fact. He lived and worked in Al Ula
as a youth. The site's residents were trucked, en masse, to modern
apartments in the 1970s.

"I remember," he says, smiling. And he talks of traveling merchants loading bales of Egyptian textiles. Of farmers stalking in at
dusk from the fields. Of women talking to each other from windows latticed for modesty.

Twin wells of memory: Almutlaq's glasses, flashing excitedly
amid the dim archaeology of his childhood.

We are all pilgrims in the Hejaz. Wanderers through time. We stop
at its wells, or we pass them by. It matters little. Used or not, the
wells remain. In their basements shine disks of pale sky—the un-
blinking eyes of memory.

After six months of walking, I say goodbye to my guides Ali and
Awad. I cross the Haql border from Saudi Arabia to Jordan. I carry
little. A shoulder bag of notebooks bound with rubber bands.
Seven hundred miles of words. Pages crazed with jottings about
devastating heat. Inked maps of pilgrim roads. Divinations of Bedouin fire doctors. Bearings for remote wells.

I reach a modern tourist resort. No one pays me any mind.
There is the novelty of women driving cars. I watch couples stroll-

ing beaches in sarongs. I stop at a minimart and buy a bottle of filtered water: a small plastic well, an artifact from the main channel of history. I peer south, beyond the Gulf of Aqaba—toward the Hejaz. A cloaked place. The lips of its ancient wells are grooved by ropes turned to dust. Dust long since blown away. I sip my water. It tastes utterly ordinary.

III. Blessed. Cursed. Claimed.

Jerusalem is not a city of war. Avner Goren is stubborn on this point.

We are on foot, walking under a cloudless morning sky in the Levant, following a river of raw sewage that foams in torrents from East Jerusalem—12 million gallons a day, Goren informs me—a foul discharge that runs for 23 miles down to the Dead Sea. We are trailing the waste as a form of pilgrimage. Goren, one of Israel's leading archaeologists, thinks like this.

"There have been seven hundred conflicts here since Jerusalem was founded," he says over his shoulder, wedging his way through religious tourists in the Old City. "But there were long times without war, too. And people lived peacefully together."

There are three of us.

Goren: a native Jerusalemite, a tousle-headed intellectual with the watery blue eyes of a dreamer, and a Jew. Bassam Almohor: a Palestinian friend and photographer, a tireless walking guide from the West Bank. I join them both after trekking north over the course of 381 days from Africa, out of the biological cradle of humankind in the Rift Valley of Ethiopia, and into the rise of agriculture, the invention of written language, the birthplace of supreme deities: the Fertile Crescent. My slow journey is part of a project called the Out of Eden Walk, whose aim is to retrace, step by step, the pathways of the Stone Age ancestors who discovered our world. I plan to ramble for seven years to the last corner of the earth reached by our species: the southernmost tip of South America. When I describe my trajectory to Goren, he replies, "Yes. You've come up from the south, like Abraham."

Our sewage walk—Goren's grand idea—is as compelling as it is eccentric: he wants to clean up the waste (Germany has promised support for a wastewater treatment plant) and establish miles of "green" trails along a fabled valley where 5,000 years ago Jerusalem was founded. These walking paths would unspool from the spiritual core of the Old City through the biblical desert, where the pollution oozes under a yellow sun. Because the effluent crosses the separation barrier between Israel and the West Bank, such a route would bridge the lives of Palestinians and Israelis. The purified river, by collecting in its arid watershed the sacred and profane, would help build peace between the Middle East's two archenemies.

"This pilgrimage will be different on many levels," Goren says. "It follows an important cultural and religious corridor, true. But it also connects Palestinians and Israelis in a very real way. And of course there is the clean water."

We start among the shrines of the three Abrahamic faiths: the Dome of the Rock, the spires of the Church of the Holy Sepulchre, and the towering blocks of the Western Wall, bristling with prayers inked on paper. We sweat down shadeless streets in Palestinian neighborhoods. We follow the sludge through barren hills, where it encircles a sixth-century monastery like a grim moat. The effluent slides through an army firing range. In airless canyons we breathe through our mouths to blunt its stench. Two days later we reach the terminus: the salt sea between Israel and Jordan.

"Monotheism was born here," Goren tells me atop a cliff overlooking the sheet of iron-colored water. "Once we invented agriculture, we didn't need nymphs at every spring anymore. The old gods of wild nature were no longer required."

Only ultimate mysteries remained.

It seems so impossible, so unworkable, so naive, Goren's dream. (Weeks later, yet another round of Palestinian-Israeli fighting would flare. Rockets would scratch the skies. Israel would invade nearby Gaza. "This will set me back by two years," Goren would sigh. "But I'll wait.") This is how we must have advanced, originally, across the dawn world. Against laughable odds. Across 2,500 generations of setbacks, despair, blows, crises of faith.

Yet surely it is the quest that matters.

We walk north, Hamoudi Alweijah al Bedul and I, from the Saudi Arabian border. We climb the brow of Syria.

What is the brow of Syria?

A rampart of rock: a colossal knuckle of sandstone punching

up from the Hisma, the pale frontier plains of south Jordan. Arab mapmakers of the Middle Ages drew this high barrier as an edge, a fulcrum point, a divide. To the south, the vast geometrical deserts of Arabian nomads, a redoubt of feral movement, of fickle winds, of open space, of saddle leather—home to the wild Bedouin tribes. To the north, the lusher, more coveted fields of settled peoples, of walled civilizations, of layered borders drawn and scratched out —the many-chambered heart of the Levant. We walk into the Fertile Crescent, the prime incubator of human change. A cockpit of empires. A palimpsest of trade roads. A place of exile and sacrifice. Of jealous gods. The oldest of promised lands.

Hamoudi, my guide, sings his way uphill. He leads a pack mule by a chain, bowed against an icy wind. His faded kaffiyeh snaps like a flag. I walk ahead, pulling another loaded mule. Hamoudi steers me, too, like a dumb beast. "Left!" he cries in Arabic. "Right!" And "No, no, straight ahead!" In three days of walking together, my Bedouin traveling companion and I pass life-sized Neolithic bulls etched into rocks at Wadi Rum, a fabulous corridor of tangerine sand—a primordial valve of human migration that T. E. Lawrence called a "processional way greater than imagination." We trace our fingers over 2,000-year-old inscriptions pecked by Nabataean incense traders and nomadic herders. We stagger over rubble from Roman forts. We camp beside ruined churches of Byzantium—the eastern Christian empire—their naves caved in, roofed now by desert skies marbled with cirrus. Everywhere we spot the prayers carved by long-dead Muslim pilgrims walking south to Mecca.

The storm belts us on the rim of the Jordan Valley. Gusts chuck up fistfuls of dirt. The mules moan. Deranged by lightning, a hobbled camel lopes past screaming like some mocking portent, only to vanish in the gloom. Bedouin women refuse us shelter. In violet twilight they warn us away, shouting objections from the interiors of their belled and tottering tents. Night falls. We walk on.

"Palestine," Hamoudi tells three lean, unshaven, deeply filthy sheepherders of the Sayadeen tribe who finally take us in. It's as good a destination as any.

The shepherds stir the cherry embers of their hearth. They accept our instant coffee sweetened with condensed milk, sipping from plastic cups with pinkies held out like lords. They ask politely after our well-being. They praise God that we are content. My feet are frozen. Hamoudi winks and grins. He will sleep with his dagger on a rug of sand. Tomorrow is Christmas.

Humankind paused, midstep, while ambling through the Middle East. Wolfish bands of hunter-gatherers, weary from 200,000 years of wandering, sat down in the chalky valleys of the Levant. They sought out reliable springs of sweet water. They learned to sow wild grasses—barley, emmer wheat, flax. They tamed wild oxen with horns 6 feet wide. The nomadic imperative of hunting was set aside forever. Instead these newly settled peoples began stacking stone upon stone, building the first villages, towns, cities. Smelted metal appeared. So did commerce and armies. A new world entire, bustled, unfolded, expanded—one we still inhabit. This "Neolithic revolution" occurred between 9,000 and 11,000 years ago. It erupted, independently, in the earliest agricultural societies in China, Mesoamerica, and Melanesia. But it bloomed first in the rumpled dun hills and forested riverbanks along our route out of Africa.

Or so say the textbooks.

Hamoudi and I trudge 300 miles north through the lavender shadows of the Transjordan range. We tug our hammer-headed mules along the tourist trails of Petra, the fabled Nabataean capital cut from rock the color of living muscle. We walk past Bronze Age graveyards that contain dead so old and unloved they hardly seem human anymore—Fayfa and Bab edh Dhra, the famous boneyards of the sort that some biblical scholars link to the destroyed cities in Genesis, Sodom and Gomorrah. Wadi Faynan 16 holds no such notoriety.

Discovered in 1996, the site sits atop a remote gravel terrace above the gaunt and dusty Jordan River valley. This obscure site is an enigma, a paradox. It upends the usual narratives of human progress. Circular dwellings, grinding stones, stone tools— its village relics date back an astonishing 12,000 years, deep into our nomadic Stone Age. The people who settled here weren't farmers. They hunted. Yet they built a large amphitheater of mud, a platform carefully runneled to carry liquid—possibly blood. They came, apparently, to witness some ritual. To pray. And like Göbekli Tepe in Turkey, another profoundly antique cultic monument that has gained worldwide fame, Wadi Faynan

16 suggests that organized religion—spiritual hunger, not empty bellies—may finally have stopped our ramblings, kindled our urbanism, made us modern.

"The amphitheater looks designed for communal worship," says Mohammad Dafalla, an archaeological guide who helped dig up Faynan 16. "Something very old ended here. Something new began."

Hamoudi gathers twigs for a campfire. The Jordan Valley sprawls below in a broth of yellow light: a vast and barren causeway trodden by the feet of prophets. By Abraham and Moses. By Jesus and John the Baptist. Early humans strode past out of Africa nearly 2 million years ago, earlier probably. Hippos, now extinct, grazed in the valley's vanished swamps. Yesterday the walls of Jericho came tumbling down. Not an inch of this antique vista hasn't been fought over, cursed, blessed, claimed for one divinity or another. It is a land worn smooth like a coin traded through countless fingers.

Hamoudi boils a pot of tea. We squint from the first house of god through a hot desert wind, down at the Holy Land's novel idea: home.

A miraculous desert rain. We slog, dripping, into As Safi, Jordan. We drive the sodden mules through wet streets. To the town's only landmark. To the "Museum at the Lowest Place on Earth."

This whitewashed building sits near the Dead Sea, exactly 1,329 feet below sea level. Inside its exhibit hall, behind panes of glass, in a white-lit lab, a team of restorers works on an ancient Byzantine floor: 44 square yards of stone shards rescued from Lot's Cave Monastery. (Lot: the Old Testament refugee from Sodom.) The floor dates from the fifth century A.D. and contains 300,000 jumbled tesserae in hues of red, brown, yellow, olive green, and white. Greek, Australian, and Jordanian experts have gathered here to piece the small stone cubes back into a whole. They have been doing this for 14 years.

Stefania Chlouveraki, the project leader, stands at a long sorting table. She turns the colored fragments over and over in her fingertips. She fits each one into its place: a magnificent tableau of lions, crosses, pomegranate trees.

"There's a trick to it," Chlouveraki says. "One small piece can bring a whole section together."

Chlouveraki, a tenacious archaeological conservator, has salvaged antiquities all over the Middle East. There is so much history here—so much that needs to be preserved, documented, rescued. Chlouveraki is particularly fond of the neighboring country of Syria. She has many friends in the old Syrian city of Hamah, a major cultural hub. She worries about them—about their safety. Much of that city has been destroyed by the Assad dictatorship in Syria's brutal civil war. She doubts she will ever see Hamah again. Yet she is wrong. Because Hamah is all around her.

Hundreds of thousands of Syrians shelter beneath UN canvas in Jordan. In the irrigated fields of As Safi, these refugees survive hand to mouth, picking tomatoes for $11 a day. We have been staying with them, Hamoudi and I, almost every night. It is remarkable. All are from Hamah. An entire metropolis has taken to its heels, walked away from apocalypse, spilled across borders, over mountain passes, to scatter in the Jordan Valley. The women bring out delicate tea sets saved from blown-up houses. They pin fine Syrian embroideries, called *sarma,* inside their dusty tents as reminders of home. Their faces, as they remember their dead, become sadly luminous.

Such is the deeper mosaic of the Levant. Here, long ago, we invented cities. Here we scatter again from war, like broken tesserae, back into nomadism.

The Holy Land is coveted. It is profoundly walled. Few outsiders realize to what extent.

In Amman, at the banks of the Jordan River between Jordan and the Israeli-occupied West Bank, people gather for Epiphany. This is a New Year's rite for Orthodox Christian believers. The faithful come to the sacred stream to sing hymns, to be rebaptized. They also exchange shouted greetings across 5 yards of sliding brown water: "How is Auntie?" "Hold up the baby!" And "Tell Mariam we will call her tonight!"

These are Christian Arab families divided by the 1967 war between Israel and its Arab neighbors. A striped metal pole, almost within arm's reach of each shoreline, juts midcurrent above the water, delineating the border. Israeli soldiers in olive fatigues and Jordanian police in navy blue stand ready to halt anyone who might dare wade across it. A few days later I ford the Jordan River on a bus: foot travel across Allenby Bridge checkpoint is strictly prohibited.

"Checkpoints. Checkpoints. Checkpoints," Bassam Almohor tells me. "We have checkpoints in our minds. We wouldn't even know what to do with free movement."

Almohor is middle-aged, a storyteller. He is a compulsive walker, a Palestinian who expects the worst in life in order to be pleasantly surprised—a relisher of irony. Over the course of two sweltering days of rambling the West Bank, we squeeze through a thicket of visible and imaginary borders, fences, walls, frontiers, barriers, no-go zones. After a year steeped in the oceanic vistas of Arabia, of Africa, such a dicing of landscape into countless microturfs makes me dizzy. My head spins.

Smaller than Delaware, packed with 2.7 million people, the core of a proposed future Palestinian state, the occupied West Bank is partitioned by the Oslo Accords into zones of Palestinian and Israeli control: Areas A, B, and C. Each of the zones has its own restrictions, guidelines, regulations. A political map of the territory looks like an X-ray: a diseased heart, mottled, speckled, clotted, hollowed out. We inch past Hisham's Palace, in Jericho, a little-visited treasure of eighth-century Islamic art (Area A). Sweating under the sun, we scale the barren eastern scarp of the Great Rift Valley (Area B), edging carefully around controversial, razor-wired Israeli settlements (Area C). Plodding 26 miles on through a nature reserve and an Israeli artillery range (Area C again), we collapse in Bethlehem (back in Area A).

A line of clocks in our cheap hotel displays the time in Lagos, Bucharest, Kiev: the capitals of pilgrims who come to kneel at the birthplace of Christ. In reality the entire world funnels through the Church of the Nativity. The next morning, on blistered feet, Almohor and I join long lines of Argentines, of Russians, of Americans, of French. In clouds of incense, they lay their palms on flesh-polished stones where the Godhead touched Earth.

A medieval Greek Orthodox church controls access to the grotto of the manger. Next door a newer Roman Catholic cathedral makes do with a peephole. Catholic visitors peer through this hole into the yellowed light of the holy birthplace. The hole is big enough, I note by testing, to admit my pencil. Here is a classic West Bank arrangement: a celestial Oslo Accord.

See the men dance. Arms draped on shoulders, kick-stepping in circles, they swing bottles of wine. Purpled thumbs cork the bottles. The wine leaps and jumps behind green glass. They throw back their heads, the dancing men. They laugh at the sky. They are happy. They lurch into streets. They reel among cars to the blare of horns. On the sidewalks their children walk, oddly attired—a carnival of pygmy soldiers, ninja, geisha, Roman centurions.

"Everything we hate," one man explains in broken English. He means sin. Laughing, he dances on.

He is Haredi, a member of the conservative Jewish sect that rejects modern secular culture. Bene Beraq—a low-income, ultra-Orthodox satellite of Tel Aviv—broils on the Mediterranean plain of Israel. Its male residents dress like crows: heavy black suits, black Borsalino hats, the old grandfathers hugely whiskered and the boys in *peot*, the curled sidelocks of the pious. The women pale and staring under the sun. In plain skirts, drab shoes. In hair scarves. Their drunken revelry jars. A fiesta of Quakers. An imams' jamboree. A bacchanal of Mennonites.

These godly folk—have they gone mad?

No. It is simply this: after walking the timeworn horizons out of Africa, I have entered a corrugated maze, a knotted crossroads of the world where landscape is read like sacrament, a labyrinth of echoing faiths called the Middle East. The strange zeal at Bene Beraq is a festival of joy, of survival: Purim. Purim commemorates the deliverance of the Jews from a genocide under the Persians almost 2,500 years ago. That slaughter, plotted by the courtier Haman, was foiled by two brave Jews, Esther and her stepfather, Mordecai. Every fourteenth day of Adar, Jews celebrate their continued existence. They exchange gifts. They make themselves "fragrant with wine." They drink until they "cannot tell the difference between 'Cursed be Haman!' and 'Blessed be Mordecai!'" It is a holiday one feels one can get behind.

I join in. Unkempt, in threadbare clothes, with holed shoes and sun-cured hide, my costume is permanent: the traveler, the man from far away. At Bene Beraq the masked children laugh. They ask for coins.

My walk is a dance.

The anthropologist Melvin Konner writes how the *num* masters of the Kung San, the shamans of the Kalahari—members of perhaps the oldest human population on the planet—induce a spiritual trance through hours of dancing around campfires. Such arduous rituals deliver up to 60,000 rhythmic jolts—the number of footfalls in a long day's trekking—to the base of their skulls. The result, Konner says, is a psychological state that we have been questing for since our species' first dawn, "that 'oceanic' feeling of oneness with the world."

This may explain the neurology of rapture. But why the pursuit of it?

I will exit the cauldron of the Levant at the Israeli port of Haifa. I buy passage on a cargo ship that will carry me around the abattoir of Syria to Cyprus. From there, it's on to Turkey.

One day's walk south of Haifa gape the Mount Carmel caves. They hold *Homo sapiens* bones 100,000 years old. This famous archaeological site marks the farthest limit of human migration out of Africa in the middle Stone Age—the outer edge of our knowledge of the cosmos. I trudge to the caves in a squall. The government has seen fit to prop mannequins inside these rock shelters: plaster cave people dressed in skins. In gray stormy light, their painted eyes stare out at the Mediterranean—at Homer's wine-dark sea, at a corridor into modernity. But in memory my walk's true coda in the Middle East came earlier.

I had camped months before, on the shore of the Dead Sea, with a family of Bedouin.

The father, Ali Salam, was poor. He gathered aluminum cans alongside the highway. His teenage wife, Fatimah, a shy, smiling girl in a filthy gown, rocked her sick baby under a plastic tarp. She cooked tomatoes pilfered from nearby fields. We ate from a sooty cook pot. Across the asphalt, not 200 yards away in the night, blazed a pod of luxury resorts. I imagined, back then, another couple standing behind plate glass windows: Glasses of minibar wine in their hands, they might have stared out into the dark. Did they see our campfire? Could they hear the child's persistent cough? Of course not. I tried to resent them. But they weren't bad, the people in that well-lit room. Certainly no worse or better than anyone else traveling the lonesome desert road. Such was the walk's only theology. The Bedouin. The people in the hotel. The road that divided and united them.

Behind Closed Doors at Hotels

FROM *Travel + Leisure*

WHEN I TRAVEL alone, when my only companion and source of affection is the hypoallergenic wedge of pillow with some silly hotel monogram on it, when the jet lag and the unfamiliar sun make me feel like a dust speck blown across the earth (an alien dust speck that will never know the love of another human being again), when all these planets align, one thing will happen: someone in the room next to me will be having very loud sex. Not just loud sex, but the most emotive, bizarre, animalistic, post-structuralist, post-human sex ever. The men will moan as if the hotel staff is extracting state secrets out of them, the women will reach a crescendo of foreign syllables that always sounds to my ears like "You're so alone, you're so alone, you're so ahhhhhh-lone!"

And I am alone. At three in the morning, in a distant land, unsure of who I am, my iPhone set to the wrong time zone, my passport forgotten at reception, my wallet out of Albanian leks, my bed floating through nothingness like a spacecraft that's slipped out of Earth's orbit and beyond Houston's range, as above me, below me, beside me, two people join up in outrageous, pornographic ecstasy, some of them clearly trying to create a third person by the early morning's light.

Different hotel chains seem to elicit different kinds of sex. W Hotels, contrary to the boutique leanings of many of its properties, seem to get going early, say 10 p.m., and some of the sex sounds vaguely romantic, with occasional kind laughter and even a precoital Italian *"Ti amo!"* The international range of the Marriott brand is unmistakable and admirable: if you want to hear sex in Tagalog in Manila, this is probably your best bet. Hands down, the lustiest hotel chain in the world in my experience is Hyatt. I don't know if every encounter is registered in its loyalty rewards program, but Hyatt may be one reason why the world's population is topping 7 billion. When I had to place Misha Vainberg, the amorous hero of my second novel, *Absurdistan,* inside a Western brand-name hotel, I really didn't have to think twice.

Of course, where you are makes a difference. At a too-cool-for-school hotel on the outskirts of Bangkok, the Japanese couple next door went at it so vocally, I was absolutely sure the woman had just recited the entire *Tale of Genji.* Even the deeply cynical Thai water bug staring at me pensively from the ceiling seemed to stop in its tracks, utterly shocked. The next morning Mr. and Mrs. Osaka were at the pool next to me nibbling on spicy scrambled eggs. Inevitably during "the morning after" the young man will be staring ahead in his most cool and sullen pose, or heartlessly flipping through his cell phone, while the young woman hums with purpose and fulfillment. This discrepancy is yet another reason to worry for our species.

(Important note: if you have recently broken up with someone and are feeling particularly blue, do not stay in a hotel in Naples, Italy, or anywhere south of Naples.)

Often I feel the people next to me are having sex with the express purpose of showing off. At a luxurious hotel in my native St. Petersburg, Russia, I was placed in a duplex suite, the kind where the second-floor mansard bedroom is just centimeters away from another person's lovemaking. By their outrageous *okh*s and *oooh*s I had immediately pegged the next-door couple as rich Muscovites come to the relatively impoverished Venice of the North to show off their advanced earning power and perfectly calibrated reproductive skills. The next morning at the hearty breakfast table, they were cinematically feeding each other sturgeon and kielbasa, cooing and mooing, laughing and loving, reminding me that the only thing sadder than a lonely traveler with sex all around him is a lonely traveler staring at a plate of cold kasha.

Sometimes the sex itself is sad. At an airport hotel in Des Moines, Iowa, the young farmers of America next door were so desperately trying to fall into a rhythm, to find a language that could accommodate that other, uncertain side of them, I almost called room service to send them up an oyster. Their meaningless call-and-response led me to open my window so that I could better hear the drone of an early-morning flight taking off for a better-sexed destination. Minneapolis, say.

Needless to say that when I travel with my partner, there is complete silence in the rooms next to us. When I'm asleep in her arms, the universe has no reason to taunt me. Enjoy the silence, it says to me. Someone loves you. Now love her back.

Ship of Wonks

FROM *The Atlantic*

THE LAUNDROMAT IS a great place to meet men, dating experts say. Also, sports bars. But what do you do when you have your own washer and dryer? When you quit drinking six years ago? What do you do when you want to meet someone who, like you, is not at that Super Bowl party but home alone watching the Science Channel, contemplating the certain collision of the Milky Way and Andromeda and the romantic ramifications of quantum entanglement, what Einstein called "spooky action at a distance"?

As I sat in my parents' kitchen last fall, thumbing through my dad's back issues of *Scientific American,* my mother warned me again about my hurtling headlong into a lonely void. "You don't have forever," she said. I was reading about the possibility that time doesn't exist but is simply "emergent." Still, I didn't argue. I nodded and opened another issue, to an ad for Insight Cruises featuring a trip with a strong physics theme.

"You're too picky," my mother went on, noting my age—"nearly forty!" "Thirty-five," I corrected her as I perused the cruise itinerary. Following a tour of CERN, on the Franco-Swiss border, home of the Large Hadron Collider, participants board the *AmaDagio* for a trip down the Rhone River, enjoying 23 onboard lectures about the latest developments in physics and cosmology punctuated by tours of five French port cities en route to Arles. *What kind of people take these trips?* I wondered. *Could this be my laundromat?*

The day before my flight, I was still packing. Casual attire was advised, but I wasn't about to meet my soulmate in a T-shirt. And visiting the largest particle accelerator in the world, where the elusive Higgs boson (the "God particle") was finally discovered, surely warrants a little dressing up. I settled on practical Hepburn-esque menswear for daytime and gowns for the evening—perfect for a transatlantic steamer setting sail in 1925.

An overnight flight later, I was standing amid a crowd of T-shirted septuagenarian couples, waiting to board a bus that would take us to CERN. I was about to give up all romantic hope when a fantastically young man in his late fifties, an English astrophysicist, asked whether he could sit next me. "Of course!" I said. And then I noticed his wedding ring, fat and gold, shaped like the Large Hadron Collider we were about to see.

Three hundred thirty feet underground, a 17-mile ring straddles the Franco-Swiss border. Whizzing through the accelerator at speeds approaching that of light, particles smash into each other, reproducing collisions that occurred in our newborn universe nearly 14 billion years ago. I was still thinking about this the next day as I stared out from the deck of the *AmaDagio*. Swathed in secondhand mink, I watched the French countryside drift by, the trees an autumn medley of orange and red, and then bare.

Belowdecks, I lunched with an American couple who reminded me of my parents. "The boeuf bourguignon is delicious," I said, smiling. "The meat is tender, but none of that matters if you don't have a person to share it with," the wife replied, after learning that I was traveling alone. I was grateful when her husband, a gynecologic pathologist, changed the subject. He asked whether I'd gotten the HPV vaccine. "My doctor says I'm too old." He nodded gingerly before estimating my age, probable number of sexual partners, and the statistical likelihood that I already had the cancer-causing virus. His wife took his hand and beamed. "My husband's work has been honored all over the world."

For dinner I selected a dramatic houndstooth gown paired with my favorite polar-bear earrings. The only one in formal attire, I blushed and quickly took a seat beside a roguishly handsome retired art history professor from Bath. An Insight Cruise veteran (this was his fifth), he had spiky white hair, dark eyebrows, and a back problem that made him look sulky and rebellious.

We bonded right away—I have a similar pain in my hip from too many hours at my desk—and I began fantasizing about becoming the wife of Bath and accompanying him on his sixth cruise.

Over dessert, he took out his iPhone to show me photos of his collection of clocks and barometers. He was going on about time and pressure when it hit me: I was not being courted but visited by the Ghost of Science Cruise Future. With a start, I realized that all of his clocks were grandfathers.

Like sand through one of the professor's hourglasses, the days of our cruise slipped by. Some mornings brought lectures on the subatomic world—"Electrons come in pairs." Several afternoons, talks on space—"We live in a time of cosmic collision, but eventually the galaxies will settle down." We toured the Roman ruins of Vienne—"The Temple of Augustus and Livia. What a pair!" And on one of our last evenings, we walked through the medieval ghost town of Viviers. Two by two we disembarked, like Noah's animals, onto dry land. The professor gallantly offered his arm.

That night I stayed up late with the captain, the married astrophysicist, the gynecologic pathologist and his wife, and a couple from China. Together in the ship's lounge, we talked excitedly about ideas the way we had when we were in college, when we were young, when we had forever. We talked about the Big Bang, about what came before the beginning, about what came before that, and before that . . . "You don't want to end up alone," I remembered my mother saying. But there, alone among the over-70 set, it dawned on me: I've seen the end, and it's not so bad. I adjusted my vintage turban and leaned into the conversation. So what if electrons come in pairs? The Higgs boson, that special thing that took almost 40 years to find, goes it alone.

CHRISTOPHER SOLOMON

Baked Alaska

FROM *Outside*

JIMMY'S STORE IN Port Heiden, population 102, stocks all the staples of Alaskan bush life, at bush prices: $14 cans of Folgers, $7.50 packs of sunflower spits, something called the Jerky Master. And on the wall, hanging from a nail: very large steel leg traps, without price or explanation.

"You're goin' up there today?" Jimmy asks from behind the counter, in what passes for a formal greeting. Jimmy's gaze trails across the ample gray acreage of his sweatshirt and settles on the window, where right now a slasher-film fog is sticking to what little scenery presents itself. Tundra. Truck. Still more tundra, unspooling to a horizon so unbroken by man or mountain range that the sky would start at your shoelaces if only you could see them. Welcome to July on the Alaska Peninsula.

Twenty minutes ago, our bush plane nosed down into the soup and left us on a gravel airstrip, where we hitched a ride to Jimmy's along with the mail sacks in the back of a gutted eighties Econoline van. QUAYANA (Thank you), the door read. NO PETS.

Jimmy Christensen is half Aleut, and like many of the native Aleut here, he's broad, quiet, and kind and in possession of his people's sly, dry sense of humor. The way everybody is always asking Jimmy for advice or to borrow his dozer until next Friday, he seems to run his hometown. He's sort of the gentle Tony Soprano of Port Heiden. There's not much new here for a man like Jimmy, and our sudden appearance and determination seem to amuse him. He sells us a gallon of white gas and offers to drive us to the road's end.

Grabbing his keys, Jimmy says we're the first backpackers he's seen in weeks. This doesn't surprise us. Nobody comes to the Alaska Peninsula by accident. Even fewer come here for fun. The peninsula marks the start of the Aleutian island chain, the 1,400-mile tail that wags west toward Kamchatka. It's a slim, Vermont-sized piece of nearly trackless green with a population of fewer than 3,000 residents, almost all of whom live in just a few villages that sit uneasily on the map, as if nature might evict them at any time. Naknek. South Naknek. Port Heiden. It's a tortured land-scape, pummeled by unrelenting storms and warted with semi-active volcanoes. In a state grinning with superlatives, this is one of the wildest, rowdiest, most remote places around. It remains a question mark to even the most sporting Alaskans.

Which is exactly why we're bouncing in the back of Jimmy's king cab. I'm obsessed with blank spots on the map, the places nobody goes. I've learned to follow my cell phone like a reverse Geiger counter: the poorer the coverage, the more enticing the destination. For 10 years, I've tried without luck to visit the most promising one of all, the one that now lurks out there in the murk: Aniakchak National Monument and Preserve, the least visited of the entire 401-unit national park system.

Already it has taken my companions—guide Dan Oberlatz and photographer Gabe Rogel—and me three flights from Seattle to reach Port Heiden, which sits about 450 miles southwest of An-chorage. Our plan is to backpack 22 miles into the monument's centerpiece, an ancient and massive crater, and then float 38 miles to the Pacific using ultralight, stowable rafts crammed deep in our packs. From there we hope to hoof and paddle nearly 80 miles down the coast to the native community of Chignik Lagoon, where the closest airstrip awaits.

Inconvenience is the least of the obstacles that Aniakchak throws up for the would-be visitor. The central peninsula is home to one of the largest concentrations of the biggest brown bears on earth. Then there are the man-eating vegetables, alder jungles that swallow bushwhackers, and cow parsnip with poison leaves that blister the skin. Add routinely nasty meteorology—"This is where a lot of the weather is made for the rest of the country," a guide once told me—and the challenge we face is pretty stark.

We're not even out of sight of Port Heiden's last house when Jimmy starts in on his version of Alaska's familiar "out of the car, into the food chain" axiom. "Just remember there's a bear up here, he's about twelve foot," Jimmy says. "The worst thing up here, though, are the wolves," he adds. "They've been hanging out now in packs of forty." The leg traps suddenly make sense. In 2010, wolves in Chignik Lake killed a petite schoolteacher while she was out for a run. The incident was only the fourth documented account in North America of unhabituated wolves killing a human being.

The truck stops where the muddy track meets a creek, and we pile out.

"What kind of gun you got?" Jimmy asks.

Dan introduces Jimmy to Pepe, his handgun and the fourth member of our group. Pepe is a brawny, confident-looking .44 Magnum. Dirty Harry's gun. I liked Pepe the moment I met him in Anchorage—a fondness that grew once Dan discouraged me from bringing my bear spray, explaining that not only is bear Mace unpredictable, it's also not allowed on commercial planes.

Feeding Pepe ammo at the trailhead, Dan suddenly seems apologetic. "Probably won't do more than piss off a twelve-footer," he says to Jimmy.

The Aleut's silence is a verdict. Jimmy then says that he prefers to carry a shotgun with slugs, the Alaska-approved way to stop 1,000 pounds of charging meat.

Before we shoulder our packs, Jimmy pauses to offer some parting native wisdom. "What you gotta do is file the tip of the sight off," he says, eyeing Pepe. "So it won't hurt so much when the bear shoves it up your ass."

In 2012, 9.7 million visitors drove through the gates of Great Smoky Mountains National Park, the country's busiest. That's nearly 19 people per minute. Meanwhile, 19 people stopped by Aniakchak all year. This isn't because Aniakchak lacks merit; it may be the coolest place you've never heard of. Around the time the Egyptians were at the height of their powers, a 7,000-foot stratovolcano blew its top with a force equal to 10,000 nuclear bombs. Bowels emptied, the peak collapsed on itself, leaving a 6-mile-wide crater with walls rising as much as 2,500 feet from the floor. For the next few thousand years, it sat resting in near anonymity. Then, in 1930, the Glacier Priest arrived.

Father Bernard Hubbard was a Jack London character sprung

to life—a self-promoting Jesuit and peripatetic head of the geology department at California's Santa Clara University who was as quick with a bear-felling shot as he was with a Hail Mary. Hubbard's scrambles all over pre-statehood Alaska, sometimes accompanied by a crew of strapping Santa Clara footballers who wore their leather helmets for protection, made the Glacier Priest a household name at a time when a depressed nation hungered for heroes. His exploits appeared in the *Saturday Evening Post* and *National Geographic;* for a time, he was said to be one of the top-paid speakers on the planet. "The world's most daring explorer," one magazine declared.

Hubbard's visit to unknown Aniakchak, though, really shot the Glacier Priest to fame. Inside the "great moon crater," as he called the long-quiet caldera, his crew discovered "paradise found . . . a world within a mountain," where orchids bloomed in the volcanically warmed soil and the rabbits were so guileless that the padre and his crew felt guilty eating them (but did anyway).

Then Aniakchak erupted again, in the spring of 1931. When the holy man returned that summer and peered over the crater's edge, he likened himself to Dante on the edge of the Inferno. "It was the abomination of desolation . . . the prelude of hell," he wrote in his book *Mush, You Malemutes!* "Black walls, black floor, black water, deep black holes and black vents; it fairly agonized the eye to look at it." Hubbard's Eden had been obliterated, replaced by a Hieronymus Bosch canvas of cauldrons bubbling with sulfurous yellows and greens and fumaroles hot enough to cook his crew's beans.

Eighty years later, Aniakchak is a quiescent member of the Pacific's volcanic Ring of Fire but is considered "potentially active" by the Alaska Volcano Observatory. The crater and surrounding areas have started to recover. So why does nobody come? Access, for one. No roads reach Aniakchak. The aforementioned nasty weather, for another. Stuck between the raging Bering Sea and North Pacific Ocean, the Alaska Peninsula is forever buffeted by storms like a beleaguered referee trying to separate heavyweights. Skies are cloudy 300 days a year, with low ceilings. Flying here is akin to navigating inside an old gym sock. Parties can wait days to get in or out.

Then there are the brown bears Jimmy warned us about. "The Alaska Peninsula has, if not the highest density in the world, then close to it," Dave Crowley, a biologist for the Alaska Department of Fish and Game who manages the area's bears, told me before I left. Recent studies have found up to 400 brown bears per 1,000 square kilometers. (By comparison, it's estimated that just 718 of the famous, feared Yellowstone grizzlies are sprinkled across 72,500 square kilometers in the greater park area.) The peninsula's bears are genetically similar to the famed Kodiak brown bears, which along with polar bears are the largest bears on earth.

If you do manage to reach Aniakchak, you will find no broad-brimmed park rangers. No Winnebagos. Not a single marked trail. As the National Park Service's website for Aniakchak puts it, "No lines, no waiting!"

"We gotta get up and outta this shit," Dan says as he climbs back into the tent on the second morning. He's soaked. After our group left Jimmy yesterday afternoon, we squished southward for 7 miles across tundra and through low grasses that felt like someone's overwatered lawn. Just a dozen miles from the grumpy Bering Sea, the landscape almost cowered; bent beneath our 65-pound packs, we were still the tallest things for miles. We eventually pitched camp in what felt like the inside of a milk jug. Now we can't see 50 feet. I thought back to two days ago, when we'd stood in the airport departure lounge in sunny, 75-degree Anchorage before a mural highlighting marquee destinations like Lake Clark National Park and Katmai that read GATEWAY TO ALASKA'S SOUTHWESTERN WILDLANDS. Aniakchak wasn't on the mural.

If this trip is a fool's errand, I can't think of better fools-in-travel than my companions. Dan, 45, is a smart-ass native of Northern California with sharp blue eyes behind his geek-chic horn-rimmed eyeglasses. A ball cap that hides a backpedaling hairline advertises Alaska Alpine Adventures, his 16-year-old company that guides trips ranging from ski-touring from a yacht to climbing in the Brooks Range and then floating to the Arctic Ocean in inflatable canoes. A few years ago, Dan also launched Adventure Appetites, a gourmet backcountry food company that has supplied the fare for our trip. Gabe, 37, from Washington, is an up-for-anything photographer whose goofiness makes it easy to forget that he's a former mountain guide who has worked everywhere from the top of 8,000-meter Shishapangma to the unclimbed vertical walls of Ethiopia.

"Chimps in the mist," Dan dubs us after breakfast as we hunch under our packs and trudge into the never-ending whiteout. The land rises almost imperceptibly in a long, green, mossy ramp that, the map tells, is the volcano's flank. We see bear tracks. We see caribou tracks. We see wolf tracks that stalk the caribou tracks.

The fog machine is on full. We steer by GPS. Condensation drools from Dan's hat brim and from Pepe's barrel, which rides holstered within easy reach on his hip. Gabe and I are jittery in the spooky murk. Wolves appear at the corners of our vision, only to resolve themselves into shrubs. Bruins become boulders. "Alaskan rock bear," Dan says after I yelp at one. With no bear spray to comfort me, I calm myself by recalling what bear expert Crowley had told me: Aniakchak bears live at the largest buffet table on earth —berries, salmon, moose. They're so well fed they "tend to be fat and lazy," he said; he'd watched bears catch salmon and only lick them, they were so full. "If you don't do anything stupid, you'll be all right." I repeat the words *buffet table* like a mantra.

Eventually the moss gives way to black-pebbled plains and ash piles and rivers of pumice. There is no wind, no birdsong, as if even sound itself has abandoned us.

"This place is so otherworldly," says Dan. "Dead. Not a thing alive."

Up and up, we chimps walk through the monochrome for hours. Finally a black line materializes from the white mist: the crater lip. Now the wind rouses, as if Aniakchak has awakened to the trespass. It roars, grabs backpacks, lifts us like bright bits of cloth and practically tosses us over the rim, sending us running down the steep pumice ramp into the crater.

Inside the caldera, the wind relents. The clouds lift. The sun shines. Finally we can see where we've arrived.

"Oh, my God," I say, looking at Gabe.

"Oh, my God," says Gabe, looking at Dan.

"Oh, my God," says Dan, looking everywhere.

A "bewitched stadium" is how Hubbard described the crater the first time he stepped inside. My initial thought is less poetic. It feels like we've stumbled into a gargantuan gopher hole. Inside it's sunny and dry: an ash-filled bowl more than 6 miles across whose floor is so large—nearly 30 square miles—that Manhattan could easily fit inside. Before us spreads a scene that's *Land of the Lost* meets nuclear holocaust. Eighty years on, the ground underfoot still looks charred. A few sprigs of dwarf fireweed flower bravely in the dry ash. Cinder cones pimple the crater floor, and all around us queer volcanic monuments pepper the landscape. To our left is a huge scoop in the earth called Half Cone, remnant of some bygone blowout. Behind us lies a scab of hardened lava the size of a neighborhood that oozed up during the 1931 eruption. As if the scene lacked for drama, high above us fog pours over the crater rim in spectacular cascades that shred and evaporate on the descent. "Cloud Niagaras," Hubbard called them.

There's green water in the distance. We head toward it instinctively, kicking up ash like postapocalyptic pilgrims.

After the 1931 eruption, the Glacier Priest had damned Aniakchak as the pit of Hades. The intervening years have softened the place slightly, rinsing off the heaviest soot and endowing it with a flinty beauty. Call it desolation sublime. We hike past walls candy-striped in sherbet pinks and reds. A caribou prances by, a sole welcoming host. In the middle of the crater, we tramp past the huge cone of 3,350-foot Vent Mountain—"a volcano within a volcano!" Hubbard had exclaimed upon first seeing it—looking sullen with its burned top. In the distance, glaciers cling to the shadier walls.

Then there's Surprise Lake, the crater's psychedelic gem, which glows the unreal green of Imodium A-D, thanks to suspended volcanic particles in the water. The specially evolved sockeye salmon that spawn here are essentially raised on soda water. "It's like nothing I've ever seen in Alaska, that's for sure," Dan says that evening after we make camp in a sheltered elbow along the lake and tuck into his company's reindeer rotini.

The next morning, wearing only daypacks, we explore the crater's oddness. It's like taking a walking tour of our dyspeptic planet. We cross electric green moss and dunes of black sand so full of iron it sticks to the magnet on the chest strap of Gabe's Camel-Bak. We hoof across otherworldly plains of dust staged with small rocks, where I'm pretty sure NASA faked the Mars rover landing. We peer into springs bubbling with a witchy brew of ferric browns and pumpkin oranges. I keep thinking of how one early geologist described Aniakchak: a "pleasing weirdness," he wrote. And all the more pleasing for our aloneness.

Or at least we seemed alone. "Now that's a big bear right there. That's a coastal brown. That's huge," Dan says, looking down at muddy paw prints along the lake near our campsite. The claws on the front paw print are as long as Swiss Army blades. The rear print swallows my XL hand with inches to spare. "Definitely a ten-footer," Dan says.

"So, uh, how old do you think those are?" I ask, second-guessing our solitude. I search to see if Pepe is still strapped to Dan's hip.

"At least a few days." I exhale.

That afternoon, as the guys nap in warm 70-degree sunshine, I tie a fly to the end of my line. Standing atop some of those bear tracks, I'm soon yanking in Dolly Varden trout, their polka dots pink in the yellow sun, from where the Aniakchak River exits the lake. Every few casts, I swivel around to make sure my fly hasn't foul-hooked the 10-footer. Some people prefer meditation to make them feel present; for me, nothing focuses the mind quite like knowing I'm a potential crudité.

From the moment it tumbles out of the crater, the 38-mile Aniakchak River runs south toward the Pacific as if it's late for dinner. It will be our escape route. We'll use our packable Alpacka rafts to float right out of the caldera. At one time the inside of the crater had been filled with a 600-foot-deep lake. That changed about 2,000 years ago, when an earthquake or eruption or massive rockslide cracked the crater wall. A biblical flood gushed through the gap, with a flow close to the Mississippi's, overwhelming the landscape downstream. Today the designated Wild and Scenic Aniakchak River still charges through that 1,000-plus-foot cleft, called the Gates, as it carries Surprise Lake to the sea.

Yesterday we'd climbed high onto the crater rim to scout our departure.

"Not a lot of volume," Gabe had said, watching the small river squeeze through the Gates before uncoiling on distant green plains. "Looks like it might be hard to get in a lot of trouble."

More careful inspection showed garage-sized boulders frothing the green waters. I knew the river dropped 75 feet per mile through here—honest rapids. I also knew that my entire whitewater experience consisted of Mom letting me ride the log flume, twice, at Virginia's Kings Dominion amusement park.

The next morning we wisely portage past the chewing rocks and Class III-plus rapids of the Gates. Downstream, we suit up in ultralight drysuits for a practice run. Dan gives us whitewater kayaking 101. "They're super-agile," he says of our micro rafts. "They'll bounce off rocks. You'll spin around," he adds. "You'll be fine."

For its first third, the Aniakchak is as wide and shallow as a sluice box. This late in summer, it's a fun-house ride of mostly Class II rapids. We bounce downstream for 13 miles of unbroken whitewater, hooting and hollering.

It's comforting to see Pepe riding high on Dan's life jacket. Which reminds me—what should I do if I see a bear standing in the river?

"Enjoy the experience," Dan says. Then, after a short pause, he flashes a wide grin. "And paddle to the deepest water."

Later that afternoon, we finally see our first: a honey-colored beauty who quickly bolts deeper into the nearby willows after spotting our odd armada.

The river slows dramatically the second day, as the land palms open into perfect bruin country. The terrain even looks bearlike— humped, alder-furred hills that seem to root around in the underbrush. We find the calm pace of this new land, sometimes dozing off while seated upright in our kayaks, other times tossing pumice stones at one another and watching them float.

As we drift languidly, I remember something Dan told me over lunch before we left Anchorage. "I could grow my business and do stupid touristy shit," he said, making a sour face. "But the soul of my business is in the wilderness." He's led 50-some trips in Alaska since founding his company, but these days he personally guides only those, like Aniakchak, that he hasn't done yet. Alaska is too big and too cool, he said, to not keep exploring.

That afternoon, the Pacific Ocean welcomes us with a stiff-arm breeze and an incoming tide. After a short struggle against both, we spy an old cannery cabin refitted by the Park Service above the beach. After five days of so much expansiveness, the confines of four walls and a small space is a relief. Inside, the cabin's logbook records many wild things: Trips of 30-bear sightings. Parties pinned down for days by hurricane winds. Savaged boats. I turn to the most recent entry and count backward. Just 11 visitors so far this year, not including us—and three of them were here for work.

Most visitors to Aniakchak get picked up by floatplane at the cabin after their paddle to the sea. The reason that Dan suggested we keep going on foot is simple: he'd never hiked the rarely trammeled, four-day, 80-mile route along the Pacific to Chignik Lagoon and wanted to do some recon for a possible client trip. Gabe and I were game.

Our trek along the beach is no Tahiti vacation. We spend long days bent under our still-heavy packs. We make decent time cruising never-ending stretches of firm sand and sneaking around barnacled headlands at low tide. Sometimes, though, we're forced upland into thickets of alder that grow as tight as prison bars and slow progress to a heartbreaking quarter-mile per hour. Whenever possible, Dan sniffs out bear trails, centuries-old bruin interstates that are the path of least resistance through the tangle. One is so disturbingly popular that it's trenched 3 feet deeper than the abutting alders.

The miles blur in a fever dream of suffering and spectacle. I remember bald eagles posing atop sea stacks like hood ornaments for the continent. I remember inflating the pack rafts nervously for a 13-mile paddle around a headland on the rolling Pacific, only to be pleasantly distracted by orange-beaked puffins and curious sea lions. I remember Pepe, drawn and ready to shout, after we surprise a chuffing brownie on a kill. And how that bear is the last of 19 we see in 24 hours as we leave the preserve and enter the Alaska Peninsula National Wildlife Refuge.

Mostly what I remember, though, is the feeling of a different rhythm taking hold, not of the wristwatch but of natural places. Each day as we hike, the sun sets a little sooner. We see salmon gather in the bays, sniffing for their home rivers—and see bears come down to the shore, ready to flick their sushi onto the sand. My fancy GPS watch dies; I don't much care. I go days without thinking of e-mail or my iPhone. This is what we want from our Aniakchaks, isn't it? Places that help us shake off the dross and find a surer and more ancient pulse.

Four days after leaving the cabin, on the puddle jumper out of Chignik Lagoon, a familiar green ramp comes into view. From 15,000 feet, it appears as smooth as pool felt. I press my forehead to the window and stare for a long time as the ramp finally climbs higher and higher, until it vanishes in a smother of white clouds. I look up. Gabe and Dan are smiling. For a moment we grin like idiots at one another. Then we press our foreheads against the cold of the Cessna's tiny portholes. Seeing all this, some of our fellow passengers look out their windows, perplexed. If you hadn't been there, it would be easy to think there was nothing worth seeing at all.

Bonfire of the Humanities

FROM *Outside*

PEOPLE DRESS LIKE kings and queens in the capital of Mali, even in the dirt streets on the far side of the river. The women walk down mud lanes wearing immaculate gowns with puffed shoulders, gold detailing, and beadwork. The dudes are natty, too, in safari suits, crisp office-boy outfits, or the grand boubou, the national robing that makes any man walk like a giant. Only the heroic boys everywhere—young teens carrying loads, pushing groceries, directing trucks—go around in recycled jeans and T-shirts. In squalor the people must be regal.

We'd been circling the outskirts of Bamako for an hour, driving in a taxi from street to street, block to block, the confusion more effective than any blindfold. Out here, far from the government compounds and hotel towers of downtown, was the striving Africa, endless rows of two-story cement houses, barbershops, and mobile-phone kiosks. Finally a boy on a motorcycle was sent to fetch us, and we followed him back through the sprawling neighborhood and into a courtyard, where the gate was quickly locked behind us.

Here a man in a red fez escorted me through the cool, dark house to an iron door painted red and freshly reinforced with cement and a strong padlock. It took a while for my eyes to adjust. Boxes. Boxes and boxes. There were 2,400 footlockers in this room.

The air reeked of decaying paper, the acid tang of the back stacks at a forgotten university. The trunks were brightly painted in the Malian style: black, green, and silver, with waving lines and diagonals and dots. They shone even in the deep shade of this cavernous room. Some were as small as suitcases, others large enough to hold a body. They climbed to the ceiling on three sides, with only a narrow passage down the middle.

The man who opened the door to this trove was Abdel Kader Haidara, 44, a round-bellied scholar from the Sahara, with a cloudy left eye and a simple white robe.

"Here," said Haidara, gesturing for me to advance.

Before me was a vast cache of knowledge pulled literally from the fires of war. These were the famed manuscripts of Timbuktu, the legendary caravan town that had thrived here between the twelfth and sixteenth centuries. Relics of a sophisticated African trading culture that stretched from Mauritania to Zanzibar, they had emerged in the past decade as one of the great archaeological discoveries of our time, a hidden-in-plain-sight secret. Inside wrappings of rag paper or gazelle leather, scribed onto camel- and goatskin parchments, written on Italian Renaissance paper and even stones, the Timbuktu books were a mountain of literature in a supposedly illiterate part of Africa, the secret history of a continent before Europeans arrived.

And then, in January 2013, they were burned. Jihadi rebels occupying Timbuktu entered the town's great library and set the manuscripts ablaze. The world condemned it as the most despicable act of vandalism since the Taliban dynamited the monumental Bamiyan Buddhas in Afghanistan in 2001.

So how could this room exist?

I was having an Indiana Jones moment. I opened a trunk and gently swept my fingers over the tooled-leather bindings and the soft edges of rag paper. I picked out a book and opened it, the pages crackling, the calligraphy stunning after some 500 years of sitting in dark rooms. I found myself stroking the books, inhaling their smell.

I opened cases at random, discovering treasures that I would never be allowed to touch in a museum. The pages were caverned out by millimeter-wide bookworms, some more tunnel than text. I opened another metal trunk and a cloud of dust emerged, the books inside more confetti than pages.

I won't look good in 500 years, either.

The bonfire was the last act in a war that has simmered for decades in the Sahara desert, pitting the nomads who have traditionally

controlled northern Mali against its weak national government.
It's no wonder you don't know where Mali is: one of the world's
25 poorest countries, this landlocked nation has 7 neighbors
and no luck, more than 30 languages, including the French of
its colonizers, and its feet in wet West Africa and its head in the
arid Arab north; it lies where the Sahara yields to the Sahel, the
grassy promise of the tropics. The northerners are mostly Tuareg,
the blue-clad tribesmen who've roamed across borders for centuries, recognizing no governments unless paid to do so. (They've
rebelled against Mali three times just since the 1990s.) Their version of Islam has long been relaxed and idiosyncratic, allowing
relative freedom to women and embracing music, especially the
electric guitar. In the 1990s, before things took a harder turn,
Tuareg leader Iyad Ag Ghali wrote a song for the biggest rock
band in the Sahara.

Timbuktu was known for tolerance as well, and for its love of
sensual pleasures like music and tobacco. Founded around A.D.
1100 where the Sahara meets the Niger River, it became a trade
hub fed by caravans that crossed the desert with salt and books,
connected by camel to Córdoba and Constantinople. By the fifteenth century, Timbuktu was home to 100,000 people, with as
many as 25,000 scholars crowding its dirt lanes. One urban quarter served as a medieval Xerox machine, lined with scriptoriums
where calligraphers churned out handmade copies. Only the rise
of European sailing ships pushed it into obscurity.

In modern times, Timbuktu attracted musicians and Western
seekers, a mixture of Afropop gods, young rockers, and ecstatic
backpackers who gathered every January for the Festival in the
Desert in the dunes west of town. That groovy vibe peaked in 2007,
when Bono and Jimmy Buffet crashed the party, but the consensus
of desert life was breaking down. Ag Ghali stopped smoking and
dancing and embraced the arch-conservative Islam of Ansardine, a
homegrown jihadi group, and AQIM, the North African affiliate of
al-Qaeda, run by a one-eyed Algerian named Mokhtar Belmokhtar,
who'd perfected the art of kidnapping for profit. In 2009, a Briton
was grabbed—and later executed—after another music festival,
and soon there were nine Western hostages in northern Mali.
European governments paid $65 million in ransoms, which only
emboldened the Tuareg and drew in more cash-hungry fighters.
Malian musicians were threatened with death for participating in

the Festival in the Desert, and the 2012 event—held right outside
Timbuktu, for safety—was the last.

Then the jihad arrived. Belmokhtar united about 2,000 Tuareg
fighters with a smaller, hardened force of jihadis—a quicksand
mixture of smugglers and holy warriors bolstered by perhaps 1,000
heavily armed mercenaries returning from Libya. That April, the
Malian army abruptly collapsed and the rebels captured Timbuktu, Gao, and Kidal, the desert's main population centers. In
Timbuktu, the Tuareg promised tolerance and respect. But when
the troops of Ansardine arrived, flying the black flags of al-Qaeda,
the rebels set up Taliban-style rule across northern Mali, a place
they called Azawad and governed with harsh sharia laws.

In previous wars—a Moroccan invasion at the end of the sixteenth century and a jihadi uprising in the fifteenth—manuscripts
had been destroyed or looted, too. But centuries later, mountains
of old paper were still there, in small family collections, preserved
by the desert climate and Islam's reverence for the written word.
"We don't care about books," one Tuareg rebel had assured a local
collector, but that didn't last. While overwhelmingly Islamic, the
books embraced secular science, Sufi magic, and intellectual argument—the wrong kind of Islam, at least for al-Qaeda.

The occupation lasted 10 months. Then, on January 26, 2013,
as a French military expedition approached the city, the retreating rebels paused to commit one final crime. Entering Timbuktu's
modern new library, the Ahmed Baba Institute of Higher Learning
and Islamic Research, they carried more than 4,000 manuscripts
into a courtyard, where they built a bonfire of words. One match
and about 30 minutes of stirring was all it took.

The mayor of Timbuktu told the *Guardian* that the fire had destroyed not one but two libraries, "a devastating blow." But smoke
gets in your eyes. Although pictures emerged of torched manuscripts lying in piles, Malian officials soon backtracked. Only *some*
books had been lost. Over the next few months, news reports
emerged of a remarkable effort by ordinary Malians to smuggle
out these treasures, by truck and trunk, donkey and canoe. The
jihadis never knew how badly they themselves had been burned:
before they lit their blaze of ignorance, the vast majority of the
city's manuscripts were already gone.

I learned some details about all this by speaking with Stephanie
Diakité, a Seattle attorney and expert in West African law. She'd

been so taken with the books when she first saw them 20 years ago that she'd trained as a conservator. Months after the war, Diakité was still preoccupied with their security and would not reveal their whereabouts or how Abdel Kader Haidara, with her assistance, had orchestrated much of the daring escape. Even in their current hiding places—that secret location I'd later visit in Bamako, as well as homes along the roads to Timbuktu—the books were at risk, she said, vulnerable to rain, theft, or another war.

Haidara revealed even less, concerned that the Timbuktu citizens who actually moved the books would be punished if the jihadis returned. The government's official catalog listed 9,000 manuscripts, but rumors were circulating that the town had held 20 or even 30 times that. Less than 1 percent had been cataloged, let alone copied, and almost no scholars could reach the books or even read the necessary languages. Surprises were waiting inside those crumbling pages.

The problem with paper is that it goes out of date. My Lonely Planet *West Africa* was only two years old but radically, dangerously obsolete. It was August, seven months after the liberation of Timbuktu, and after glimpsing the surviving books in Bamako, Italian photographer Marco Di Lauro and I were determined to reach the old city, to meet the heroic, but unnamed, smugglers who'd gotten the books out. We wasted 10 full days in Bamako trying to catch one of the rare UN flights that carried African peacekeeping troops into Timbuktu. There is a northern road through the Sahara and a southern route through the Sahel, but fresh reports of shootings and kidnappings convinced us to avoid both. Instead we'd travel down the Niger, a 2,600-mile watercourse that flows west to east through five countries, curving like a question mark toward the Sahara. The river was the way many of the books had escaped and would be our route back.

After a day of driving, we spent the night in Djenné, a magical, mud-walled city surrounded by the rushing waters of the Bani River. Djenné is a sister city to Timbuktu, equally venerable, with a mind-blowing mud mosque and its own small library of worm-eaten medieval manuscripts in gold leaf.

An hour up the road was Mopti, the main port on the Niger. We slipped down the stone quay at 4:15 a.m., picking our way over exhausted stevedores sleeping on cardboard. Hundreds of these men and boys crowd Mopti's teeming waterfront by day, shouting and dusty, but here was Africa motionless, silent, and cool. After shimmying over smaller pirogues to reach our boat, the captain cast off, and we drifted into the current of Africa's third largest river.

LP's cigarette-paper pages described a peacetime world of swift tourist boats here, with cabins and meals, gliding backpackers past riverside mosques. What we got was a smelly cargo vessel on a rescue mission. Called a pinnace, it had the proportions of a river canoe but was larger: 130 feet long and 12 feet wide, made from planked boards held together with hope. A waterline cargo deck supported two thundering diesels made in France, a score of crated motorcycles, and 6,300 sacks of yellow split peas donated by the World Food Program. The food was destined for the war-displaced nomads and starving villagers we would pass during the next 300 miles of riverbank. The motorcycles were a side business.

Swinging up an exterior ladder brought you to the lido deck, a passenger area sheltered by a very low roof of corrugated tin. There was room only to sit or lie down; bed was the tin deck and dinner was riz sauce, a fiery brown stew made with goat (once) or fish heads (the rest of the time). There were 14 others onboard, all crew or their families. Seven months after the war, people were still paying to get out of Timbuktu, not in.

August was the low point for the river, but the first rains had arrived upstream, and our *capitaine* was attempting his debut passage of the season. Sitting at a wood steering wheel at the front of the top deck, he assured me that we would make the trip between Mopti and Timbuktu in two days and one night. *"La nonstop,"* he said. It turned out neither of us spoke French.

The boat marched down the brown river at the pace of a slow bicyclist, hour after hour of featureless mud banks and a couple of barren villages where police officers looked over our credentials. Twice on the first day we paused to pass down the heavy bags of yellow peas or the motorcycles, which were placed in canoes and paddled ashore by strong men.

But that afternoon, we came through widening channels to a village on an island and, despite all plans and pleas, *la stop*. Our captain and crew were members of the Bozo tribe, known since ancient times as the masters of the river. This was their largest village, Barkinelba, on the reedy edge of Lake Débo, a seasonal body of water that forms in the Niger.

In a gibberish of Bozo to Bambara to French to English, we heard that it was too windy to cross the lake. A quick walk across the island proved the point: whitecaps tore up the surface, and the Bozo fishing pirogues were all sheltered in back creeks, tied fore and aft. We were spending the night right here.

Barkinelba was nice, in the way of insanely poor places at sunset. A few thousand people lived in reed huts with dirt floors, but they were clean, well dressed, and working hard. By day the men fished with monofilament nets while the women pounded millet. At night I sat on the roof of our boat as people with flashlights wandered the dark lanes. The average lifespan in Mali is 55; children in villages like this die all the time for lack of clean water. Yet there was something romantic, even immortal, in the sight of women embroidering by the light of a battery-powered television set, filling the darkness with gossip and laughter.

The skies had been smudged with Saharan sands all day, but this blew out at night, leaving an enormous Milky Way overhead. When Scottish explorer Mungo Park first came down this river in 1795, he was astonished by what people requested: they wanted paper. In the 1840s, the explorer Heinrich Barth gave away reams of the stuff and described traders wandering the desert with nothing but books to sell. Illiterate Africa was a myth. Words—books —had always been necessary.

If going there is a dream, and getting there a nightmare, arriving in Timbuktu is one of the world's great disappointments. Hungry and nearly insane with boredom, we endured days three and four of the two-day trip, staring limply at the banks of the Niger until the north shore gradually turned into the high khaki dunes of the Sahara. The south shore, the Sahel, offered a smattering of restorative grass, and this was Timbuktu's real advantage. On the desert crossings that connected the Mediterranean world to Africa, it was the first or last stop, the place, they said, where the camel met the canoe.

Our big canoe ran aground just 400 yards off the quay at Kabara, Timbuktu's port. We crossed through a sandy no man's land in a dented Mercedes taxi with desert-soft tires. In ancient times, attacks on travelers were so common here that this patch of sand had its own sinister name, They Don't Hear, reflecting the cries of victims.

We passed through rings of increasingly tense security, first Malian soldiers cradling AK-47s, then technicals (weaponized pickup trucks), then African Union soldiers lurking behind sandbagged positions. There had been five suicide bombings linked to al-Qaeda affiliates in northern Mali since the occupation ended; now UN and African diplomats were overseeing the deployment of Minusma, a West African peacekeeping force that was supposed to replace French troops and create stability.

But the streets of Timbuktu seemed empty, the population of 54,000 gutted by war. Only a trickle of men attended prayers at the fourteenth-century mosque, built by the great emperor Musa, the ruler who gilded Timbuktu's reputation forever by marching all the way to Mecca with so much West African gold that he crashed the Egyptian economy. Europeans absorbed this story like blood absorbs alcohol and spent centuries searching the Sahara for Tombouctou, a wondrous city of golden castles. When Frenchman René-Auguste Caillié finally reported in 1828 that it was actually a small and downtrodden oasis of mud houses, he was initially met with suspicion.

Alas, he was right. The Atlantis of the desert was a dumpy little place, 600 years past its prime, with sand in the streets and plastic bags in the trees. Almost every hotel and restaurant had closed, and when we found a room it was just in time, for a sandstorm blew in, followed by a chilly downpour that flattened the wattle roofs of poor herders in the backstreets, turning the avatar of mystery into a shivering hovel of mud.

In the morning, we went straight to the Ahmed Baba Institute. After seven months, you could still see not merely the sooty starburst left on the floor by the bonfire of books, but the actual shreds and cinders of manuscripts themselves, which were swirling around in a sheltered area by the men's room. I took a step to investigate and heard the crunching of ancient knowledge under my feet. Had I just crushed the only existing copy of an Ottoman geography or the final verses of a Moorish poet? It smelled like the fire happened yesterday.

The institute was founded in 1973 but only gained real traction in 1984, when Haidara joined, bridging the gap between state researchers and some 65 families with private collections. Like most, he retained physical control of his books, and his own 45,000 items make up by far the largest collection in Timbuktu. These were not just piles of old scraps. Often they were high-quality works with spectacular Arabic calligraphy, illuminated with bright red and blue inks and graced with gold-leaf arabesques that wrapped in infinite loops, reflecting the never-ending nature of God. In 2000, Mali greatly expanded the institute, and this new building opened in 2009 with a staff of 50 Malians trained to protect and digitize the books.

This was Big Data, Saharan edition. The books are "heirlooms of an African renaissance," says South African historian Shamil Jeppie, who runs the Tombouctou Manuscripts Project at the University of Cape Town. They include everything from astronomy to zoology, from Turkish maps to Jewish wedding contracts, along with a mother lode of commercial records about caravans and the salt trade. One of the few scholars to have examined the works firsthand, Jeppie has found law and theology but also poetry, a history of tea, and two sex manuals, which he describes as "very practical—I mean, very impractical."

Yet, by 2012, the institute had digitized just 2,000 manuscripts. You couldn't exactly slap them on a scanner: the paper was as fragile as a mummy, and the ink (typically made of charcoal mixed with gum arabic) could burst into flames from the hot beam of light. When the jihadis arrived to trash the library, this inefficiency turned out to be a partial blessing: compared with the tens of thousands in state hands, there were hundreds of thousands still in private homes, waiting their turn for restoration and copying with cold-circuit photography. The people of Timbuktu had been careful, even grudging, with their books. As in centuries past, this was a winning strategy.

The State Library building is big for Timbuktu—a whole block—but blends in nicely, with the trapezoidal walls and open galleries of a Saharan home. Out in the ochre-colored courtyard was Bouya Haidara. Short and sober-faced, with a scruff of white chin hair and a white scholar's cap, he was the guardian of the library, an important position with elements of security chief and casino greeter. From a loose pile of burned books sitting against a wall—books that had been outdoors for seven months—he pulled a cardboard box, black all over. Inside were stacked pages of beautiful calligraphy, perhaps a hundred sheets, all scorched around the edges. I asked Bouya what this manuscript had been. A consultation

was held; a bony man lounging on a mattress by the front door
turned out to be a locally prominent scholar. He casually flicked
through the charred contents, turning ancient pages that crum-
bled at his touch. "Botany," he said, in French. "The useful plants
of the desert. Flowers. Herbal medicines."

He probed deeper into the pile. "Verses of the Holy Koran."
Yes, the jihadi warriors had thoughtlessly burned their own sacred
book—multiple copies were destroyed in the fire, Bouya noted.

I leaned over for a whiff, but a desert blast swept the fine,
powdery ash up my nose, into my eyes, into my suddenly gasping
mouth. I gagged and couldn't find water anywhere. In Mali, Koranic scholars sometimes sell amulets that contain tiny verses, and
in extreme cases of need customers may soak the paper in a glass
of water and drink the inky result, literally absorbing the words
into their bodies. Maybe snorting parts of the Holy Koran was not
blasphemy but a blessing.

We followed Bouya into the basement, where he showed me
how he stood back that afternoon as the rebels ripped a locked
gate off its hinges and entered the storage rooms, tossing books
into piles on the floor.

Thousands of manuscripts were added to the fire, but French
fighter jets were overhead, and the rebels left many behind.
Even better, they missed two rooms entirely, including the Salle
de Manuscripts No. 4, which held 14 shelves of uncataloged vol-
umes. These were recent donations that no one had even opened
yet: piles of paper were stacked everywhere. Some manuscripts
were big and neatly bundled; others were tiny scraps, stuffed into
French airmail envelopes from decades ago.

Aboubacrine Abdou Maiga, the library director's representative, was grieving like a man who had been stabbed—"Four hundred books from Andalusia were burned!" he moaned to me—but
he produced a final tally: 4,203 books had been destroyed by fire,
but another 10,487 had survived.

That's not counting the works that had already been spirited
out. Even though the rebels had been camping for 10 months in
the institute's courtyard, Bouya and others had smuggled out some
of the most important books inside their robelike boubous. He
mimed stuffing a parchment into his underwear and laughed at the
awkward gait and unseemly bulge that ancient literature created.

This is why I had gone all the way to Timbuktu. To see how people acted under pressure, when there was no plan, only instinct. The librarians simply grabbed books and walked out, passing with fake confidence by armed men ready to kill them. The sound of a culture surviving was the discreet rustling of men's underpants.

The news kept getting better. Bouya pointed out that thousands of other books were still across town at an old archive called the dispensary. The next day, we drove over to a one-story mud-and-stone building in a walled compound. There we met Hassine Traore, a 32-year-old whose grandfather had been the dispensary's official guardian.

"The first day they penetrated the town, the rebels came," Traore said. They looted computers and other equipment. The dispensary books—another mound of uncataloged mysteries—were in locked storerooms, and the rebels demanded entry.

"They came and faced us and said, 'Give me the key to the manuscripts,' and we answered that we didn't have it," Traore said. "They pushed. They came every day, asking, 'Where are the manuscripts?'"

The rebels were put off again and again, for four long months, but the pressure was continuous, Traore said, and he and his father grew desperate. They talked with neighbors, with families that had donated the books, and with Haidara, who had fled to Bamako. Government officials in the capital were sympathetic but helpless.

"Then, in August, we found the solution," Traore said. Late at night, they began to pack up manuscripts, stuffing them into old rice sacks. Just the packing took a full month and involved dozens of men from several book-owning families. Traore hired five donkey drivers to carry the thousands of manuscripts—no one could count them all—out of the dispensary around midnight, every night for a week. They loaded the donkeys, and then Traore's 72-year-old grandfather, the retired guardian, walked point, scouting for jihadi patrols. Each night they distributed books to a different house, joining the small number of high-priority works smuggled out of the main library by underwear.

Traore's grandfather, Abba al-Hadi, was dozing in a chair nearby, his beard of white scruff touching his chest. He woke up when I approached; like me, he spoke little French, but he understood my question well enough: Can you read?

Non. An illiterate old man had gone out ahead, keeping the ink moving, the blood flowing in this system of survival.

By August 2012, it was clear that the books had to escape not just the library buildings but Timbuktu itself. That meant transporting them over one of two roads. The road through the Sahara was one of the world's most unsafe and difficult pieces of terrain, controlled partly by Tuareg sentries who regarded looting as a kind of divine right. The road through the Sahel began in rebel territory but reached Mopti and government control after 10 hours. That was in the best vehicle and conditions; now the rainy season was here. On August 28, Bouya and his colleagues at the state institute loaded 781 manuscripts into boxes, rolled them across town in a vegetable cart, and put them in the back of a *quatre-quatre,* the 4x4s that plow the desert. It was a test shipment. When it reached Mopti safely, they began shipping every day. They got about 24,000 state-owned manuscripts out by vehicle. But rain made the passages worse, and bandits were taking advantage of the war, robbing people in any part of Mali.

Although Haidara had fled Timbuktu by car himself, he left behind his own collection. In addition to the manuscripts escaping the library in those donkey-borne rice sacks, there were 27 major family collections still in Timbuktu houses, totaling at least 200,000 books. During the fall of 2012, Haidara urged those families to set up their own smuggling route. They bought up all the shipping trunks in Timbuktu's Grand Marché and started sending them out by road to Bamako or hiding places along the way.

More than half the books were still stuck in Timbuktu, but war and chaos were about to close off the roads. The only other escape route—the Niger itself—was dangerous to the manuscripts in a new way.

Old rag paper and soluble inks do not belong on a river. Stephanie Diakité, the lawyer and conservator, said she nearly panicked when Haidara told her of his scheme. One tippy canoe could erase centuries of irreplaceable work. Reluctantly, she agreed. During early January 2013, cargo motorcycles and beater taxis began carrying a few trunks at a time away from the family libraries, to Kabara, the river port. Only light pirogues were available, and each could hold maybe a dozen boxes. Strong boys carried the footlockers down to the waterline, working for coins. The little chugging motors of the canoes kicked in, and the books of Timbuktu went out of the desert and onto the water for the first time in their lives. Three or four canoes left every day, headed upriver toward Djenné or Mopti.

By mid-January, the war had entered a more deadly phase: a French rapid-reaction force was attacking the rebel coalition, and Gazelle gunships appeared over the Sahara. Moving a few boxes at a time was suddenly no longer enough.

Haidara used his cell phone to encourage a book breakout. Diakité sat next to him some days. In the fall, she had been raising support from her international contacts: a Dutch royal charity gave money, and at one point a European embassy donated a paper bag full of cash. Now they had to funnel money to help comrades in Timbuktu pay off soldiers and functionaries. These traditional *cadeaux,* or gifts, are unsavory yet inescapable in Mali —when I refused to pay for an interview, one Koranic scholar told me, "You have your culture, we have ours."

This makeshift book club then put together a bigger shipment: about 25 pirogues, leaving Timbuktu in one convoy. But as the boats crossed Lake Débo, they were intercepted by a French helicopter gunship. The Bozo skippers understood the innocence of paper; they opened some footlockers, showing that their cargo was not RPGs but worm-eaten books. The French pilot also understood; Diakité said that he saluted before flying away.

The conspirators now made one final push, sending a true fleet upriver past Mopti to Djenné. This lengthy convoy—45 pirogues in a row—drew more unwelcome attention. In the narrow channels west of Lake Débo, armed men stopped the convoy and demanded (and eventually got) a large ransom. They were robbers, not holy warriors; once paid, they let the boats move on.

The final convoy reached Djenné just two weeks before the squad of jihadis arrived at the main library with orders to destroy everything they could find. But they were too late, or nearly so: hundreds of thousands of books had already escaped. Not one had been lost to the road or the river.

The threat now is from nature, not man. The arid Sahara has preserved this paper for centuries; Bamako's humidity is a prescription for destroying it. (A calligrapher showed me works on salt slabs that were already fading.) Haidara's stash, perhaps 90 percent of the known manuscripts, is still at risk, despite his efforts to install dehumidifiers and air-conditioning in the still-secret rooms. He estimated it would cost $10 million just to put them in acid-free boxes; conserving and copying them could take a decade. But, like the scores of families who trusted him with their books, he was determined to return them eventually, when Timbuktu was stable. "The books must go back," he said.

Aside from the occasional suicide bombing, Mali was in recovery mode, and Marco and I witnessed a round of peaceful elections that returned popular ex-president Ibrahim Boubacar Keita, known as IBK, to the national palace. The environment was hardly safe: in November, two French radio journalists working in the desert were kidnapped and then executed, presumably by al-Qaeda leftovers, and French and Malian forces were still conducting sporadic raids on jihadi holdouts in the far north. Yet normalcy kept building, and in 2014, Malians would restage a Festival on the Niger, in the town of Ségou, with some of Afropop's biggest stars.

Last August, early in the rainy season, Timbuktu felt safe, even joyous. Marco and I walked the streets with caution, greeted with extraordinary warmth by a people hungry for outsiders, for tourists, for stability and trust. Grateful old men took my hand like I was Bill Clinton. We stumbled on an Islamic wedding, a noisy, wild event full of rapturous Sufis and unveiled women gyrating on the dance floor like so many Aretha Franklins. After the somber soldiers patrolling in technicals, after the nearly yearlong rule of the jihadis, the *dames* of Timbuktu were literally letting their hair down, bursting out of short skirts and tight tops, throwing off head scarves and going down in butt-bumping contests.

Verdict from the dance floor: the jihad was over, and Timbuktu had won. Yet we left the party quickly, Marco warning that our very presence could draw a suicide bomber down on these people.

We spent days touring the small libraries of Timbuktu, empty for the first time in centuries. In one low adobe home, a robed Koranic teacher named Dramane Moulaye Haidara opened a small trunk and displayed what he'd hidden from the occupiers: a few illuminated manuscripts in vermilion and gold, works full of astrological diagrams. He made a living casting fortunes and putting blessings on people. This was how the war had been won, he told us, not with bombs but with magic. "We bombed them with charms," he said of the jihadis. "So many charms."

We looked up. It had started raining. The books were sitting outside, the rag pages getting pelted with fat drops of water. We rushed out and pulled the sixteenth century back to safety.

Marco and I left soon after that, catching a ride on an elderly MD-80 jet painted white and labeled UNITED NATIONS—the flight we had waited for in vain back in Bamako. It was extracting a fact-finding mission, which arrived in a convoy of commando-staffed pickup trucks and some black SUVs, delivering a vital top-level Italian diplomat shaped like a meatball and his boss, a lean and silent Nigerian general. On the plane I squeezed in next to a red-bearded Swedish officer sweating in his jungle fatigues.

Under my arm I had a book. Not one of the actual books, just a single page, copied out in calligraphy by a Timbuktu artist. The passage was from Ahmed Baba, the namesake of the research institute. In 1591, an army from Morocco had sacked Timbuktu, destroying many books and forcing scholars like him to flee across the desert. The lonely passage urged any traveler to "make a detour by Timbuktu, murmur my name to my friends and bring them the scented greeting of the exile."

In the end, after many trials, Ahmed Baba was able to return. Someday, scanned and measured, conserved and protected, the books of Timbuktu will follow him home.

PAUL THEROUX

The Soul of the South

FROM *Smithsonian*

THE SOUTH IS easy to find but hard to sort out, and it is full of paradoxes. Once I was talking southern fiction with William Styron and he said, "I come from the High South"—he was from Virginia, and he was mildly boasting. Like many writers who had left the South to find a life in the North, he often talked fondly about the region that had formed him.

There is plenty to boast of in the Deep South, with its cultural pleasures, where the cities in particular are vibrant, the art galleries of Atlanta, the gourmet restaurants of Charleston, the cities with pro sports or great college teams. The Alabama Symphony Orchestra in Birmingham is scheduled to perform César Franck's Symphony in D minor, as I write, and the Mississippi Symphony is scheduling six concerts for its Bravo Series (Mozart, Beethoven) in Jackson. There are presidential libraries, playhouses, and botanical gardens. Civil War battlefields abound—these solemn places are well kept and enlightening: you could spend months profitably touring them. The golf courses of Georgia and Alabama are famous, there is motor racing, and every large city has a grand hotel or two, and a great restaurant.

Parts of the Deep South are commercially prosperous, too, with booming industries—medical research and technology, aerospace and aviation, car manufacturing. The Mercedes you bought could have been made in Alabama, BMW's plant in South Carolina will soon be its largest in the world, Nissan makes cars in Mississippi, and so does Toyota. There are many associated businesses, suppliers of car-related components. This is a testament to the enduring pride and work ethic of the South, not to mention labor laws.

I think most people know this. They may also be aware that the Deep South has some of the highest rates of unemployment, some of the worst schools, the poorest housing and medical care, a vast number of dying and depopulated towns. As for being hard up, the states I visited in the Deep South have nearly 20 percent of their people living below the poverty line, more than the national average of 16 percent.

This other Deep South, with the same pride and with deep roots —rural, struggling, idyllic in places, and mostly ignored—was like a foreign country to me. I decided to travel the back roads for the pleasure of discovery—doing in my own country what I had spent most of my life doing in Africa and India and China—ignoring the museums and stadiums, the antebellum mansions and automobile plants, and, with the fiftieth anniversary of the civil rights struggle in mind, concentrating on the human architecture, in particular the overlooked: the submerged fifth.

Part One: South Carolina

The South began for me in Allendale, in the rural Lowcountry of South Carolina, set among twiggy fields of tufted white, the blown-open cotton bolls brightening the spindly bushes. In a lifetime of travel, I had seen very few places to compare with Allendale in its oddity; and approaching the town was just as bizarre. The road, much of it, was a divided highway, wider than many sections of the great north-south interstate, Route 95, which is more like a tunnel than a road for the way it sluices cars south at great speed.

Approaching the outskirts of Allendale I had a sight of dooms-day, one of those visions that make the effort of travel worthwhile. It was a vision of ruin, of decay and utter emptiness; and it was obvious in the simplest, most recognizable structures—motels, gas stations, restaurants, stores—all of them abandoned to rot, some of them so thoroughly decayed that all that was left was the great concrete slab of the foundation, stained with oil or paint, littered with the splinters of the collapsed building, a rusted sign leaning. Some were brick-faced, others made of cinder blocks, but none was well made and so the impression I had was of astonishing decrepitude, as though a war had ravaged the place and killed all the people.

Here was the corpse of a motel, the Elite—the sign still legible —broken buildings in a wilderness of weeds; and farther down the road, the Sands, the Presidential Inn, collapsed, empty; and another fractured place with a cracked swimming pool and broken windows, its rusted sign, CRESENT MOTEL, the more pathetic for being misspelled.

Most of the shops were closed, the wide main road was littered. The side streets, lined by shacks and abandoned houses, looked haunted. I had never seen anything quite like it, the ghost town on the ghost highway. I was glad I had come.

Just as decrepit, but busy, was a filling station and convenience store, where I stopped to buy gas. When I went inside for a drink, I met Suresh Patel. "I came here two years ago from Broach," Mr. Patel told me, from behind the counter of his cluttered shop. Broach is an industrial river district of 1.5 million in the state of Gujarat. Mr. Patel had been a chemist in India. "My cousin call me. He say, 'Come. Good business.'"

Many Indian shopkeepers, *duka-wallahs,* whom I knew in East and Central Africa, claimed Broach as their ancestral home, where the Patel surname identifies them as members of a Gujarati, primarily Hindu subcaste. And Mr. Patel's convenience store in Allendale was identical to the *dukas* in East Africa, the shelves of food and beer and cheap clothes and candy and household goods, the stern hand-lettered sign, NO CREDIT, the same whiff of incense and curry. A 1999 story in the *New York Times Magazine* by Tunku Varadarajan declared that more than 50 percent of all motels in the United States are owned by people of Indian origin, a statistic supplied by the Asian American Hotel Owners Association—and the figure is even greater now.

All the convenience stores, the three gas stations, and the one motel in small, unpromising Allendale were each owned by Indians from India. The presence of Indian shopkeepers, the heat, the tall dusty trees, the sight of plowed fields, the ruined motels and abandoned restaurants, the somnolence hanging over the town like a blight—and even the intense sunshine was like a sinister aspect of that same blight—all these features made it seem like a town in Zimbabwe.

Later I saw just outside Allendale proper the campus of the

University of South Carolina Salkehatchie, with 800 students, and the old main street, and the handsome courthouse, and a small subdivision of well-kept bungalows. But mostly, and importantly, Allendale, judging from Route 301, was a ruin—poor, neglected, hopeless-looking, a vivid failure.

"We Have to Change the Worst"

In an office tucked inside a mobile unit, signposted ALLENDALE COUNTY ALIVE, I found Wilbur Cave. After we shook hands, I mentioned the extraordinary weirdness of Route 301.

"This was a famous road once—the halfway point from up north to Florida or back," Wilbur said. "Everyone stopped here. And this was one of the busiest towns ever. When I was growing up, we could hardly cross the road."

But there were no cars today, or just a handful. "What happened?"

"Route 95 happened."

And Wilbur explained that in the late 1960s, when the interstate route was plotted, it bypassed Allendale 40 miles to the east, and like many other towns on Route 301, Allendale fell into ruin. But just as the great new city rising in the wilderness is an image of American prosperity, a ghost town like Allendale is also a feature of our landscape. Perhaps the most American urban transformation is that very sight; all ghost towns were once boomtowns.

And this was why Wilbur Cave, seeing the area where he grew up falling to ruins—its very foundations conducing to dust—decided to do something to improve it. Wilbur had been a record-breaking runner in his high school, and after graduation from the University of South Carolina in Columbia, worked locally and then ran for the state representative's seat in this district. He was elected and served for more than four years. He became a strategic planner, and with this experience he joined and reenergized the nonprofit Allendale County Alive, which helps provide decent housing to people. The town itself had a population of 4,500, three quarters of them black, like the county.

"It's not just this town that needs help," Wilbur said. "The whole county is in bad shape. In the 2010 census we are the tenth poorest county in the United States. And, you know, a lot of the others are Indian reservations."

Wilbur Cave was 61 but looked 10 years younger, compact,

muscular, still with an athlete's build, and energetic, full of plans. His family had lived in the area for many generations. His mother had been a teacher at Allendale County Training School. "The black school," Wilbur explained. "The white one was Allendale Elementary."

I remarked on how recently social change had come to the South.

"You have to know where we come from," Wilbur said. "It's hard for anyone to understand the South unless they understand history—and by history I mean slavery. History has had more impact here."

Without realizing it, only smiling and tapping a ballpoint on the desktop blotter, he sounded like one of the wise, admonitory southern voices in a Faulkner novel, reminding the northerner of the complex past.

"Take my mother's family. Some were farmers, for generations, right here in Allendale County. They had a hundred acres or so. It was a family activity to pick cotton. The children did it, the grandchildren. It was a normal afterschool job. I did it, I sure did—we all did it."

The small cotton farms were sold eventually to bigger growers, who introduced mechanical harvesters. That was another reason for the unemployment and the decline in population. But farming was still the mainstay of Allendale County, home to 10,000 people, 36 percent of whom lived below the poverty line.

Once there had been textile factories, making cloth and carpets. They'd closed, the manufacturing outsourced to China, though a new textile plant is scheduled to open. The lumber mills —there were two in Allendale, turning out planks and utility poles —did not employ many people.

Wilbur drove me through the backstreets of Allendale, and as we passed along the side roads, the lanes, the dirt paths on which there were two-room houses, some of them fixed up and painted, others no more than wooden shanties of the sort you might see in any third-world country, and some shotgun shacks that are the emblematic architecture of southern poverty.

"That's one of ours," Wilbur said of a tidy, white wood-framed bungalow on a corner, one of 150 houses his organization had fixed up or rebuilt. "It was a derelict property that we rehabbed and now it's part of our inventory of rentals."

"My feeling is—if South Carolina is to change, we have to change the worst," Wilbur said as we passed a small, weathered house of sun-blackened planks and curling shingles, an antique that was beyond repair. But a man had lived in it until just recently, without electricity or heat or piped water.

"You hungry?" Wilbur asked.

I said I was and he took me on a short drive to the edge of town, to a diner, O' Taste & See, sought out for its soul food, fried chicken and catfish, biscuits, rice and gravy, fruit pies, and friendliness.

"Money is not the whole picture, but it's the straw that stirs the drink," Wilbur said over lunch, when I mentioned the hundreds of millions in U.S. aid that was given to foreign countries. "I don't want hundreds of millions. Give me one thousandth of it and I could dramatically change things like public education in Allendale County."

Wilbur said that he didn't begrudge aid to Africa, but he added, "If my organization had access to that kind of money we could really make a difference."

"What would you do?"

"We could focus our energy and get things done." He smiled. He said, "We wouldn't have to worry about the light bill."

The Massacre

With accommodations scarce in sunny, desolate Allendale—most of the motels abandoned or destroyed—I drove up Route 301, the empty, glorious thoroughfare, 45 miles to Orangeburg. It was a small town, kept buoyant by revenue from its schools and colleges.

Walking along the main street, I fell into step with a man and said hello. And I received the glowing southern welcome. He wore a dark suit and carried a briefcase. He said he was a lawyer and gave me his card, *Virgin Johnson Jr., Attorney at Law*. I asked about the history of the town, just a general inquiry, and received a surprising answer.

"Well," Mr. Johnson said, "there was the massacre."

Massacre is a word that commands attention. This bloody event was news to me, so I asked for details. And he told me that Orangeburg was still segregated in 1968 in spite of the fact that the Civil Rights Act had been in force for four years. A bowling alley, the only one in town, refused to allow black students inside.

One day in February '68, objecting to being discriminated against, in the bowling alley and elsewhere, several hundred students held a demonstration at the campus of South Carolina State College across town. The event was noisy but the students were unarmed, facing officers from the South Carolina Highway Patrol, who carried pistols and carbines and shotguns. Alarmed by the jostling students, one police officer fired his gun into the air—warning shots, he later said. Hearing those gunshots, the other police officers began firing directly at the protesters, who turned and ran. Because the students were fleeing they were shot in the back. Three young men were killed, Samuel Hammond, Delano Middleton, and Henry Smith; 27 were injured, some of them seriously, all of them students, riddled with buckshot.

When I mentioned Kent State to Mr. Johnson, how everyone knew the name, he smiled and said, "But you know those kids that died were white."

Before I went on my way I remarked on how odd it was to me to be holding this conversation with someone I'd met by chance, simply asking directions on a public street. I was grateful for his taking the time with a stranger who had so many questions.

"People here understand how it is to need help," he said. "To be neglected." He tapped the business card I'd been holding. "You let me know if you want to meet some people who know more than I do. Why not stop in to my church this Sunday? I'll be preaching."

"Your card says you're an attorney."

"I'm a preacher, too. Revelation Ministries over in Fairfax. Well, Sycamore, actually."

"God Has a Plan for You"

The back roads from Orangeburg to Sycamore were empty on this Sunday morning—empty and beautiful, passing along the margins of more twiggy cotton fields, many of them puddled and muddy, the ripe tufts (the linty so-called locks) in open bolls sodden and the bushes beaten down by yesterday's rain.

Reverend Johnson's church was the large industrial-looking structure near Barker's Mill and the flag-draped meetinghouse of the Sons of Confederate Veterans. At the church a group of older men, formally dressed in suits, welcomed me and introduced themselves as deacons and ushers.

On the back wall, a scroll-shaped sign in gold: REVELATION

MINISTRIES — REVEALING GOD'S WORD TO THE WORLD — WE
LOVE YOU — AIN'T NOTHING YOU CAN DO ABOUT IT!

After the preliminaries — music, singing — when the church was full, the familiar dark-suited figure of Virgin Johnson Jr. rose from his high-backed, thronelike chair. He began to preach, a well-thumbed Bible in his right hand, and his left hand raised in admonition.

"Hear me today, brothers and sisters," he began, and lifted his Bible to read from it. He read from Luke, he read from Mark, he read from Jeremiah, and then he said, "Tell your neighbor, 'God has a plan for you!'"

The woman in front of me and the man beside me took turns saying to me in a grand tone of delivering good news, "God has a plan for you!"

Reverend Johnson described the children of Israel taken into captivity in Babylon and paraphrased Jeremiah's epistle: "Even though it look like stuff mess up in your life, it gon' to be all right, after a while! Stop distressing, stop worrying. Even though your circumstances don't look prosperous, you gon' be all right!"

Thirty minutes of his warm encouragement, and then the music began again in earnest and the whole church was rocked in song.

"I'm just a country boy, from bottom-line caste, born and raised in Estill, Hampton County," Virgin Johnson told me that night over a meal up the road in Orangeburg, where he lived. Estill was the sticks, he said, deep country, cotton fields. Then with a mock-resigned sigh, he said, "Po' black."

Still in his dark suit, he sipped his iced tea. This was another man speaking, not the excited Sycamore preacher, not the shrewd Orangeburg trial lawyer, but a quiet, reflective private citizen in a back booth at Ruby Tuesday, reminiscing about his life as a loner.

"I was born in 1954, in Estill. In 1966, as a result of what they called 'voluntary integration,' I was the only black student at Estill Elementary School. Happened this way. There were two buses went by our place every morning. I had said to my daddy, 'I want to get the first bus.' That was the white bus. He said, 'You sure, boy?' I said, 'I'm sure.'

"The day I hit that bus everything changed. Sixth grade — it changed my life. I lost all my friends, black and white. No one talked to me, no one at all. Even my white friends from home. I knew they wanted to talk to me, but they were under pressure, and so was I. I sat at the back of the bus. When I went to the long table for lunch, thirty boys would get up and leave.

"The funny thing is, we were all friendly, black and white. We picked cotton together. My daddy and uncle had a hundred acres of cotton. But when I got on the bus, it was over. I was alone, on my own.

"When I got to school I knew there was a difference. There was not another African American there—no black teachers, no black students, none at all. Except the janitors. The janitors were something, like guardian angels to me. They were black, and they didn't say anything to me—didn't need to. They nodded at me as if to say, 'Hold on, boy. Hold on.'

"I learned at an early age you have to stand by yourself. That gave me a fighting spirit. I've had it since I was a child. It's destiny. What happens when you let other people make your decisions? You become incapable of making your own decisions.

"I was the first African American to go to law school from my side of the county. University of South Carolina at Columbia. I was in a class of one hundred—this was in the eighties. I was the only black person. Passed the bar in 1988. Got a license to preach.

"There's no contradiction for me. I'm happy doing both. I just wish the economy was better. This area is so poor. They got nothin' —they need hope. If I can give it to them, that's a good thing. Jesus said, 'We have to go back and care about the other person.'

"This is a friendly place—nice people. Good values. Decent folks. We have issues—kids having kids, for one, sometimes four generations of kids having kids. But there's so little advance. That does perplex me—the condition of this place. Something's missing. What is it?"

And then he made a passionate gesture, flinging up his hand, and he raised his voice in a tone that recalled his preaching voice. "Take the kids away from this area and they shine!"

Part Two: Alabama

Greensboro, Alabama, less than 40 miles south of Tuscaloosa, lies under the horizon in a green sea of meadows and fields, a small, pretty, somewhat collapsed and haunted town. Up the road from Greensboro, around Moundville, lies the farmland and still-substandard houses where James Agee and Walker Evans spent a summer collecting material for the book that would become *Let Us Now Praise Famous Men*. Published in 1941, it sold a mere 600 copies. Its commercial failure contributed to Agee's heavy drinking and early death at the age of 45. Twenty years later, it was republished, and in the early 1960s it found many more readers and admirers.

Cherokee City in the book is Tuscaloosa, Centerboro is Greensboro, the subject of some of Evans's photographs, and where I was eventually headed.

Greensboro was beautiful—hardly changed architecturally since Agee's visit in 1936—but it was struggling.

"Our main problems?" Greensboro's mayor, Johnnie B. Washington, said with a smile. "How much time do you have? A day or two, to listen? It's lack of revenue, it's resistance to change, it's so many things. But I tell you, this is a fine town."

One of the largest personal libraries I have ever seen belonged to Randall Curb, who lived in a white frame house on a corner, near the end of Main Street, in Greensboro. He was legally blind, but as it had been a progressive decline in his vision, he had continued to buy books—real tomes—while adjusting to audio books. He was 60, kindly, generous, eager to share his knowledge of Greensboro, of which he was the unofficial historian. He was also steeped in the lore of *Let Us Now Praise Famous Men*. He impressed me by calling its prose "incantatory."

Randall knew all the readers round about. He gave talks—on Agee, on Eudora Welty, on the English writers he loved (he spent a few months in London almost every year), on historical figures such as Ben Franklin. He knew the writers, too.

"You should meet Mary T," he said to me, his way of referring to Mary Ward Brown, who lived in the town of Marion, in the next county. "She writes short stories—very good ones. She's ninety-five," he added. "Ninety-six in a few months."

"Perhaps you could introduce me," I said.

Days passed. I read a dozen of her stories and her memoir. I called Randall and said, "I'd like to see her soon."

When I came to Marion, I realized how moribund Greensboro was. The shops in Marion were still in business; Marion had a courthouse, and a military institute, and Judson College, which Mary T (she insisted on the name) had attended. There were bookstores in Marion and a well-known soul food restaurant, Lottie's. Coretta

Scott King had been raised in Marion, and voting rights activist
Jimmie Lee Jackson had been shot and killed by an Alabama state
trooper in the town in 1965 during a peaceful protest, a catalyz-
ing event in the civil rights movement that provoked the protest
marches from Selma to Montgomery.

"Notice how it's desolate here," Randall said as I drove outside
town. Though he was unable to see, he had a clear memory of the
flat land, the fields of stubble, the wet clay roads, the thin patches
of woods, the absence of houses, now and then a crossroads.
"You'll know it when you see it. It's the only house here."

After 5 miles of fields, he said, "This must be Hamburg," and
a white bungalow appeared, and on the porch—we had called
ahead—Mary T and a much younger woman, wearing an apron.

"Is Ozella with her?" Randall said, trying to see. He explained
that Ozella was the daughter of a previous housekeeper. Ozella was
standing closely next to Mary T, who was tiny, watchful, like a bird
on a branch, and smiling in anticipation. Very old and upright
people have a dusty glow that makes them seem immortal.

"My father built this house in 1927," Mary T said when I praised
the house. It was a modest two-story bungalow, but squat and solid,
fronted by the bulging porch, a dormer above it, so unlike the
shotgun shacks and rectangular houses we'd passed at the edge
of Marion. Inside, the walls were paneled in dark wood, a planked
ceiling, an oak floor. Like Randall's house it was filled with books,
in the bookcases that were fitted in all the inner rooms and upstairs.

Mary T opened a bottle of blueberry wine from a winery in Har-
persville, and though it was a warm noontime, a fly buzzing behind
the hot white curtains in the small back dining room, we stood
and clinked schooners of the wine and toasted our meeting—the
ancient Mary T, the nearly blind Randall, and myself, the traveler,
passing through. Something about the wood paneling, the quality
of the curtains, the closeness of the room, the sense of being in
the deep countryside holding a glass of wine on a hot day—it was
like being in old Russia. I said so.

"That's why I love Chekhov," Mary T said. "He writes about
places like this, people like the ones who live here—the same situations."

The sunny day, the bleakness of the countryside, the old bungalow on the narrow road, no other house nearby; the smell of the

muddy fields penetrating the room—and that other thing, a great and overwhelming sadness that I felt but couldn't fathom.

"Have a slice of pound cake," Randall said, opening the foil on a heavy yellow loaf. "My mother made it yesterday."

Mary T cut a crumbly slab and divided it among us, and I kept thinking, *This could only be the South,* but a peculiar and special niche of it, a house full of books, the dark paintings, the ticking clock, the old furniture, the heavy oak table, something melancholy and indestructible but looking a bit besieged; and that unusual, almost unnatural tidiness imposed by a housekeeper—pencils lined up, magazines and pamphlets in squared-up piles—Ozella's hand, obvious and unlikely, a servant's sense of order.

In *Fanning the Spark* (2009), a selective, impressionistic memoir, Mary T had told her story: her upbringing as a rural shopkeeper's daughter; her becoming a writer late in life—she was 61 when she published her first short story. It is a little history of surprises—surprise that she became a writer after so long, a period she called "the 25-year silence"; surprise that her stories found favor; surprise that her stories won awards.

Setting her glass of wine down on the thick disk of coaster, she said, "I'm hungry for catfish"—the expression of appetite a delight to hear from someone 95 years old.

She put on a wide-brimmed black hat the size, it seemed, of a bicycle wheel, and a red capelike coat. Helping her down the stairs, I realized she was tiny and frail; but her mind was active, she spoke clearly, her memory was good, her bird claw of a hand was in my grip.

And all the way to Lottie's diner in Marion, on the country road, she talked about how she'd become a writer.

"It wasn't easy for me to write," she said. "I had a family to raise, and after my husband died it became even harder, because my son Kirtley was still young. I thought about writing, I read books, but I didn't write. I think I had an advantage. I could tell literature from junk. I knew what was good. I knew what I wanted to write. And when I came to it—I was more than sixty—I rewrote hard. I tried to make it right."

At last we were rolling down Marion's main street, Washington Street, then past the military academy and the courthouse, and over to Pickens Street, the site of Mack's Café—the places associated with the shooting of Jimmie Lee Jackson. We came to Lottie's.

I parked in front and eased Mary T out of the passenger seat and into the diner.

"I've been reading a book about interviews with people who are over one hundred years old," Mary T said, perhaps reminded of her frailty. "It was called something like *Lessons from the Centenarians*. The lesson to me was, I don't think I want to live that long."

People seated at their meals looked up from their food as Mary T entered, and many of them recognized her and greeted her. Though Mary T was moving slowly, she lifted her hand to greet them.

"See, the Yankee's having the grilled catfish," Randall said, after we seated ourselves and ordered. "We stick with the fried."

"My mother worked in the store—she was too busy to raise me," Mary T said over lunch, pausing after each sentence, a bit short of breath. "I was raised by our black housekeeper. She was also the cook. I called her Mammy. I know it's not good to call someone Mammy these days, but I meant it—she was like a mother to me. I leaned on her."

"If my mother ever sat and held me as a child I don't remember, but I do remember the solace of Mammy's lap," she had written in *Fanning the Spark*. "Though she was small, light-skinned and far from the stereotype, her lap could spread and deepen to accommodate any wound. It smelled of gingham and a smoky cabin, and it rocked gently during tears. It didn't spill me out with token consolation but was there as long as it was needed. It was pure heartsease."

Randall began to talk about the changes in the South that he knew.

What will happen here? I asked.

"Time will help," Mary T said. "But I think the divisions will always be there—the racial divisions."

And I reminded myself that she'd been born in 1917. She had been in her teens during the Depression. She was only seven years younger than James Agee, and so she had known the poverty and the sharecroppers and the lynchings in the Black Belt.

"I did my best," she said. "I told the truth."

After, I dropped her at her remote house, the sun lowering into the fields; she waved from the porch. I dropped Randall in Greensboro. I hit the road again. The following week Mary T sent me an e-mail, remarking on something I'd written. I wrote again in the following days. I received a brief reply, and then after a week or so, silence. Randall wrote to say that Mary T was ill and in the hospital; and then, about a month after we met, she died.

Traveling in America

Most travel narratives—perhaps all of them, the classics anyway —describe the miseries and splendors of going from one remote place to another. The quest, the getting there, the difficulty of the road is the story; the journey, not the arrival, matters, and most of the time the traveler—the traveler's mood, especially—is the subject of the whole business. I have made a career out of this sort of slogging and self-portraiture, travel writing as diffused autobiography; and so have many others in the old, laborious look-at-me way that informs travel writing.

But traveling in America is unlike traveling anywhere else on earth. It is filled with road candy, and seems so simple, sliding all over in your car on wonderful roads.

Driving south, I became a traveler again in ways I'd forgotten. Because of the effortless release from my home to the road, the sense of being sprung, I rediscovered the joy in travel that I knew in the days before the halts, the checks, the affronts at airports— the invasions and violations of privacy that beset every air traveler. All air travel today involves interrogation.

Around the corner from Main Street in Greensboro, Alabama, tucked into a brick building he'd financed himself, was the barber- shop of the Reverend Eugene Lyles, who was 79. He was seated at a small table peering at the Acts of the Apostles, while awaiting his next customer. In addition to his barbershop, Reverend Lyles was a pastor at the Mars Hill Missionary Baptist Church just south of town, and next door to the barbershop, Reverend Lyles's soul food diner, nameless except for the sign DINER out front.

Marking the page in his Bible, and shutting it, then climbing onto one of his barber chairs and stretching his long legs, he said, "When I was a boy I bought a pair of clippers. I cut my brothers' hair. Well, I got ten boy siblings and three girl siblings—fourteen of us. I kept cutting hair. I started this business sixty years ago, cutting hair all that time. And I got the restaurant, and I got the church. Yes, I am busy.

"There are good people in Greensboro. But the white core is rooted in the status quo. The school is separate yet. When it was

integrated the whites started a private school, Southern Academy.
There's somewhere above two hundred there now." Reverend
Lyles laughed and spun his glasses off to polish them with a tissue.
"History is alive and well here."

And slavery is still a visitable memory because of the persistence
of its effects.

"I went to segregated schools. I grew up in the countryside, outside Greensboro, ten miles out, Cedarville. Very few whites lived in
the area. I didn't know any whites. I didn't know any whites until
the sixties, when I was in my thirties.

"Most of the land in Cedarville was owned by blacks. There was
a man, Tommy Ruffin, he owned ten thousand acres. He farmed,
he had hands, just like white folks did, growing cotton and corn.
He was advised by a white man named Paul Cameron not to sell
any of that land to a white person. Sell to blacks, he said, because
that's the only way a black man can get a foothold in a rural area.

"My father was a World War I vet. He ran away from here in
1916—he was about twenty. He went to Virginia. He enlisted
there, in 1917. After the war, he worked in a coal mine in West
Virginia. He came back and married in 1930, but kept working in
the mine, going back and forth. He gave us money. I always had
money in my pockets. Finally he migrated into Hale County for
good and bought some land."

We went next door to Reverend Lyles's diner. I ordered baked
chicken, collard greens, rice and gravy. Reverend Lyles had the
same. His younger brother Benny joined us.

"Lord," Reverend Lyles began, his hands clasped, his eyes shut,
beginning grace.

The Gift

At the edge of County Road 16, 10 miles south of Greensboro,
an old white wooden building stood back from the road but com-
manded attention. It had recently been prettified and restored
and was used as a community center.

"That's the Rosenwald School. We called it the Emory School,"
Reverend Lyles told me. "I was enrolled in that school in 1940.
Half the money for the school came from Sears, Roebuck—folks
here put up the difference. My mother also went to a Rosenwald
School, the same as me. The students were black, the teachers

were black. If you go down Highway 69, down to the Gallion area, there is another Rosenwald School, name of Oak Grove."

Julius Rosenwald, the son of German Jewish immigrants, made a success of his clothing business by selling to Richard Sears, and in 1908 became president of Sears, Roebuck and Co. In midlife his wish was to make a difference with his money, and he hatched a plan to give his wealth to charitable causes but on a condition that has become common today: his contribution had to be met by an equal amount from the other party, the matching grant. Convinced that Booker T. Washington's notion to create rural schools was a way forward, Rosenwald met the great educator and later began the Rosenwald Fund to build schools in backlands of the South.

Five thousand schools were built in 15 states beginning in 1917, and they continued to be built into the 1930s. Rosenwald himself died in 1932, around the time the last schools were built; but before the money he had put aside ran its course, in 1948, a scheme had been adopted through which money was given to black scholars and writers of exceptional promise. One of the young writers, Ralph Ellison, from Oklahoma, was granted a Rosenwald Fellowship, and this gave him the time and incentive to complete his novel *Invisible Man* (1952), one of the defining dramas of racial violence and despair in America. Rosenwald Fellowships also went to the photographer Gordon Parks, the sculptor Elizabeth Catlett (who later created Ellison's memorial in New York City), W. E. B. DuBois, Langston Hughes, and many other black artists and thinkers.

The schools built with Rosenwald money (and local effort) were modest structures in the beginning, two-room schools like the one in Greensboro, with two or at the most three teachers. They were known as Rosenwald Schools, but Rosenwald himself discouraged naming any of them after himself. As the project developed into the 1920s the schools became more ambitious, brick-built, with more rooms.

One of the characteristics of the schools was an emphasis on natural light through the use of large windows. The assumption was that the rural areas where they'd be built would probably not have electricity; paint colors, placement of blackboards and desks, even the southerly orientation of the schools to maximize the light were specified in blueprints.

The simple white building outside Greensboro was a relic from an earlier time, and had the Reverend Lyles not explained its history, and his personal connection, I would have had no idea that almost 100 years ago a philanthropic-minded stranger from Chicago had tried to make a difference here.

"The financing was partly the responsibility of the parents," Reverend Lyles told me. "They had to give certain stipends. Wasn't always money. You've heard of people giving a doctor chickens for their payment? That's the truth—that happened in America. Some were given corn, peanuts, and other stuff instead of cash money. They didn't have money back in that day." Reverend Lyles, who came from a farming family, brought produce his father had grown, and chickens and eggs.

"My grandfather and the others who were born around his time, they helped put up that school building. And just recently Pam Dorr and HERO"—the Hale Empowerment and Revitalization Organization—"made a plan to fix up the school. It made me proud that I was able to speak when it was reopened as a community center. My grandfather would have been proud, too."

He spoke some more about his family and their ties to the school, and added, "My grandfather was born in 1850."

I thought I had misheard the date. Surely this was impossible. I queried the date.

"Correct—1850."

So Booker T. Washington (1856–1915) was younger than Reverend Lyles's grandfather. "My grandfather wasn't born here but he came here. He remembered slavery—he told us all about it. I was thirteen years old when he passed. I was born in 1934. He would have been in his nineties. Work it out—he was ten years old in 1860. Education wasn't for blacks then. He lived slavery. Therefore his name was that of his owner, Lyles, and he was Andrew Lyles. Later on, he heard stories about the Civil War, and he told them to me."

Fruit Pies and Bamboo Bikes

A corner shop on Main Street in Greensboro was now called PieLab, a café associated with HERO and well known locally for its homemade fruit pies, salads, and sandwiches.

"The idea was that people would drop in at PieLab and get to know someone new," Randall Curb had said. "A good concept, but it hasn't worked out—at least I don't think so." Shaking his head, he had somewhat disparaged it as "a liberal drawing card."

The next day, quite by chance, having lunch at PieLab, I met the executive director of HERO (and the founder of its Housing Resource Center), Pam Dorr.

The more appealing of the skeletal, fading towns in the South attracted outsiders, in the way third-world countries attracted idealistic volunteers, and for many of the same reasons. With a look of innocence and promise, the places were poor, pretty, and in need of revival. They posed the possibility of rescue, an irresistible challenge to a young college graduate or someone who wanted to take a semester off to perform community service in another world. These were also pleasant places to live in—or at least seemed so.

The desperate housing situation in Greensboro, and Hale County generally, had inspired student architects of the Rural Studio (a program of the School of Architecture, Planning and Landscape Architecture at Auburn University) to create low-cost housing for needy people. The Auburn houses are small, but simple, and some of them brilliantly innovative, looking folded out and logical, like oversized elaborations of origami in tin and plywood. The studio determined that in Greensboro the right price for a small, newly built house would be no more than $20,000, "the highest realistic mortgage a person receiving median Social Security checks can maintain."

Hearing about the Auburn Rural Studio, Pam Dorr had traveled from San Francisco to Greensboro 10 years before to become an Auburn Outreach fellow. It was a break from her successful career as a designer for popular clothing companies, including Esprit and the Gap and Victoria's Secret ("I made cozy pajamas"). She had come to Greensboro in a spirit of volunteerism, but when her fellowship ended, she was reluctant to leave. "I realized there was so much more I could do," she told me at PieLab, which grew out of an entrepreneurial group she was in. Another idea, to make bicycle frames out of bamboo, resulted in Hero Bikes, one of the businesses Pam has overseen since starting the Housing Resource Center in 2004.

"We build houses, we educate people on home ownership, and working with nontraditional bankers we help people establish credit." Local banks had a history of lending mainly to whites.

Blacks could get loans but only at extortionate rates—27 percent interest was not uncommon.

"It seemed to me a prime opportunity to start a community again," Pam said. "We have thirty-three people on the payroll and lots of volunteers. HERO is in the pie business, the pecan business —we sell locally grown pecans to retail stores—the bamboo bike business, the construction business. We have a daycare center and afterschool program. A thrift store."

Some of these businesses were now housed in what had been a hardware store and an insurance agency. They had redeveloped or improved 11 of the defunct stores on Main Street.

"I worked free for two years," Pam said. "We got a HUD grant, we got some other help, and now, because of the various businesses, we're self-sustaining."

She was like the most inspired and energetic Peace Corps volunteer imaginable. Upbeat, full of recipes, solutions, and ideas for repurposing, still young—hardly 50—with wide experience and a California smile and informality. The way she dressed—in a purple fleece and green clogs—made her conspicuous. Her determination to effect change made her suspect.

"You find out a lot, living here," she told me. "Drugs are a problem—drive along a side road at night and you'll see girls prostituting themselves to get money to support their habit. Thirteen-year-olds getting pregnant—I know two personally."

"What does the town think of your work?" I asked.

"A lot of people are on our side," she said. "But they know that change has to come from within."

"Reverend Lyles told me you had something to do with fixing up the Rosenwald School here."

"The Emory School, yeah," she said. "But we had help from the University of Alabama, and volunteers from AmeriCorps—lots of people contributed. Reverend Lyles was one of our speakers at the reopening dedication ceremony. That was a great day." She took a deep calming breath. "But not everyone is on our side."

"Really?"

This surprised me, because what she had described, the renovation of an old schoolhouse in a hard-up rural area, was like a small-scale development project in a third-world country. I had witnessed such efforts many times: the energizing of a sleepy community, the fund-raising, the soliciting of well-wishers and sponsors, engaging volunteers, asking for donations of building material, applying for grants and permits, fighting inertia and the naysayers' laughter, making a plan, getting the word out, supervising the business, paying the skilled workers, bringing meals to the volunteers, and seeing the project through to completion. Years of effort, years of budgeting. At last, the dedication, everyone turned out, the cookies, the lemonade, the grateful speeches, the hugs. That was another side to the South, people seeing it as a development opportunity, and in workshops talking about "challenges" and "potential."

"So who's against you?" I said.

"Plenty of people seem to dislike what we're doing," Pam said. She rocked in her clogs and zipped her fleece against the chilly air. "Lots of opposition." She laughed, saying this. "Lots of abuse. They call me names." Once, she said, someone spit on her.

Part Three: Mississippi

Hardly a town or a village, Money, Mississippi (pop. 94), was no more than a road junction near the banks of the Tallahatchie River. There, without any trouble, I found what I was looking for, a 100-year-old grocery store, the roof caved in, the brick walls broken, the facade boarded up, the wooden porch roughly patched, and the whole wreck of it overgrown with dying plants and tangled vines. For its haunted appearance and its bloody history it was the ghostliest structure I was to see in the whole of my travels in the South. This ruin, formerly Bryant's Grocery and Meat Market, has topped the list of Mississippi Heritage Trust's Ten Most Endangered Historic Places, though many people would like to tear it down as an abomination.

What happened there in the store and subsequently, in that tiny community, was one of the most powerful stories I'd heard as a youth. As was so often the case, driving up a country road in the South was driving into the shadowy past. A MISSISSIPPI FREEDOM TRAIL sign in front of it gave the details of its place in history. It was part of my history, too.

I was just 14 in 1955 when the murder of the boy occurred. He was exactly my age. But I have no memory of any news report in a Boston newspaper at the time of the outrage. We got the *Boston*

Globe, but we were subscribers to and diligent readers of family magazines, *Life* for its photographs, *Collier's* and the *Saturday Evening Post* for profiles and short stories, *Look* for its racier features, *Reader's Digest* for its roundups. This Victorian habit in America of magazines as family entertainment and enlightenment persisted until television overwhelmed it in the later 1960s.

In January 1956, *Look* carried an article by William Bradford Huie, "The Shocking Story of Approved Killing in Mississippi," and it appeared in a shorter form in the *Reader's Digest* that spring. I remember this distinctly, because my two older brothers had read the stories first, and I was much influenced by their tastes and enthusiasms. After hearing them excitedly talking about the story, I read it and was appalled and fascinated.

Emmett Till, a black boy from Chicago, visiting his great-uncle in Mississippi, stopped at a grocery store to buy some candy. He supposedly whistled at the white woman behind the counter. A few nights later he was abducted, tortured, killed, and thrown into a river. Two men, Roy Bryant and John William "J.W." Milam, were caught and tried for the crime. They were acquitted. "Practically all the evidence against the defendants was circumstantial evidence," was the opinion in an editorial in the *Jackson Daily News.*

After the trial, Bryant and Milam gloated, telling Huie that they had indeed committed the crime, and they brazenly volunteered the gory particularities of the killing. Milam, the more talkative, was unrepentant in describing how he'd kidnapped Emmett Till with Bryant's help, pistol-whipped him in a shed behind his home in Glendora, shot him, and disposed of the body.

"Let's write them a letter," my brother Alexander said, and did so. His letter was two lines of threat—*We're coming to get you. You'll be sorry*—and it was signed, *The Gang from Boston.* We mailed it to the named killers, in care of the post office in Money, Mississippi.

The killing prompted a general outcry in the North, and my brothers and I talked of little else for months. Yet there was limited response from the authorities. The response from the black community in the South was momentous—TILL'S DEATH RECEIVED INTERNATIONAL ATTENTION AND IS WIDELY CREDITED WITH SPARKING THE AMERICAN CIVIL RIGHTS MOVEMENT, the commemorative sign in front of the Bryant store said—and the response was unusual because it was nonviolent. On December 1 of that same year of the Till trial, 1955, in Montgomery, Alabama,

Rosa Parks refused to surrender her seat to a white passenger on a city bus. She was arrested for her act of disobedience, and she became a symbol of defiance. Her stubbornness and sense of justice made her a rallying point and an example.

Though the *Jackson Daily News* editorialized that it was "best for all concerned that the Bryant-Milam case be forgotten as quickly as possible," the paper also had published a robust piece by William Faulkner. It was one of the most damning and gloomiest accusations Faulkner ever wrote (and he normally resisted the simplifications of newspaper essays), and his anguish shows. He must have recognized the event as something he might have imagined in fiction. He wrote his rebuttal hurriedly in Rome while he was on an official junket, and it was released through the U.S. Information Service.

He first spoke about the bombing of Pearl Harbor, and the hypocrisy of boasting of our values to our enemies "after we have taught them (as we are doing) that when we talk of freedom and liberty, we not only mean neither, we don't even mean security and justice and even the preservation of life for people whose pigmentation is not the same as ours."

He went on to say that if Americans are to survive we will have to show the world that we are not racists, "to present to the world one homogeneous and unbroken front." Yet this might be a test we will fail: "Perhaps we will find out now whether we are to survive or not. Perhaps the purpose of this sorry and tragic error committed in my native Mississippi by two white adults on an afflicted Negro child is to prove to us whether or not we deserve to survive."

And his conclusion: "Because if we in America have reached that point in our desperate culture when we must murder children, no matter for what reason or what color, we don't deserve to survive, and probably won't."

Nowhere in the piece did Faulkner use Emmett Till's name, yet anyone who read it knew whom he was speaking about.

Forget him, the Jackson paper had said, but on the contrary the case became a remembered infamy and a celebrated injustice; and Emmett Till was eulogized as a hero and a martyr. Suppression of the truth is not merely futile but almost a guarantee of something wonderful and revelatory emerging from it: creating an opposing and more powerful and ultimately overwhelming force, sunlight breaking in, as the Till case proved.

Near the ghostly ruin of Bryant's store, I walked around in the chill air—no one outside on this winter day. I drove east down Whaley Road, past Money Bayou and some narrow ponds, hoping to find Dark Ferry Road and the farm of Grover C. Frederick, where the little house of Emmett's great-uncle, Mose Wright, had stood, where he'd worked as a sharecropper and where the boy stayed during his visit. But my map didn't help, and there was no one to ask, and some parts of the past had been erased, but negligible parts. Night was falling when I drove back to Money, the same sort of darkness into which Emmett Till had been dragged. The next day I visited the Emmett Till museum in nearby Glendora, in a forbidding former cotton gin.

Rowan Oak

Oxford, where Faulkner had lived and died, was the university town of Ole Miss. Off well-traveled Route 278, the town vibrated with the rush of distant traffic. There is hardly a corner of this otherwise pleasant place where the whine of cars is absent, and it is a low hum at Rowan Oak, Faulkner's house, which lies at the end of a suburban street, at the periphery of the campus and its academic splendors.

The road noise struck an odd and intrusive note because, though Oxford resembles Jefferson in Faulkner's work, the town and its surroundings are in all respects as remote from Faulkner's folksy, bosky, strife-ridden, plot-saturated, and fictional Yoknapatawpha County as it is possible to be. The town is lovely. The university is classically beautiful in the Greek Revival southern style, of columns and bricks and domes, suggesting a mood both genteel and scholarly, and backward-looking.

And for a century this esteemed and vividly pompous place of learning clung to the old ways—segregation and bigotry among them, overwhelming any liberal tendencies. So here is an irony, one of the many in the Faulkner biography, odder than this self-described farmer living on a side street in a fraternity-mad, football-crazed college town.

Faulkner—a shy man but a bold, opinionated literary genius with an encyclopedic grasp of southern history, one of our greatest writers and subtlest thinkers—lived most of his life at the center of this racially divided community without once suggesting aloud, in his wise voice, in a town he was proud to call his own, that a black student had a right to study at the university. The Nobel Prize winner stood by as blacks were shooed off the campus, admitted as menials only through the back door, and when their work was done told to go away. Faulkner died in July 1962. Three months later, after a protracted legal fuss (and deadly riots afterward), and no thanks to Faulkner, James Meredith, from the small central Mississippi town of Kosciusko, was admitted as its first black student.

Fair-minded, Faulkner had written in *Harper's Magazine:* "To live anywhere in the world today and be against equality because of race or color is like living in Alaska and being against snow." But he asked for a gradual approach to integration, and, as he wrote in *Life* magazine, he was against the interference of the federal government—"forces outside the south that would use legal or police compulsion to eradicate that evil overnight." We'll do it ourselves, in our own time, was his approach; but, in fact, nothing happened until the federal government—the South's historical villain—intervened.

Restless when he was not writing, always in need of money, Faulkner traveled throughout his life; but Oxford remained his home, and Rowan Oak his house, even when (it seems) a neighborhood grew up around the big, ill-proportioned farmhouse previously known as "the Bailey Place." He renamed it Rowan Oak for the mythical powers of the wood of the rowan tree, as the docents at the house helpfully explained to me.

This street—orderly, bourgeois, well tended, tidy, conventional—is everything Faulkner's fiction is not and is at odds with Faulkner's posturing as a country squire. On this road of smug homes, Rowan Oak rises lopsidedly like a relic, if not a white elephant, with porches and white columns, windows framed by dark shutters, and stands of old, lovely juniper trees. The remnants of a formal garden are visible under the trees at the front—but just the symmetrical brickwork of flowerbed borders and walkways showing on the surface of the ground like the remains of a neglected Neolithic site.

He was anchored by Oxford but lived a chaotic life; and the surprising thing is that from this messy, lurching existence that combined the asceticism of concentrated writing with the eruptions of binge drinking and passionate infidelities, he produced an enormous body of work, a number of literary masterpieces, some near misses, and a great deal of garble. He is the writer all aspiring

American writers are encouraged to read, yet with his complex and speechifying prose he is the worst possible model for a young writer. He is someone you have to learn how to read, not someone anyone should dare imitate, though unfortunately many do.

Some of Faulkner's South still exists, not on the land but as a racial memory. Early in his writing life he set himself a mammoth task, to create the fictional world of an archetypical Mississippi county where everything happened—to explain to southerners who they were and where they'd come from. Where they were going didn't matter much to Faulkner. Go slowly, urged Faulkner, the gradualist.

Ralph Ellison once said, "If you want to know something about the dynamics of the South, of interpersonal relationships in the South from, roughly, 1874 until today, you don't go to historians; not even to Negro historians. You go to William Faulkner and Robert Penn Warren."

I walked through the rooms at Rowan Oak, which were austerely furnished, with a number of ordinary paintings and simple knickknacks, a dusty piano, the typewriter and the weird novelty of notes puzzling out the plot of *A Fable* written by him on the wall of an upstairs room. Notes clarifying the multilayered, if not muddled, plot were, for Faulkner, a good idea, and would serve a reader, too. Nothing to me would be more useful than such handwriting on a wall. Baffled by seven pages of eloquent gabble, you glance at the wall and see: "Charles is the son of Eulalia Bon and Thomas Sutpen, born in the West Indies, but Sutpen hadn't realized Eulalia was of mixed race, until too late . . ."

"We'll be closing soon," the docent warned me.

I went outside, looked at the brick outbuildings and sheds, a stable, and meandered past the plainness of the yard, among the long shadows of the junipers in the slant of the winter sun. From where I stood, the house was obscured by the trees at the front, but still it had the look of a mausoleum; and I was moved to think of Faulkner in it, exhausting himself with work, poisoning himself with drink, driven mad in the contradictions of the South, obstinate in his refusal to simplify or romanticize its history, resolute in mirroring its complexity with such depth and so many human faces—all this before his early death, at the age of 64. No other region in America had a writer who was blessed with such a vision. Sinclair Lewis defined the upper Midwest, and showed us who we were in *Main Street* and *Elmer Gantry;*

but he moved on to other places and other subjects. Faulkner stayed put, he achieved greatness; but as a writer, as a man, as a husband, as a delineator of the South's arcane formalities and its lawlessness, his was a life of suffering.

Pearl Handle Pistols

Natchez is dramatically sited on the bluffs above the wide brown Mississippi facing the cotton fields in flatter Louisiana and the town of Vidalia. A small, well-kept city, rich in history and river lore, architectural marvels — old ornate mansions, historic houses, churches, and quaint arcades; its downtown lined with restaurants. But none of its metropolitan attributes held much interest for me.

The cultural event that got my attention was the Natchez Gun Show at the Natchez Convention Center. It was the main event in town that weekend, and the size of the arena seemed half as big as a football field, with a long line of people waiting to go in.

Entering was a process of paying an admission of $7 (CHILDREN 6 TO 11, $1), and, if you had a firearm, showing it, unloading it, and securing it with a plastic zip tab.

After that lobby business, the arena, filled with tables and booths and stalls, most selling guns, some selling knives, others stacked with piles of ammo. I had never seen so many guns, big and small, heaped in one place — and I suppose the notion that they were all for sale, just lying there waiting to be picked up and handled, sniffed and aimed, provided a thrill.

"Pardon me, sir."

"No problem, scoot on bah."

"Thank you much."

No one on earth — none I had ever seen — is more polite, more eager to smile, more accommodating and less likely to step on your toe, than a person at a gun show.

"Mississippi is the best state for gun laws," one man said to me. We were at the coffee and doughnut stall. "You can leave your house with a loaded gun. You can keep a loaded gun in your car in this state — isn't that great?"

Most of the gun-show goers were just looking, hands in pockets, sauntering, nudging each other, admiring, and this greatly resembled a flea market, but one smelling of gun oil and scorched metal. Yet there was something else in the atmosphere, a mood I could not define.

Civil War paraphernalia, powder flasks, Harpers Ferry rifles, spurs, canes, swords, peaked caps, insignia, printed money, and pistols—a number of tables were piled with these battered pieces of history. And nearly all of them were from the Confederate side. Bumper stickers, too, one reading, THE CIVIL WAR—AMERICA'S HOLOCAUST, and many denouncing President Obama.

"My uncle has one of them powder flasks."

"If it's got the apportioning spigot spout in working order, your uncle's a lucky guy."

Some were reenactors, a man in a Confederate uniform, another dressed in period cowboy costume, looking like a vindictive sheriff, black hat and tall boots and pearl handle pistols.

It was not the first gun show I'd been to, and I would go to others, in Southhaven, Laurel, and Jackson, Mississippi. In Charleston, South Carolina, I'd seen a table set up like a museum display of World War I weapons and uniforms, as well as maps, books, postcards, and framed black-and-white photos of muddy battlefields. This was a commemorative exhibit put on by Dane Coffman, as a memorial to his soldier-grandfather, Ralph Coffman, who had served in the Great War. Dane, who was about 60, wore an old infantryman's uniform, a wide-brimmed hat, and leather puttees, the getup of a doughboy. Nothing was for sale; Dane was a collector, a military historian, and a reenactor; his aim was to show his collection of belts and holsters, mess kits, canteens, wire cutters, trenching tools, and what he called his pride and joy, a machine gun propped on a tripod.

"I'm here for my grandfather," he said. "I'm here to give a history lesson."

Back in Natchez, a stall-holder leaning on a fat black assault rifle was expostulating. "If that damn vote goes through, we're finished." He raised the gun. "But I would like to see someone try and take this away from me. I surely would."

Some men were wandering the floor, conspicuously carrying a gun, looking like hunters, and in a way they were, hunting for a buyer, hoping to sell it. One private seller had a 30-year-old weapon—wood and stainless steel—a Ruger .223-caliber Mini-14 assault rifle with a folding stock, the sort you see being carried by sharpshooters and conspirators in plots to overthrow wicked dictatorships. He handed it to me.

"By the way, I'm from Massachusetts."

His face fell, he sighed and took the gun from me with big hands, and folded the stock flat, saying, "I wish you hadn't told me that."

As I walked away, I heard him mutter, "Goddamn," not at me but at regulation generally—authority, the background checkers and inspectors and paper chewers, the government, Yankees.

And that was when I began to understand the mood of the gun show. It was not about guns. Not about ammo, not about knives. It was not about shooting lead into perceived enemies. The mood was apparent in the way these men walked and spoke: they felt beleaguered—weakened, their backs to the wall. How old was this feeling? It was as old as the South perhaps.

The Civil War battles might have happened yesterday for these particular southerners, who were so sensitized to intruders and gloaters and carpetbaggers, and even more so to outsiders who did not remember the humiliations of the Civil War. The passing of the family plantation was another failure, the rise of opportunistic politicians, the outsourcing of local industries, the disappearance of catfish farms, the plunge in manufacturing, and now this miserable economy in which there was no work and so little spare money that people went to gun shows just to look and yearn for a decent weapon that they'd never be able to buy.

Over this history of defeat was the scowling, punitive shadow of the federal government. The gun show was the one place where they could regroup and be themselves, like a clubhouse with strict admission and no windows. The gun show wasn't about guns and gun totin'. It was about the self-respect of men—white men, mainly—making a symbolic last stand.

"Where I Could Save My Kids"

You hear talk of people fleeing the South, and some do. But I found many instances of the South as a refuge. I met a number of people who had fled the North to the South for safety, for peace, for the old ways, returning to family, or in retirement.

At a laundromat in Natchez, the friendly woman in charge changed some bills into quarters for the machines and sold me some soap powder, and with a little encouragement from me, told me her story.

Her name was Robin Scott, in her midforties. She said, "I came here from Chicago to save my children from being killed by gangs. So many street gangs there—the Gangster Disciples, the

Vice Lords. At first where I lived was OK, the Garfield section. Then around the late eighties and early nineties the Four Corners Hustlers gang and the BGs—Black Gangsters—discovered crack cocaine and heroin. Using it, selling it, fighting about it. There was always shooting. I didn't want to stay there and bury my children.

"I said, 'Gotta get out of here'—so I quit my job and rented a U-Haul and eventually came down here where I had some family. I always had family in the South. Growing up in Chicago and in North Carolina, we used to visit my family in North Carolina, a place called Enfield, in Halifax County near Rocky Mount."

I knew Rocky Mount from my drives as a pleasant place, east of Raleigh, off I-95 where I sometimes stopped for a meal.

"I had good memories of Enfield. It was country—so different from the Chicago streets. And my mother had a lot of family here in Natchez. So I knew the South was where I could save my kids. I worked at the casino dealing blackjack, but after a time I got rheumatoid arthritis. It affected my hands, my joints, and my walking. It affected my marriage. My husband left me.

"I kept working, though, and I recovered from the rheumatoid arthritis and I raised my kids. I got two girls, Melody and Courtney —Melody's a nurse and Courtney's a bank manager. My boys are Anthony—the oldest, he's an electrician—and the twins, Robert and Joseph. They're twenty-one, at the University of Southern Mississippi.

"Natchez is a friendly place. I'm real glad I came. It wasn't easy. It's not easy now—the work situation is hard, but I manage. The man who owns this laundromat is a good man.

"I got so much family here. My grandmother was a Christmas —Mary Christmas. Her brother was Joseph. We called my grandmother Big Momma and my grandfather Big Daddy. I laughed when I saw that movie *Big Momma's House*.

"Mary Christmas was born on a plantation near Sibley. They were from families of sharecroppers. My grandfather was Jesse James Christmas."

I mentioned Faulkner's *Light in August* and Joe Christmas, and how I'd always found the name faintly preposterous, heavy with symbolism. I told her the plot of the novel, and how the mysterious Joe Christmas, orphan and bootlegger, passes for white but has a black ancestry. Before I could continue with the tale of Lena Grove and her child and the Christian theme, Robin broke in.

"Joe Christmas was my uncle," she said, later explaining that he lived in a nursing home in Natchez until he died recently, in his nineties. "It's a common name in these parts."

"Repent"

Another beautiful back road in the Deep South—a narrow road past pinewoods and swamps, the hanks of long grass in the sloping meadows yellowy-green in winter. Some orderly farms—a few —were set back from the road, but most of the dwellings were small houses or bungalows surrounded by a perimeter fence, a sleepy dog inside it, and scattered house trailers detached and becalmed under the gum trees; and shacks, too, the collapsing kind that I only saw on roads like these. I had crossed into Jefferson County, one of the poorest counties in the nation and well known to public-health experts for having the nation's highest rate of adult obesity. Every few miles there was a church—no bigger than a one-room schoolhouse and with a similar look, a cross on the roof peak and sometimes a stump of a steeple, and a signboard on the lawn, promoting the text for the week's sermon: LORD JESUS HAS THE ROADMAP FOR YOUR JOURNEY.

I was as happy as I had ever been driving in the South. There is a sense of purification that seems to take place in sunshine on a country road, the winking glare in the boughs passing overhead, the glimpses of sky and the stands of trees, wall-like pines in some hollows, enormous oaks and columns of junipers in others, and a fragrance in the air of heated and slightly decayed leaf litter that has the aroma of buttered toast. Oaks and pine trees lined the road for some miles and narrowed it and helped give the impression of this as an enchanted road in a children's story, one that tempted the traveler onward into greater joy.

And it was about that point that the ominous signs began to appear, real signs nailed to trees. For some miles, large, lettered signs were fastened to the thick trunks of roadside trees, their messages in black and red letters on a bright white background.

PREPARE TO MEET THY GOD
— AMOS 4:12

HE WHO ENDURES TO THE END SHALL BE SAVED
— MARK 13:13

THE EYES OF THE LORD ARE IN EVERY PLACE BEHOLDING THE EVIL
AND THE GOOD
—PROVERBS 15:3

FAITH WITHOUT WORKS IS DEAD
—JAMES 2:26

STRIVE TO ENTER AT THE STRAIT GATE
—LUKE 13:24

REPENT
—MARK 6:12

In a church of believers, these sentiments, spoken by a pastor
in a tone of understanding, could be a consolation, but painted
on a tree in the backwoods of Mississippi they seemed like death
threats.

"One of the Great Places"
In my ignorance, I had believed the Delta to be solely the low-lying
estuary of the Mississippi River, round about and south of New Or-
leans, the river delta of the maps. But it isn't so simple. The Delta
is the entire alluvial sprawl that stretches northward of that mud
in Louisiana, the floodplain beyond Natchez, emphatically flat
above Vicksburg, almost the whole of a bulge west of Mississippi,
enclosed in the east by the Yazoo River, all the way to Memphis. It
is a definite route, as well; it is Highway 61.

I swung through Hollandale, which was just as boarded-up as
other places on and off the highway I'd been through, but I heard
music, louder as I entered the town. It was a hot late-afternoon,
dust rising in the slanting sunlight, the street full of people, a man
wailing and a guitar twanging: the blues.

When I hesitated, a police officer in pressed khakis waved me
off the road, where cars were parked. I got out and walked toward
a stage that had been set up against a stand of trees—this was the
limit of the town, and a powerful, growly man was singing, backed
by a good-sized band.

"That's Bobby Rush," the police officer said to me as I
passed him.

A banner over the stage was lettered HOLLANDALE BLUES FES-
TIVAL IN HONOR OF SAM CHATMON. Stalls nearby were selling

fried chicken and corn, ice cream and soft drinks and T-shirts. Bobby Rush was screaming now, finishing his last set, and as he left the stage to great applause from the people—about 200 of them —standing in the dust, another group took the stage and began stomping and wailing.

A black biker gang in leather stood in a group and clapped, old women in folding chairs applauded and sang, children ran through the crowd of spectators, youths dressed as rappers, with low-slung trousers and hats turned back to front—they clapped, too, and so did 17-year-old Shu'Quita Drake (purple braids, a sweet face), holding her little boy, a swaddled 1-month-old infant named D'Vontae Knight, and Robyn Phillips, a willowy dancer from Atlanta, who had family in Hollandale and said, "This is just amazing."

But the music was so loud, so powerful, splitting the air, making the ground tremble, conversation was impossible, and so I stepped to the back of the crowd. As I was walking, I felt a hand on my arm.

It was a man in an old faded shirt and baseball cap.

"Welcome to Hollandale," he said.

"Thank you, sir."

"I'm the mayor," he said. "Melvin L. Willis. How can I help you?"

Melvin Willis was born in Hollandale in 1948 and had grown up in segregated Delta schools. (And, alas, in November 2013, some months after I met him, he died of cancer.) He went to college and got a job teaching in York, Alabama, a small town near the Mississippi state line. He had become a high-school principal in York.

"I worked there forty years, then retired and came back home to Hollandale in 2005. I ran for mayor in 2009 and won. I just got my second term. This festival is an example of the spirit of this town."

The music, the crowds, the many cars parked under the trees, the food stalls, and the festive air—none of it could mask the fact that, like Rolling Fork and Anguilla and Arcola and other places I'd visited, the town looked bankrupt.

"We're poor," he said. "I don't deny it. No one has money. Cotton doesn't employ many people. The catfish plant was here. It closed. The seed and grain closed. The hospital closed twenty-five years ago. We got Deltapine—they process seeds. But there's no work hereabouts."

A white man approached us and put his arm around Mayor Willis. "Hi. I'm Roy Schilling. This man used to work for my daddy at the grocery."

The grocery was Sunflower Food Store in the middle of Hollandale, one of the few stores still in business. Roy, like Mayor Willis, was an exuberant booster of Hollandale and still lived nearby.

"Over there where the music is playing?" Roy said, "That was Simmons Street, known as the Blue Front, every kind of club, all sorts of blues, bootleg liquor and fights. I tell you it was one lively place on a Saturday night."

"One of the great places," Mayor Willis said.

But it had ended in the 1970s. "People left. Mechanization. The jobs dried up."

More people joined us—and it was beautiful in the setting sun, the risen dust, the overhanging trees, the children playing, the music, the thump and moan of the blues.

"My father had a pharmacy over there, City Drug Store," a man said. This was Kim Grubbs, brother of Delise Grubbs Menotti, who had sung earlier at the festival. "We had a movie theater. We had music. Yes, it was very segregated when I was growing up in the sixties, but we were still friendly. We knew everyone."

"It was a kind of paradise," Kim said.

Mayor Willis was nodding, "Yes, that's true. And we can do it again."

"Closed. Went to Mexico."

"What you see in the Delta isn't how things are," a woman in Greenville, Mississippi, told me.

"But they don't look good," I said.

"They're worse than they look," she said.

We sat in her office on a dark afternoon, under a sky thick with bulgy, drooping clouds. Scattered droplets of cold rain struck the broken sidewalks and potholed street. I had thought of the Delta, for all its misery, as at least a sunny place; but this was chilly, even wintry, though it was only October. For me, the weather, the atmosphere was something new, something unexpected and oppressive, and thus remarkable.

Things are worse than they look was one of the more shocking statements I heard in the Mississippi Delta, because as in Allendale,

South Carolina, and the hamlets on the back roads of Alabama, this part of the Delta seemed to be imploding.

"Housing is the biggest challenge," said the woman, who did not want her name published, "but we're in a Catch-22—too big to be small, too small to be big. By that I mean, we're rural, but we don't qualify for rural funding because the population is over twenty-five thousand."

"Funding from whom?"

"Federal funding," she said. "And there's the mindset. It's challenging."

I said, "Are you talking about the people living in poverty?"

"Yes, some of those people. For example, you see nice vehicles in front of really rundown houses. You see people at Walmart and in the nail shops, getting their nails done."

"Is that unusual?"

"They're on government assistance," she said. "I'm not saying they shouldn't look nice, but it's instant gratification instead of sacrifice."

"What do you think they should do?"

"I grew up in a poverty-stricken town"—and having passed through it the day before I knew she was not exaggerating: Hollandale looked like the plague had struck it. "At any given time there were never less than ten people in the house, plus my parents. One bathroom. This was interesting—we were never on any kind of government assistance, the reason being that my father worked. His job was at Nicholson File. And he fished and hunted and gardened. His vegetables were really good. He shot deer, rabbits, squirrels—my mother fried the squirrels, or made squirrel stew." She laughed and said, "I never ate that game. I ate chicken."

"What happened to Nicholson File?" The company made metal files and quality tools, a well-respected brand among builders.

"Closed. Went to Mexico," she said. This was a reply I often heard when I asked about manufacturing in the Delta. "I could see there wasn't much for me here. I joined the military—I did 'three and three'—three active, three reserve. I was based in California, and I can tell you that apart from Salvation it was the best decision I've made in my life. The service provided me with a totally different perspective."

"But Greenville is a big town," I said. I'd been surprised at the extent of it, the sprawl, the downtown, the neighborhoods of good, even grand houses. And a new bridge had been built—one yet to be named—across the Mississippi, just west of the city.

"This is a declining town. River traffic is way down. We've lost population—from about forty-five thousand in 1990 to less than thirty-five thousand today. This was a thriving place. We had so much manufacturing—Fruit of the Loom men's underwear, Schwinn Bikes, Axminster Carpets. They're all gone to Mexico, India, China. Or else they're bankrupt. There was once an Air Force base here. It closed."

"What businesses are still here?" I wondered.

"Catfish, but that's not as big as it was. We've got rice—Uncle Ben's, that's big. We've got a company making ceiling tiles, and Leading Edge—they put the paint on jet planes. But there's not enough jobs. Unemployment is huge, almost twelve percent, twice the national average."

"People I've talked to say that better housing helps."

"It's fine to have a home, but if you don't have the subsidies to go with the home, you're just treading water—but that's how a lot of people live."

"Do people fix up houses?"

"Very few homes get rehabbed. Most are in such bad shape it's cheaper to tear them down than fix them. A lot are abandoned. There's more and more vacant lots."

"If Greenville happened to be a city in a third-world country, there would probably be lots of aid money pouring in.

"This was a federal Empowerment Zone—ten years, ten million dollars pumped into the economy."

"Ten million isn't much compared to the hundreds of millions I've seen in U.S. aid to Africa," I said. "I was in Africa last year. Namibia got three hundred five million—sixty-nine million to the Namibian tourist industry."

"That's news to us," she said. "We do what we can. Things have been improving slowly. There's Greenville Education Center. They have both day and night classes for people to study."

Later I checked the curriculum of the Mississippi Delta Community College, which was part of this program, and found that they offered courses in bricklaying and tile-setting, automotive mechanics, commercial truck driving, heavy equipment operation, electronics, machine tool expertise, welding, heating and air-conditioning, office systems, and much else. But there are few jobs.

"People get educated and they leave," she said. "There's a high rotation in doctors and teachers. We've got to come together. It doesn't matter how. Some healing has to take place."

Given the seriousness of the situation and the blight that was general over the Delta, I wondered aloud why she persevered.

"Me? I was meant to be here," she said.

At Hope Credit Union in Greenville, I met Sue Evans and asked her about the local economy. She gave me helpful replies, but when I changed the subject talked about the musical history of the Delta, the blues, the clubs that had been numerous up and down the Delta, she became animated.

"My mother had a blues club in Leland," Sue said.

I had passed through Leland, another farming town on Highway 61, well known for its blues history. "She was a great gal, my mother—Ruby—everyone knew her." There were still some clubs, she said. There were blues museums. People came from all over the world to visit these places associated with the blues, and to see the birthplaces and the reference points—the farms, the creeks, the railways, the cotton fields.

"I heard that in Indianola there's a B. B. King museum," I said.

This produced a profound silence. Sue and a colleague of hers exchanged a glance, but said nothing. It was the sort of silence provoked by an unwelcome allusion, or sheer confusion, as though I had lapsed into an unfamiliar language.

"He was born there, I understand," I said, flailing a bit, and wondering perhaps if I had overstayed my visit.

Sue had a mute and somewhat stubborn gaze fixed away from mine.

"Berclair," Sue's colleague said. "But he was raised in Kilmichael. Other side of Greenwood."

It seemed very precise and obscure information. I couldn't think of anything more to say, and it was apparent that this topic had produced an atmosphere in the room, a vibration that was unreadable, and that made me feel like a clumsy alien.

"Shall we tell him?" Sue's colleague said.

"I don't know," Sue said.

"You tell him."

"Go ahead," Sue said.

This exchange, a sort of banter, had the effect of lifting the mood, diffusing the vibe.

"Sue was married to him."

"Married to B. B. King?"

Sue said, "Yes, I was. I was Sue Hall then. His second wife. It was a while back."

Now that the subject had been raised, Sue was smiling. "One night my mother booked him," she said. "He kind of looked at me. I was just a kid. I had an idea of what he was thinking, but my mother wouldn't stand any nonsense or fooling around. He played at the club a lot—a great musician. He waited until I turned eighteen—he waited because he didn't want to deal with my mother. He was afraid of her."

She laughed at the memory of it. I said, "This would have been when?"

"Long ago," Sue said. "We were married for ten years."

"Did you call him B. B.?"

"His proper name is Riley. I called him B."

I was writing down *Riley*.

"Which was confusing," Sue was saying. "Because Ray Charles's wife was named Beatrice. We called her B, too. We often got mixed up with the two B's."

"You traveled with him?" I asked.

"All the time. B loved to travel. He loved to play—he could play all night. He loved the audiences, the people, he lived to talk. But I got so tired. He'd say, 'You don't like to hear me,' but it wasn't that. I just hated staying up all hours. I'd be in the hotel room, waiting for him."

"Are you still in touch?"

"We talk all the time. He calls. We talk. He still tours—imagine. Last I talked to him he said he had some dates in New York and New Jersey. He loves the life, he's still going strong."

And for that 15 or 20 minutes there was no blight on the Delta; it was a cheery reminiscence of her decade with B. B. King, the man who'd brought glory to the Delta and proved that it was possible and could happen again.

Epilogue: Arkansas

A great number of blacks in the Delta who had been farmers and landowners lost their land for various reasons, and so lost their livelihood. Calvin R. King Sr. had spent his life committed to reversing that loss and founded, in 1980, the Arkansas Land and Farm Development Corporation, which is in Brinkley, Arkansas. "When you look at the Delta," he asked me, "do you see businesses owned by blacks, operated by blacks? In manufacturing? In retail?" He smiled, because the obvious answer was: Very few. He went on, "Compare that to the black farmers here, who are part of a multibillion-dollar business."

Through him I met Delores Walker Robinson, 42, a single mother of three sons, ages 22, 18, and 12, in the small town of Palestine, Arkansas, less than 50 miles west of the Mississippi. After more than 20 years of travel with her serviceman husband, and work, and child-rearing, and a sudden divorce, Delores had returned to the place where she'd been born. "I didn't want my sons to live the harsh life of the city," she told me as we walked through her cow pasture. "I felt I would lose them to the city—to the crimes and problems that you can't escape."

With her savings as a certified nursing assistant, she bought 42 acres of neglected land. With help from friends and her sons, she fenced the land, built a small house and began raising goats. She enrolled in Heifer International, a charity based in Little Rock devoted to ending hunger and alleviating poverty, attended training sessions, and got two heifers. She now has 10 cows—and, keeping to the organization's rules, she has passed along some cows to other farmers in need. "I wanted something I could own," she said. She'd been raised on a farm near here. "I wanted to get my sons involved in the life I knew."

She also had sheep, geese, ducks, and chickens. And she grew feed corn. Because the cash flow from the animals was small, she worked six days a week at the East Arkansas Area Agency on Aging as a caregiver and nursing assistant. Early in the morning and after her day at the agency, she did the farm chores, feeding and watering the animals, repairing fences, collecting eggs. She went to livestock management classes. "I made a lot of friends there. We're all trying to accomplish the same things."

Easygoing, uncomplaining, yet tenacious, Delores Walker Robinson had all the qualities that made a successful farmer—a great work ethic, a strong will, a love of the land, a way with animals, a fearlessness at the bank, a vision of the future, a gift for taking the long view, a desire for self-sufficiency. "I'm looking ten years down the road," she said as we tramped the sloping lane. "I want to build up the herd and do this full-time."

Many southerners I met asserted—with grim pride, or with sorrow, or misquoting Faulkner—that the South doesn't change. That's not true. In many places, the cities most of all, the South has been turned upside down; in the rural areas the change has come very slowly, in small but definite ways. The poet William Blake wrote, "He who would do good to another must do it in Minute Particulars," and the Delta farmers I visited, and especially Delores Robinson, were the embodiment of that valiant spirit. She had shaken herself loose from another life to come home with her children, and she seemed iconic in her bravery, on her farm, among friends. It goes without saying that the vitality of the South lies in the self-awareness of its deeply rooted people. What makes the South a pleasure for a traveler like me, more interested in conversation than sightseeing, is the heart and soul of its family narratives—its human wealth.

Contributors' Notes
Notable Travel Writing of 2014

Contributors' Notes

Based in Copenhagen, **Lisa Abend** is a correspondent for *Time* magazine and a contributing writer for *AFAR*. She is also the author of *The Sorcerer's Apprentices: A Season in the Kitchen of Ferran Adrià's elBulli.*

Scott Anderson is a veteran war correspondent, a novelist, and a contributing writer for *The New York Times Magazine.* "Lawrence's Arabia," his first piece for *Smithsonian* magazine, was inspired by the five years he spent researching and writing his international bestseller, *Lawrence in Arabia: War, Deceit, Imperial Folly and the Making of the Modern Middle East.* "After poring so long over historical documents in archives," Anderson says, "I was anxious to visit — or in some cases revisit — those places in the Middle East that played a key role in T. E. Lawrence's story. It was fascinating to see the physical disparity, with some places all but unrecognizable from a century ago while others have barely changed at all." On a more political level, Anderson discovered a dispiriting change. "There have always been two camps in the Arab world in regard to the Lawrence legend, those who believe he truly did try to help the Arabs gain their independence in World War I, and those who believe he was a scheming agent for British imperialism all along. It's a measure of how deeply the West is distrusted throughout the Middle East today — a distrust amply earned — that the latter view is now almost universally held."

Kevin Baker is the author of five novels, most recently *The Big Crowd* (2013), set mainly in postwar New York and based closely on the greatest unsolved murder in Mob history. He is also the author or coauthor of a contemporary novel, a graphic novel, two works of American history, and an as-told-to memoir by Reggie Jackson, *Becoming Mr. October.* Baker is a contributing editor at *Harper's Magazine* and a frequent contributor to the

New York Times, and has written for many other newspapers and magazines. He is a member of the executive board of the Society of American Historians and lives in New York City.

Along with two books of travel essays, *Guatemalan Journey* and *Green Dreams: Travels in Central America,* **Stephen Connely Benz** has published essays in *Creative Nonfiction, River Teeth, TriQuarterly,* and other journals. One of his essays appeared in *The Best American Travel Writing 2003.* He teaches professional writing at the University of New Mexico and leads workshops in travel writing at the Taos Summer Writers' Conference.

Benjamin Busch is a writer, filmmaker, and photographer. He served 16 years as an infantry and light armored reconnaissance officer in the United States Marine Corps, deploying to Iraq in 2003 and again in 2005. As an actor he is best known for his portrayal of Officer Colicchio in the HBO series *The Wire.* He is the author of a memoir, *Dust to Dust* (2012), and his essays have appeared in *Harper's Magazine, The New York Times Magazine, Newsweek/The Daily Beast,* and NPR's *All Things Considered.* His poetry has appeared in *North American Review, Prairie Schooner, Five Points, The Florida Review, Oberon,* and *Michigan Quarterly Review,* among others.

Madeline Drexler is an award-winning journalist, author, and travel essayist. She is editor of *Harvard Public Health* magazine and a senior fellow at Brandeis University's Schuster Institute for Investigative Journalism. Drexler's articles have appeared in the *New York Times,* the *Wall Street Journal, The Nation, Tricycle,* and many other national publications. Her book *Emerging Epidemics: The Menace of New Infections* (2010) drew wide praise. Drexler began her career as a staff photographer for the Associated Press. She is currently working on a new series of essays based on a return reporting trip to Bhutan.

David Farley is the author of *An Irreverent Curiosity: In Search of the Church's Strangest Relic in Italy's Oddest Town,* which most recently became a documentary by the National Geographic Channel. He's a contributing writer at *AFAR* and also writes regularly for the *New York Times,* the *Wall Street Journal,* and *Bon Appétit,* among other publications. Farley teaches writing at New York University. Find him online at www.dfarley.com.

Lauren Groff is the author of the novels *Fates and Furies, Arcadia,* and *The Monsters of Templeton* and the short story collection *Delicate Edible Birds.* Her work has appeared in *The New Yorker, The Atlantic,* and *Harper's Magazine,* as well as in three editions of the *Best American Short Stories* anthology and *100 Years of The Best American Short Stories.* She lives in Gainesville, Florida.

In 1996, **Peter Hessler** arrived in China as a teacher with the Peace Corps, and he stayed on for more than a decade, writing a trilogy of nonfiction books about the country: *River Town, Oracle Bones,* and *Country Driving.* He is also the author of *Strange Stones,* a collection of his articles. He currently lives with his wife and twin daughters in Cairo, where he is working on a book about post-revolution Egypt.

Rachael Maddux is a writer and editor whose essays and features have appeared in *Oxford American, The Believer, Guernica,* and elsewhere. She was raised in Tennessee and lives in Atlanta.

Patricia Marx is a staff writer for *The New Yorker.* Her latest book is *Let's Be Less Stupid: An Attempt to Maintain My Mental Faculties* (2015). She overpacks for everything, including once for jury duty.

Tim Neville is a correspondent for *Outside, Ski,* and *Skiing* magazines and a frequent contributor to the *New York Times* travel section. His work has also appeared in *The Best American Sports Writing.* He lives in Oregon with his wife and daughter. Follow him @tim_neville.

Maud Newton is a writer and critic whose work has appeared in *Harper's Magazine, The New York Times Magazine, Narrative, Oxford American, Granta, Bookforum, The Awl,* and many other publications. She received the 2009 Narrative Prize and is writing a book about the science and superstition of ancestry.

Adriana Páramo is a cultural anthropologist, writer, and women's rights advocate. Her book *Looking for Esperanza* (2012), winner of Benu Press's 2011 Social Justice and Equity Award in Creative Nonfiction, was named one of the top 10 best books by Latino authors in 2012 by thelatinoauthor.com and the Best Women's Issues Book at the 2013 International Latino Book Awards, and was also an award winner at the 2012 Book of the Year Awards. She is the author of *My Mother's Funeral,* a work of nonfiction set in Colombia. Páramo's work has won numerous awards and honors, including multiple Pushcart Prize nominations, and it has been noted in *The Best American Essays* of 2012, 2013, and 2014. She has been named one of the top 10 Latino authors in the USA by LatinoStories.com. Her work has appeared or is forthcoming in *The Sun, The Georgia Review, Southern Sin, Brevity, The Fourth Genre, Columbia: A Journal of Literature and Art, Going Om,* and others. She keeps a travel blog: www.paramoadriana .com/travelblog.

Nick Paumgarten is a staff writer at *The New Yorker.* He lives in New York City.

Raised in Australia and a denizen of the East Village of Manhattan for many years, **Tony Perrottet** is a contributing writer at *Smithsonian* and a regular at the *New York Times, WSJ Magazine,* and other publications. He is the author of five books, most recently *Napoleon's Privates: 2,500 Years of History Unzipped* and *The Sinner's Grand Tour: A Journey Through the Historical Underbelly of Europe.* He is currently working on a book about adventurers in 1930s China. This is his sixth appearance in the *Best American Travel Writing* series.

Lauren Quinn is a writer and teacher currently living in Los Angeles. Her work has appeared in *The Believer, Guernica, The Guardian,* and *Hazlitt,* among others.

Monte Reel is the author of the books *Between Man and Beast* and *The Last of the Tribe.* His essays and articles have appeared in publications including *The New York Times Magazine, Harper's Magazine, Outside, Businessweek,* and *The Believer,* among others. He lives in Evanston, Illinois.

Paul Salopek is a freelance journalist who has reported on conflicts in Africa, the Middle East, Central Asia, the Balkans, and Latin America. His work has appeared in the *New York Times, National Geographic,* the *Chicago Tribune, The Atlantic, Foreign Policy, American Scholar, The Best American Travel Writing,* and other publications. His reportage has earned two Pulitzer Prizes. He is currently walking across the world as part of a seven-year narrative project called the Out of Eden Walk; see www.outofedenwalk.com.

Gary Shteyngart was born in Leningrad in 1972 and came to the United States seven years later. His debut novel, *The Russian Debutante's Handbook,* won the Stephen Crane Award for First Fiction and the National Jewish Book Award for Fiction. His second novel, *Absurdistan,* was named one of the Ten Best Books of the Year by *The New York Times Book Review,* as well as a best book of the year by *Time, Washington Post Book World,* the *San Francisco Chronicle,* the *Chicago Tribune,* and many other publications. He has been selected as one of *Granta*'s Best Young American Novelists. His work has appeared in *The New Yorker, Esquire, GQ,* and *Travel + Leisure,* and his books have been translated into more than 20 languages. He lives in New York City. His most recent work is the memoir *Little Failure.*

Iris Smyles's stories and essays have appeared in *The Atlantic,* the *New York Times,* the *New York Observer, BOMB,* and other publications. She has written two books of fiction: *Iris Has Free Time* and the forthcoming *Dating Tips for the Unemployed.* She lives in New York and Greece. Visit her online at IrisSmyles.com.

Christopher Solomon writes about travel, outdoor pursuits, science, and the environment for the *New York Times, Scientific American, Popular Mechanics,* and other publications. He is a contributing editor at both *Outside* and *Runner's World.* This is his second appearance in *The Best American Travel Writing.* His work also appeared in *The Best American Sports Writing 2014.* A former reporter for the *Seattle Times,* Solomon lives in Seattle. Find more of his work at chrissolomon.net.

Patrick Symmes writes: "I am a correspondent and travel writer for national magazines and the author of two books on the Cuban Revolution, *Chasing Che* (2000) and *The Boys from Dolores* (2007). The latter made the *New York Times* Ten Best Books list for 2007. I have been a contributing editor at *Harper's Magazine, Outside,* and *Condé Nast Traveler,* and after more than 20 years of writing about the remote regions of the world and the ragged edges of geopolitics, I am surprised to find that I crave even more."

Paul Theroux is the author of many highly acclaimed books. His novels include *The Lower River* and *The Mosquito Coast,* and his renowned travel books include *Ghost Train to the Eastern Star* and *Dark Star Safari.* He lives in Hawaii and Cape Cod.

Notable Travel Writing of 2014

Selected by Jason Wilson

DOUGLAS FOX
  The Time I Got Stranded in Antarctica. *TheAtlantic.com*, January 7.

J. MALCOLM GARCIA
  Praying in Reyhanli. *Tampa Review*, Fall.
KEITH GESSEN
  Waiting for War. *The New Yorker*, May 12.
ANNE GOLDMAN
  Travels with *Jane Eyre*. *Georgia Review*, Fall.
ADAM GOPNIK
  Stones and Bones. *The New Yorker*, July 7 & 14.
JEFF GUNDY
  The Other Side of Empire. *Georgia Review*, Fall.

GABRIELLE HAMILTON
  Big Night in Uruguay. *Travel + Leisure*, April.
KATE HARRIS
  Lands of Lost Borders. *Georgia Review*, Fall.
EVA HOLLAND
  Birth of a Birder. *World Hum*, June 24.

ANDY ISAACSON
  Island at the End of the World. *National Geographic Traveler*, August/
    September.

LESLIE JAMISON
  It Does Not Happen by Machine. *Witness*, Spring.
GEORGE JOHNSON
  The Nuclear Tourist. *National Geographic*, October.

GIDEON LEWIS-KRAUS
  Story A. *Harper's Magazine*, June.

LAURA MILLER
  Romancing the Stones. *The New Yorker*, April 21.
JON MOOALLEM
  A Journey to the Center of the World. *New York Times Magazine*,
    February 23.

DAVID NAIMON
  Third Ear. *Fourth Genre*, Spring.
JOSIP NOVAKOVICH
  Jerusalem According to Cats. *Narrative*, Winter.

DAVID OWEN
    Floating Feasts. *The New Yorker,* November 3.
    Game of Thrones. *The New Yorker,* April 21.

STEPHANIE PEARSON
    The Devil Made Me Do It. *Outside,* February.
TONY PERROTTET
    The Cave Dwellers. *Smithsonian,* February.
BRIAN PHILLIPS
    The Sea of Crises. *Grantland,* November 5.

DAVID QUAMMEN
    Franz Josef Land. *National Geographic,* August.

EMILY RABOTEAU
    Who Is Zwarte Piet? *Virginia Quarterly Review,* Winter.
ANDREW REINER
    One Man's Beat. *Washington Post Magazine,* March 23.
NATHANIEL RICH
    Hitler's Airport. *The Atlantic,* April.
CHRIS RYAN
    Cuba, Undistilled. *World Hum,* December 20.

DAVE SEMINARA
    Day of the Goose. *Morning News,* March 20.
GARY SHTEYNGART
    Wet Hot Israeli Summer. *New York Times Magazine,* February 23.
FLOYD SKLOOT
    To Land's End and Back. *Boulevard,* Spring.
CHRISTOPHER SOLOMON
    The Soul of Skiing in the Great White North. *Outside,* November.

JEFFREY TAYLER
    Bogotá's Bohemian Renaissance. *National Geographic Traveler,* October.

SCOTT WALLACE
    Over the Horizon. *National Geographic Traveler,* February/March.
JASON WEIL
    Back in the U.S.S.R. *New York Times Magazine,* June 29.
GRAEME WOOD
    Burmese Daze. *The Atlantic,* March.

ESTHER YI
    Pistachio Politics. *The Atlantic,* September.